Wissenschaftliche Untersuchungen
zum Neuen Testament · 2. Reihe

Herausgeber / Editor
Jörg Frey (München)

Mitherausgeber / Associate Editors
Friedrich Avemarie (Marburg)
Judith Gundry-Volf (New Haven, CT)
Hans-Josef Klauck (Chicago, IL)

233

Thomas R. Blanton, IV

Constructing a New Covenant

Discursive Strategies in the Damascus
Document and Second Corinthians

Mohr Siebeck

THOMAS R. BLANTON, IV, born 1968; 1991 B. A. (Psychology) University of North Carolina at Chapel Hill; 1994 M. T. S. Duke Divinity School; 2006 PhD (Biblical Studies) Divinity School, University of Chicago; Visiting Assistant Professor of Religion at Luther College in Decorah, Iowa.

ISBN 978-3-16-149207-5

ISSN 0340-9570 (Wissenschaftliche Untersuchungen zum Neuen Testament, 2. Reihe)

The Deutsche Nationalbibliothek lists this publication in the Deutsche Nationalbibliographie; detailed bibliographic data is available in the Internet at *http://dnb.d-nb.de*.

The book was printed by Laupp & Göbel in Nehren on non-aging paper and bound by Buchbinderei Nädele in Nehren.

Printed in Germany.

Preface

This book constitutes a revision of my 2006 University of Chicago doctoral dissertation, written under the supervision of Prof. Hans-Josef Klauck. Prof. Klauck, along with the other two readers on my dissertation committee, functioned as an academic "dream team" on my behalf. Prof. Klauck allowed me the freedom to pursue my own ideas, even when in some cases they differed from his own. In his writings on Paul, Prof. Klauck describes the apostle as one who wins his authority through diligent, behind-the-scenes service to the community. I think he will take it as a compliment if I say that, in my experience, this has also been the model according to which Hans-Josef has accrued some of his own personal authority. Even if often behind the scenes, such service does not go unnoticed or unappreciated.

My other readers, Professors Bruce Lincoln and James VanderKam, have also proven to be valuable assets as I have prepared my manuscript. Prof. VanderKam has improved my discussion both in matters of substance and detail. He has an especially keen editorial eye, and has saved me from many errors that otherwise might have gone unnoticed. Professor Lincoln has been a mentor in matters of critical methodology, and I hope that his influence will be evident throughout this work. Of course, my committee members are not to be held responsible for any errors that might remain in the finished product.

I would also like to thank Elaine Bonner, Access Services Manager at the Jesuit-Krauss-McCormick Library in Hyde Park, who often went out of her way in helping me to check out – and check in – the books that I needed. Even on the day in which I carted in moving boxes full of well over one hundred books to be returned, Elaine retained her characteristically good humor.

Dr. Steven Holloway of the American Theological Library Association, as well as my brother, Prof. Ward Blanton, now at the University of Glasgow, both read portions of my manuscript and provided valuable feedback and advice. May May Latt, a doctoral student at the Lutheran School of Theology, on several occasions provided technical assistance as I attempted to perform unfamiliar operations on my MacIntosh. Thanks are also due to my parents, Tom and Beth Blanton who, in addition to offering encouragement, love, and occasional advice, also provided significant material support during my final year of graduate school.

I am grateful to the editorial board of Mohr Siebeck Publishing House, and in particular Dr. Henning Ziebritzki and Prof. Jörg Frey for accepting my work for publication in the *Wissenschaftliche Untersuchungen zum Neuen Testament* series. My commendation goes to Jana Trispel of the Production Department, who skillfully resolved several problems that I encountered in formatting the text.

Finally, I would like to dedicate this book to my son, Zachary. I am told that one Christmas, when I was nearing the completion of my doctoral program, Zach expressed the wish that Santa Claus would bring me a completed version of my dissertation. It is fitting that this work should now be published in time for Christmas, 2007.

Decorah, August 2007   *Thomas R. Blanton, IV*

Table of Contents

Chapter 1

Introduction

1. Methodological Orientation

Only two groups are known in antiquity to have made use of the Jeremianic phrase "new covenant" in their own ideological constructions. These two groups are the Essenes and the early Christians. Even within these groups however, the use of the phrase was limited. What prompted the Essenes, on the one hand, and the Christians, on the other, to reach into the deposit of scriptural tradition in order to withdraw the phrase for their own use? To date, there has been no extended treatment of this question. This study aims to fill that lacuna by examining the ways in which two important texts, the Damascus Document from among the Dead Sea scrolls, and Paul's Second Epistle to the Corinthians, constructed discourses involving the phrase "new covenant" in response to salient features of the respective local situations within which each discourse was written.

A study of the use of the phrase "new covenant" in the Damascus Document and in Paul's 2 Corinthians implies two critical procedures that have been characteristic preoccupations in the writings of Jonathan Z. Smith: comparison and classification. The ideologies which the Damascus Document, one the one hand, and Paul on the other, employ in their discussions of the new covenant are disparate. The characteristic concern of this study will be to redescribe these differences in terms suggested by a particular theoretical perspective. The theoretical perspective adopted here is in principle neither new nor particularly daring – Biblical scholars will recognize it as an expression of the principle of interpreting a text according to its *Sitz im Leben*, combined with a measure of *Tendenzkritik* – but its application yields results that serve to correct some older scholarly notions about the relationship between the study's objects of comparison. This process however, necessitates an act of classification.

There has been a strong tendency among scholars who compare early Jewish texts with early Christian ones to engage in an essentialist interpretation of the two "religions" that are supposed to be represented by the texts compared: Judaism, construed as "essentially" a religion of "works," whereby one earns one's salvation based on one's own efforts, and Christianity as "essentially" a religion of grace, whereby individuals are acquitted at the divine judgment solely on the basis of God's mercy. Although this tendency was most pronounced during the nineteenth and throughout much of the twentieth century, it is still evident today. Both the dichotomy of works/grace and the essentialism that supports this dichotomy have been shown to have arisen as the product of a Protestant polemic against Catholicism, a polemic that was subsequently applied to Judaism as well.[1] This study will undermine the essentialist classificatory scheme by treating early Christianity as a Jewish sect, and not as a separate "religion." (Reasons for adopting this classificatory scheme are adduced in chapter 7.) The comparison between the Damascus Document and Paul is therefore not to be taken as a comparison between two "religions," but as a comparison of two groups within the broader rubric of Judaism in the Second Temple period.

A diagram of the relationship between early Jewish and early Christian literature, understanding Judaism and Christianity as "essentially" different religions, would look like this:

Figure 1: *Essentialist Construction of the Relationship Between Judaism and Christianity*

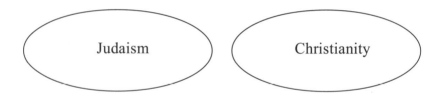

---

[1] See for example J. Z. Smith, *Divine Drudgery: On the Comparison of Early Christianities and the Religions of Late Antiquity* (Chicago: University of Chicago Press, 1990); "Fences and Neighbors: Some Contours of Early Judaism" in *Imagining Religion: From Babylon to Jonestown* (Chicago and London: University of Chicago Press, 1982) 1–18; "Religion, Religions, Religious" in *Relating Religion: Essays in the Study of Religion* (Chicago and London: University of Chicago Press, 2004) 179–196; Tessa Rajak, "Jews and Greeks: The Invention and Exploitation of Polarities in the Nineteenth Century" in T. Rajak, *The Jewish Dialogue with Greece and Rome: Studies in Cultural and Social Interaction* (Leiden: Brill, 2001) 535–557; Dale Martin, "Paul and the Judaism/Hellenism Dichotomy: Toward a Social History of the Question" in T. Engberg-Pederson, ed., *Paul Beyond the Judaism/Hellenism Divide* (Louisville: Westminster John Knox Press, 2001) 29–61.

A diagram representing the classificatory scheme adopted in this study, which takes the early Christian movement as a Jewish sect,[2] appears below. (I have taken the liberty here of filling out the diagram by including other Jewish sects. The implication of the diagram is that each of the groups that composed Judaism in the last half-century of the Second Temple period were sects; there was no non-sectarian Judaism at that time.)

Figure 2: *Jewish Sects in the Late Second Temple Period*

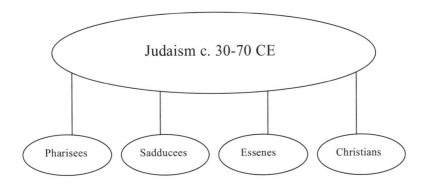

The classificatory scheme adopted here does not abolish differences among the various groups; in fact rivalries between Jewish groups fueled civil war both in the Hasmonean and in the Herodian period. However, comparisons involving the early Christian literature and other Jewish material of this period constitute not a comparison between two different religions, but within a single, albeit variegated entity, Judaism.

If classifying the early Christian movement as a Jewish sect does not entail the thesis that it exhibits complete homogeneity with other Jewish sects, it is only the comparison of these groups that reveals what is distinctive to each. Following the logic and method of classification, one could perhaps be content with listing and describing the system of similarities and differences between the use of the phrase "new covenant" in the Damascus Document and 2 Corinthians. However, classification is not this study's objective, rather it is the application of a particular theoretical perspective, already alluded to but not yet defined, that constitutes the study's main objective. This theoretical perspective seeks to correlate

---

[2] I define "sect" as a group that may be in competition with other groups, each of which identifies itself as a (or "the") representative of a larger social entity.

ideological expressions, such as are constituted by the texts that employ the phrase "new covenant," with local political and social situations.

The correlation of textually encoded ideological expressions with the specific local situations within which they were produced entails a three step procedure. Firstly, one must construct an account of the local historical situation in which a particular text is thought to have been produced. This historical construct will identify certain social or political features of the local context as salient to the interpretation of the ideological expressions encoded within a particular text. These salient factors are those which are deemed to have constituted factors that significantly influenced the text's production as well as the specific terms in which it was formulated. The second step in this process is to provide an interpretation of a given text. This interpretation is one that correlates the text's ideological formulations with those features of the local historical context which are deemed to have influenced the text's production. This method then involves the construction of two complementary narratives: this first concerning a specific historical situation, and the second an interpretation of a particular text or textual unit, here denoted a "source text." A third step involves the comparison of these two narratives. Such a comparison in theory may reveal elements in which a particular source text stands in tension with the local context in which it was produced. This act of comparison should reveal any significant omissions, distortions, or creative redescriptions of the local situation that are evident in the source text. That is, the comparison of text and context should allow the interpreter to delineate the procedures that were employed in the construction of a particular discourse. Can falsifications be detected in the source text? Omissions? Distortions? Such a procedure allows the interpreter to formulate answers to these questions.

We may note that any interpretation that takes into account only the formal semeiotic and rhetorical structures encoded within a text, inasmuch as these focus on the internal formulation of the text to the neglect of salient external factors – which because they are external to the text are rendered imperceptible to formal and structural textual analysis – cannot begin to answer these questions. This methodology serves as a corrective to and extension of methodologies which focus only on structures that are evident within a given text. Within this category I would include both formal rhetorical analysis and structuralist analysis. These types of analysis provide a necessary but not a sufficient method for examining the discursive strategies employed within a given text. Such procedures can never, for example, detect a lie. In order to succeed in detecting such, one must juxtapose textual analysis with a construction of the local situation in which the text was produced. In this one way one can identify with greater precision the discursive strategies employed within a text.[3]

If the scheme of classifying the Dead Sea sect as well as early Christianity alike as Jewish sects undermines the essentialist scheme of opposing "Christianity" and an undifferentiated "Judaism" as opposing religions or "religious principles," to borrow a phrase from F. C. Baur,[4] the method of correlating discursive formulations with aspects of the local situation in which they were produced does likewise. If a plausible link may be constructed between a discursive formulation and the situation within which it was produced, the discursive formulation must then be interpreted as a contingent, social and historical production, rather than the manifestation of a religious "essence," construed as trans-historical and supra-cultural. Such a conclusion would not preclude a position such as that of Adolf von Harnack, who wished to distinguish between a religion's essential (and essentialist) "kernel" and the culturally conditioned "husk" which served as the vehicle of its communication.[5] Harnack's position however suffers from a fatal flaw; every attempt to recover a religion's trans-historical kernel is undertaken by a person whose perceptual apparatus is constructed as the result of inhabiting a particular body and living in a particular place or places at particular moments in history. The act of interpretation transmutes that which is interpreted; everything is rendered husk.

The careful reader has no doubt noticed that I have chosen to relate my key concepts, "discursive formulation" and "local situation" by employing

---

[3] I borrow the phrase "discursive strategies" from Bruce Lincoln. My own approach has been influenced by Lincoln, whose work incorporates semeiotic and structuralist approaches, often in the service of delineating the procedures whereby discourses construct taxonomies and hierarchies encoding ("naturalizing" or "mystifying") relations of dominance and subordination among groups. Most relevant in this respect are Lincoln's *Theorizing Myth: Narrative, Ideology, and Scholarship* (Chicago, IL and London, UK: University of Chicago Press, 1999); *Authority: Construction and Corrosion* (Chicago, IL and London, UK: University of Chicago Press, 1994); *Discourse and the Construction of Society: Comparative Studies of Myth, Ritual, and Classification* (New York, NY and Oxford, UK: Oxford University Press, 1989); *Holy Terrors: Thinking About Religion After September 11* (Chicago, IL and London, UK: University of Chicago Press, 2003); part II of *Death, War, and Sacrifice: Studies in Ideology and Practice* (Chicago, IL and London, UK: University of Chicago Press, 1991); as well as the special issue of *Cultural Critique* (No. 12, Spr. 1989: *Discursive Strategies and the Economy of Prestige*) inspired by the work of Pierre Bourdieu. Succinct methodological statements can be found in Lincoln's "Theses on Method" in *Method & Theory in the Study of Religion* 8.3 (1996) 225–227, and more recently, "How to Read a Religious Text: Reflections on Some Passages of the Chāndogya Upaniṣad," *History of Religions* 46.2 (2006) 127–139.

[4] Baur's formulations are discussed briefly in chapter 4 herein.

[5] *What is Christianity?* (Philadelphia, PA: Fortress Press, 1986; trans. of *Das Wesen des Christentums*, originally published in 1900).

the language of correlation rather than causality. "Discursive formulation" refers to any discursive act, written or uttered; it is constituted by a linguistic performance. This performance may employ an ideological formulation or formulations, but is not limited to such. "Local situation" refers to the salient features of the social, ideological (and I subsume "religion" within this category), institutional, political, and/or economic context in which a discursive formulation is created. As "ideology" falls within the purview of both the category "discursive formulation" and "local situation," clearly I do not intend to imply the reductionist view that ideology is a societal effect; rather I assume that ideology and society exert a reciprocal influence. Both terms, society and ideology, exist at once as cause and effect of the other. Existing as both cause and effect of the local, societal situation within which it appears, ideology and its embodiment within discrete discursive formulations can only be said to correlate with, and not per se to be caused by, any given factor judged to be constitutive of the local societal situation. For this reason, I prefer a model of historical change that views acts as calculated responses to factors construed as influences, rather than the mechanistic historiographical model of the nineteenth and early twentieth century that posited causes and their inevitable (albeit unpredictable) results. Eschewing the language of causality, my own formulations will seek rather to identify correlations between aspects of a local situation, construed not as causes but as influences, and the discursive formulations produced within the context of that situation. Local situations influence discursive formulations, which themselves become a constitutive part of the evolving local situation.

As briefly indicated already, the essentialist interpretation which posits Christianity and Judaism as two religions separated by irreconcilable religious "principles" has not entirely disappeared. It is alive and well, for example, in the *Anchor Bible Dictionary*'s article, "New Covenant." The article invokes essentialist notions of what constitutes Christianity and Judaism:

> As a Christian, Paul has a major problem knowing what to do with the law ... In Romans, Paul says Christians are discharged from the law (Rom. 7:6), that Christ is the end of the law (10:4). Yet Paul does not want to dispense with the law; in fact, he claims to uphold it (3:31). His other statements, however, distance him irrevocably from Judaism, for whom the law is central and eternally binding. For Paul, Christ is central, and the new covenant written by his life-giving Spirit surpasses all other covenants and is eternal.[6]

"As a Christian," Paul "has a major problem knowing what to do with the law." Christianity is construed in essentialist terms; it is a religion of grace, not law. Judaism is placed at the opposite pole: "for [Judaism] the

---

[6] J. Lundbom, *ABD* 4:1091.

law is central and eternally binding." Judaism is a religion of works; it is characterized by legalism. Commenting on the Dead Sea sect, the author writes, "The community bore an unmistakable stamp of legalism ..." The Dead Sea sect furthermore was characterized by an ethical life that was followed only as the result of external stricture, not an internal desire to do what is right: "[T]he individual responsibility presupposed in the Manual [of Discipline] appears not to result from any inner motivation, at least not the sort envisioned by Jeremiah in his new covenant prophecy ... [because] they still need admonitions to obey ..." Jeremiah's "new covenant prophecy" is taken as emblematic of an internally motivated ethical practice, one which the Dead Sea sect fails to embody. Christianity, on the other hand, is characterized as a religion whose adherents act according to an internal motivation, and so embody Jeremiah's understanding of the new covenant:

Paul's precise understanding of how the new covenant manifests itself among the gentiles is by no means transparent in these verses [i.e., Rom. 2:14-15], but one should note that his thinking nevertheless runs parallel to Jeremiah's new covenant passage where the promise of a law written on the heart is followed by the promise of a new inner motivation to know and do the law ...[7]

The internal/external and legalism/grace dichotomies have been standard items in Christianity's polemic against Judaism at least since the time of the schism between Protestant and Catholic Christianity.

2. Sociology and Theology in a Recent Study of Covenant

Dichotomizing tendencies are equally evident in the Ellen Juhl Christiansen's study of covenant entitled, *The Covenant in Judaism and Paul: A Study of Ritual Boundaries as Identity Markers.*[8] The dichotomy which is operative throughout the book, and which in fact dictates the results of Christiansen's exegesis of the various writings from the Hebrew Bible (Christiansen's "Old Testament"), the Pseudepigrapha and Dead Sea scrolls, and finally several of the letters of Paul is that of particularism versus universalism. As one might predict, universalism is construed as the positive term, particularism the negative. Christiansen also employs the "religion of works"/"religion of grace" dichotomy, although her use of this dyad is much more restrained. As Christiansen's is the most extensive work by a single author on the idea of covenant in early Judaism and early Christianity that has been written in the last decade, and because it exhibits

---

[7] Lundbom, "New Covenant," 1091.
[8] Published in Leiden, New York, and Köln by E.J. Brill, 1995.

some of the main oppositions that are called into question in this study, her work deserves sustained attention.

Christiansen's study employs a contradictory set of ideological commitments, both of which inform her method throughout the book. Firstly, as the subtitle of her book, *A Study of Ritual Boundaries as Identity Markers*, indicates, Christiansen employs analytical tools that are drawn from sociological studies. Christiansen takes an introductory textbook on the sociology of religion by Meredith McGuire[9] to provide her primary theoretical and analytical perspectives. Christiansen summarizes her sociological project as follows:

> It is my *thesis ... that the characteristic identity features of a group*, the basic forms of socio-religious belonging, are *mirrored by the entrance rites ... Entrance rites* [such as circumcision and baptism] ... *express a change in social identity*. Because they are rites of crossing a boundary, and mark becoming a part of a community, they serve as a means to *differentiate socially one group from another.*[10]

Alongside this sociological perspective however, Christiansen espouses another, quite contradictory, ideological commitment. This commitment is provided by a particular form of Christian theology. Christiansen's theological commitment becomes evident from the first page of her book, on which she criticizes previous studies for privileging "soteriology over ecclesiology," that is, by focusing on covenant, but more particularly baptism, as a category pertaining to individual salvation, as opposed to expressing a corporate identity ("ecclesiology"). Christiansen opines, "It is, however, theologically illegitimate to give priority to soteriology over ecclesiology."[11] The issue of theological legitimacy is in fact central to Christiansen's project, and the results obtained from her theological method stand in sharp contrast to those obtained by her sociological one.

The foundation of Christiansen's theological method is provided by a lecture delivered by Dietrich Bonhoeffer in 1936, and subsequently translated into English and published under the title, "The Question of the Boundaries of the Church and Church Union."[12] Christiansen summarizes Bonhoeffer's essay in the following terms:

> Thus, for Bonhoeffer, the nature of the church, in the Reformation tradition, is not determined by those who de facto belong to it, but it is determined by the Word and

---

[9] *Religion: The Social Context* (5th ed., Belmont, CA: Wadsworth Thomson Learning, 2002).

[10] *Covenant in Judaism and Paul*, 16. The italics in this and following quotations are Christiansen's.

[11] *Covenant in Judaism and Paul*, 1.

[12] The essay appears *The Way to Freedom: Letters, Lectures and Notes 1935–1939*, Vol. 2 (London: Collins, 1966) 75–96. First delivered as a lecture in April, 1936, the essay was published two months later in the journal *Evangelische Theologie*.

sacrament of Jesus Christ. Whenever the church reflects on its boundaries it is conscious that its message and call to salvation are either accepted or rejected. When the message is not believed, boundaries are set. 'It is not the church that sets the boundaries; it comes up against boundaries that are imposed on it from the outside.' Because the encounter between church and unbelief always leads to an act of decision, the boundary is between salvation and rejection ... The idea ... raises some theological questions. Most important are the identity questions related to a consciousness of true and false in the ongoing inner-confessional dialogue ...[13]

Christiansen subsumes Bonhoeffer's comments within the standard depiction of Christianity as a universal religion. Of course, it is clear that as a point of sociological fact, Christianity does exhibit social boundaries: it is a particular religion, with an "inside" and an "outside," an "us" and "them." This fact calls for explanation. Following Bonhoeffer, Christiansen asserts that external boundaries are not endemic to Christianity; they are imposed "from the outside," as the result of the rejection of the Christian message by non-Christians. Christianity is a bounded, and thus a particularistic religion, but Christianity is not culpable for this attribute: it is the non-Christian who "imposes" boundaries, and thus particularity, upon what by rights ought to be a universal religion. This exculpatory procedure is taken as a justification for Christiansen's preference, consistent throughout the book, for referring to early Christianity as a universalistic religion. This theological procedure stands in stark contrast to a quite apt comment that she had made in her section on sociological method: "True social identity is almost unimaginable if not ethnic (national) or particularistic ..."[14] Although according to a sociological analysis, Christianity is a boundaried, and thus particularistic religion, nevertheless Christiansen prefers the idealistic and essentialist theological construction of Christianity as a universalistic religion.

If Christiansen reinscribes the familiar construction of Judaism as a particularistic religion juxtaposed with Christianity as a universalistic, and therefore superior religion, she is nevertheless to be commended, in my view, for her sensitivity to Jewish-Christian relations. She objects to the notion that the covenantal relationship between Jews and God has been superceded by a new covenant that encompasses only Christians. Instead, Christiansen prefers the more recent idea, arising "from a Jewish perspective[, that] the two covenants have been understood as separate relationships that exist without mutually excluding each other by focusing on the *diversity* of the two."[15] Christiansen construes Judaism and Christianity as partners in dialogue.

---

[13] *Covenant in Judaism and Paul*, 12.

[14] *Covenant in Judaism and Paul*, 15.

[15] *Covenant in Judaism and Paul*, 10.

The dialogue that Christiansen proposes between Judaism and Christianity however, includes a significant element of "challenge, especially in a context of dialogue."[16] Christiansen does not define the nature of the "challenge" that her methods entail until the latter third of her book, in the section that deals with covenant and baptism in Paul's letters. In this section however, Christiansen's theological agenda becomes clear. In the context of her discussion of Gal 4:21–5:1, she states:

> Paul seems to imply both the point that he has made in Gal 3, that the line of inheritance is through promise, and also that *faith is more important than ethnic descent.* This is expressed here in the language of adoption in 4:31: *we are the children, not of the slave girl but of a free woman.* Having thus identified the Galatian community, including himself, as the *true children of God*, Paul can answer the question regarding identity in a powerful way: *true identity is primarily to have a child relationship with God.* By implication there is a contrast to false identity.
>
> Moreover, by operating not with historically successive covenants, but with two principles, Paul presupposes two simultaneously existing identities ... If humanity's relationship with God is constituted as a community[,] this is visible in mutual love and it builds on inclusiveness as ideal.[17]

Christiansen enlists Paul as a mouthpiece of the non-supercessionist construction of the Jewish and Christian covenants. The Pauline, and therefore Christian covenant, Christiansen argues, is based on faith, as opposed to the Jewish covenant, based on ethnic descent. Christian faith constitutes one as a "true child of God," which is construed as a form of "true identity," in opposition to Judaism, the "child of the slave girl," which, since it is not a universalistic religion (it does not "build on inclusiveness as an ideal"), "[b]y implication ... [exhibits a] false identity." A few pages later Christiansen continues:

> Paul has reinterpreted and *widened covenant identity*, from identity based on ethnic criteria to it being based in creation [and therefore a universal category] ... Moreover, as in Romans, because identity is redefined according to different criteria, covenant in its narrow sense, that is in its association with law, is no longer an obvious term for the present community's relationship with God. Rather, Paul prefers the expression children of God, and thus *widens the ethno-centric to a universal relationship* ...[18]

In this passage, a covenant based on "ethnic criteria" functions analogously to one defined "in its association with law" in that both are contrasted with a covenant that is characterized by a familial relationship ("children of God"). In terms of Christiansen's discussion of Gal 4:21–5:1, quoted above, "*true identity is primarily to have a child relationship with God.* By implication there is a contrast to false identity." True identity is provided by one of the key Pauline characterizations of his congregations

---

[16] *Covenant in Judaism and Paul*, 11.

[17] *Covenant in Judaism and Paul*, 242.

[18] *Covenant in Judaism and Paul*, 249.

as "children of God," whereas identity that is associated with ethnic or legal criteria is described as "false identity." Returning again to Christiansen's model in which Judaism and Christianity are construed as "dialogue partners," by this point in the argument Judaism's implied role in this dialogue becomes clear: it is to acknowledge its "false identity," convert to a "true identity" by espousing faith in Christ, and thereby contribute to the universalization of Christianity. The incorporation of Jews into Christianity would remove an "other" that contributes significantly to the "imposition" of boundaries upon Christianity. If there is no "other" to be encountered, then the church would be able to construe itself as unbounded, and therefore universal. With this in mind we gain a new apprehension of the significance of Christiansen's formulation quoted earlier, the implications of which are strategically left for the reader to infer:

'It is not the church that sets the boundaries; it comes up against boundaries that are imposed on it from the outside.' Because the encounter between church and unbelief always leads to an act of decision, the boundary is between salvation and rejection ... The idea ... raises some theological questions. Most important are the identity questions related to a consciousness of true and false in the ongoing inner-confessional dialogue ...

In light of its stated "challenge" to Christianity's dialogue partner, Judaism, Christiansen's book may be classified as an evangelistic discourse, inviting Jews to "an act of decision" that would situate them safely across the "boundary ... between salvation and rejection," the act of assuming an identity as a "child of God" by espousing faith in Jesus Christ.

The formulations that arise as the result of Christiansen's theological bias stand in some cases in stark contrast to the results that she achieves from the application of her sociological method. When she analyzes texts from the "Old Testament," Pseudepigrapha, and Dead Sea scrolls, both the theological bias and the sociological method lead to the same results: Judaism is defined as a religion that is characterized by the construction of ritual and ideological boundaries: it is a particularistic religion. However, Christiansen fails to apply the same type of sociological analysis to the Pauline material that she surveys, and which in her study implicitly constitutes the exemplar for the category "Christian." Christiansen insulates Christianity from sociological analysis. According to her theological outlook, Christianity is a universalistic religion; according to her sociological method it, like the Judaism with which it is juxtaposed, is a boundaried and therefore particularistic religion. Christiansen formulates her conclusions in such a way as to escape the implications of her sociological method, in preference for her theological outlook.

Reflecting on Paul's formulation in Gal 3:29 ("And if you belong to Christ, you are therefore Abraham's offspring, inheritors according to promise."), Christiansen writes:

Because Paul has a comprehensive view of what relationship with God is and what covenant relationship implies, he can *no longer* define identity in particularistic terms of covenantal belonging. When identity builds on and derives its content from a relationship with God, imaged as Father, such a relationship is open to *both Jews and Gentiles* ... Paul demonstrates that Christian identity is wider than ethnic belonging, and simultaneously that it is *narrow* inasmuch as it is based on faith in Christ.[19]

And again:

[W]hen Paul reads the Old Testament prophecy ecclesiologically, his reinterpretation of identity forces him to argue for exclusion. The community consists of those who believe in Christ, who act out their faith according to the law of love and freedom ... Therefore it becomes necessary to establish a dividing line between freedom and slavery ... [Describing the community's relationship with God], Paul prefers the expression children of God, and thus *widens the ethno-centric to a universal relationship, and narrows it to a christo-centric faith relationship*.

Inasmuch as Christian boundary distinctions do not correspond do ethnic distinctions, Christianity is construed as a universalistic religion. At the same time, Christiansen recognizes that Christian identity is formulated in accordance with a "narrow" ideological criterion, constituted by "faith in Christ." In formulating her conclusions in this way, Christiansen introduces a major methodological inconsistency. Her stated sociological method, followed consistently with regard to the "Jewish" material that she surveyed in the Old Testament, Pseudepigrapha, and Dead Sea scrolls, consists of interpreting theological constructs in terms of the sociological function that they serve; that is, the construction and maintenance of social distinctions. So for example we read: "Covenantal identity has not only a temporal, historical dimension, a theological dimension of having a relationship with God, but also a social dimension."[20] And again: "[the theological construct of a covenant] with God is never a purely religious, vertical relationship, but it always has a social dimension"[21] inasmuch as it is constitutive of a social distinction. However, Christiansen fails to apply her sociological analysis to Paul's "Christian" theological formulations. They are simply restated in theological terms similar to those in which they were expressed in the Pauline sources: identity is "based on faith in Christ," it "narrows ... to a faith relationship." The "Christian" theological language is not subjected to the same sociological analysis to which the "Jewish" sources had been. Although Christianity is viewed as a "narrow" religion, it is never said to be particularistic; to do so would overturn the fundamental theological distinction upon which Christiansen's entire work

---

[19] *Covenant in Judaism and Paul*, 239.
[20] *Covenant in Judaism and Paul*, 1.
[21] *Covenant in Judaism and Paul*, 8.

is predicated, that Judaism is a particularistic religion, Christianity a universalistic one.

In fact, had Christiansen applied her sociological method to the Pauline sources, she would have had to formulate an entirely different conclusion: both Christianity and Judaism are particularistic religions, although the particularism is in each case defined according to different criteria. Had she applied her own type of sociological analysis to the Pauline material, Christiansen would have been faced with a Christianity, the social boundaries of which were constituted on the basis of a "narrow ... faith relationship" or, translating this theological language into sociological terms, on the basis of a particular religious ideology and the specific sets of practices that are associated with it and by which it is constituted. Had she followed through with her sociological analysis however, this would have undermined the theological framework upon which her entire book is structured, and which serves as the basis of her evangelical appeal. The basic distinction between Christianity, construed as a universal and therefore, according to Christiansen, implying a "true identity," based on the order of creation, and Judaism construed as a particularistic religion, based on an ethnic distinction and therefore implying a "false identity," is rendered false by the consistent application of Christiansen's sociological method. However, rather than abandoning her theological model, she chose to apply her sociological model selectively; that is, only to the "Jewish" material that she surveyed. Christiansen's study entails an act of methodological boundary-setting: the border between Judaism and Christianity is also the boundary at which sociological analysis ceases. Christianity is off-limits to sociological analysis.

In those rare instances in which Christiansen does grant that Christianity is a religion that is constituted on the basis of an act of social delimitation, she exculpates Christianity from the charge of particularism, as we have already seen, by asserting that "Christianity itself does not impose boundaries, rather they are imposed from the outside ..." However, this defense is inadequate: the same is true of any social grouping. Any social grouping can only define itself in relation to other groups: to be a member of a particular group, x, implies that one is not also at the same time a member of the particular group, y.[22] Thus, membership in any group implies an analytical act both of inclusion and exclusion: to define oneself as x is also to define oneself as *not y*.

---

[22] Here I assume an agonistic model of inter-group dynamics for heuristic purposes; it is the model that Christiansen's study implies. For her, both Judaism and Christianity, since they are predicated on "opposed principles" (p. 244), entail mutually exclusive "identities." The truth of the one entails the falsity of the other.

My own study will address only tangentially the central sociological question raised by Christiansen, the question of the ways in which the idea of covenant is used to construct social boundaries. Rather, my own study explores the way in which covenant, more particularly the phrase "new covenant," is deployed within discourses that attempt to influence the perceptions of certain target audiences, and thereby to influence the local situation within which those discourses were produced. Christiansen's sociological method is undoubtedly correct in positing a link between theological constructs and the construction of social identity. However, these theological constructs are deployed in a nuanced way, such that the construction of identity is but one of a number of social functions that discourses on "covenant" and "new covenant" served. I will try to identify several of these functions during the course of the study.

3. Outline of the Project

This study follows the three step methodology outlined. I will construct an account of the local conditions in response to which the texts were produced, attempt to delineate some of the discursive strategies involved in the construction of particular narratives, and finally, juxtapose my readings of those narratives with salient aspects of the local situations as I have (re)constructed them. This juxtaposition facilitates comparison, highlights contrast, and provides the data whereby one may make reasonable inferences about the interests that are served by the discourses under investigation.

This study is divided into two main sections; the first, in chapters 2 and 3, treating the conception of the new covenant entailed by the Damascus Document and the second, in chapters 4 and 5, dealing with Paul's discourse on the new covenant in 2 Corinthians 3–4. In chapter 2, I briefly outline the use of the term "covenant" in ancient Near Eastern treaties, in the Hebrew Bible, and in Second Temple Jewish literature. Subsequently, I discuss the covenantal ideology of D, setting it in the context of rivalries with the Hasmoneans over priestly legitimacy, and the Pharisees over authority in matters of halakhic interpretation. In chapter 3, I examine the use and significance of the Damascus Document's phrase, "the new covenant in the land of Damascus." Turning to the relevant Pauline material, in chapter 4 I advance a new hypothesis regarding the identity and ideology of Paul's missionary rivals in Corinth. In the following chapter, I examine the discursive interests at work in Paul's construction of the new covenant in 2 Cor 3–4. In chapter 6, I draw some conclusions regarding the relationship of the discourses of the Damascus Document and 2 Corinthians to the two local situations in response to which those texts were written, and formulate hypotheses regarding the interests served by those texts. Finally, I make some methodological proposals about the way in which comparative work between early Christian and (other) early Jewish texts ought to proceed.

Chapter 2

The Covenant According to
the Damascus Document

1. Prolegomenon: Texts and Dates of Composition

The Damascus Document contains an extensive collection of halakhot, or legal precepts, that were followed by the members of the Essene sect.[1] These legal precepts are prefaced by a series of homilies addressed to members of the sect on the occasion of the sect's annual covenant renewal ceremony. At this ceremony the members of the sect listened to a recitation of the sect's halakhot, after which the members of the sect pledged an oath to follow all of the legal precepts that they had just heard. The annual covenant renewal ceremony was a special occasion within the sect; it was during this ceremony that the members of the sect ritually entered into the ancient covenant that God had first established with Israel during the time of Abraham. According to the ideology of the sect, the only way in which one could participate in the ancient covenant with Israel was by participating in the sect's covenant renewal ceremony.

The legal precepts that the Damascus Document contains pertain to all aspects of Jewish life. Some of the precepts legislate the proper processes whereby a male member of the sect should choose a bride, while others defined limits within which sexual interaction between married members of the sect could take place. The Damascus Document includes the sect's

---

[1] There has been intensive discussion as to the relation of the Essene sect, as described by Philo and Josephus, to the sect that produced much of the material in the Dead Sea scrolls. For overviews of the discussion and bibliography, I refer the reader to the article by T. Beall, "Essenes," *EDSS* 1:262–269, and J. VanderKam, "Identity and History of the Community" in *The Dead Sea Scrolls After Fifty Years: A Comprehensive Assessment* (P. W. Flint and J. VanderKam, eds., Leiden, Boston, and Köln: Brill, 1999) 487–533. My own view follows the consensus that Philo and Josephus described the same sect that produced the scrolls. However, in the following discussion, my characterizations of the sect will be based on the material from the Dead Sea scrolls. Philo and Josephus will be adverted to only occasionally to provide supporting information. I will follow the standard practice of referring to the sect that was largely responsible for writing and copying the Dead Sea scrolls as "the Essenes." However, I will also refer to the same group by the designation, "the Association," "the *yaḥad*," or simply "the sect," when the context makes it clear that the Essene sect is being referred to.

interpretation of the Sabbath laws in the Pentateuch, laws governing the presentation of offerings at the Jerusalem Temple, various precepts regarding impurity, priestly laws for the diagnosis of skin disease, and laws pertaining to other matters as well. The collection of laws that is preserved in the Damascus Document was meant to order the practices of all members of the Association, as well as those of their wives, children, and servants.

The Document was not written in its entirety at one particular point in time, but probably had a long history during which various portions were added to the text.[2] Many of the legal precepts in the Damascus Document probably originated with the group that started the Dead Sea sect, perhaps during the 150s BCE.[3] Other precepts in the Damascus Document undoubtedly originated at later points in the sect's history, as the group engaged in ongoing reflection on Scripture, the source from which many of the sect's laws were derived. Even the homiletical sections of the Damascus Document probably represent a collection that grew over a period of time. We will briefly discuss the dating of the Damascus Document, but only after we have discussed the provenance and dating of the various manuscripts in which the Damascus Document has been preserved.

1.1. The Text of the Damascus Document

Copies of portions of the Damascus Document (abbreviated D) come from two different locations. Two versions of the Damascus Document were

---

[2] So for example, P.R. Davies, who states that "the opinion of most scholars has been that the Admonition is a complex work" (*The Damascus Covenant: An Interpretation of the "Damascus Document"* [Sheffield, UK: JSOT Press, 1982]) 48. Davies interprets 1–8, 19–20 as an organized literary product with a coherent plot and structure, while recognizing that it incorporates earlier literary elements. Ben Zion Wacholder has recently argued the contrary, assigning D to a single author in *The New Damascus Document: the Midrash on the Eschatological Torah of the Dead Sea Scrolls: Reconstruction, Translation, and Commentary* (STDJ 56; Leiden and Boston: Brill, 2007) 9–11, 139–40.

[3] The majority of scholars place the activity of the sect's early leader, the Righteous Teacher, in the time of Jonathan (High Priest from 152 to 143 BCE). The literature on this subject is vast; here I only refer the reader to the articles by Michael Knibb, "Teacher of Righteousness," *EDSS* 2:918–921 and Hanan Eshel, "Jonathan (Hasmonean)," *EDSS* 1:422-423 and the literature cited in those articles. However, John J. Collins ("The Time of the Teacher: An Old Debate Renewed" in *Studies in the Hebrew Bible, Qumran, and the Septuagint Presented to Eugene Ulrich*; P. W. Flint, E. Tov, and J. C. VanderKam, eds. [Leiden and Boston: Brill, 2006] 212–229), in dialogue with Michael O. Wise ("Dating the Teacher of Righteousness and the Floruit of his Movement," *JBL* 122 [2003] 53–87), has recently offered serious criticisms of the standard view, and it can no longer be regarded as secure.

found in the Cairo Genizah in 1896 or 1897.[4] (The Genizah versions are designated by the abbreviation "CD," indicating "Cairo Damascus Document.") The first version (MS-A) contained the section from 1:1–14:23 and the second version (MS-B) had material from 19:1–20:34. The material contained in MS-B overlaps, with some variation, the material preserved in MS-A, cols. 7–8. These two versions of the Damascus Document, however, are incomplete. Additional material that belonged in the Damascus Document was found in the caves near Qumran. This material contains a section at the beginning of the Damascus Document that was not preserved in the Cairo Genizah versions. Also, the ordering of the material in the versions found at Qumran differs from the two versions found in the Cairo Genizah. However, scholars have been able to piece together a composite version of the Damascus Document by comparing and combining the Qumran versions with the Cairo Genizah versions of the text.[5]

The versions of the Damascus Document found in the Cairo Genizah are medieval copies, and so are of no value in determining the earliest date at which the Damascus Document must have been copied and circulated. The versions found in the Qumran caves, however, were copied and disseminated at a time that was much closer to the period in which the latest portions of D were being written. The earliest version of the Damascus Document from among the Dead Sea scrolls fragments was copied during the first half or middle of the first century BCE (approx. 100–50 BCE).[6] This copy includes material that was previously known from the

---

[4] Solomon Schechter obtained a large collection of medieval manuscripts from the Cairo Genizah during the winter of 1896–1897. He published two manuscripts of CD in 1910 under the title, *Documents of Jewish Sectaries, Vol. 1: Fragments of a Zadokite Work* (Cambridge: University Press). Stefan Reiff gives an overview of the genizah finds in his article, "Cairo Genizah," *EDSS* 1:105–108.

[5] I will refer to the composite text that results when the Qumran fragments are integrated with the Cairo Genizah manuscripts as D, and retain the designation CD only when referring specifically to the Cairo Genizah manuscripts. Although H. Stegemann announced in 2000 plans to edit a composite version of D, incorporating all of the extant Qumran fragments with the Cairo Genizah manuscripts ("Towards the Physical Reconstruction of the Qumran Damascus Document Scrolls," pp. 177–200 in *The Damascus Document: A Centennial of Discovery*, J. Baumgarten, et al., eds., Leiden: Brill, 2000), he has now been preempted in this endeavor by Ben Zion Wacholder, whose recent publication of a composite edition will be a welcome addition to the tools available for the study of the Damascus Document (*The New Damascus Document*).

[6] Cross dates this MS to the first half of the first century BCE (*Ancient Library of Qumran* [3rd ed., Sheffield: Sheffield Academic Press, 1995; 1st ed. 1958] 95–96). H. Stegemann prefers a date between 75–50 BCE, as asserted in his book, *The Library of Qumran: On the Essenes, Qumran, John the Baptist, and Jesus* (Grand Rapids, MI and Cambridge, UK: Eerdmans and Leiden: Brill, 1998; trans. of *Die Essener, Qumran,*

homilies in the Cairo Damascus Document (MS-A and MS-B). In addition to the material that overlaps with the Cairo Damascus Document, 4Q266 also includes material from the beginning of the Damascus Document that was not included in the MSS found in the Cairo Genizah. From among the fragments of CD that were found in the Qumran caves, the latest copy was made during the "beginning of the second half of the first century CE" (c. 50 CE).[7] The remaining eight copies of CD from which fragments were found at Qumran indicate that these copies were made during the span from the latter half of the first century BCE to the middle of the first century CE. The period of time during which these ten copies of CD were made corresponds well with the period during which Qumran was used as a meeting place for the sect's community council, from roughly 100 BCE until 68 CE, when the site apparently was burned by the Romans. However, the dates when the Qumran copies of CD were made are indicative of the period of time when the group that held its meetings at Qumran used CD, copying and recopying it as old scrolls became worn and illegible. The dates during which the copies of CD were made, of course, do not indicate when CD was originally composed. The latest portions of CD may very well have been composed before the date of the earliest copies that we have from Qumran. A full list of the copies of the Damascus Document, along with the approximate dates at which they were copied, appears below.

Johannes der Täufer und Jesus [Freiburg im Breisgau: Verlag Herder, 1993]) 117. J. Baumgarten in *DJD* 18 gives a paleographical date of "from about the first half or the middle of the first century BCE." A portion of 4Q266 was subjected to Accelerator Mass Spectrometry, which yielded a date from 5–80 CE for the sheepskin on which 4Q266 was written (Charlotte Hempel, *The Damascus Texts* [Companion to the Qumran Scrolls 1; Sheffield: Sheffield Academic Press, 2000] 21). There are still unresolved issues regarding the efficacy of radiocarbon dating vis-à-vis paleographical (cf. G. Bonani, et al., "Report and Discussion Concerning Radiocarbon Dating of Fourteen Dead Sea Scrolls," pp. 441–453 in *Methods of Investigation of the Dead Sea Scrolls and the Khirbet Qumran Site*, M. Wise, et al., eds., New York: New York Academy of Sciences, 1994; I. Carmi, "Radiocarbon Dating of the Dead Sea Scrolls" in L. Schiffman, E. Tov, and J. VanderKam, eds., *The Dead Sea Scrolls Fifty Years After Their Discovery: 1947–1997* [Jerusalem: Israel Exploration Society, 2000] 881–888). I will follow the standard paleographical dating in my own arguments.

[7] Hempel, *The Damascus Texts*, 22.

1.2. The Manuscripts of the Damascus Document[8]

Text Number	Paleographical Date
4Q266	100–50 BCE
4Q267	late 1st century BCE–early 1st century CE
4Q268	mid-first century CE
4Q269	late 1st century BCE
4Q270	1–50 CE
4Q271	50–25 BCE
4Q272	late 1st century BCE
4Q273	late 1st century BCE[9]
5Q12	50–1 BCE
6Q15	1st century CE
Cairo Genizah MS-A	10th century CE
Cairo Genizah MS-B	12th century CE

1.3. Dating the Damascus Document

The Damascus Document is a composite work. Various portions of the document were probably written at different points in the history of the Dead Sea sect. The earliest portions of D probably consist of some of the sect's laws.[10] According to D, many of these laws originated with a group that was active in Damascus[11] and was led by the "Righteous Teacher" (CD 20:31–33a). If we assume the standard view that the Righteous Teacher was active during the middle of the second century BCE, during the time of Jonathan, we would have reason to believe that some of the sect's laws probably originated during this period. However, since the sect did not cease the exegetical activities that resulted in the propagation of new laws (cf. 1QS 6:6b–8a; 8:11b–12a), many of the laws in D probably arose after the period in which the "Righteous Teacher" was active. One of the narrative portions of D mentions the death of the "Righteous Teacher" (cf. CD 19:35–20:1; 20:14, 32). However, since it is difficult to establish a

---

[8] This list is indebted to the succinct presentation of the manuscript fragments in Hempel, *The Damascus Texts*, 19–25.

[9] Three unidentified fragments were photographed together with these fragments of D. The paleographical dating of the unidentified fragments has been set at the middle or late second century BCE (Baumgarten, *DSD* 18:194). However, it is not at all certain that these fragments actually constitute a part of the Damascus Document. They do not correspond with any of the text of CD that is known from the other manuscripts.

[10] Cf. P. R. Davies, *The Damascus Covenant* and C. Hempel, *The Laws of the Damascus Document: Sources, Tradition, and Redaction* (STDJ 29; Leiden: Brill, 1998).

[11] I take "Damascus" to be a reference to a city or region in Syria, and not a veiled reference to Qumran. This problem will be discussed more fully later in this chapter.

date for the teacher's death, all that we can safely conclude is that the section of D that mentions the teacher's death must have been written at some time after the 150's BCE, perhaps significantly later.

A more secure point of reference is provided by D's reference to the Book of Jubilees (CD 16:2–4). James VanderKam argues that Jubilees must have been written between 160 and 150 BCE.[12] The portion of the Damascus Document that mentions Jubilees must have been written subsequent to this period. This information provides a firm *terminus a quo* for the production of D, or at least the portion of it that includes the reference to Jubilees.

The *terminus ad quem* for the CD in its final form falls in the first half of the first century BCE, the date of the earliest extant copy of the work, 4Q266.[13] Combining the *termini a quo* and *ad quem*, we conclude that the final form of D must have been attained between the 150s BCE and 50 BCE (the latest likely date for the copying of 4Q266).

Both Michael Knibb[14] and Hartmut Stegemann[15] have used CD 19:35b–20:1a and 13b–15a, which refer to the death of the sect's Righteous Teacher, in attempts to date D. Both Knibb and Stegemann argue that D had reached its final form by 100 BCE. However, in light of recent criticisms of the standard view that the Teacher was active during the middle of the second century BCE,[16] any attempt to date D on the basis of calculations involving the purported date of the Teacher's death must be rejected.

Dupont-Sommer also attempted to provide a narrow range of dates for the production of D. Dupont-Sommer argued on the basis of CD 8:8–12a that this section was written after 63 BCE, when Pompey captured Jerusalem.[17] This argument has been adopted most recently by Gregory

---

[12] "Jubilees, Book of" in Schiffman and VanderKam, eds., *The Encyclopedia of the Dead Sea Scrolls* (2 vols., Oxford: Oxford University Press, 2000) 1:434.

[13] Stegemann, *Library of Qumran* 117, attempts to supply a more precise paleographical date: 75–50 BCE. We will continue to use the less precise, but more generally accepted, range of c. 100–50 BCE.

[14] "The Place of the Damascus Document" in *Methods of Investigation of the Dead Sea Scrolls and the Khirbet Qumran Site: Present Realities and Future Prospects* (M. O. Wise, N. Golb, J. J. Collins, and D. Pardee, eds., Annals of the New York Academy of Sciences 722; New York: New York Academy of Sciences, 1994) 149–150.

[15] *The Library of Qumran*, 117.

[16] See Collins, "The Time of the Teacher," and Wise, "Dating the Teacher of Righteousness."

[17] *The Dead Sea Scrolls: A Preliminary Survey* (Oxford, UK: Basil Blackwell, 1954) 54. Dupont-Sommer argued on the basis of other evidence that D should be dated to 45–40 BCE (p. 57).

Doudna.[18] The cornerstone of this position is that D refers to a certain "head of the kings of Greece." Since during the Hellenistic period, the various Greek kingdoms were not ruled by a single ruler, the "head" referred to in D was not Greek. However, as Doudna argues, after Pompey received a grant of *imperium* from the Roman Senate, he could be thought of as being the "head" of the kings of Greece, as he *de facto* possessed overwhelming power throughout the eastern Mediterranean.[19]

The criticism that can be made of Dupont-Sommer in this regard is relevant to Doudna's restatement of the position, despite his attempts to forestall it: if the author of D had intended a reference to a Roman general, why are the *Kittîm*, "Romans," not mentioned? Why instead do we have only a reference to Greeks? Besides this criticism, we may also note that D's reference to the "head" serves to link the Greek kings with the scriptural citation in Deut 32:33. The "head of adders" mentioned in the scriptural citation is identified, in pesher-like manner, with the "head of the kings of Greece" (ראש מלכי יון). Due to the fact that the term "head" serves as the catchword by which the "kings of Greece" are identified as the referent of Deuteronomy's "head of adders," it may be unwise to place much emphasis on this word as the key to identifying a particular historical referent. More important is the fact that the pesher-style of interpretation was used to identify Deuteronomy's text with the "kings of Greece." Rather than referring to the Roman Pompey, it is more likely that the "head of the kings of Greece" refers to a Hellenistic king. One might suggest that the text refers to Demetrius III Eukairos, who according to Josephus (*Ant* 13.5–14.2, §§372–383), engaged in an abortive attempt to capture Jerusalem in 88 BCE, inflicting a defeat on Alexander Jannaeus in the process. Demetrius is referred to in 4QPesher Nahum, frag. 3, col. 1, lines 2–3.[20] In this passage, the "kings of Greece" (מלכי יון) are clearly distinguished from the "rulers of the Romans" (מושלי כתיים). In the same passage, Demetrius is referred to as a "king of Greece" (מלכ יון). The designation מלכי יון, "kings of Greece," is common to D and Pesher Nahum. Whether or not CD 8:8–12 encodes a reference to Demetrius III Eukairos, the passage in Pesher Nahum weakens the argument that would identify D's "head of the kings of Greece" with Pompey. Roman rulers are referred to as מושלים, and Rome and Greece are clearly distinguished.

If we are to take CD 8:8–12 as a reference to an imminent attempt of Demetrius III Eukairos to enter Jerusalem, then this section of D must have been written ca. 88 BCE. Any attempt to relate CD 8:8–12 to a particular

---

[18] *4Q Pesher Nahum: A Critical Edition* (JSPsSupp. 35; New York, NY and London, UK: Sheffield Academic Press, 2001) 639–674.

[19] *4Q Pesher Nahum*, 640–642.

[20] On the incident, see Doudna, *4Q Pesher Nahum*, 632–635.

historical situation, however, must remain tentative. Therefore, the *termini* established on the basis of D's citation of Jubilees (CD 16:2–4) and the latest likely date at which 4Q266 was copied indicate a date range between ca. 150 BCE and ca. 50 BCE. If CD 8:8–12 refers to Demetrius, it is possible that this section of D was one of the latest portions added to the text, perhaps during the first quarter of the first century BCE.

2. Precursors to D's Construal of "Covenant"

The members of the Association[21] described entry into their group as "entering into the covenant." The ideology and language of the "covenant" has a long and rich history both within the Hebrew Bible and in the political history of the Mediterranean and Mesopotamian regions. In order to establish a broad context within which we may situate the use of the term בְּרִית in the Dead Sea scrolls as well as its Greek counterpart in the LXX and in the New Testament, διαθήκη, let us survey the relevant material from the Hebrew Bible and other sources.

Moshe Weinfeld has offered an analysis of the two types of covenants that are present in the Hebrew Bible that will prove to be particularly useful to us in this study. Weinfeld has argued that the two types of covenants present in the Hebrew Bible, "the obligatory type reflected in the Sinai covenant and the promissory type reflected in the covenants with Abraham and David,"[22] are modeled on two types of treaties evidenced throughout Mesopotamia from the middle of the second millennium onward. The two treaty types include the political treaty, in which a sovereign imposes conditions of vassalship upon a weaker state, and the royal land grant, in which a master rewards a servant for service faithfully rendered.[23] Stipulations for the continuance of the agreement are neces-

---

[21] I use "Association" here as a translation of the noun יַחַד, which the sectarian scrolls use as a self-designation. I am anticipated in this by Bruno Dombrowski, *Ideological and Socio-structural Developments of the Qumran Association as Suggested by Internal Evidence of Dead Sea Scrolls* (Kraków: Enigma Press, 1994). On the structural similarities between the *yaḥad* and Hellenistic associations, see Matthias Klinghardt, "The Manual of Discipline in Light of Statutes of Hellenistic Associations" in M. O. Wise, et al., eds., *Methods of Investigation* 251-270. The classic study is that of Moshe Weinfeld, *The Organizational Pattern and the Penal Code of the Qumran Sect: A Comparison with Guilds and Religious Associations of the Hellenistic-Roman Period* (NTOA 2; Göttingen: Vandenhoeck & Ruprecht, 1986).

[22] "The Covenant of Grant in the Old Testament and in the Ancient Near East" *JAOS* 90 (1970) 184.

[23] George E. Mendenhall's pioneering work provided a foundation for the study of the Biblical covenants in the light of ancient Near Eastern treaties ("Ancient Oriental and

sarily involved in the vassal treaty. The land grant, on the other hand, may or may not involve stipulations to be followed by the donee.

The vassal treaty provided the model upon which the covenant in the book of Deuteronomy was based. In Deuteronomy, YHWH offers protection and a perpetual homeland to the Hebrew people in return for their adherence to certain stipulations that YHWH had set forth. These stipulations included the Decalogue. The covenant at Sinai is the premier example of this type of conditional covenant in the Hebrew Bible. The covenant remains in force so long as both parties continue to uphold their end of the bargain: YHWH bestows the land to his people, while YHWH's people are expected to obey the laws that he has set forth.

The covenant of grant, on the other hand, need not entail stipulations for the covenant to remain in force. Weinfeld adduces instances in which Mesopotamian kings reward their servants (or vassals) with grants of land, or with the rule over some region, in return for their loyal service to the overlord. The premier example of this type of grant in the Hebrew Bible is YHWH's covenant with Abraham in Gen 15:7–12, 17–18 (the J version), in which YHWH is said to have given to Abraham the gifts of progeny and land. Similarly, YHWH is said to have granted David a royal dynasty that was to rule in perpetuity (e.g., 2 Sam 7). In these instances, the covenant functions as a gift offered by YHWH in return for the fidelity of his servants.

While the treaty-type of covenant by definition is a bilateral agreement, with both parties expected to fulfill certain obligations, the grant type does not necessarily involve any obligation on the part of the donee. However, even in this latter type, stipulations are involved in some cases. Weinfeld draws attention to a Hittite grant between Mursili II and Abiradda, in which "the Hittite suzerain guarantees the rights of DU-Tešup, Abiradda's son, to throne, house, and land, only on the condition that DU-Tešup will not sin ... against his father".[24] This grant parallels the conditional contract of Ps 132:11b-12, in which YHWH declares that he will give David an enduring dynasty, on the condition that his descendants observe the covenant and treaty that YHWH will teach them (זו אלמדם אם ישמרו בניך בריתי ועדתי[25]). In the Priestly retelling of the covenant with Abraham

---

Biblical Law," *BA* 17.2 [1954] 26–46; "Covenant Forms in Israelite Tradition," *BA* 17.3 [1954] 50–76). The fundamental work on the covenant in early Judaism is that of Klaus Baltzer, *The Covenant Formulary in Old Testament, Jewish and Early Christian Writings* (Philadelphia: Fortress Press, 1971; trans. by David E. Green of *Das Bundesformular* [Heidelberg, 1959]).

[24] *The Promise of the Land: The Inheritance of the Land of Canaan by the Israelites* (Berkeley: University of California Press, 1993) 245–246.

[25] MT incorrectly points וְעֵדֹתִי, "and my testimonies."

(Gen 17), YHWH's promise of land is clearly subject to a set of stipulations.

Not only could the covenant of grant be subject to a set of stipulations, but in some cases the covenant includes a clause stating that, even though the grant is given in perpetuity, nonetheless the donee could be punished for failing to act with loyalty towards the donor. Weinfeld cites a Hittite pact in which land is granted in perpetuity, although the pact includes a punishment clause, in the case that the donee's progeny fail to serve the donor loyally:

> After you, your son and grandson will possess it, and nobody will take it away from them. If one of your descendants sins ... the king will prosecute him at his court. Then when he is found guilty ... if he deserves death he will die. But nobody will take from the descendant of Ulmi-Tešup *either his house or his land* in order to give it to a descendant of somebody else.[26]

In the Hebrew Bible, the perpetual grant with a punishment clause is found in 2 Sam 7:14–16 and in Ps 89:27–33, which states,

> I will make him (i.e., David) the firstborn, the highest of the kings of the earth. Forever I will keep my steadfast love (חסד) for him, and my covenant (ברית) with him will stand firm. I will establish his line forever, and his throne as long as the heavens endure. If his children forsake my law and do not walk according to my ordinances, if they violate my statutes and do not keep my commandments, then I will punish their transgression ... but I will not remove from him my steadfast love ... (NRSV).

A recognition of these two broad categories of covenant; 1) the treaty-type which involves mutual obligations by both parties, and 2) the covenant of grant, which may or may not involve obligations on the part of the donee and sometimes included a punishment clause for the failure of the donee's progeny to act with loyalty towards the donor, is a prerequisite to understanding the later development of the idea of covenant as it was employed within the sectarian Association, on the one hand, and the LXX and NT, on the other. But before we examine the DSS and NT, let us take a closer look at YHWH's covenant with Moses at Sinai. It is this covenant that the Association takes as the ideological, and to some extent, ritual precursor of its own formulation of the covenant.

2.1. Translating ברית *and Related Terms*

The term "covenant" in English is defined as "a solemn agreement between two or more groups; compact."[27] Even given this definition, however, many readers often overlook the element of mutual obligation that is

---

[26] Quoted in Weinfeld, *The Promise of the Land*, 237. The italics in the quotation are Weinfeld's.

[27] "Covenant" in *The World Book Dictionary* (2 vols., Chicago, IL: Doubleday & Co., 1976) 1:478.

the defining characteristic of many of the uses of the term "covenant" in English translations of the Bible. In those instances in which "covenant" refers to that which was established at Sinai, we must keep in mind the element of mutual obligation that binds both parties to the covenant. In the case of the Sinai covenant, as we have noted, YHWH is expected to deliver to his people the land of Canaan in return for their obedience to his Torah. The element of mutual obligation is expressed in such English terms as "treaty" or "pact." Alan Segal suggests the translation "contract."[28]　The German terms *Vereinbarung* and *Übereinkunft* may imply an element of reciprocal obligation, as does the French *alliance*. However, none of the terms used to translate the Hebrew ברית is sufficient on its own to indicate the content of the "agreement" that has been reached. One must be sensitive to the contexts in which the term ברית occurs in order to determine the stipulations upon which a ברית/covenant is based in any given instance.

However, as soon as we mention the "stipulations" of the ברית/ covenant, we must introduce another important term, Heb. עֵדָה. This term is synonymous with ברית and may appear in parallelism with it in poetic texts (Ps 25:10; 132:12). Cognate with the Heb. עדת is an Aramaic word, עָדַיָּא used only in the plural to denote "treaty stipulations," or in a collective sense to refer to the "treaty" itself.[29] The Priestly writer uses the term עדת to refer to the "treaty" or "covenant" in its physical manifestation: the two stone tablets inscribed at Sinai. It is the inscribed stone tablets that are referred to in the Priestly writer's phrase, ארון העדת, the "ark of the covenant."[30] The ark was the box in which, according to P, the stipulations of the covenant between Yahweh and Israel were housed.

The term ברית and the related term עדת imply a treaty that involves stipulations which obligate two parties. The term ברית, however, was also used in the Hebrew Bible to refer to donations that corresponded to the pattern that Weinfeld designated the "covenant of grant." Some of the formulations of YHWH's gift of the land to Abraham fall into this category. It is this usage of the term ברית that gave rise to one of the most

---

[28] *World Religions: Western Traditions*; edited by W. G. Oxtoby (2nd ed., Oxford and New York: Oxford University Press, 2002) 41.

[29] See J. Fitzmyer, *The Aramaic Inscriptions of Sefire* (Rome: Biblical Pontifical Institute, 1995 [1967] 57–59) and C. L. Seow, "The Designation of the Ark in Priestly Theology," *HAR* 8 (1984) 192–194.

[30] The mistaken translation, "ark of the testimony" is the result of relating עדת to the root עוד, "to warn, admonish, testify" (as per *BDB*, s.v.) rather than the root עהד, "to bind, to make a covenant," according to Seow, "The Designation of the Ark," and F. M. Cross, *Canaanite Myth and Hebrew Epic: Essays in the History of the Religion of Israel* [Cambridge, MA: Harvard Press, 1997; 1st ed. 1973] 267). However, Fitzmyer's discussion of the term and its relation to the Akkadian *adû* would seem to imply a biconsonantal root, עד (*Sefire* 57–59).

common understandings of the English "covenant," "the solemn promises of God to man as set forth in the Old and New Testaments."[31] The Septuagintal translation of the term ברית by the Greek διαθήκη reinforced this understanding of "covenant." Since the Greek διαθήκη was most often used to designate a "will," the διαθῆκαι in the LXX became associated with the "promises" whereby God bequeathed some gift to humankind.

While the connotation of the Greek term διαθήκη was appropriate to some of the uses of ברית in the Hebrew Bible, such as certain formulations of God's "covenant" with Abraham, it was highly inappropriate for others, such as the Sinai covenant, which was not a "donation," but a pact which mutually obligated both parties to adhere to certain stipulations. The Greek language certainly did have suitable translation equivalents for the Heb. ברית in its use to designate a bilateral treaty. The Greek term συνθήκη designates a bilateral treaty.[32] However, the translators of the LXX generally avoided using this term, presumably because they wished to present the biblical "covenants" as enduring "promises" (which the translation διαθῆκαι implies), which God would at some point see fit to uphold.[33]

In the NT, the impact of the LXX's translation of ברית by διαθήκη is clearly felt. The construction of "covenant" in the NT is devoid of any sense of mutual obligation between two parties, as had been the case in many of the instances of ברית in the Hebrew Bible. In a few instances, it is clear that the term διαθήκη is interpreted as referring to the document by which a person bequeaths his property to his posterity, contingent upon his death (cf. Heb 9:16–17). At this point, let us examine in more detail the ways in which the term ברית is used in a few key books in the Hebrew Bible.

2.2. The "Covenant with the Ancients" and the Sinai Covenant

The ideology of the covenant in D depends heavily on Scriptural prototypes. Chief among these are the covenant between YHWH and Abraham and the later Sinaitic covenant. Briefly, the covenant with Abraham is narrated in two different accounts, once in Gen 15 (the account of the "J"

---

[31] "Covenant" in *The World Book Dictionary* 1:478.

[32] Cf. M. Weinfeld, "Covenant Terminology in the Ancient Near East and Its Influence on the West," *JAOS* 93 (1973) 190–199.

[33] The term διαθήκη appears in works that were translated from Heb. or Aram. almost 300 times, whereas the term συνθήκη occurs only seven times as a translation of words such as ברית or מישרים, according to Hatch and Redpath's *Concordance to the Septuagint* (2nd ed.; Grand Rapids, MI: Baker, 1998). The recent dictionary of the LXX by J. Lust, E. Eynikal, and K. Hauspie glosses διαθήκη as "treaty, covenant," but it is not clear that the Greek translation actually retained the connotations of the Hebrew term, as this gloss supposes (*A Greek-English Lexicon of the Septuagint* [Stuttgart: Deutsche Bibelgesellschaft, 2003] 137–138).

source) and again in Gen 17 (from the Priestly redactor). In the account in Gen 15, YHWH speaks to Abram/Abraham, promising him two things: that Abraham's descendants would be exceedingly numerous (v. 5) and that those descendants would in time take possession of the land from the Euphrates southward to the Nile (i.e., from Mesopotamia to Egypt; v. 18). The treaty is ratified when YHWH, in the form of a smoking fire-pot, passes between the two halves of a series of dismembered sacrificial animals: a heifer, a goat, and a ram (v. 9). The two halves of the dismembered animals graphically depicted the penalty under which YHWH placed himself in the event that he did not adhere to his covenantal obligation: he would suffer the same dismemberment. Of course on the level of J's narrative, this threat is metaphorical: YHWH is not depicted as having a body at all, but is symbolized by the fire-pot. The dismemberment of animals in a ceremony of treaty ratification however, was a widespread practice in the ancient Mediterranean region. Generally, the two parties to the treaty passed through the two halves of some animal, sometimes repeating some oath formula such as, "If I do not adhere to the stipulations of the treaty, so may it be done to me."[34]

The account in Gen 17, added by the Priestly writer in the sixth century BCE, is very different. It lacks the reference to the ritual of dismemberment and adds new material. In P's account, Abram/Abraham is again promised land, but in this version the extent of the territory to be given is reduced. In this latter version, YHWH deeds to Abraham the territory of Canaan, whose southern border stretched from the Wadi el-Arish eastward to ancient Kadesh Barnea and then northward past Damascus to ancient Lebo Hamath. The Mediterranean formed the western border, while the Jordan River and Jebel Druze (modern Jabal ad Duruz) marked the eastern extremity.[35] In another innovation vis-à-vis the J account, the Priestly writer connects the Abrahamic covenant with the practice of circumcision. Circumcision, according to Gen 17:9–14, was both a stipulation of the covenant and a visible symbol that the covenant had been enacted. Incidentally, circumcision retained this dual signification into the Hellenistic period. According to some accounts, circumcision constituted the primary requirement of the Torah (cf. *Ant* 20.44),[36] while according to other

---

[34] Compare the treaty from Sefîre, in which among other curses to be enacted should one of the parties to the treaty prove unfaithful to it, we read, "(Just as) this calf is cut in two, so may Matiʿel be cut in two, and may his nobles be cut in two!" (Stele 1, face A, l. 40). The translation is that of Fitzmyer, *Sefîre* 47.

[35] Carl G. Rasmussen, ed., *NIV Atlas of the Bible* (Grand Rapids: Zondervan, 1989) 91.

[36] In this section the strictly observant Jew Eleazar admonishes King Izates of Adiabene, "In your ignorance, O king, you are guilty of the greatest offense against the law ... For you ought not merely to read the law but also, and even more, to do what is com-

sources, circumcision constituted a "sign" that one was a member of God's chosen people.[37]

The promise made to Abraham subsequently devolved upon his progeny Isaac and then Jacob (Gen 26:3–5; 28:3–4). In the Priestly account of the giving of the law at Sinai, the older covenant with Abraham, Isaac, and Jacob is recalled (Lev 26:42). In CD 1:4, the covenant with Abraham, Isaac, and Jacob is referred to as the "covenant of the ancestors" (ברית הראשנים). The "covenant of the ancestors," for CD as well as for Leviticus (cf. 26:45), recalls YHWH's giving of the land to Abraham's posterity. This will form a fundamental element in the Damascus Document's ideology of the covenant.

If the covenant with Abraham in Gen 15 represented the grant type according to Weinfeld's typology, then the Sinaitic covenant represents a treaty type of covenant. In the Sinaitic covenant, both YHWH and his people must follow specifically defined parameters in order for the covenant to remain in effect. Those parameters are most clearly defined in the book of Deuteronomy, the formulation of which, as Weinfeld and others have shown, was deeply influenced by Assyrian vassal treaties. Deuteronomy displays significant parallels with the vassal treaties of Esarhaddon, both in terms of its formulation of a bilateral agreement between vassal and suzerain, in which both parties undertake certain obligations to one another, and in terms of its vocabulary. The Assyrian vassal treaties often include a provision that Assyria will serve to protect the vassal state in the event that the latter is attacked, while the vassal agrees to support unconditionally the Assyrian overlord and his progeny, who will succeed him on the throne.[38]

In Deuteronomy, YHWH takes the place of the Assyrian overlord in initiating the treaty (ברית). YHWH imposes certain stipulations on the Hebrews. Among other things, they are to worship no gods other than YHWH and they are to fashion no image of him. These stipulations are familiar as the ten commandments (Deut 5:6–21; cf. Ex 20:2–17). In addition, YHWH imposes rules to govern many aspects of civic life, including dietary laws, rules concerning tithing, care for the indigent, the

---

manded in it. How long will you continue to be uncircumcised?" The translation is that of Feldman, *LCL*, Josephus, vol. 9:413.

[37] Cf. Jubilees 15:26: "Anyone who is born, the flesh of whose private parts has not been circumcised by the eighth day does not belong to the people of the pact which the Lord made with Abraham .... Moreover, there is no sign on him that he belongs to the Lord ...." Translation is that of J. VanderKam, *The Book of Jubilees* (Corpus Scriptorum Christianorum Orientalium, Scriptores Aethiopici 88; Louvain: Peeters, 1989) 93.

[38] See D. J. McCarthy, *Treaty and Covenant: A Study in Form in the Ancient Oriental Documents and in the Old Testament* (Rome: Biblical Institute Press, 1981) and M. Weinfeld, *The Promise of the Land*, 222–264, for examples of this type of treaty.

"year of release" (15:1–23), a cultic calendar (16:1–17), rules for the local administration of justice, laws pertaining to adultery, and regulations pertaining to the conduct of the king, in the event that one should materialize (16:18–17:20). A collection of various civic and cultic laws is preserved in 18:1–25:16. Certainly this body of disparate laws had existed prior to the composition of Deuteronomy, but it was part of the literary and theological artifice of the Deuteronomist to bring these elements together and to present them as stipulations in the *berît* between God and his people. YHWH, for his part, is to make good on his promise to the patriarchs to deliver the land of Canaan to Abraham's posterity (cf. Deut 1:7–8 and *passim*).

Although it is never stated in Deuteronomy, the Sinaitic covenant establishes a system of exchange: in return for their absolute loyalty and exclusive worship of YHWH, YHWH gives to the people the land of Canaan. However, Deuteronomy often reiterates that, should the people fail to uphold their end of the bargain, YHWH also will cease to fulfill his covenantal commission: the result will be the people's exile (cf. 28:63–64; 29:28).

The final form of the book of Deuteronomy was in fact brought about by a group of Judeans who were themselves exiles from their homeland. According to F. M. Cross, Deuteronomy had achieved its final form by 550 BCE.[39] This redaction of the book was brought about by a group who had been exiled after the Babylonian invasion of Judea early in the sixth century. Part of the rhetoric of Deuteronomy serves to provide a theological justification for the fact of the exile: it constituted YHWH's response to his people's apostasy. But on the other hand, Deuteronomy holds forth the hope that, if the people should recall the covenantal stipulations and begin to adhere to them once again, YHWH would also respond by restoring to them their promised land (30:1–10).

Deuteronomy provides the model of the Sinaitic covenant, and presents clearly the ideology of the covenantal pact whereby the people are expected to abide by YHWH's stipulations (including the ten commandments, adherence to a festal calendar, and various other cultic and civic laws), while YHWH was expected to deliver the land of Canaan into the hands of the Israelites. This covenantal model, however, is not the only pattern that Deuteronomy bequeathed to the sectarian Association. Deuteronomy also provided an equally important model of covenant renewal. As we have already noted, the final version of the Book of Deuteronomy was completed by tradents writing in exile during the sixth century BCE. For these tradents the idea of covenant renewal became an important theme. Given the Deuteronomistic motif that linked Israel's faithfulness

---

[39] *Canaanite Myth and Hebrew Epic*, 274–289.

to YHWH's covenantal stipulations with Israel's control of the "promised land," as well as the historical situation of the exile, it was taken as a theological as well as a social imperative to impress upon the exiles the possibility that, if they diligently adhered to the stipulations of the Sinaitic covenant, they might be restored their "promised land." For this reason, presenting a program of "covenant renewal" by reiterating a collective commitment to the stipulations of YHWH's treaty, became an important part of the Deuteronomist's program.

The Book of Exodus likewise presents a ready pattern for exile and restoration in the story of the wilderness wandering. After the abortive attempt at ratifying the Sinaitic covenant presented in Ex 19–32 (which represents the combined work of JEP), in which the people had broken one of the ten commandments even before they had been brought down from the mountain (the golden calf incident), Moses shatters the two stone tablets of the law. Moses' shattering of the tablets gives physical expression to the status of the pact (ברית) between YHWH and the people: it was nullified even before it had been ratified. Moses and his band of refugees were forced to wander in the desert for a generation, until all of the members of the "rebellious generation" had died. It is at the end of this forty years of wandering, when the people are poised to enter into the land of Canaan in order to take possession of it, that the covenant between YHWH and the people must finally be ratified.

Returning to the Book of Deuteronomy, we find that when the Israelites are poised to enter Canaan to take possession of it, Moses delivers an oration and presides over a ceremony that provides the prototype for later attempts at covenant renewal, including the Damascus Document's. It is in this section of Deuteronomy that we find some of the elements that the sectarian Association will later incorporate into their own covenant renewal ceremony.

The basic structure of this ceremony according to Deut 5:1–6:25 is simple:

1) Moses convenes "all Israel." This undoubtedly includes women and children (5:1a).
2) Moses begins his oration with the exhortation, שמע ישראל, "Listen, Israel!" (5:1b).
3) Moses briefly recounts the prior covenant attempt at Horeb (5:1b–5).
4) The stipulations of the covenant are outlined and interpreted (5:6–6:25).

At the conclusion of the ceremony, the participants bind themselves to the covenantal agreement by invoking a series of curses upon any who would transgress the covenant's stipulations, "Cursed be anyone who makes an idol ..." "Cursed be anyone who does not uphold the words of this law by observing them!" (Deut 27:15 and 26, NRSV). Each curse is recited by the Levites, and in response to each recited curse the people acknowledge their assent by shouting "Amen!" The Association's *Serekh ha-Yahad* also includes a series of curses, recited by priests and assented to with a resounding, "Amen." Like D's, the *Serekh*'s version of the covenant renewal ceremony was influenced by Deuteronomy.

Deuteronomy also attests to the observance of a periodic covenant renewal ceremony. According to Deut 31:9–13, every seventh year during the Festival of Booths, all of the people of Israel, including men, women, children, and even resident aliens, were to assemble for a covenant renewal ceremony in which the law was read aloud. In this way the stipulations of the covenant between YHWH and his people could be rehearsed and presumably, the people's adherence to them reinforced.

2.3. Covenant Renewal in Ezra-Nehemiah

The books of Ezra-Nehemiah offer information that bears on the covenant renewal ceremony. In 539 BCE, the Persian King Cyrus had issued an edict releasing various peoples who had been exiled under the Babylonian regime.[40] The Persian king Artaxerxes I Longimanus authorized Ezra to return to Judea with a group of exiles, probably in 458 BCE.[41] Nehemiah led a group of returnees to Jerusalem in 445 BCE.[42] Artaxerxes had charged Ezra with reconstructing Judean society along lines stipulated in a version of the Torah which appears to have incorporated legislation from the Deuteronomic and Priestly strands of the Pentateuch (cf. Ezra 7:11–26).[43]

Nehemiah 8:1–10:39 brings together accounts from disparate sources, and which stand in some tension with one another, to form a single narrative that recapitulates the pattern of the covenant renewal ceremony. The redactor of Ezra-Nehemiah, whose editorial work is usually thought to have been undertaken around 400 BCE,[44] presents Ezra and Nehemiah as contemporaries (Neh 8:9; 12:26), although within the sources utilized by the redactor, "Nehemiah plays no part in Ezra's reform, and Ezra plays no part in Nehemiah's attempt to fortify Jerusalem."[45] The editor juxtaposes

---

[40] J. M. Miller and J. H. Hayes, *A History of Ancient Israel and Judah* (Philadelphia: Westminster Press, 1986) 443.

[41] Miller and Hayes, *A History*, 468–469. The chronology of the periods in which Ezra and Nehemiah operated has been the subject of debate. Here we follow what appears to be the most likely view.

[42] Miller and Hayes, *A History*, 469–470.

[43] After pointing out a number of contradictions between Ezra and the present form of the Pentateuch regarding calendrical matters, John Collins concludes, "Nonetheless, it remains true that the law of Ezra corresponds substantially to the Torah as we know it, including both Deuteronomy and some form of the Priestly Code" (*Introduction to the Hebrew Bible* [Minneapolis, MN: Fortress Press, 2004] 433).

[44] R. Klein, art. "Ezra-Nehemiah, Books of," *ABD* 2:734.

[45] Collins, *Introduction to the Hebrew Bible*, 437.

material relating to Ezra (8:1–18; 9:1–5), Nehemiah (10:1–39), and an apparently independent corporate confession (9:6–37). The editorial juxtaposition however, suggests the pattern of the covenant renewal ceremony. We may compare the composite narrative in Nehemiah with the earlier account of the covenant renewal ceremony from Deuteronomy. The structure of the composite narrative in Nehemiah may be outlined as follows:

1) Prolegomenon (8:1–18): during the Festival of Booths in the seventh month, Ezra reads the law (apparently including material from the D and P strands of the Pentateuch) in Hebrew and explains it to the gathered assembly. The assembly includes "men and women and all who could hear with understanding" (8:2).

2) The eighth day of the festival was declared a day of fasting and penitence (9:1–5).[46] The people confess their sins and listen to the law read for "a fourth part of the day." They participated in a communal confession and worship session for the following "fourth part of the day."

3) The assembled people[47] recite a communal prayer on the twenty-fourth day of the seventh month. The confession includes the following elements:

    a. Address to YHWH and recollection of the covenant with Abraham (9:6–8);
    b. The mighty acts of God are recalled. The mighty acts referred to include
       YHWH's deliverance of the Hebrews from Egypt (9:9–15);
    c. YHWH's faithfulness to the covenant is contrasted with the people's
       disobedience to it (vv. 16–31);
    d. The people complain that they are "slaves in the land that you gave to our
       ancestors" (vv. 32–37).

4) The people, led by Nehemiah, pledge themselves to adhere to the law of Moses (10:1–39).

The pattern that is created by the editorial juxtaposition of the various materials at his disposal incorporates the elements that one would expect of a covenant renewal ceremony.[48] As in Deuteronomy, a ceremony is held during the Festival of Booths, in the seventh month. As in Deuteronomy, the ceremony includes women, although children are apparently excluded.[49] In both the Deuteronomy ceremony and in that in Nehemiah, some version of the sacred history is recalled. This involves a recollection of the "mighty acts of God" in some form and inevitably culminates in an

---

[46] This material sits uneasily after the section in chap. 8, in which the Festival of Booths was described as a time of "great rejoicing" (8:12, 17).

[47] Following the MT version. According to the LXX, it was Ezra who recited the prayer on the people's behalf (LXX inserts καὶ εἶπεν Ἐσδρας at the beginning of 9:6).

[48] These elements may be compared with D. J. McCarthy's reconstruction of the "covenant formulary," with the caveat that the examples that we have selected from Deut and Neh. both represent examples in which an older covenant/treaty is being recalled and renewed, and not made for the first time, as in the bulk of McCarthy's examples in *Treaty and Covenant*.

[49] The category "all who could hear with understanding" in Neh 8:2 is probably meant to exclude those who, for any reason, were mentally incapacitated.

account of the covenant between YHWH and the people that was made at Sinai-Horeb. Following this account, the stipulations of the covenant are read aloud (i.e., the reading of the law). The account in Nehemiah does not include a recitation of the curses that the people invoked upon themselves should they fail to adhere to the stipulations of the covenant. Perhaps the account in Nehemiah implies that the curses have already befallen the people (cf. 9:35–37), and are therefore not recited. Another difference between the accounts in Deuteronomy and Nehemiah is the addition of the penitential prayer in Neh 9. Such prayers became characteristic during and after the exilic period,[50] and would certainly be appropriate in a covenant renewal context in the post-exilic period. It is difficult to ascertain the editor's intention in juxtaposing the materials that he had at his disposal in the manner and order in which he did. It is possible that he wished to present the post-exilic community under the leadership of Ezra and Nehemiah (at the same time) as having accomplished a renewal of the covenant upon their return to Judea.[51]

It is important to note, however, that while D and the *Serekh ha-Yaḥad* rely on the covenantal patterns established within the biblical narratives, the literature of the sectarian Association appears to bypass the Ezra-Nehemiah account. This is an important elision, the reason for which is not hard to deduce: the literature of the Association does not countenance a successful attempt at covenant renewal during the Persian Period. In fact, the Association's construal of Israel's history contradicts the idea that the Sinaitic covenant had been renewed prior to the sect's own formation. In order to appreciate the Association's position on this matter, we must pause briefly to delineate the differences between the Association's view of Israel's history and that of modern biblical scholars.

Most modern chronologies of the "history of Israel," following the lead of the canonical scriptures, including Ezra-Nehemiah, delineate an "exilic period" beginning in 586 BCE and lasting until successive waves of exiles returned to Judea from the late sixth to the middle of the fifth century BCE. The "exilic period" ends when the "Persian period" begins. Books written during the Persian period, such as Ezra-Nehemiah and the books of Chronicles, are considered "post-exilic" works.

---

[50] For examples, see Rodney A. Werline, *Penitential Prayer in Second Temple Judaism: The Development of a Religious Institution* (Atlanta, GA: Scholars Press, 1998).

[51] Michael Duggan's study of Neh 8-10 treats this section as depicting a covenant renewal ceremony in a revision of his dissertation entitled, *The Covenant Renewal in Ezra-Nehemiah (Neh 7:72B—10:40): An Exegetical, Literary, and Theological Survey* (SBL Dissertation series 164; Atlanta: Society of Biblical Literature, 2001). Duggan notes the use of the verb כרת, idiomatic for "cutting (a covenant)," as well as the nouns אמנה, "firm agreement," and שבעה, "oath," indicative of the ratification of a covenant (pp. 256–257, 286–287).

However, the distinction of "exilic" and "post-exilic" periods does not occur in D. From the perspective of D, the circumstances of the exile had persisted until the present time. The author of CD 1 considered that his own time (perhaps the late Hasmonean period) was a time of exile for the Jewish people. It apparently seemed self-evident to the author of D that "the promise of the land" and the expected return of Diasporic Jews to that land had not yet been fulfilled. This idea was widespread during the Second Temple period, as M. Knibb has shown.[52] Since Ezra-Nehemiah reports a return of Diasporic Jews to Jerusalem and may imply an attempt at covenant renewal there, D does not make mention of these books, as they provided information that would have weakened D's claim that the covenant, broken prior to Jerusalem's destruction by Nebuchadnezzar, was only renewed during the time of, and by the Association.

2.4. Covenant Renewal in Jubilees and Jeremiah

If the Association chose to ignore the accounts of Ezra-Nehemiah, its appropriation of the Book of Jubilees was much more enthusiastic. Jubilees provides important precedents for the covenant renewal festival as it was practiced within the Association. Jubilees recounts a series of covenants between God and various figures including Noah, Abraham, Isaac, Jacob, and finally Moses. These covenants, according to Jubilees, were made in each case except Noah's on the fifteenth day of the third month, during the Feast of *Shavu ʿot* (cf. Jub 14.1, 10, 18, 20; 15:1–14; 16:13–14; 22:15,30).[53] Jubilees cites this date (3/15) as the occasion of a yearly covenant renewal ceremony (Jub 6:17): "For this reason it has been or-dained and written on the heavenly tablets that they should celebrate the Festival of Weeks during this [i.e., the third] month – once a year – to renew the covenant (*laḥaddis kidan*) each and every year."[54]

Like Deuteronomy before it, Jubilees connects the covenant with the promise of the land, and explains the diaspora as being the result of the people's violation of the covenant's stipulations (1:5, 9–10, 13). However, Jubilees predicts that the people will in the future return to the law of Moses, at which time God will "build [his] temple among them and dwell with them" (1:17). The people are expected to make confession of their

---

[52] Knibb, "The Exile in the Literature of the Intertestamental Period," *Heythrop Journal* 17 (1976) 253–272; idem, "Exile in the Damascus Document," *JSOT* 25 (1983) 99–117, esp. 109–110.

[53] Noah's covenant was established instead on 3/1 (cf. Jub 6:1, 10).

[54] Trans. of VanderKam, cited in his art., "Covenant," *EDSS* 1:152. I have added to VanderKam's translation the transliteration of the Ethiopic text that appears in parentheses. A critical text of the Ethiopic versions is available in VanderKam, *The Book of Jubilees: A Critical Text* (Corpus Scriptorum Christianorum Orientalium; Scriptores Aethiopici 87; Louvain: Peeters, 1989).

past transgressions, and to engage in an act of corporate repentance. In response to this anticipated act of repentance, Jubilees cites God as declaring (1:23b–24),

I will cut away the foreskins of their minds and the foreskins of their descendants' minds. I will create a holy spirit for them and will purify them in order that they may not turn away from me from that time forever. Their souls will adhere to me and to all my commandments ... I will become their father and they will become my children.[55]

As we will see a bit later, the sectarian Association found Jubilees' ideology very congenial. The sect agreed with Jubilees that the age in which they lived was an age of exile; but they, like the author of Jubilees, expected that God would at some point regather the people to the promised land.[56] The sect speaks of times of corporate repentance (e.g., CD 2:5; 4:2), and sees Jubilees' promise that God would "create a holy spirit for them and ... purify them" as fulfilled in the act of joining the sect (cf. 1QS 3:6b-8).

There remains one important biblical antecedent to the way in which the "covenant" was construed within the Association. This is the Book of Jeremiah, which likely provided the inspiration for the phrase "new covenant" (ברית חדשה) that is used in D (CD 6:19; 8:21; 20:12). If Deuteronomy provided an ideology that had proven to be very serviceable to the sectarian Association, Jeremiah's construction of the "new covenant" did not prove so unambiguously useful. Far from it, for while the sect appears to have appropriated the phrase "new covenant" from Jeremiah, Jeremiah's own construction of what constituted the "new covenant" was in some ways diametrically opposed to the practices of the Association.

Jeremiah is the only biblical or non-biblical book in which the term ברית חדשה, "new covenant" is known to have occurred, prior to D. As we have seen, Jubilees did use the phrase "to renew the covenant" (Eth. *laḥaddis kidan*). Although this formulation is very close conceptually to the usage in Jeremiah and D, it is only in these latter two texts that we encounter the noun-adjective combination that seems to point to D's literary dependence on Jer 31. Although Jeremiah seems to have bequeathed the phrase "new covenant" to D, other characteristic elements of Jeremiah's "new covenant" are notably absent from D. Jer 31:31-34 reads as follows:

Behold! Days are coming (oracle of YHWH), when I will make a new covenant with the house of Israel and the house of Judah; (one) not like the covenant that I made with their

---

[55] Trans. of VanderKam, *The Book of Jubilees*, 5.

[56] The volume edited by James M. Scott, entitled *Restoration: Old Testament, Jewish, and Christian Perspectives* (Supplements to the Journal for the Study of Judaism 72; Leiden and Boston: Brill, 2001), treats the theme of return from exile in texts from the Hebrew Bible to early rabbinic and Christian literature.

fathers when I strengthened their hand to bring them out of the land of Egypt, my covenant which they broke, though I ruled over them (oracle of YHWH). For this is the covenant that I will make with the house of Israel: after these days (oracle of YHWH) I will set my law within them, and I will write it on their hearts, and I will be their God and they will be my people. And no one will teach his companion or his brother any longer, saying, "Know YHWH"; for all of them will know me, from the least to the greatest of them, for I will forgive their transgression, and their sin I will remember to longer.[57]

Jeremiah follows Deuteronomy in viewing the exile as a punishment for the people's transgression of the stipulations of the covenant. Jeremiah looks forward to a time in which Israel and Judah will have completely internalized the stipulations of the covenant (i.e., the Torah). Jeremiah presents YHWH as saying, "I will set my law within them, and I will write it on their hearts." While the members of the Association presumably would have been very open to appropriating this language, verse 34 posed more of a problem for the sect. According to Jer 31:34, when the "new covenant" is established, "no one will teach his companion or his brother any longer, saying, 'Know YHWH.'" However, the teaching and study of the Torah constituted a very important part of the sect's practice. Each year, the sect's halakhot were read during the covenant renewal ceremony. According to 1QS 6:7, members of the sect were to stay awake for a portion of each night of the year studying the law, and reporting to one another the results of their exegetical labors (1QS 8:11–12). The intense focus on studying and teaching the law within the sect did not correspond with Jeremiah's optimistic view that when the new covenant was established, the law would be so internalized among YHWH's people that they would not have any need to study it. This rather important discrepancy between Jeremiah's construction of the "new covenant" and the later practice of the Association is the probable reason why the sect adopted only the phrase "new covenant" from Jeremiah, while steering clear of Jeremiah's construction of the new covenant in other respects. Jeremiah's phrase, ברית חדשה, proved both memorable and useful to the writer(s) of D's admonitions. Jeremiah's ideology, however, was utopian, and stood in stark contrast with the necessary practice of a group that considered itself the recipient of God's "new covenant." In order for the sect to maintain strict order as it attempted to enforce adherence to sectarian halakhah, teaching the law became a key element in the sect's regime of praxis.

Each of the texts that we have reviewed is important either as a precursor or a model for D's construction of the new covenant. However, the sect evidenced a complex mode of reception with regard to these texts. While D and 1QS largely assimilated Deuteronomy's ideology of the

---

[57] All translations are my own unless noted otherwise.

covenant, they passed over the account of the covenant renewal in Ezra-Nehemiah. Although the sect's own covenant renewal ceremony has some structural parallels with the one recorded in Neh 8, D does not mention this attempt at covenant renewal in its historical survey in CD 1. Since the author(s) of D's exhortations considers that the exile continued until the writer's own time, it seems unlikely that he considered Ezra-Nehemiah's attempt at covenant renewal to have been effective.

Jubilees is an important precursor to D inasmuch as it presents a pattern in which the covenant is renewed on a yearly basis, on the fifteenth day of the third month, during the Feast of Weeks. The Book of Jeremiah also appears to have influenced D. The sect's reception of Jeremiah, however, was limited. The sect adopted Jeremiah's phrase ברית חדשה, while at the same time avoiding Jeremiah's utopian construction of the new covenant, whereby YHWH's people would have the law "written on their hearts," and thus had no need of studying it. The sect passed over in silence those texts from scripture that did not cohere with or which contradicted its own practice and ideology, while adopting and utilizing the ideologies or language of those texts that the sect deemed useful.

3. The Covenant According to D

The Damascus Document evinces a rich ideology of the covenant, which depends to some degree on the covenantal theology of biblical precursors such as Deuteronomy, but which also develops this ideology in significant ways. The ideology of the covenant in D is well suited to represent the interests of the sect that produced and utilized it. D's ideology of the covenant is dualistic; all of humanity may be classified into two categories: those who adhere to the precepts of the covenant and those who do not. The principle of classification involved in this categorical dualism is sociological: those who are identified as members of the sect are classified as "within the covenant" and those who are not members of the sect are classified as "without." Those who are categorized as existing outside of the covenant include both Gentiles and more importantly, Jews who do not belong to the sectarian Association. Pharisees, Sadducees, and other Jews who did not belong to any of the Jewish sects of the time were construed as existing outside of God's covenant.

The ideology of the covenant is alluded to multiple times in the hortatory section at the beginning of D. In many instances, even when the term ברית is not used, nonetheless the ideology of the covenant is still clearly present. The hortatory sections in CD-A 1:1–8:21 and CD-B 19:1–20:34 contain much material that is relevant to the sect's construction of the covenant. Three Qumran texts, 4Q266, 4Q267, and 4Q268 preserve material that originally preceded the beginning of the text as it appears in CD-A.[58] This material, although fragmentary, also has some information relevant to D's construction of the covenant.

3.1. The Prologue

The 4Q material that precedes the beginning of CD-A and overlaps it is preserved in 4Q266 1.1–2.1.1-6, 4Q267 1.1–8, and 4Q268 1.1–8. The most extensive of these fragments, 4Q266, includes a blank space just before the point of its overlap with CD-A, indicating a section break. The material that precedes CD-A 1.1 has been referred to as a prologue, and as J. G. Campbell has remarked, "there are numerous turns of phrase which link this passage to the language of Qumran in general and to the remainder of the Admonition in particular."[59]

Several of the themes that are prominent in the prologue to D are treated in more detail in the sections that begin with CD 1.1, and will be treated more fully in connection with those passages. Two themes however, deserve mention from the outset. The first is the idea that Israel lives in a time of divine punishment. This punishment, as we will see in connection with CD 1.1–4a and 11b–18, was inaugurated as the result of violations of the stipulations of the covenant, and takes the form of a covenant lawsuit (ריב). The members of the sect are instructed to keep separate from non-Essene Jews who, because they do not adhere to sectarian halakhot,[60] are deemed guilty of violating the terms of the covenant. The relevant lines read as follows:[61]

```
]                 לב]ני אור הנזר מדרכי רשעה
]                 [עד תום מועד פקודה ברוח עולה
]                 [ישמיד אל את כול מעשיה להבי כלה
בת]ועי רוח    [למסיגי גבול וכלה יעשה לפועלי
רשעה
```

[...for the so]ns of light to separate from the paths of wickedness
...until the completion of the appointed time of visitation upon the spirit of transgression
...God will destroy all its deeds, so as to bring destruction

---

[58] H. Stegemann, "Towards the Physical Reconstruction," 193–197.

[59] *The Use of Scripture in the Damascus Document 1–8, 19–20* (Berlin and New York: de Gruyter, 1995) 42.

[60] Non-Essene Jews are referred to as מסיגי גבול, which refers to halakhic transgressions.

[61] The texts of 4Q266–268 are printed in García Martínez and Tigchelaar, *DSSSE* 1:580–605; J. M. Baumgarten, *DSSR* 1:78–131; idem, *DJD* 18:23–121; Ben Zion Wacholder, *New Damascus Document*, 22–27. The text presented here is based on that of Baumgarten in *DSSR*.

on those of iniqui[tous spirit ...]for the movers of the boundary and he will bring
   about destruction for those who work
wickedness.

According to D, a time if visitation (מועד פקודה) has been set which will
involve the destruction/annihilation (ישמיד/כלה) of those guilty of halakhic
transgressions. Fragment 2 of 4Q266, lines 3–4 juxtapose the time of
God's wrath against his enemies with times of favor for those who adhere
perfectly to the stipulations of the Torah.

הו[∘א חקוק קץ חררון לעם לא ידעהו   ]

[והוא הכין מועדי רצון לדור]שי מצוותו ולהולכים בתמים דרך

...a time of wrath is decreed for a people who does not know him,
[but he has established appointed times of favor for those who exam]ine his commandments and act perfectly.

The criterion that distinguished whether one would be destroyed or receive
divine favor was clear: in order to receive God's favor, one needed to
examine the commandments and follow them perfectly (הולכים בתמים
דרך). Following the commandments, of course, required that one interpret
them, and this interpretation was supplied by the Essene community.

3.2. CD 1:1–4

The prologue preserved in 4Q266–268 is followed by material that corre-
sponds with the A manuscript from the Cairo Genizah, and which develops
themes alluded to in the prologue, notably that of the covenant lawsuit.
CD-A opens its hortatory section with a call to listen that is reminiscent of
Moses' injunctions for the people to listen to his sermons in Deuteronomy.
CD 1:1-4a reads as follows:

ועתה שמעו כל יודעי צדק ובינו במעשי

אל כי ריב לו עם כל בשר ומשפט יעשה בכל מנאציו

כי במועלם אשר עזבוהו הסתיר פניו מישראל וממקדשו

ויתנם לחרב

And now listen, all who know righteousness, and understand the works of God; for he
has a legal dispute with all flesh, and he will execute judgment against all who despise
him. For because of their treachery (with) which they abandoned him, he hid his face
from Israel and from his sanctuary and he gave them over to the sword.

This is a well-crafted passage, which succinctly lays out many of the
principles of D's covenantal ideology. The first point that we will wish to
notice is the statement that God has a ריב, a "legal dispute" or "covenant
lawsuit," with all humanity. The term ריב in this context refers to the
deity's legal case against humans: all humans are held to be guilty of
violating the stipulations of the covenant that God had made with Israel.
The stipulations of the covenant are expressed in the sect's interpretation

of the law of Moses (CD 15:8–10). Lines 3 and 4 invoke the topos of Israel's exile as resulting from its failure to adhere to the stipulations of the covenant. Line 3 adds to this topos an element that Ezekiel had earlier explored: as a result of the people's transgression of the Torah, God was forced to leave the temple (Ezek 10:18–19; 11:22–23). The phrase "he hid his face from Israel and from his sanctuary," refers at once to God's withdrawal of his divine protection as the result of the people's sin as well as alluding to God's departure from the temple immediately prior to the time of the exile.

It may seem strange that Israel's failure to adhere to the stipulations of God's covenant with Israel would result in God's opening a ריב with all humanity (כל בשׂר). Whereas D had precursors in asserting that God had a covenant lawsuit with Israel (Hos 4:1) and Judah (Hos 12:3),[62] exilic texts such as the Book of Jeremiah had already broadened the scope of the ריב so that it encompassed all humanity. Jer 25:31, from which D seems to have borrowed, reads, כי ריב ליהוה בגוים נשפט הוא לכל בשׂר הרשעים נתנם לחרב, "For Yahweh has a legal dispute with the nations. He has entered into judgment with all flesh; the wicked he will deliver to the sword." Jeremiah's words adumbrate the apocalyptic worldview that would later permeate the sectarian Association. The Fourth Book of Ezra also illustrates the idea that God holds all humanity accountable to the Torah. In a meditation of the fate of the Gentiles, an angel says to Ezra (7:21–22, 24):

> For God strictly commanded those who came into the world, when they came, what they should do to live, and what they should observe to avoid punishment. Nevertheless, they were not obedient ...
> They scorned his Law, and denied his covenants,
> they have been unfaithful to his statutes
> and have not performed his works.[63]

Jeremiah, D, and IV Ezra agree that God holds not only Israel, but also the other nations accountable to covenantal stipulations. D's use of the term ריב in the beginning of its discourse hints at the judgment that is in store for those who have, in the eyes of the author of the narrative, violated the stipulations of God's covenant.

Humanity's culpability in the face of God's covenant lawsuit is dramatically heightened by the use of the phrase, במועלם אשׁר עזבוהו, "because of the treachery (with) which they abandoned him." The term מועל, "treachery" or "perfidy," like the term ריב, has legal connotations here. It refers to the faithlessness that is involved when one party fails to adhere to

---

[62] Although in Hosea the dominant image is one of marital infidelity: Israel is accused of leaving its husband, YHWH, in order to have relations with foreign gods.

[63] Trans. of B. Metzger in *OTP* 1:537.

the stipulations set forth in an agreement; in this case it refers to human-ity's failure to adhere to the Torah.[64]   However, it should be remembered that one of the stipulations of the Torah was that the people should worship only YHWH. D may be invoking the connotation that God's people had abandoned him to worship foreign gods. The "legal case" would involve a charge of adultery: God's wife, Israel, had abandoned him to fornicate with foreign gods. The term עזב, "to abandon" has legal connotations,[65] and could be used to describe the abandonment of a marital contract.[66]   In 1 Enoch 1:9, God is described as coming "to execute judgment against all, and he will slay all the impious, and he will convict all flesh for all their impious deeds." Here impiety (ἀσέβεια) is the main charge which is brought against "all flesh." It seems that in D, as in 1 Enoch, the failure to worship Israel's God was viewed as an offense for which "all flesh," including Gentiles, were to be held responsible. D however, like Fourth Ezra, views this as a halakhic transgression; it involves a failure to adhere to a stipulation of the Torah "given through the hand of Moses."

3.3. CD 1:4–8

The opening passage continues in the next few lines, adding more infor-mation pertinent to understanding D's construction of the covenant. Lines 4–8a read:

ובזכרו ברית ראשנים השאיר שארית

לישראל ולא נתנם לכלה ובקץ חרון שנים שלוש מאות

ותשעים לתיתו אותם ביד נבוכדנאצר מלך בבל

פקדם ויצמח מישראל ומאהרן שורש מטעת לירוש

את ארצו ולדשן בטוב אדמתו

And when he recalled the ancestral covenant,[67] he left a remnant for Israel, and he did not deliver them to destruction. And during the time[68] of wrath – when he had deliv-

---

[64] Cf. the use of מעל, in both its nominal and verbal forms, in Lev 26:40, where Is-rael's "treachery" in forsaking the stipulations of the covenant results in YHWH's leading the people into exile.

[65] Cf. 1 Kgs 19:10, 14 for the phrase עזב ברית. See also Weinfeld, *The Promise of the Land*, 227–228, where he notes that עזב is often used in conjunction with the term חסד, "faithfulness" to a covenant, and is equivalent in meaning to the verb סור – which itself is often used to refer to departure from a former covenantal relationship.

[66] Cf. Isa 54:6–7.

[67] Lit., "covenant of the first ones."

[68] This phrase is usually translated, "At the end of wrath ..." Although the term קץ may itself denote an "end" in some cases, in CD it does not seem to carry this sense. Apart from the use in CD 1:5, the term occurs sixteen times, each time with reference to a specific period of time (cf. CD 2:9; 4:5, 9; 5:20; 6:10, 14; 7:21; 12:23; 15:7, 10; 16:2; 19:10 (bis); 20:15, 13:20 (restored) and perhaps 14:18). In light of this evidence for the use of קץ to refer to a period of time, we should probably read the use in CD 1:5 in the

ered[69] them into the power of Nebuchadnezzar, king of Babylon for three hundred ninety years[70] – he turned his attention to them[71] and caused a cultivated root to sprout from Israel and Aaron, in order to inherit his land and to enjoy the bounty of his earth.

In this passage once again we encounter the leitmotif that the time of the exile, here specifically presented as inaugurated when God "delivered" Israel into the power of Nebuchadnezzar, occurred as punishment for Israel's lack of fidelity to the stipulations of the covenant. The figure of 390 years is derived from Ezek 4:1–8, which stipulates that Israel will remain in captivity in Babylon for this period. These lines of D add a crucial point to D's construal of covenantal theology: whereas Israel had become unfaithful to the stipulations of the covenant, nevertheless God remained faithful. CD 8:14–15 cites Deut 7:8, "Not by your righteousness or your uprightness of heart do you come to dispossess these nations, but rather from his love of your fathers and his keeping of the oath."[72] God is

---

same light. Read in this way, the phrase parallels the expression in CD 5:20, ובקץ בקץ מעל ,6:10, בכל קץ הרשע ;6:14; 12:23; 13:20 (restored); 15:7; 20:23, חרון הארץ; ישראל, and most relevant, 7:21, בקץ הפקודה (cp. 19:10).

[69] The ל+ infinitive constr. of נתן + 3d pers. masc. sg. possessive suffix as a temporal expression, as in Isa 7:15, "when he knows." The phrase is usually translated, "after he had delivered," which, despite Rabinowitz's protestation ("A Reconsideration of 'Damascus' and '390 Years' in the 'Damascus' ('Zadokite') Fragments," *JBL* 73 [1954] 14, n. 8b), is grammatically possible. Since the infinitive construct does not indicate time of action, a temporal indication must be supplied in translation. The temporal significance assigned to לתיתו depends on the prior question of how one understands the phrase ובקץ חרון.

[70] The clause שנים שלוש מאות ותשעים ... נבוכדנאצר מלך בכל represents a rather glaring example of anacoluthon, interrupting the construction ... ובקץ חרון פקדם ויצמח. R. H. Charles (*APOT* 2:800), followed by Rabinowitz ("A Reconsideration" 13-14, n. 8a) and M. Boyce ("The Poetry of the *Damascus Document* and its Bearing on the Origin of the Qumran Sect," *RQ* 14 [1990] 617, 620), views the intrusive phrase as an interpolation. If so, it may have stemmed from the same hand that added CD 16:2b–4a.

[71] The verb פקד is used ten times in CD (in the Cairo Genizah versions, duplicate passages being counted only once). In the hortatory sections the term is used to refer to God's "visitation" or "inspection" that precedes his judgment or results in his wrath (5:15; 7:9=19:6; 8:2=19:14). In the halakhic/community discipline section, the term is used to refer to the "mustering" of the community for inspection, or the *mevaqqer*'s "inspection" or "examination" of an individual or group (15:6, 8; 10:2; 13:11; 14:3, 6). A third usage of the verb occurs in contexts in which someone turns attention toward a third party, motivated by concern for that party's welfare (cf. Ps 8:5; Jer 23:2). Baumgarten's translation (*PTSDSSP* 2:13), "he turned his attention to them and caused to grow ..." reflects this usage. Baumgarten's translation understands פקד as a favorable "viewing" that resulted in or was contemporaneous with the action of the following verb, ויצמח, and I have adopted it here.

[72] Trans. of Baumgarten, *PTSDSSP* 2:29.

presented as faithful to the oath of the covenant,[73] even though Israel was not. This passage construes the covenant as unconditional, on the pattern of the royal land grant that Weinfeld delineated. As we have seen, one of the patterns on which the biblical covenants were constructed is that of the land grant with a clause stipulating that punishment is warranted should the progeny of the donee fail to act loyally toward the donor. The "ancestral covenant," according to D, was a perpetual covenant. While the progeny of "the ancestors" (הראשנים) were liable to punishment, should they fail to remain loyal to Yahweh, nevertheless the donation of the land to Abraham's seed remained in force.

3.4. Covenant in Jubilees and D

D's mention of the "ancestral covenant" provides a suitable cause to examine the larger covenantal context within which D places the "ancestral covenant." James VanderKam has made some observations that constitute an appropriate starting-point for our discussion:[74]

> Covenant is an important concept in the *Serekh ha-Yaḥad* and the Damascus Document. The covenant mentioned in these works is the same as the one made and renewed in the Hebrew Bible. It is the covenant made with the ancestors (see CD 1:4; 8:17–18; 19:30–31 ...)[75] and is eternally valid (... CD 3:4). The group(s) reflected in the texts are the chosen ones who maintain the agreement in the present evil age (... CD 20:17). In their time God had again remembered the covenant and renewed it with them (see ... CD 1:4; 6:2; 19:1 ...). The primary difference between the biblical covenant involving Israel and the one in the sectarian texts is that in the latter the covenantal community now embraces only those who pledged to adhere to the covenant in sectarian terms.

VanderKam included his observations about the nature of the covenant in the Qumran texts within the context of a discussion of the covenant as it is used in the Book of Jubilees. It appears that D has much in common with Jubilees in its understanding of the covenant. An examination of Jubilees' account of the covenant offers comparative material by which we may clarify D's understanding of the covenant.

The Book of Jubilees recounts a version of Israel's sacred history from the time of the creation of the world to the giving of the law at Sinai, recasting much of the material that appears in the Pentateuch. However, Jubilees does not, as does the Pentateuch, adhere to a chronological scheme, according to which the story of the creation of the world is followed by that of Noah, and so on. Rather, Jubilees recounts its version of

---

[73] On the role of the taking of oaths in covenant ratification, see J. VanderKam, "Covenant and Biblical Interpretation in Jubilees 6" in L. Schiffman et al., *The Dead Sea Scrolls Fifty Years After Their Discovery*, 96–98; 101–102.

[74] "Covenant and Biblical Interpretation in Jubilees 6," 101.

[75] In the quotation, I omit all of VanderKam's references to Qumran material except his citations of CD.

the Pentateuchal history in the form of a speech delivered from an angel to Moses at Sinai. The effect of this narrative device is strategic: by subsuming its version of the Pentateuchal narrative within the context of the story of the giving of the law at Sinai, Jubilees is able to recontextualize and to reinterpret events that occurred in the Pentateuchal narrative prior to the giving of the law at Sinai from the perspective of the Sinaitic covenant. The idea of the Pentateuchal Priestly writer that God established a series of covenants, each more specific than the last, is modified. For Jubilees, there is but one "eternal covenant," which is first established between God and Noah (Jub 6:4, 10), and subsequently renewed by Abraham (Jub 14:20), Jacob (Jub 22:15, 30), and Moses (Jub 6:19).[76] As VanderKam states, "the writer [of Jubilees] took seriously the implications of the word 'eternal' that modifies Noah's covenant. If there was an eternal covenant, then a new one was not necessary; the ancient one had simply to be renewed."[77]

There is evidence that D may have shared Jubilees' idea of a single "eternal covenant" that was renewed at various points in Israel's history. This evidence occurs in CD chapters 1–6, which recount a version of the history of God's covenant with Israel. According to CD 3:2–3, Abraham "kept God's commandments (מצות אל) and did not follow his own desire,[78] and he transmitted (them) to Isaac and to Jacob, and they kept (them) and were inscribed as lovers of God and parties to the covenant forever (ובעלי ברית לעולם)."[79] In this passage, Abraham, Isaac, and Jacob are described as "parties to the covenant," a status bestowed on them as the result of "keeping the commandments of God." Jacob's posterity however, failed to follow the commandments of the covenant, and were punished (3:4). The narrative then turns its attention to the generation immediately preceding Israel's entrance into the land of Canaan (3:5–10a). Because "they did not heed the voice of their maker, the commandments of their teacher" (3:7–8), a reference to the commandments that God gave to his people "through the agency of Moses" (cf. 5:21). In 3:10–12a, "those who entered into the covenant of the first ones were delivered up to the sword"

---

[76] Jubilees 1:1 states that Moses ascended Sinai on 3/16, but its citation of Ex 24:12 at this point hints that the author of Jubilees read the material in Ex 24:1–11 as a story of covenant renewal accomplished the preceding day, 3/15. On this point I follow VanderKam, "Covenant and Biblical Interpretation in Jubilees 6" 92–104.

[77] "Covenant and Biblical Interpretation in Jubilees 6," 98.

[78] Lit., "he did not choose the desire of his spirit."

[79] The term ברית lacks the article. Baumgarten and Schwartz (*PTSDSSP* 2:17) attempt to provide determinacy by inserting a possessive pronoun in their translation, which reads, "(his) covenant." Perhaps the noun is considered determinate on the basis of its unique status, as in the phrase אהל מועד in Ex 27:21, although unique nouns are more often designated as determinate by being marked by the definite article (cf. Joüon-Muraoka, §137h).

(ויסגרו לחרב) as the result of transgressing against the covenant (בו חבו; 3:10). These lines probably refer to the beginning of the Babylonian exile, which was referred to in similar terms in CD 1:3–4, which states that God "gave them up to the sword (ויתנם לחרב)." However, a select few remained faithful to the stipulations of the covenant through the period that culminated in Israel's exile; with these "God established his covenant with Israel forever" (3:10–11). This passage is connected with the discussion in 1:1–17, not only by the mention of the period of exile, referred to as "giving them over to the sword," but also by the theme that a remnant inherits covenantal promises made to the patriarchs (1:3–4; 3:13). It is this remnant, subsequent to the time of Nebuchadnezzar, with which the sect identifies itself. This identification is made clear in 1:5–11, in which the remnant is said to have been taught by the Righteous Teacher.

The wording of the text allows us to make some inferences by which we may fill out D's somewhat hasty summary of covenantal history. First, because CD 3:1 reads, "because of it (i.e., "stubbornness of heart," 2:17–18) was the straying of *the sons of Noah* and their clans," we may infer that Noah himself was not party to this "straying" in "stubbornness of heart." In this regard, D probably presupposes the idea that Noah was one with whom God established his "eternal covenant" as in Jub 6:4, 10–11. In Jub 6:18, we read that "from the day of Noah's death his sons corrupted (it) [i.e., the yearly observance of covenant renewal] until Abraham's lifetime and were eating blood."[80] D seems to presuppose a view of the role of Noah and his offspring in relation to covenantal obligations similar to that of Jubilees. Secondly, D seems to presuppose Jubilees' view that Moses was associated with a time of covenant renewal. Even though Moses is nowhere mentioned in CD 3:5–10, the citation of Deut 9:23 in CD 3:7 and Deut 1:27 in the following line establish a context in which Moses would be assumed. The phrase in CD 3:8 that the people were "grumbling in their tents" alludes to Deut 1:27, in which the people grumbled against Moses' authority because they did not wish to challenge the inhabitants of the land of Canaan, as Moses had suggested that they do. The outcome of the story in the biblical narrative is that the generation which had accompanied Moses out of Egypt would not live to enter the land of Canaan (cf. Num 14:26–35), an outcome reflected in CD 3:8–10: "God's anger was kindled against their congregation ... through it their heroes perished."[81] In light of CD 5:21, which links the "commandments of God" with the "hand of Moses," we may presume that the author of D saw the time of Moses as one of covenant renewal. Similarly, in Jub 6:19,

---

[80] Trans. of VanderKam, *The Book of Jubilees*, 40.
[81] Trans. of Baumgarten and Schwartz, *PTSDSSP* 2:17.

we read, "During your [i.e., Moses'] lifetime the Israelites had forgotten (it) [i.e., the covenant] until I renewed (it) for them at this mountain."[82]

We can summarize CD's presentation in chapters 1–5 as follows: an original covenant made at least by the time of Noah was followed by a period in which Noah's sons refused to obey the stipulations of the covenant. The covenant was renewed with Abraham, who transmitted the stipulations of the covenant to Isaac and Jacob. Subsequent generations failed to follow these stipulations. The covenant was renewed in the time of Moses, but again, subsequent generations failed to adhere to its stipulations. This failure to adhere to covenantal stipulations eventually culminated in the Babylonian exile. Subsequent to the exile, God renewed his covenant once again with a "remnant," identified with the Essene sect. This pattern generally coheres with that established in the Book of Jubilees.

In addition to a pattern of various moments of covenant-making or covenant renewal associated with Noah, Abraham, Isaac, and Jacob, Moses, and finally the Essene sect itself, D also presumes that the interim periods between moments of covenant renewal were marked by "blindness." According to CD 3:13–14, God revealed to the Essene sect "hidden things (נסתרות) in which all Israel had erred." The "hidden things" are also mentioned in the portion of D's prologue preserved in 4Q266 1.5–6 and 4Q268 1.7–8: ויגל עיניהם בנסתרות ואוזנם פתחו וישמעו עמוקות ויבינו בכול נהיות עד מה יבוא בם, "and he opened their eyes to hidden things and they opened their ears,[83] and they heard deep things and understood everything that will be, until[84] it comes upon them." The theme of blindness occurs in CD 16:2–4: "And the explication of their times, when Israel was blind to all these [i.e., the specifications of the law of Moses]; behold, it is specified in the Book of the Divisions of the Times in their Jubilees and in their Weeks."[85] The book referred to in these lines is the Book of Jubilees,

---

[82] Trans. of VanderKam, *The Book of Jubilees*, 40.

[83] According to the reading of 4Q266. 4Q468 reads: ואוזנמה פתח, "and he opened their ears ..."

[84] Baumgarten (*DSSR* 1:129; *PTSDSSP* 2:15) translates the phrase, עד מה, "before," both here and in CD 2:10. Tigchelaar and García Martínez hedge their bets, translating the same phrase "before" in 4Q266/4Q268 and "until" in CD 2:10 (*DSSSE* 1:585, 605, 553). Although normally the preposition עד carries the sense "until," Koehler and Baumgartner (*HALOT* 1:786–787) indicate another temporal usage, "just before." However, the passages that they cite (Judg 16:2; 1 Kings 18:29) offer only dubious support for this category. In BH, the phrase has the sense, "how long" (e.g., Num 24:22; Ps 4:3), but this is far from the meaning in D. The identical phrase occurs in Syriac (ܥܕܡܐ) in the sense, "until" (cf. J. Payne Smith, *Compendious Syriac Dictionary* [Repr. ed., Winona Lake, IN: Eisenbrauns, 1998] 401). My translation assumes that the usage in D is analogous.

[85] Trans. of Baumgarten, *PTSDSSP* 2:39.

as the incipit to the Ethiopic manuscripts of the book opens with an almost identical designation.[86] These lines may well be a gloss, as Baumgarten, following Ginzburg, suggests.[87] Nevertheless, they provide a link between D's mention of "hidden things, in which all Israel erred" and the periods of "blindness" to the stipulations of the covenant, which according to Jubilees occurred between periods of covenant renewal. According to Jub 1:9 and 14, following the days of Moses, the people "forgot" or "forsook" the commandments. According to Jub 6:34, Noah's posterity "forgot" God's ordinances concerning the calendar. Following the death of Moses, Jubilees 50:5 states that "[t]he jubilees will pass by until Israel is pure of every sexual evil, impurity, contamination, sin, and error."[88] The frame-work provided by positing periods of covenant renewal followed by periods of forsaking or forgetting the stipulations of the covenant are common to Jubilees and D.

3.5. Remnant Theology

CD 1:4–5 introduces the reader/hearer of the discourse to another very important element in D's construction of its ideology of the covenant. This is D's "remnant theology." D's remnant theology finds its prototypes in the Hebrew Bible, particularly in the prophetic books such as Isaiah, Jeremiah, and Ezekiel. The logic of remnant theology is simple: since the people have abandoned the stipulations of the covenant, they have merited destruction. God, in his mercy however, spares some of the people, who are designated the "remnant" or "remainder" from among the condemned (cf. Isa 10:20–23; 37:4, 32). The fact that God is portrayed as sparing a remnant is viewed as an act of divine mercy, a self-imposed limitation on the extent of wrath that the deity would inflict on his wayward people. The remnant theology in this way is able to emphasize God's mercy even in the context of an act of divine judgment, such as the exile was consid-ered to have been.

Jeremiah and Ezekiel, both of whom were exiles themselves, molded the remnant theology into an ideological tool that would serve the interests of exiles: the remnant would, by an act of divine deliverance that was reminiscent of Yahweh's actions in bringing his people out of Egypt, be regathered from their places of exile in order to return to Judea (Jer 23:3; 29:10–14; 31:1–14). Not only would the exiles be able to return to Judea, but they would also regain control over the area when they arrived there,

---

[86] "These are the words regarding the divisions of the times of the law and of the testimony, of the events of the years, of the weeks of their jubilees throughout all the years of eternity ..." Trans. of VanderKam, *The Book of Jubilees*, 1.

[87] *PTSDSSP* 2:39, n. 132.

[88] Trans. of VanderKam, *The Book of Jubilees*, 325.

wresting it from those who had not been deported, that is, the "people of the land." According to this exilic ideology, those who had remained in Jerusalem during the time of the exile had become corrupt and, when the exiles returned to regain control of Jerusalem, would be destroyed (Ezek 9:1–11; 11:14–21). Jeremiah constructs a parable on the basis of this ideology: the exiles in Babylon were likened to a basket full of ripe figs, while those who had remained in Jerusalem were likened to a basket of rotten figs. The "ripe figs" would be rewarded, whereas the rotten were destined for destruction (Jer 24:1–10). The Damascus Document relies heavily on remnant theology, construing the members of the sect as the exiled remnant that would one day return to regain control of Jerusalem and the temple (cf. CD 3:18–4:4).

The remnant theology also included an important temporal aspect. The exile was to last only for a specified period. In Ezek 4, the prophet was commanded to enact dramatically his prophecy that Israel would be punished with exile in Babylon for 390 years. The prophet was commanded to lie down beside an inscribed brick, symbolizing Jerusalem, that was surrounded by a mound of dirt, symbolizing the siegeworks that would be laid around the city. Ezekiel was bidden to lie beside this symbolic city under siege for 390 days, one day for each year in which Israel, it was prophesied, would remain in exile in Babylon (Ezek 4:1–8).

CD alludes to Ezekiel's prophetic enactment when it states, "in the period of wrath, he punished them for 390 years ..." Apparently, the "period of wrath" (קץ חרון) corresponds to the time during which the author of D believed the exile to have lasted. Here, as in the remnant theology espoused in Jer 5:10–11, 18–19, even the remnant is held culpable for transgressing the stipulations of the covenant. D does not employ the theology of a "righteous remnant" such as espoused in Zeph 3:12–13. Instead the remnant, though it is held guilty of transgressing the stipulations of the covenant, awaits a time of renewal in which its sins will be forgiven and its fortunes and position in Israel restored (cf. Jer 31:1–14). The reason given in D for God's sparing of the remnant is that he "recalls the ancestral covenant" (ברית הרשונים) which as we have seen, refers to the covenant with Abraham, Isaac, and Jacob as well as to the covenant at Sinai. On this point, D agrees fully with the theology of the Deuteronomist, who opined, "It is not because of your righteousness that you will inherit this land, but because of the promise that I made to your forefathers" (Deut 9:4–6; paraphrase).

3.6. CD 1:7–8

Lines 7–8 describe God's gracious act of shaping a group who would become the recipients of God's promise of the land to Abraham. The section reads: "he turned his attention to them and caused a cultivated root to sprout from Israel and Aaron, in order to inherit his land and to enjoy the bounty of his earth."

These lines recall God's promise of the land. The reference to the "bounty of (God's) earth" may be intended to connote the terms in which Deuteronomy had earlier described the land that Moses' people would come to inhabit as one "flowing with milk and honey." The agricultural imagery is extended into the social realm when D refers to God as one who "caused to sprout" a group who would inherit the promise of the land. As we have seen in ll. 4–5, the reason for this act is that God called to mind his ancient Abrahamic covenant. Though the people had transgressed it, God chose to remain faithful. The designation of the "root" as arising out of "Israel and Aaron" connotes the military/political authority on the one hand, and the priestly authority on the other, that the sect claimed it would embody at the end of the "last days." The phrase מישראל ומאהרן resonates with the sect's messianism, whereby they expected two anointed figures to arise, one kingly (מישראל) and one priestly (מאהרן).[89] However, CD 1:7–8 does not here refer to messianic figures, per se, but to the continuation of the lineages that would eventually give rise to those figures.

The language of "root/shoot" combined with the planting imagery is related to biblical passages such as Isa 11, to Jewish texts of the Second Temple Period such as Jub 1:16; 21:24; 1 Enoch 10:16, and to other texts that were produced by the sectarian Association, such as 1QS 8:5.[90] Using this imagery the sect is able to establish its pedigree as a group that was founded by an act of divine election, as God chose and nourished the "root" that would later constitute the sect. Through a creative use of the remnant theology, D is able to present itself as the sole legitimate heir to Israel's traditions, while at the same time designating the Hasmoneans and their supporters in Jerusalem as those who were destined to be destroyed in the coming judgment (cf. CD 8:2b–19; 19:5b–14). Although D does not cite Jeremiah on this point, its dichotomy between exiles and non-exiles, with the concomitant positive valuation of the exiles (the "good figs," destined to rule in Jerusalem) and negative valuation of the non-exiles (the "rotten figs," destined for destruction), was one that Jeremiah had explored centuries earlier (Jer 24:1–10).

---

[89] On dual messianism in QL, see J. J. Collins, *The Scepter and the Star: the Messiahs of the Dead Sea Scrolls and Other Ancient Literature* (ABRL; New York: Doubleday, 1995) 74–101.

[90] Shozo Fujita reviews the use of plant/planting imagery in PsSol, 1 Enoch, T12P, Jub, and some QL in "The Metaphor of Plant in Jewish Literature of the Intertestamental Period," *JSJ* 7 (1976) 30–45. Patrick Tiller examines the same imagery in QL, 1 Enoch, and Jubilees in "The 'Eternal Planting' in the Dead Sea Scrolls," *DSD* 4 (1997) 312–335.

3.7. CD 1:8–11

Lines 8b–11 continue as follows:

ויבינו בעונם וידעו כי

אנשים אשימים הם ויהיו כעורים וכי מגששים דרך

שנים עשרים ויבן אל אל מעשיהם כי בלב שלם דרשוהו

ויקם להם מורה צדק להדריכם בדרך לבו

And they perceived their sin, and they knew that they were guilty men.[91] And they were like blind men and like ones who grope[92] for the way for twenty years. And God perceived their works, how they sought him wholeheartedly, and he raised up for them a Righteous Teacher to lead them in they way of his (i.e., God's) heart.

The "root" that, according to D, is to fall heir to the promise to Abraham, "perceive their sin" and recognize their guilt. Although the recognition of guilt that resulted in the exile is a prominent aspect of the penitential prayers that abounded in Second Temple Judaism (e.g., Dan 9:4–19; Ps 106:6),[93] these lines apply this recognition only to the group that would later (from the perspective of D) become organized around the instruction of the Righteous Teacher.

The proto-sect, according to D, "groped for the way" like blind men. This metaphor develops the idea common in Hellenistic Judaism that one's behavior is likened to walking along a path (the term *halakhah* is related to the root הלך, "to walk"). God's instruction may be likened to a lamp to guide one's way (Ps 119:105). It is precisely this divine guidance that was lacking at this point in Israel's history, according to D. Though the proto-sect was conscious that it shared in the guilt that had led to the exile, God as yet had provided no remedy; the people recognized their guilt but as yet had no one to "guide them in the way of (God's) heart." D refers here to a period of "blindness," during which no one had a proper knowledge of the law. Such periods occurred after successive acts of covenant renewal. D, as we have seen, probably borrowed this idea from Jubilees. CD 3:12b–15 lists those matters which were at that point "hidden" from Israel: "his holy Sabbaths, his glorious appointed times, his righteous statutes, his true ways, and the desires of his will." The first two of these concerns relate to calendrical matters, the third to legal interpretation, and the last two constitute general categories, but may include issues both of calendar and legal interpretation. Whatever set of halakhic norms was being followed

---

[91] The scribe who copied CD-A had inserted dots in the letters of this word. Apparently this signaled that the word so marked did not belong in the text. If so, was the offending term erased for stylistic reasons (pleonasm), or was אשימים read by mistake for אשימים?

[92] Written as a single word in CD-A: וכימגששים.

[93] More examples appear in R. A. Werline, *Penitential Prayer*.

during this period of Israel's "blindness," it was according to D's account incomplete, and did not represent God's "true ways, the desires of his will."

However, God provided a way out of this impasse, ויקם להם מורה צדק, raising up (or: appointing) for them a Righteous Teacher. Here the Righteous Teacher is presented as fulfilling a function analogous to that of Moses. The verb that is used to indicate the "raising up" of the teacher echoes a similar formulation in Deut 18:15, which states, "The LORD your God will raise up (יקים) for you a prophet"[94] like Moses. As Moses preached the Torah with the authority of God himself, so the teacher "led them in the way of God's heart" (להדריכם בדרך לבו). Both Moses and the Righteous Teacher delivered the authoritative Torah at the end of a period that was Torah-bereft, and neither the teacher nor Moses lived to see the entry of their people into the promised land. D does not overtly state these parallels, but nonetheless it seems that D viewed the Righteous Teacher as having filled a role that was in some ways analogous to that of Moses', teaching in exile the divinely-sanctioned Torah.

3.8. CD 1:11–18

CD 1:11b–18 continues as follows:

ויודע
לדורות אחרונים את אשר עשה בדור אחרון בעדת בוגדים
הם סרי דרך היא העת אשר היה כתוב עליה כפרה סוריריה
כן סרר ישראל[95] בעמוד איש הלצון אשר הטיף לישראל
מימי כזב ויתעם בתוהו לא דרך להשח גבהות עולם ולסור
מנתיבות צדק ולסיע גבול אשר גבלו ראשנים בנחלתם למען
הדבק בהם את אלות בריתו להסגירם לחרב נקמת נקם ברית

And he made known to the last generations what he would do[96] in the last generation, among the congregation of traitors – they are ones who depart[97] from the way. This is

---

[94] Trans. NRSV.

[95] The *ʾaleph* and *lamed* are indicated by a single symbol in MS-A. Yoseph Ofer presents a brief discussion of the significance of this orthographic feature in *PTSDSSP* 2:11. Ofer lists the occurrences of the symbol in MS-A, but overlooked its use in 1:14.

[96] The verb עשה must be taken as a prophetic perfect. Baumgarten states (*PTSDSSP* 2:13, n. 8), "'did' here means 'will do.'" While Baumgarten's note does capture the predictive element implicit in the verb here, we may be a little more precise in assigning a tense and mood in our translation of this verb. The phrase את אשר עשה, since it serves as the object of a verb of knowing, constitutes indirect discourse. When an utterance that was originally stated in the future tense (i.e., "I/he will do") is reported in indirect discourse, the future tense is appropriately rendered by an English subjunctive (thus, "He made known what he would do ...").

[97] The term סרי is a Qal participle, masc. pl. constr. derived either from the geminate root סרר, "to be stubborn, rebellious" or the weak root סור, "to turn away, depart."

the time about which it is written, "Like a rebellious cow, so Israel rebelled (Hos 4:16)" – when[98] the scoffer arose, who dripped deceptive waters for Israel and mislead them in a wasteland with no path, bringing low the eternal heights and departing from righteous paths and removing the border which the ancestors had established as their inheritance. Therefore he caused the curses of the covenant to adhere to them, delivering them to the sword (which) executes the covenant's vengeance.

These lines hint at an important aspect of the sect's construction of the covenant. Whereas prototypical constructions of the covenant such as that of Deuteronomy viewed the blessings that followed from adherence to the stipulations of the covenant (such as good harvests, peace, and longevity; Deut 28:1–14) and the curses that were to result from non-adherence (famine and blight, war and deportation; Deut 28:15–68) as events which occurred within a historical sequence, the sect's construction of the covenant introduced a note of eschatological finality to the blessings and curses. Whereas Deuteronomy viewed the effects of God's curse as potentially reversible if the people began once again to adhere to the stipulations of the covenant, D envisions a time in which God will "once and for all" reward those who have kept the covenant and punish those who had not. And whereas in Deuteronomy, Yahweh's punishments and rewards accrued to Israel as a whole, in D God is presented as discriminating between Israelites who had kept the covenant and those who had not. This is a major departure from the prototypical theology of earlier works such as Deuteronomy, but was entirely in keeping with the apocalyptic tradition that was developing within Second Temple Judaism.

The phrase דורות אחרונים refers to the "last generations" who live prior to the time of God's judgment. Related designations occur in 4Q166 (4QpHos[a]) 1.10, which mentions the "generation of the visitation/ punishment" (דור הפקודה), and 4Q177 (4QCatena[a]) 2.16, which refers to those who have "circumcised the foreskin of their fleshly heart in the last generation ([בדור הא]חרו[ן])." Each of these references invokes the eschatological horizon that was central to D's construction of the covenant. God has a ריב with all of humanity and soon, according to the sectarian ideology, the day of reckoning would come. The sectarian Association, of

---

The following quote from Hos. 4:16, which employs the verb סרר, may be taken to support the former option. However, the connection with the following term, דרך, "way, path" indicates that a derivation from סור is more likely.

[98] The syntax of this section is awkward. The main verb is ויודע at the end of 1:11. The object of the main verb is constituted by the clause, את אשר עשה .... Syntactically, the section in lines 13-14a (הם סרי דרך ... כן סרר ישראל) is an anacoluthon. Pronouns used demonstratively are often used in the DSS to introduce explanatory glosses, as is the case here (היא, הם). The clause beginning, בעמוד איש הלצון, functions as an adverbial temporal clause, modifying the verb אשה of line 12. Finally, the phrase למען הדבק introduces a result clause.

course, shared this expectation with other groups within Second Temple Judaism. We may cite one non-sectarian source that expresses particularly well the idea that the outcome of God's covenant lawsuit with humanity would result in a great "last judgment" in which the wicked would be destroyed and the righteous rewarded.

I Enoch 1:9, 7–8 provides a nice parallel with the theologoumenon of eschatological judgment as espoused in D.[99]

ἔρχεται σὺν ταῖς μυρίασιν αὐτοῦ καὶ τοῖς ἁγίοις αὐτοῦ, ποιῆσαι κρίσιν κατὰ πάντων, καὶ ἀπολέσει πάντας τοὺς ἀσεβεῖς, καὶ ἐλέγξει πᾶσαν σάρκα περὶ πάντων ἔργων τῆς ἀσεβείας αὐτῶν ... καὶ μετὰ τῶν δικαίων τὴν εἰρήνην ποιήσει, καὶ ἐπὶ τοὺς ἐκλεκτοὺς ἔσται συντήρησις καὶ εἰρήνη, καὶ ἐπ' αὐτοὺς γενήσεται ἔλεος ...

He is coming with all the myriads of his holy ones[100] to execute judgment against all, and he will slay all the impious, and he will convict all flesh for all their impious deeds ... And he will make peace with the righteous, and there will be preservation and peace for his elect, and for them there will be mercy ...

Like D, 1 Enoch 1 envisions a "covenant lawsuit" between God and humanity. The conviction (ἐλέγξις) will be lodged, and the penalty for the impious (ἀσεβεῖς) is death. However, the righteous (οἱ δίκαιοι) will be acquitted. They will receive mercy on the day of judgment. D employs this basic scenario, but modifies some of the key elements involved. According to D, the righteous and the wicked are distinguished not simply on the basis of their deeds, but on the basis of whether they had become members of the sect. We will return to develop this point more fully when we treat CD 1:11b–17.

The phrase עשׂה אשׁר את ... וידע expresses the sect's contention that God had revealed the future to the Righteous Teacher, along with other members of the sect. The Teacher, through his inspired exegesis of scripture, and in particular of the prophetic books, had acquired knowledge of what would befall Israel during "the final age" (האחרון קץ; cf. 1QpHab 2.7–10; 7.1–6). On this point, D and the pesharim agree with a statement that Josephus makes about the Essenes (*BJ* 2.159):

Εἰσὶν δ' ἐν αὐτοῖς οἳ καὶ τὰ μέλλοντα προγινώσκειν ὑπισχνοῦνται, βίβλοις ἱεραῖς καὶ διαφόροις ἁγνείαις καὶ προφητῶν ἀποφθέγμασιν ἐπαιδοτριβούμενοι· σπάνιον δ' εἴ ποτε ἐν ταῖς προαγορεύσεσιν ἀστοχοῦσιν.

---

[99] I have reordered the text so that its logic will be easier to follow. The Greek text, edited by Matthew Black, appears in *Apocalypsis Henochi Graece* (Pseudepigrapha Veteris Testamenti Graece 3; Leiden: E. J. Brill, 1970).

[100] The phrase ταῖς μυρίασιν αὐτοῦ καὶ τοῖς ἁγίοις αὐτοῦ, is hendyadic.

There are some among them who even profess to know beforehand what is to come, since they are educated in the holy books and in different (kinds of) purifications and in the sayings of the prophets, and they rarely if ever fail in their predictions.[101]

However, we should also point out the tensions between Josephus' Essenes and the sect that produced D and the pesharim. Josephus' Essenes were interested in predicting non-eschatological events, such as the death of Antigonus, the brother of Aristobulus I (*BJ* 1.78–80; *Ant* 13.311). The Teacher's predictions, on the other hand, concerned "what (God) would do at the end of days." Regarding the failure rate of the Teacher's predictions, we need only point out that throughout history, eschatological prediction has proven to be one area in which success invariably has been elusive.[102]

The phrase in 1:13–14 that refers to the עדת בוגדים, "the congregation of the rebels," who are characterized as those who have "rebelled from the way" (הם סרי דרך), also reveals important aspects of D's covenantal theology. The "congregation of the rebels" refers to Jews, living in the "last generation," who do not belong to the Association. The use of the term בוגדים to refer to this group is significant. The verb בגד can be used to characterize the act of refusing to behave in accordance with the stipulations of a treaty or covenant. The term is so used in Isa 48:8, where YHWH addresses Israel, "for I knew that you would surely rebel, since from the womb you were called a rebel" (כי ידעתי בגוד תבגוד ופשע מבטן קרא לך). Similarly, the verb סור here refers to the act of "turning aside" from "the way" stipulated by the covenant. The use of the verb סור here probably suggested to the author the passage from Hosea 4:16 that follows in the next two lines (כפרה סוריריה כן סרר ישראל). The author puns on the similarity between the root סור "to turn away, depart," and סרר, "rebel." Of course when the metaphor of the "way" is applied to Israel's covenant, "departing" from that way is tantamount to rebellion. The absolute use of דרך, "the way" here refers to the way of life that was

---

[101] *BJ* 2.159; cp. also *BJ* 1.78–80 (*Ant* 13.311); 2.113 (*Ant* 17.345–348). These passages are conveniently collected in Vermes and Goodman, *The Essenes According to the Classical Sources* (Sheffield: JSOT Press, 1989).

[102] Two millennia after its utterance, the self-assured remark attributed to Jesus of Nazareth, which followed a series of eschatological predictions, can only be viewed with irony: Ἀμὴν λέγω ὑμῖν ὅτι οὐ μὴ παρέλθη ἡ γενεὰ αὕτη μέχρις οὗ ταῦτα πάντα γένηται, "Truly I say to you that this generation will by no means pass away until all these things (i.e., the foregoing predictions) have happened" (Mk 13:30). On the failure of the eschatological predictions made by members of the Association, see Stegemann, *The Library of Qumran* 128-129. Even if one does not agree with every aspect of Stegemann's scheme for reckoning the "time of the end" according to D, his point remains valid.

stipulated by sectarian halakhah,[103] which according to the ideology of the sect recapitulated the law of Moses and so faithfully represented the conditions of God's covenant with Israel.

3.9. "The Scoffer"

Line 14 refers cryptically to "the scoffer" (איש הלצון). The same figure appears to be mentioned again in CD 4:19 and 8:13. "The scoffer" may be the same as the one whom CD 4:12 refers to as צו. This person appears as a leader of the Pharisees (the group that is likely referred to as the בוני החיץ in the same line). In CD 8:12, the בוני החיץ are presented as having fallen under the influence of "one who sprinkles falsehood" (מטיף כזב). Each of these three designations is linked by the use of a form of the root נטף to refer to the activities of the one designated. This verb is regularly associated with the activity of prophets in the Hebrew Bible (Amos 7:16; Ezek 21:2). This led J. T. Milik to identify the "scoffer" with John Hyrcanus, who according to Josephus (*Ant* 13.300) had received the "gift of prophecy."[104]

The designation, "the scoffer," constitutes an allusion to Isaiah 28:14,[105] which uses the plural designation, אנשי לצון, "men of scoffing" or simply, "scoffers." In the Isaianic context, the epithet refers to those who rule in Jerusalem (אנשי לצון משלי העם הזה אשר בירושלם). The supposition that CD 1:14 alludes to Isa 28:14 is strengthened by the reference to צו (a designation which, although it could be translated "(legal) precept," is usually simply transliterated, *tsaw*) in CD 4:19, which also may allude to the same section of Isaiah (cf. Isa 28:10, 13).

In CD 4:19, as in CD 8:12, the figure referred to as *tsaw* or as "the scoffer" appears to be associated with the Pharisees. The references to the "builders of the wall" in these lines may be taken as a reference to the Pharisees, who by means of oral halakhah attempted to "build a fence" around the Torah[106] (i.e., they made halakhot more stringent than the Torah required so as to prevent inadvertent transgression). The hypothesis that the phrase, "builders of the wall" refers to the Pharisees is rendered more probable by the phrase that is connected with it in 8:12, where the same group is referred to as "plaster-coaters" (טחי התפל). This latter epithet recalls Ezek 13:10–15, in which the prophet uses the practice of covering a wall with white plaster to hide the cracks that lay underneath (although in

---

[103] For an early Christian parallel to this absolute use of "the way," see Acts 19:23; 22:4.

[104] According to the report of Cross, who cites Milik's position without referring to any of Milik's written works (*Ancient Library of Qumran* 117, n. 4).

[105] So Campbell, *The Use of Scripture in the Damascus Document*, 56, 63.

[106] *Avoth* 1:1: ועשא סיג לתורה.

Ezekiel the metaphor is used to refer to false prophecy). In the NT, Matthew 23:27 reports that Jesus derided the Pharisees in terms that relied on the metaphor of plastering. In the Matthean passage, Jesus refers to the Pharisees and scribes as "plastered tombs (τάφοι κεκονιαμένοι), which look beautiful on the outside, but which on the inside are filled with the bones of dead men and every kind of uncleanness."

Since "the scoffer" is associated with the Pharisees, and since the allusion to Isa 28:14 in CD 1:14 suggests that he was a ruler in Jerusalem, it is possible that he should be identified as either Jonathan, Simon, or John Hyrcanus I. Each of these seems to have been associated with the Pharisees. Hyrcanus I, however broke decisively with the Pharisees during his reign[107] (although the date of this break is unknown).

The attempt to identify "the scoffer" with either Jonathan, Simon, or Hyrcanus has produced mixed results. While Vermes has argued that the "scoffer" refers to Jonathan,[108] Milik, as noted earlier, identified this figure with Hyrcanus. Discretion is probably the better part of valor in this matter. Without trying to identify the figure with any one person, we may simply conclude that the "scoffer" may have been one of the early Hasmoneans. On the other hand, if we place less emphasis on the possibility of an allusion to the העם משל י of Isa 28:14 in CD 1:14, then the "scoffer" may refer to an unnamed Pharisaic leader.

The phrase that the scoffer "dripped on Israel lying waters" relies on biblical imagery related to public speaking, particularly prophetic preaching. The metaphor of "dripping waters" is applied to the preaching of Amos in Amos 7:16 and to the preaching of Ezekiel in Ezek 21:2. On the basis of this biblical usage, we may conclude that "the scoffer" was engaged in some sort of preaching endeavor. However, this endeavor, according to D is grievously misguided. The outcome of this preaching is that Israel is (mis)led into a "wasteland with no path" (לא ויתעם בתוהו דרך). This phrase employs the common metaphor whereby the Torah establishes the "path"; i.e., the set of halakhic norms according to which Israel is to order its practice. D's metaphor implies that "the liar" advocated an inadequate or flawed set of halakhic norms. This flawed set of halakhic norms, as we have seen, are those of the Pharisees, the "builders of the wall."

D views the imposition of Pharisaic halakhah upon Israel as an innovation. A series of active verbs is used to characterize the "liar's" influence: he "moves the eternal boundaries," "departs from paths of righteousness," and "moves the border which the ancients had established." Whether or

---

[107] Cf. Josephus, *Ant* 13.288–298.

[108] *An Introduction to the Complete Dead Sea Scrolls* (Philadelphia, PA: Fortress Press, 1999) 139–140.

not this construction is historically accurate, D depicts the "scoffer" as departing from ancestral tradition. The metaphors of "boundary," "border," and "path" were traditional ones, each of which referred to a set of specific legal injunctions, constituted by the Torah, that was taken as normatively establishing orthopraxy for all Israelites. These metaphors were ones whereby the "limits" of God's covenant with Israel had been set out. To transgress these limits ("move the border/boundary," "depart from the path") was to break the covenant that God had established with Israel. These metaphors refer to the transgression of the stipulations of the covenant that God had set forth in the Torah, and which the sect interpreted in the light of its own halakhic norms.

Line 17 describes the outcome of Israel's failure to adhere to the precepts of the Torah. This section of D takes its verbal and ideological inspiration from Deuteronomy 28, which describes the blessings that follow upon Israel's adherence to the stipulations of the covenant and the curses that were contingent on Israel's failure to follow the stipulations of the covenant. The curses included, among other things, the threat that Israel would be conquered by a foreign nation if she failed to obey the Torah (Deut 28:25–68). CD 1:17 recapitulates this Deuteronomic pattern: למען הדבק בהם את אלות בריתו להסגירם לחרב נקמת נקם ברית. God enacts the "curses of the covenant" that had, in Deuteronomy's construction, always formed part of Israel's covenant with Yahweh.

3.9. CD 1:18–2:1

The final section of exhortation 1 (1:18–2:1) describes in general terms the transgressions which Israel, misled by the "liar," is said to have committed.

בעבור אשר דרשו בחלקות ויבחרו במהתלות ויצפו
לפרצות ויבחרו בטוב הצואר ויצדיקו רשע וירשיעו צדיק
ויעבירו ברית ויפירו חוק ויגודו על נפש צדיק ובכל הולכי
תמים תעבה נפשם וירדפום לחרב ויסיסו לריב עם ויחר אף
אל בעדתם להשם את כל המונם ומעשיהם לנדה לפניו

Because they sought smooth things and chose deceptions and kept watch for breaches and chose the beautiful neck and acquitted the guilty and condemned the just and they transgressed the covenant and broke the statute and formed a cabal against the life of the righteous man and their soul abhorred all those who walk in perfection and they pursued them with the sword and they delighted in the strife of the people, so the anger of God burned against their congregation so that all their multitude will be laid waste, for their works are impurity before him.

The language employed in this section is heavily indebted to scripture. A catena of biblical citations is woven together into a condemnation of non-Associate Judaism. The effect is to portray Jews who do not belong to the sectarian Association as prototypical sinners. The first biblical echo that we encounter in this section is the phrase, דרשו בחלקות ויבחרו במהתלות, "they sought smooth things and chose deceptions." This passage reworks slightly its lemma, Isa 30:10, דברו לנו חלקות חזו מהתלות, "speak smooth words to us, prophesy deceit." Aside from the semantically insignificant addition of ב to mark the substantives מהתלות and חלקות as the direct objects of חזו and דברו, respectively, D changes the verb דברו of the lemma to דרשו. This change is significant. It marks the activity of the opposition as one involving an exegetical enterprise, "seek, interpret,"[109] rather than the speech activity of the prophets who were excoriated in Isaiah. The verb דרש is often used in the sectarian literature of the DSS to refer to the activity of interpreting scripture (cf. CD 1:18; 7:18; 1QS 5:11; 6:6). However, D accuses Jews who were not members of the Association of seeking חלקות, "smooth things." This is metaphorical language that refers in this instance to legal interpretations that are construed as lax.

Many scholars have seen in the phrase, "seekers of smooth things," (דורשי חלקות) a punning reference to Pharisaic legal interpretation, in which legal precepts were referred to as הלכות. John Meier has recently criticized this claim, noting that the DSS do not use the term הלכה in this sense.[110] The literature in which the term is used to refer to Rabbinic legal precepts comes from a later period.[111] So, he concludes, we do not have enough information to state with any assurance that the term חלקות in CD 1:18 puns on an established Pharisaic legal vocabulary. Even if one grants Meier's point that we cannot be confident that the pun between חלקות and הלכות was intended by D, nonetheless it remains likely that the Pharisees are referred to by the use of this epithet. As we have seen, the metaphor of "plaster-daubing" that D uses to refer to the same group that was referred to as "seekers of smooth things" was used during the Roman period in reference to the Pharisees (Mt 23:27). The legal positions argued by the "seekers of smooth things" correspond to early rabbinic rulings (i.e., niece marriage) which increases the likelihood that the group referred to was Pharisaic, whose legal system set the precedent for the later rabbinic systems. Despite Meier's negative findings on the issue of the pun in-

---

[109] Cp. 1QS 8:11–12, "Everything which is concealed from Israel and is found (ונמצאו) by somebody who studies – he shall not conceal it from them out of fear of a backsliding spirit." Trans. is that of Charlesworth, *PTSDSSP* 1:35.

[110] "Is There *Halaka* (the Noun) at Qumran?" *JBL* 122 (2003) 150–155.

[111] While we cannot equate the sages of the early rabbinic period c. 200 CE with Pharisees, it is clear that many of the first generation tannaim were Pharisees (as were Gamaliel and Hillel, for example). Many of the legal positions of rabbinic Judaism certainly originate with the Pharisees who taught prior to the destruction of the second temple.

volved in the term חלקות, it remains likely that the phrase "seekers of smooth things" refers to the Pharisees.[112]

We need not examine in detail each of the actions that are chosen to characterize the "seekers of smooth things" in CD 1:18–2:1 (i.e., "they chose deceptions and kept watch for breaches," etc.). We may simply note that each of the metaphors used was chosen in an effort to characterize the Pharisees as a group who corporately had transgressed the stipulations of the covenant between God and the people that were set forth in the Torah. CD 1:20 makes the point explicit: ויעבירו ברית ויפירו חוק, "And they violated the covenant and broke the statute."

Lines 1:21 and 2:1 outline what the author of D viewed as a fitting punishment for those who did not espouse the legal positions of the Association: "so the anger of God burned against their congregation so that all their multitude will be laid waste, for their works are impurity before him."

An important aspect of this discourse is that the opponent is defined as "Israel" (1:3, 14). In CD 1, the members of the sect are seen as having arisen from within Israel, but are nonetheless distinct from it (1:7). We should point out that here the sect does not construe itself to be the "true Israel." According to CD 1, Israel has broken the covenant and therefore will be punished (2:1).

CD 1:1–2:1 offers a good overview of D's construction of the covenant. Subsequent sections of the "Exhortations," however, provide significant elaborations on this theme. In what follows, we will briefly examine only a few of the more salient elaborations that these sections provide.

3.10. Elaborations of the Covenant Theme (CD 2:2–4:6)

CD 2:2–13 reiterates the claim made in the first discourse that judgment awaits those who do not follow the law (or, more to the point, the sect's own construal of it). In deterministic language reminiscent of that of the *Serekh ha-Yaḥad*, lines 7–13 construct a dualistic schema in which some people are chosen by God as a remnant whose offspring are destined to "fill the world" (l. 12) while others are destined for "great wrath with fiery flames in the hand of the angels of punishment" (ll. 5–6).[113] The determinism of D is summed up in l. 13: ואת אשר שנא התעה, "and whom he hated, he lead astray."[114]

---

[112] J. VanderKam reaches the same conclusion in an article entitled, "Those Who Look for Smooth Things, Pharisees, and Oral Law" in Shalom Paul, et al., eds., *Emanuel: Studies in Hebrew Bible, Septuagint, and Dead Sea Scrolls in Honor of Emanuel Tov* (Leiden and Boston: Brill, 2003) 465–477.

[113] Baumgarten's trans. in *PTSDSSP* 2:15.

[114] In addition to the determinism espoused in 1QS 3:15–4:26, one may compare Rom 9:6–26.

CD 3:12b–16a espouses an idea that is central to the Association's construction of the covenant. Israel had transgressed the stipulations of the covenant, with the result that it was nullified, or "broken." However, God reestablished (הקים) the covenant with "those who had held fast to God's ordinances" (l. 12). The ordinances in question are then outlined: "his holy Sabbaths, his glorious festivals, his righteous stipulations, his true ways, and the delights of his will, which man will do and live because of them (ll. 13–16)." These ordinances constituted "hidden matters" (נסתרות) which were "revealed" (using a form of the verb גלה) to the members of the sect.[115]

Foremost among the ordinances that were hidden to Israel are matters of Sabbath and festival. These issues divided the members of the sect from the rest of Judaism in the Second Temple Period. The sect had adopted a schematic solar calendar in which the year consisted of 364 days. The result of adopting this calendar was that the sect celebrated its festivals on different days than did the rest of Judaism – and most significantly, it celebrated its festivals on days other than those on which the Jerusalem temple, the center of national religious life, celebrated them. The issue of the Sabbath, as we have seen, also involved a calendrical dispute. Although the sect observed the Sabbath on the same day that other Jews celebrated it, the sect interpreted Lev 23:38 to mean that festival sacrifices were not to be offered on the Sabbath. This brought the sect's practice into direct conflict with that of the temple. On other respects also, the sect's halakhic norms differed from Pharisaic practice (niece marriage, remarriage, etc.). It is these practices that are alluded to by the phrases, "his righteous stipulations, his true ways," and so on.

Of course, the Association's claim that its members were the sole inheritors of the covenant represented a counter-claim to the claim of the

---

[115] L. H. Schiffman treats the categories of "hidden" and "revealed" law in his book, *Sectarian Law in the Dead Sea Scrolls: Courts, Testimony and the Penal Code* (Chico, CA: Scholars Press, 1983) 14–17. Schiffman identifies the revealed law with "those laws rooted in Scripture whose interpretations are obvious to anyone" (p. 15). The "hidden laws" are "those commandments the correct interpretation of which is known only to the sect." However, D would indicate that the terms *nistar* and *nigleh* refer not to sectarian law and non-sectarian law, respectively, but rather to two different phases in the development of sectarian law: according to CD, that which was "hidden" (*nistar*) was revealed (*nigleh*) to the sect (cf. CD 3:13; 5:4–5). In 1QS 1:9, the "revealed" laws (הנגלות) refer to calendrical matters, which clearly were not issues on which the sect agreed with other groups within Judaism, and thus were not laws "whose interpretations are obvious to everyone." "Revealed" law refers not to halakhic matters over which the Association agreed with other Jewish groups, but instead refers to the legal interpretations particular to the Association. In the DSS, both "revealed" and "hidden" laws refer to the halakhot of the Association; for that which was "hidden" from Israel is equivalent to that which was "revealed" to the Associates.

Hasmonean dynasty, which controlled the temple, to represent a return to the principles of the covenant after that had been interrupted by pro-Seleucid factions within Jewish society which had vied for power and the high priesthood prior to the Hasmonean rebellion. According to 1 Macc 2:27, the rallying cry of Mattathias was, "Let everyone who is zealous for the law and upholds the covenant come out after me!"[116] One of the hallmarks of the Hasmonean regime was its insistence that circumcision represented a visible symbol of one's adherence to the law. The Hasmoneans not only insisted that those who dwelt in Judea follow the Torah, but also those who resided in territories that were conquered by the Hasmoneans as well (cf. the coercive circumcision of Idumeans and Pereans; *Ant* 13.257–258; 395–397). Against this backdrop, D's audacity is striking when it asserts that Israel "wallowed in man's iniquity and in the ways of impurity and said, 'It (i.e., the covenant) is ours'" (CD 3:17–18).[117] In the ideology of D, the early Hasmoneans,[118] who followed a version of Torah that was influenced by the Pharisees, rather than upholding the covenant had become traitors against it.

The statement placed on the lips of the sect's opposition, "it is ours," constitutes a citation of Ezek 11:15, in which a dichotomy is established between those who had been taken into exile by the Babylonians after the conquest of Jerusalem in 586 BCE, and those who were spared being taken into exile. Those who remained in Jerusalem, according to Ezekiel, claimed the land for themselves: הארץ למורשה לנו היא נתנה, "The land has been given to us as an inheritance." According to Ezekiel, those who remained in Jerusalem had sunk into a debased religious practice, so that YHWH had promised to regather the dispersed exiles, who would return to Jerusalem in order to purify cultic practices there.

By citing Ezek 11 as it does, D implicitly makes an identification between the members of the Association and the "remnant" whom, Ezekiel predicted, would be regathered to take possession of Jerusalem. The other side of this equation is that the Hasmoneans and their supporters, who controlled the temple when this section of D was written, are identified with those who had remained in Jerusalem during the time of the exile and had debased the worship that took place within the temple. By simply citing the two words, לנו היא, the author of CD 3 is able to insinuate not

---

[116] Πᾶς ὁ ζηλῶν τῷ νόμῳ καὶ ἱστῶν διαθήκην ἐξελθέτω ὀπίσω μοῦ.

[117] והם התגוללו בפשע אנוש ובדרכי נדה ויאמרו כי לנו היא. The particle כי functions here to introduce direct discourse (R. J. Williams, *Hebrew Syntax: An Outline* [Second ed., Toronto: Univ. of Toronto, 1992], §452, cites 2 Kings 8:13 as an example of recitative כי).

[118] Here I make the assumption that John Hyrcanus, prior to his rupture with the Pharisees, continued the policy of his successors. This is by no means certain, however.

only that the Hasmonean high priesthood had debased the temple's practices, but also that the priests within the sectarian Association would
eventually take their rightful place as restorers of orthopraxy within the
temple's precincts.

The rationale for the sectarian priesthood's replacement of the Hasmonean high priesthood in controlling the temple's practice is developed
in 3:18b–4:4. These lines assert that God "atoned for their iniquity (i.e.,
that of the Association's Zadokites) and forgave their sin and built them a
sure house (בית נאמן) in Israel, the likes of which has not stood from the
past until now." The reference to the "sure house" echoes 1 Sam 2:35, in
which the prophet Samuel delivers an oracle to the priest Eli:

(YHWH says:) "I will raise up for myself a faithful priest, who shall do according to
what is in my heart and in my mind. I will build him a sure house (בית נאמן), and he
shall go in and out[119] before my anointed one[120] forever" (NRSV).

The narrative in 1 Sam 2 relates the removal of the Elide priesthood and its
replacement with the Zadokite line. CD 3:18–4:4 invokes this narrative,
and in so doing identifies its own priestly members with the Zadokites of 1
Sam 2, while identifying the Hasmonean priesthood with the Elides. The
implication is that as the Elides had been replaced, so would the Hasmoneans.[121]

The sect often identified its priestly members as "sons of Zadok" (e.g.,
1QS 5:2, 9; 1QSa 1:2). The identification of the Association's priesthood
with the Zadokite lineage further legitimated their own claims to represent
the "true" priesthood against the claims of the Hasmoneans. The Hasmoneans, for their part, legitimated their claim to the priesthood on the
basis of their religious zeal, citing as a precedent for their seizure of the

---

[119] I.e., render (priestly) service.

[120] I.e., the king.

[121] J. J. Collins has argued that there is no evidence that the Hasmonean usurpation of
the high priesthood was a "major reason for the formation of the [Essene] sect." Collins
writes that "[t]he reasons for separation given in the *Damascus Document* and 4QMMT
concern the cultic calendar and matters of legal observance. At no point is any mention
made of the legitimacy of the High Priest" ("The Time of the Teacher," 215). Collins'
observations serve as a corrective to the theory that Essene origins may be traced to a
Hasmonean ouster of Zadokite priests (particularly the Teacher of Righteousness) from
the temple. Collins leaves open the possibility that the confrontation between the
Teacher and the Wicked Priest may have occurred during the first century BCE. In light
of Collins' statement that the legitimacy of the high Priest is not an issue in D however,
it is important to point out that the Hasmonean high priesthood is implicitly critiqued in
that text. CD 3:18-20 and 4:3–4 assume the view that the Essene sect's own priesthood
would replace that of the Hasmoneans. This critique of D's however, does not necessarily carry information relevant to the sect's origins, but may have arisen in response to
events that occurred later in the sect's history.

priesthood the biblical account of the "zeal of Phinehas" (1 Macc 2:23–26). For his zeal in opposing debased cultic practices, Phinehas was rewarded with a "covenant of perpetual priesthood" (Num 25:6–15). The Hasmoneans, who were conscious of their image as interlopers in the office of high priest, were able to rely on the story of Phinehas to show that it was zeal for the law, and not lineage alone, that legitimated a priest. The argument for the legitimacy of the Association's priesthood espoused in CD 3:19–4:4 offers a good example of the way in which sectarian religious rhetoric was formulated in opposition to the claims put forward by the sect's perennial enemies, the Hasmoneans.

However, D's claim to legitimacy in CD 3:19–20 surpasses even that of their Zadokite predecessors. Whereas the Zadokite line had very obviously lost its power during the course of history, the sect claimed that the authority that it embodied had not been paralleled in the history of Israel. The "sure house" that the Association's Zadokite priesthood embodied was one such as "had not stood from before until now" (3:19). The evident instability of the old Zadokite line is not shared by the Zadokites of the sectarian Association, according to D. Not only that, but "those who hold fast to it (are destined) for eternal life, and all the glory of Adam is (or: will be) theirs" (3:20).[122] Those who support the "sure house" are destined to enter into an era in which they will regain the glory with which Adam had been clothed prior to his "fall."

The "glory" that CD 3:20 promises to those who support the Association's Zadokites is probably to be understood as entailing two qualities which were commonly imputed to divine beings in antiquity: eternal life and luminescence (cf. 4Q267 3.2; בהופע כבוד אל, "when the glory of God shines"). According to Pesiqta Rabbati 41:12, "When God created Adam he created him so that he might live forever like the ministering angels ..."[123] The History of the Rechabites 7:2 compares Adam and Eve to the

---

[122] המחזיקים בו לחיי נצח וכל כבוד אדם להם. The term אדם here may be understood either as a proper noun, "Adam," or as a generic noun, "a man/human." Both the terms אדם and אנוש are used in CD with a generic sense (cf. 3:16, 17; 9:1, etc.), but this does not of course decide the issue. The decision between understanding אדם as a generic or a proper noun must be based on exegetical grounds. To translate "human glory" here spoils the logic of the passage. Such a translation assumes that a dichotomy between divine glory and human glory is envisioned here. But such is not the case. In the eschatological age, humans will inherit a mantle of divine glory. This idea is espoused in 1QS 4:7–8. In the eschatological age, Adam's transgression, which resulted in his death and the eventual death of all his progeny is reversed: eternal life is restored (CD 3:20), along with the glory that Adam radiated in Eden (as demonstrated in the passages cited on the following page herein).

[123] Quoted in James Kugel's *The Bible as it Was* (Cambridge, MA and London: Belknap, 1977) 71.

Blessed Ones, immortal humans whose appearances are described as "luminous" (ܐܘ̈ ܐ̈ ;ܗ̈ ܐ̈ ; 11:5),[124] and who are "robed in garments of glory, that which clothed Adam and Eve before they sinned" (ܐ̈ܘ̈ ܐ̈ܘ ܐ̈ܘ ܐ̈ܘ ܐ̈ܘ ܐ̈ܘ [125]ܐ̈ܘ̈ ܐ̈ܘ; 12:3).[126] D's vision of eschatological reward is closely paralleled in 1QS 4:7–8, which states that the reward for the "Sons of Truth" is "everlasting joy in eternal life and a crown of glory with a measure of splendor in everlasting light."[127]

The claim of the Association's Zadokite priesthood to hold the keys to eternal life and everlasting splendor certainly goes far beyond the claims advanced by the Hasmonean regime which, although it saw in its own success the fulfillment of Biblical prophecies (cf. 1 Macc 3:3–9; 14:4–15), did not apparently look forward to any future time of eschatological bliss. The sectarian Association attempted to trump Hasmonean power and propaganda, both in the religious and political spheres, with its own claims that it would represent the sole repository of priestly authority in the coming messianic age. The way to achieve eschatological blessing, according to CD 3:19–20, was to support the "sure house" of the Association's Zadokite priesthood, abandoning the Hasmoneans who, like the Elides, were due to be replaced.

3.11. CD 4:7–5:11

CD 4:7–5:11 draws attention to the halakhic nature of the dispute between the sectarian Association and the rest of Judaism. Apparently citing the Aramaic Testament of Levi as its authority, D asserts that Israel is caught in the "three nets of Belial." These "nets" are three types of halakhic error. To those who engage in the practices that D describes as "nets," the practices involved seem like "three kinds of righteousness" (CD 4:16–17).

---

[124] For other examples of adjectives in construct with the nouns that they modify, see T. Nöldeke, *Compendious Syriac Grammar* (Winona Lake, IN: Eisenbrauns, 2001 [1904]), §205A; p. 162.

[125] Fem. pl. abs. form. The construct state appears to be lacking for this noun, which is a calque from the Greek στολή. On Greek nouns which, when adopted by Syriac, are defective in the absolute or construct states, see Nöldeke, *Compendious Syriac Grammar*, §91; p. 62.

[126] F. Nau edited the Syriac version of the History of the Rechabites in *Revue Sémitique* 7 (1899) 54–75. M. R. James edited the Greek version in *Apocrypha Anecdota* (Texts and Studies 2/3; Cambridge: University Press, 1893) 86–108. An English translation, which differs somewhat from my own in the passage cited above, is provided by J. Charlesworth in *OTP* 2:443–461. In its present form, the History is clearly a Christian work, stemming perhaps from as late as the sixth century CE. The present Christian version may have had roots in earlier Christian and/or Jewish traditions (cf. the discussions of Charlesworth and James just cited).

[127] ושמחת עולמים בחיי נצח וכליל כבוד עם מדת הדר באור עולמים.

This is an appropriate metaphor for understanding the nature of the disputes between the various sects within Second Temple Judaism: depending on the way in which Mosaic law is interpreted, the same action may be described by different groups alternately as "righteous" or "wicked."

The three nets are defined as illicit sex (זנות), wealth (הון),[128] and defilement of the sanctuary (טמא המקדש). The term *zenut* as used in CD is elastic; the sect used it to refer to various sexual and marital practices that were illicit according to sectarian halakhah. These include engaging in intercourse with a menstruant (CD 5:7), marriage to one's niece (5:7–11) and here, marriage to two wives during one's lifetime (4:20–21). Whereas Pharisaic practice allowed remarriage in the case of divorce or the death of one's spouse, the Association forbade remarriage as long as a man's first wife was alive (11QT 57:17–18; cp. CD 4:19–5:5).[129]

The term הון refers to dedications made to the temple illegitimately or to the misappropriation of temple funds (CD 6:15–17). The third "net" is "defilement of the sanctuary." This charge relates to the perception that the temple priesthood engaged in intercourse with their wives during their menstrual periods (5:6–7; cp. PsSol 8:13). It is difficult to see how this last charge could have had any merit, as immersion in a *miqveh* would have rendered the priest pure, thus preventing his defiling the sanctuary, even if he had engaged in intercourse with his wife during her menstrual period. Perhaps the force of this charge is to be understood as involving the delineation of the precise time at which one, having immersed in the *miqveh*, was to be considered pure again. Pharisaic practice specified that one was to be considered clean immediately upon exit from the *miqveh*,

---

[128] Although the medieval manuscript clearly reads ההין, "the arrogance," it seems likely that the medieval copyist misread an earlier (ה)הון, since *waw*'s and *yodh*'s are difficult to distinguish in many texts copied during the late Second Temple Period. This is the emendation preferred by most scholars, following the reading adopted by Solomon Schechter in his *editio princeps* (*Fragments of a Zadokite Work*, xxxvi and n. 19). See also Catherine Murphy, *Wealth in the Dead Sea Scrolls and in the Qumran Community* (STDJ 40; Leiden: Brill, 2002) 37–78. Baumgarten (*PTSDSSP* 2:21) reads הין both here and in 8:3. However, 8:3 is a quote from Hos 5:10, as Baumgarten notes, and should be read הוי, as does the Hosea text. In 8:3, the reading הוי was adopted by Qimron in *The Damascus Document Reconsidered* (ed. M. Broshi; Jerusalem: Israel Exploration Society, 1992) 25, a volume to which Baumgarten himself contributed. Qimron's reading is correct, as the photograph of col. 8 of CD-A clearly shows. In CD-A, *waw*'s and terminal *nun*'s are distinguished in that the former display a curve up and to the left at the top of the letter, whereas terminal *nun*'s are characterized by a serif that is made by a separate penstroke, clearly distinguishing it from *waw*. Also, as Murphy notes, the Genizah manuscript indicates a section break before 5:11b. The section in 5:11b-19 is not an attempt, as Baumgarten supposes, to define the content of the second net of Belial.

[129] See the discussion of Y. Yadin, *The Temple Scroll* (3 vols., Jerusalem: Israel Exploration Society, 1977–1983) 1:355–357.

whereas Essene practice specified that one was not to be declared clean until the evening following his immersion.[130] This was probably a case in point for the Associates who considered the Pharisees to have taken a lax view of the Torah, branding them as "seekers of smooth things."

Following the section on the three nets of Belial, CD 5:11b–16 constitutes a condemnation of all those who opposed the halakhic teachings of the Association. These critics of the sect's halakhic precepts are described as "opening their mouths against the statutes of God's covenant with a blasphemous tongue, saying, 'they are not well-founded'" (לא נכונו; lines 11-12). In these lines, the statutes of God's covenant (חוקי ברית אל) are identified with the sect's own halakhic precepts. It is the latter of which opposing groups alleged, "they are not well-founded."

The sectarian Association was not the only Jewish group in antiquity that received the criticism that its legal precepts were not "well-founded." One may recall the anonymous statement recorded in *m. Ḥagigah* 1.8 that certain rabbinic legal rulings "are as mountains suspended by a hair, because Scripture is meagre and the rules are many."[131] The rabbis also lived with the knowledge that the biblical basis of some of their practices was slight.

The statement, "they are not well-founded," in CD 5:11–12 constitutes a criticism of the Association's legal precepts, lodged by a rival group. Some of the Association's teachings appeared, to those who were not members of the Association, to have slight biblical justification. We may suggest that the Association's teaching which banned niece marriage on the basis of Lev 18:13, as well as the sect's prohibition of offering festal sacrifices on the Sabbath, which itself was supported merely by the biblical phrase "apart from your Sabbaths" in Lev 23:38, both fell into this category. In terms of their grounding in specific biblical texts, neither one of these rulings could be said to have been particularly well-founded.

The prohibition against marriage to one's niece is explained in CD 5:8–11a. The Torah prohibits a man from marrying his aunt (Lev 18:13), but is silent on the issue of whether a woman may marry her uncle (niece marriage). According to the early rabbis, niece marriage was not only permissible but in many instances was viewed as a favored marital arrangement.[132] According to D, however, "Now the precept of incest is written from the point of view of males, but the same law applies to

---

[130] On this matter see L. Schiffman, "Pharisaic and Sadducean Halakhah in Light of the Dead Sea Scrolls: The Case of *Ṭevul Yom*," *DSD* 1, 3 (1994) 285–299.

[131] Cited according to the trans. of P. Blackman, *Mishnayoth* (6 vols., Brooklyn, NY: Judaica Press, 2000 [1964]).

[132] Cf. L. Ginzberg, *An Unknown Jewish Sect* (New York: Ktav, 1976) 128 and n. 84.

women ..."[133]   That is, just as males are forbidden from marrying their aunts, females are forbidden from marrying their uncles. Since there is no ruling on the legality of niece marriage in the Torah, D was forced to draw an inference on the basis of a related law (i.e., marriage to a nephew).[134] This is certainly a ruling of which the sect's opponents might have said, "It is not well-founded (in the Torah)."

The Essenes utilized a calendar that consisted of a year of 364 days.[135] This calendar was wonderfully regular in that the festivals fell on the same day of the week each year. According to this calendar, festivals never fell on a Sabbath. As for the festivals that lasted for seven days (Unleavened Bread and Booths), and so normally would have included at least one, if not two Sabbaths during the festival, the sect appears not to have counted the Sabbath as a festal day. Since the Sabbath was not counted as a festal day, the festivals of Unleavened Bread and Booths were extended by one day in order to compensate for this loss.[136]   In this regard, the practice of the sect stands in direct contradiction to biblical law. According to Lev 23:38, when festivals fell on a Sabbath, the temple priests were directed to offer first the Sabbath offering, then the festal offering. Both the Sabbath and the festal days were to be recognized when these coincided. However, the Association was able to read the very text that contradicted its practice as though that text supported it. After listing each of the yearly festivals and the offerings that were appropriately made at the temple on those festivals, Leviticus concludes its festal legislation as follows (23:37–38):

These are the appointed festivals of the LORD, which you shall celebrate as times of holy convocation, for presenting to the LORD offerings by fire – burnt offerings and grain offerings, sacrifices and drink offerings, each on its proper day – apart from the Sabbaths of the LORD (מלבד שבתת יהוה), and apart from your gifts, and apart from your votive offerings, and apart from your freewill offerings, which you give to the LORD (NRSV).

The function of the prepositional phrase מלבד שבתת יהוה, "apart from YHWH's Sabbaths" appears to have been to specify that the offerings given for Sabbaths, votive offerings, etc. were to be given *in addition to* any festal offerings that were sacrificed on a given Sabbath. D however

---

[133] Trans. of Baumgarten, *PTSDSSP* 2:21.

[134] The practice of inferring an ordinance by making an analogy to a related matter is called *gezerah shawah*, and constituted one of the "seven rules of Hillel" (cf. H. Strack and G. Stemberger, *Introduction to the Talmud and Midrash* [Minneapolis, MN: Fortress Press, 1992] 19–21).

[135] For a thorough discussion of the sectarian calendar, see J. VanderKam, *Calendars in the Dead Sea Scrolls: Measuring Time* (Literature of the Dead Sea Scrolls series; London, UK and New York, NY: Routledge, 1998).

[136] See the calendrical schematic in J. Maier, *The Temple Scroll: An Introduction, Translation, and Commentary* (JSOTSupp 34; Sheffield: JSOT Press, 1985) 71–76.

understands this phrase as an absolute prohibition of mixing festal sacrifices with Sabbath sacrifices; according to D these could not be offered on the same day.[137] The effect of this reading of Lev 23:38 is that the Association's practice of keeping Sabbath and festival days separate is able to claim the support of the Torah. This support however, was weak: one prepositional phrase taken from the vast corpus of the Hebrew scriptures. Like the Association's legislation banning niece marriage, the maintenance of an absolute separation between Sabbath and festal sacrifices in the sectarian calendar was a practice that found little if any support in scripture. This was another case in which the sect's opponents would have been justified in criticizing the practice as one that was not well-founded.

However, the possibility that there may have been some truth to the opponent's claims was not countenanced by D. Instead of admitting that some of the sect's legal rulings did indeed receive only scant support from scripture, D foreclosed discussion on these matters by creating a discourse that was designed to threaten and intimidate those who might countenance the stance of the sect's halakhic opposition. CD 5:14–16 likened its opponents to those who approached Mt. Sinai too closely during the time of God's theophany and the giving of the law to Moses. Concerning the parties who opposed the Association, CD 5:14b–15 states, "One who comes close to them will not be exculpated. As (at) the mountain, his house will be held guilty, unless he was under duress."[138] Just as at the time of the giving of the original Torah, the people were not allowed to approach the mountain on pain of death (Ex 19:23–24), so all those who criticized the sectarian understanding of Torah did so only at their own peril, D implies. This section of D in particular discourages open debate with the sect's opponents,[139] resorting instead to the presumed forcefulness of threatening gestures embedded within a narrative that the opposition was never meant to have read.

---

[137] Cana Werman offers a similar interpretation and discusses the relationship of D's ruling with rabbinic legislation in "CD 11:17: Apart from Your Sabbaths" in J. Baumgarten, ed., *The Damascus Document: A Centennial of Discovery*, 201–212.

[138] Trans. of Baumgarten, *PTSDSSP* 2:21.

[139] Cp. 1QS 9:16.

Chapter 3

The New Covenant in the Damascus Document

1. Prolegomenon: The New Covenant in the Dead Sea Scrolls

Although the term ברית occurs very frequently in the sectarian texts from among the Dead Sea scrolls (74 times in CD and 1QS alone), the phrase "new covenant" (ברית חדשה) occurs only four times; three times in CD and once in the Habakkuk pesher. There are four additional instances in which the term ברית occurs with verbal forms from the root חדש ("to be new, to renew"), either as the subject of a passive verbal form or as the object of an active transitive form.[1] Three of these four instances of the verbal use of a form of חדש with ברית either as subject or object occur in 1QSb, a work now known simply as "Blessings." One final use of the same noun-verb phrase occurs in 1Q34, which represents a fragment of a liturgy either for the Day of Atonement or the Feast of Weeks.

The fragments of 1Q34 and 1Q34bis, together referred to as "1QLiturgical Prayers," were probably not compositions of the Essene sect. The text does not exhibit sectarian terminology[2] (as displayed in 1QS and D, for example) and the ideological perspective espoused therein appears to be pan-Israelite rather than sectarian. In fragment 3, col. 2, ll. 5b–7, we read:

And you have chosen for yourself a people in the time of your goodwill, for you remembered your covenant and you have appointed them to be separate[3] from all the peoples for you for (the purpose of) holiness. And you have renewed your covenant with them in the vision of glory and the words of your holy spirit, by the works of your hands, when your right hand wrote to make known to them the glorious regulations and eternal ascents/deeds.

This text is interesting in that it ascribes the "renewing of the covenant" to the time of the Sinai theophany. The combination of the Elohistic and Priestly versions of the Sinai story in Exodus resulted in two accounts of the giving of the tablets of the law. The first account is followed by the

---

[1] 1QSb 3:26; 5:5; 5:21; 1Q34 3:2:6.

[2] So J. Davila, *Liturgical Works* (Eerdmans Commentaries on the Dead Sea Scrolls; Grand Rapids, MI and Cambridge: Eerdmans, 2000) 15–24.

[3] Taking להבדל either as hophal inf. constr. or as hiphil (intrans.) inf. constr.

story of the golden calf and the apostasy of the Israelites, with the result that Moses threw down the two tablets, shattering them and thereby symbolically enacting the dissolution of covenantal bonds between YHWH and Israel. This broken covenant is explicitly re-made in Ex 34:1–28. It is possible however, that the covenant "remembered" in line 5 and renewed in line 6 is the Abrahamic covenant, renewed at Sinai, in which case 1Q34 espouses a theology of the covenant that has similarities with Jubilees.

The "vision of glory" that 1Q34 refers to is the vision of YHWH that Moses was allowed in Ex 33:17–23. The statement in 1Q34 3.2.7 that God's "right hand wrote to make known to them the glorious regulations" refers to the scene narrated in Ex 34:1b: "I (i.e., YHWH) will write on the tablets the words that were on the former tablets, that you broke." The renewal of the covenant in 1Q34, since it espouses a pan-Israelite perspective, differs in this regard from the Essene construction of the covenant.

The fragments of the sectarian composition 1QSb ("Blessings") also use forms of the verb חדש either in direct connection with the term ברית or in contexts that imply it. These contrast with the way in which "covenant renewal" was construed in 1Q34, but cohere very well with the construction of the covenant that we have delineated in CD.

The "Blessings" contain the fragments of three blessings with which the sectarian functionary known as the משכיל, "wise man," who functioned as a teacher within the sect, was to bless various groups. Charlesworth and Stuckenbruck outline the contents of 1QSb as follows:[4]

1:1–2:21	Blessing of the Faithful
2:22–28	Blessing of a Part of the Sect
3:1–16	Blessing of an Officiating Priest
3:17–21	Blessing of Another Part of the Sect
3:22–4:21	Blessing of the Sons of Zadok
4:22–28	Blessing of the Zadokite High Priest
5:1–19	Blessing of an Unidentifiable Part of the Sect
5:20–29	Blessing of the Prince of the Congregation

The final section includes the blessings to be pronounced over the "prince of the congregation," who was expected to appear at some future point in time as a messianic king who would lead an Israel that had been restored to its former glory, as in Davidic times (5:20–29). The blessings preserved in 1QSb were "reserved for (the) final session of the eschatological age ... when the Sons of Light (were expected to) receive 'all the everlasting blessings.'"[5]

In the first section (1:1–2:21), the members of the sect are described as those who have been chosen for the eternal covenant (לברית עולם; 1:2–3).

---

[4] *PTSDSSP* 1:119.

[5] J. Charlesworth, *PTSDSSP* 1:119.

This phrase echoes the language of the Priestly writer in the Pentateuch (cf. Gen 9:16; 17:7; Lev 24:8) and refers to the covenant between God and his people. However, as D amply demonstrates, the "covenant" represented for the Associates not a covenant with all of Israel, but only with those who were members of the sectarian Association. As D argued, it was only the sect that knew how properly to interpret and follow the Torah, which constituted the set of stipulations upon which the covenant was based. We may conjecture that the phrase in 5:5, ‏וחדש לכה]‏ was once completed by an object such as ‏בריתו‏ or ‏ברית עולם‏, "he will renew for you his covenant/the eternal covenant." Because the object is lacking however, we cannot place much emphasis on this small fragment.

In the blessing to be pronounced over the Zadokite priests (col. 3, l. 26), the *maskil* recites, ‏וברית כהונת [עולם יח]דש לכה‏, "and [may he re]new for you the covenant of [eternal] priesthood." Even though the section heading relates the blessings in 3:22–4:21 to the "sons of Zadok," the blessings themselves are addressed in the second person singular: "May the Lord bless you" (sing., 3:25), "[may he r]enew for you (sing.) the covenant of the [eternal] priesthood" (3:26).[6] Therefore it is possible that the blessing was intended for the messianic high priest, to whom the section in 4:22-28 was addressed. Whether it was meant specifically for the messianic high priest, or for the Zadokite priests in general, this blessing reflects the expectation that we encountered in CD 3:19–20 that God had built for the Association's Zadokites a "sure house" such as had not stood "from the past until now." The idea that the Association's Zadokites would have a permanent priesthood is expressed aptly by the phrase, ‏ברית כהונת עולם‏, "the covenant of eternal priesthood."

The final section of the Blessings, designated for the prince of the congregation, represents a very important contribution to our view of the Essene construction of the covenant. In 5:21 we read, ‏וברית היחד יחדש לו להקים מלכות עמו לעול[ם]‏, "and may he (i.e., God) renew the covenant of the Association for himself in order to establish the kingdom[7] of his (i.e., God's) people forev[er]."[8] Here the covenant is described as the

---

[6] Trans. of Charlesworth and Stuckenbruck, *PTSDSSP* 1:127.

[7] Or "dominion."

[8] The subject of the jussive verb ‏יחדש‏ is properly God, rather than the prince. Who is the subject of the possessive pronoun in the prepositional phrase ‏לו‏ is a more difficult question. The referent could be either God or the prince. Stuckenbruck and Charlesworth take God as the antecedent and translate, "the covenant of the Community he (God) shall renew for himself ..." (*PTSDSSP* 1:129). This interpretation has the benefit of referring the possessive pronoun in both ‏לו‏ and ‏עמו‏ to the same subject, God. Taking the ‏ל‏ as indicative of the *dativus commodi*, we may recall that many of the penitential prayers of Second Temple Judaism seek to remind God that it is to his own benefit to restore his covenant (e.g., Dan 9:19, where the petitioner asks God to restore his people speedily,

province of the sectarian Association, rather than as pertaining to all Israel, as in 1Q34 and in the Bible. The renewal of the covenant of the Association is linked with the establishment of the "kingdom of God's people." The *hiphil* infinitive construct להקים connotes purpose or consecution;[9] the covenant is renewed for the purpose of or with the result that the kingdom is established. In this construction, the "kingdom of God's people" consists of the members of the sectarian Association (יחד). However, it is quite possible, on the basis of 4QMMT[e] frags. 11–13, lines 5–6 ("And this is the end of days, when they will return in Israel to the L[aw] ...."),[10] that the author of 1QSb believed that those Jews who were not members of the Association would repent and join the sect to constitute a new, restored Israel. According to 1QSb, it is the sect's own covenant that serves as the basis for the establishment of this new kingdom.

1QSb offers an illuminating glimpse at the Association's construction of the covenant and covenant renewal. The ideology of 1QSb is compatible with that of D in that the covenant is not construed as belonging to all Israel, but to the sectarian Association alone. Both 1QSb and D share the view that the Association's Zadokites will inherit a "sure house" of eternal priesthood. The messianism entailed in 1QSb's last section is compatible with D's expectation of a "prince of the congregation" who will arise to "destroy all the sons of Seth" (CD 7:20–21). (The kingly messianism of 1QSb however, finds its closest parallel in the "Messianic Apocalypse," 4Q246.)

1QSb offers interesting insights into the Essene construction of the covenant and covenant renewal, but it does not include the phrase הברית החדשה, "the new covenant" that appears several times in D. The phrase does however, occur once in the Habakkuk pesher. 1QpHab 1:16–2:10a interprets Habakkuk 1:5, "Look, traitors[11] and see! Be astonished,[12] be astounded, for he is doing a deed in your days (which) you will not believe

---

"For your own sake, O my God, because your city and your people bear your name!" [NRSV]).

[9] Cf. Joüon-Muraoka, *A Grammar of Biblical Hebrew* 2:436, §124l.

[10] Trans. of García-Martínez and Tigchelaar, *DSSSE* 2:803.

[11] Due to the fragmentary state of the text, almost all of the biblical quotation must be restored on the basis of the MT. The MT however, reads בגוים, which does not accord well with the pesher given in the following lines, which mentions the בוגדים. The LXX of Hab 1:5 reads οἱ καταφρονηταί, which probably presupposes a Hebrew exemplar that read בוגדים (so Horgan, *Pesharim*, 23). In support of this view, we may note that LXX translates the בוגדים of Hab 1:13 with καταφρονοῦντας. It appears then that the author of 1QpHab utilized a Hebrew text of Habakkuk that agreed with LXX against MT.

[12] Taking the *hithpael* in a passive, rather than a reflexive sense.

(האמינו) when[13] it is recounted." The biblical text is interpreted as referring to the traitors (הבוגדים) who, along with the "liar," did not assent to
(האמינו; restored) the words of the Righteous Teacher, although those
came "from the mouth of God." The lemma is also interpreted to refer to
"those who betrayed the new covenant, for they did not assent to the covenant of God and they profaned his holy name" (הבוג]דים בברית [החדשה
קודשו [ש]ם את [ויחללו] אל בברית האמינו לוא [י][כ)[.14 The pesher subsequently describes how the "traitors" refused to believe the content of the
teacher's eschatological predictions (2:5–10). This message included
teaching about "all that is coming upon the last generation." The author of
1QpHab, and probably the Righteous Teacher as well, viewed this message
as one that had been implicit in the prophetic literature, and which the
Teacher had "discovered" as a result of his inspired exegesis of scripture
(1QpHab 2:7–9; cf. also 7:1–9). For their refusal to assent to the Teacher's
message, the author of the Habakkuk pesher asserts that the "traitors" will
be punished by the *Kittîm*, a cryptonym for the Romans (2:10b–4:13a).

In the Habakkuk pesher, betraying the covenant is connected with the
refusal to assent to the Teacher's instruction concerning the end-time. The
pesher does not make explicit any disagreements over halakhah that the
teacher's group may have had with the group represented by the "liar" and
the "traitors." However, it may very well be that the "liar" here is to be
identified with D's "one who dripped deceitful waters upon Israel," otherwise referred to as "the scoffer."[15] If so, then this in turn provides a link to
Pharisaic halakhot (see section 3.9 herein), which as we have seen were
opposed in D.

The Habakkuk pesher does not explain what is entailed in its use of the
phrase "new covenant." We do not receive a definition or description of
the content or terms of the "new covenant." As is so often the case in the
pesharim, the text presupposes a knowledge of significant people, ideas,
and events that was reserved for initiates, those schooled in the lore of the
Association. The one thing that we can conclude about the new covenant
from the Habakkuk pesher is that it was connected with the teaching of the
"Righteous Teacher."

---

[13] The particle כי is probably better understood here as a temporal particle ("when")
than as a conditional particle ("if"), although either sense is possible.

[14] Here I use the text as restored by García Martínez and Tigchelaar in *DSSSE* 1:12.

[15] So T. Lim, art. "Liar," *EDSS* 1:493.

2. New Covenant in the Damascus Document

If the Habakkuk pesher tells us precious little about the sectarian construction of the new covenant, D offers a little more data on the subject. The phrase itself occurs only three times in D, each time within the same set clause, "the new covenant in the land of Damascus." There is an important, if not constitutive, geographical component to D's construction of the "new covenant." We will return to this observation later on. First, however, let us examine in some detail the contexts in which the phrase "new covenant" occurs in D.

The first occurrence of the phrase in D is in CD 6:19. The immediate context in which the line appears is a section that extends from 6:11b–7:6a. This section is structured according to the binary oppositions of purity and defilement, the holy and the profane. The section in 6:11b–7:6a is itself composed of two thematically distinct subsections. The first extends from 6:11b–20b. This section deals with matters of cultic practice at the temple. The section in 6:20b–7:6a deals with the precepts that are meant to govern life within the covenantal community.[16] This is, it must be stressed, a thematic division, and a somewhat artificial one at that. The scribe who copied CD-A apparently thought that the section should be divided between the noun וגר and the verb ולדרוש in l. 21. However, the infinitive ולדרוש is clearly subordinate to the verb ישמרו, which governs the extended protasis of 6:14–7:1a. The author of this section of D switched from discussing cultic matters to matters of conduct within the community in mid-sentence. It is this switch that makes it so difficult adequately to assign a section-break between the material related to cultic purity and that related to holiness in relations between members of the sect.

This section does not preclude members of the sect from making offerings at the temple. This passage does, however, place constraints on the conduct of the Associate while he is within the temple's precincts. He must "remain separate from the sons of the pit" (ולהבדל מבני השחת), a reference to Jews who were not members of the sectarian Association. This was undoubtedly an issue of purity. Since the Associates were especially rigor-

---

[16] The scribe who copied CD-A divided the section differently. This MS leaves a space after וגר, "proselyte" in l. 21a. Apparently this scribe considered the support of "the poor, the destitute, and the proselyte" (trans. of Baumgarten, *PTSDSSP* 2:25) to be a cultic matter. The temple did of course take up offerings for the poor, the widow and the orphan, although I am unaware of any collection in the temple that was to be disbursed specifically to proselytes. But clearly, the phrase that precedes this one in ll. 20–21, "to love each man his brother as himself" (Baumgarten, *PTSDSSP* 2:25) deals with matters of conduct between members of the sect.

ous in sending offerings to the temple only by those who had been purified (CD 11:18-20), inadvertent contact with one who adhered to less stringent laws of purity might result in the defilement of the Associate – and thus the defilement of the sanctuary. The Associate is enjoined "to act scrupulously in accordance with the exact interpretation of the law during the age of wickedness" (6:14). The scrupulosity that is enjoined here entails a significant calendrical component. The Associates must:

[ישמרו] (ו)להבדיל בין הטמא לטהור ולהודיע בין
הקודש לחול ולשמור את יום השבת כפרושה ואת המועדות
ואת יום התענית כמצאת באי הברית החדשה בארץ דמשׁק
להרים את הקדשים כפירושיהם

[And they shall be careful] to distinguish between impure and pure, and to recognize (the difference) between the holy and the profane, and to keep the day of the Sabbath according to its exact interpretation, and (to keep) the festivals and the day of fasting in accordance with the findings[17] of those who entered the new covenant in the land of Damascus, to offer holy things in accordance with their exact specifications.

Two aspects of this section deserve special mention. The first is that "those who entered the new covenant" are credited with having "found" (כמצאת) the exact specifications of the law regarding sacred time (i.e., the appropriate dates "to offer holy things"). The term פרושׁ refers to the specification of a precise legal requirement on the basis of scripture (cp. CD 4:8; 4Q266 10.1.10, 11). This "exact specification" regards the time and manner in which one was to observe the Sabbath, the festivals, and the "day of fasting." These were issues that were connected with the Association's solar calendar. The Associates observed the festivals, including the day of atonement (the "day of fasting"), according to a different schedule than did the rest of Judaism. Although the Sabbath was observed on the same day on which other Jews observed it, a major issue arose concerning whether it was permissible for the priests to offer festal sacrifices on the Sabbath. At issue in this debate was the interpretation of the phrase "apart from the Sabbaths of YHWH" (מלבד שבתת יהוה) in Lev 23:38, which the Pharisees took to mean, "in addition to" Sabbath offerings, while the Associates took it to mean "separate from" Sabbath offerings. On days when in the temple's calendar, the Sabbath corresponded with the day of one of the yearly

---

[17] The term מצאת appears to be either a *qal* inf. constr. of the verb מצא, "to find," or a plural construct form of the noun מציאה, "finding," formed from the same root. However, the standard inf. abs. form of the verb מצא is מצֹא, not מצאת. One might argue that the final ת was acquired through the assimilation of the III-*Aleph* inf. constr. form to that of the III-*He*. But if this were so, one would have expected the form מצות. If the term is taken as a plural fem. noun, then the form should be pointed as a defectively written, מצאת (Jastrow lists the form as מציאות). It would seem that in terms of orthography, the only viable option is to take the term as a fem. pl. noun.

festivals, Pharisaic law ruled that both the Sabbath sacrifice and the festal sacrifices were to be offered during the day.[18] The Associates, on the other hand, ruled that on the basis of Lev 23:38, no festal offerings could be offered on a Sabbath. It is the Association's interpretation of this biblical passage that was "found" by "those who entered the new covenant in the land of Damascus."

The hermeneutical outlook that is perhaps implied by the use of the verb "to find" in the context of scriptural interpretation calls for some comment. The view implied here is not one that recognizes signifiers as inherently unstable and susceptible of multiple possible interpretations; rather, the scriptural text serves as a repository of legal rulings and eschatological teachings, some of which were "hidden" within the text and were in need of being "found." This must not be taken to imply that the members of the Association considered all interpretations of scripture to be equally valid. For the Associates, the "true meaning" of Scripture was latent within the text, to be found only by those to whom God had given the eyes to see, namely "those who had entered the new covenant in the land of Damascus." The result of the exegetical labors of authorized interpreters (i.e., those who belonged to the Association) was the פרוש התורה, "the exact interpretation of the law."

Of course the "exact specification of the law" was not purely a hermeneutical activity. It was an enterprise that took into account the halakhic practices of the Association as well as those of their enemies, the Pharisees. The Association's interpretation of Lev 23:38, "apart from the Sabbaths of YHWH" certainly involved an exegetical decision; but this decision was influenced by the fact that the earliest representatives of the group had decided to adopt a schematic solar year to order their festal and liturgical calendar. According to the Association's solar calendar, the festivals fell on the same day each year, and never fell on a Sabbath. So the sect was able to turn to Lev 23:38 to support the separation that was maintained between Sabbath and festival. However, it does not seem to have been the case that the Association's exegesis was overdetermined by social praxis; rather we should posit a reciprocal interaction between social practice and exegesis. It seems probable that it is Lev 23:38 that influenced the Associates to add an extra day to their observance of the festivals of Booths and Unleavened Bread,[19] so that they could observe the Sabbath as

---

[18] C. Werman ("Apart from Your Sabbaths," 201–212) argues that although the general Pharisaic approach was to perform both festal and Sabbath sacrifices on days when the two coincided, there was an inner-Pharisaic debate over the matter between the schools of Hillel and Shammai.

[19] According to J. Maier, *The Temple Scroll*.

Sabbath (and not as a festival day in addition), when it fell during these festivals.

CD 6:11b–20a attributes to "those who entered the new covenant in the land of Damascus" an exegetical activity whereby they "found" detailed legal requirements in the Torah, including some innovative calendrical reckonings.[20] But who is referred to in the phrase "those who entered ..."? And what is the significance of the location given, "the land of Damascus"? This latter phrase has in particular been the subject of much debate. This, however, is a case in which the "naive" interpretation is also the best: "Damascus" refers to a city in Syria.

3. "In the Land of Damascus": A Brief Survey of the Interpretative Options

Scholars have proposed three interpretations of the phrase "in the land of Damascus," each of which has continued to find support. The most obvious interpretation of the phrase is that it refers to a city or region in Syria. Prior to the discovery of the Dead Sea scrolls, scholars were unanimous in interpreting the "Damascus" of CD in a straightforward literal sense.[21] However, since the discovery of the Dead Sea scrolls, many scholars have been tempted to identify "Damascus" with Qumran. F. M. Cross has opined that "Damascus" is the "prophetic" or "revealed" name "referring to the desert retreat in the wilderness of Qumran."[22] According to Cross, this interpretation best fits the archaeological data as presented and interpreted by R. de Vaux (i.e., indicating date for the habitation of Qumran during or prior to the reign of John Hyrcanus).[23] Murphy-O'Connor is the leading exponent at present of yet a third option: "Damascus" is an allegorical name for Babylon.

---

[20] I would include the adoption of the 364-day calendar as an innovative practice. Although earlier Jewish sources are aware of such a calendar, they do not seem to have put it to use (so S. Talmon in his art. "Calendars and Mishmarot," *EDSS* 1:114). Even if one would disagree in seeing the Essene solar calendar as an innovation in terms of the actual practice of Jews during the second temple period, the practice of not counting the Sabbath among the festival days, at least, is unknown in sources earlier than the DSS.

[21] See P. Davies' summary of the history of interpretation of CD in *The Damascus Covenant: An Interpretation of the "Damascus Document,"* esp. 5–14.

[22] *Ancient Library of Qumran*, 72–73, n. 5.

[23] De Vaux is tentative in his conclusions regarding the date of Period 1a: "It is possible that this [building activity] would have commenced under one of the predecessors of John Hyrcanus, but we cannot push it back very far ..." (*Archaeology and the Dead Sea Scrolls* [London, UK: Oxford University Press, 1973] 5).

The idea that "Damascus" refers to Qumran is refuted succinctly by Murphy-O'Connor: "The Qumran interpretation is excluded by Damascus Document, CD-A vi.5, because Qumran is in 'the land of Judah.'" The passage that Murphy-O'Connor is referring to is part of the "well midrash" and reads (ll. 5–6): "The 'well' is the Torah and those who 'dug' it are the penitents of Israel *who departed from the land of Judah* and dwelt in the land of Damascus." Clearly, the "land of Damascus" must lie outside of Judah. Since Qumran lies within the territory of ancient Judah, "Damascus" cannot be a "code" name for Qumran.[24]

Or is "Judah," too, perhaps a cipher for a non-geographical referent, as de Vaux argued?[25] This is unlikely in CD 6:5. When D uses the term "Judah" as a coded reference, the reference is to the sectarian Association. D establishes a typological correspondence between the sectarian Association and eighth-century BCE Judah, on the one hand, and the Pharisees and eighth-century Ephraim, on the other (CD 7:11–13; 14:1; cf. 4:11). According to the eighth-century prophets Isaiah and Hosea, Ephraim had rejected Yahweh and would subsequently be punished for its rebellion (Isa 7:17; 9:9, 21; Hos 5:3, 5, 9 and throughout). According to the typology that D establishes, the Pharisees during the Hasmonean period had rejected God's commandments and would, like the Ephraim of a former age, be punished. In the designation "princes of Judah" in 8:3 and 19:15, and "wicked of Judah" in 20:27, the term "Judah" retains its geographical significance, even if in context it has a pejorative connotation. The passage in CD 6:5 yields no sense if we take "Judah" as a reference to the sectarian Association, so the geographical significance is much more likely, especially when we notice that יהודה, "Judah," is governed by a specifically geographical term, ארץ, "land."

It should also be stated that if Jodi Magness is correct in dating the habitation of the Qumran site to c. 100 BCE, then Cross' reconstruction of Qumran origins, which would have the Teacher of Righteousness leading his little band of exiles into the desert to Qumran during the middle of the second century BCE,[26] is excluded. If the Righteous Teacher's floruit is placed during the time of Jonathan in the 150s BCE, then most of his ca-

---

[24] A point made also by Devorah Dimant in an article entitled, "Non pas l'Exil au Désert mais l'Exil Spirituel: l'Interprétation d'Isaïe 40,3 dans la *Règle de la Communauté*" (A. Lemaire and S. Mimouni, eds., *Qumrân et le Judaïsme du Tournant de Notre Ère: Actes de la Table Ronde, Collège de France, 16 novembre 2004* [Paris and Louvain: Peeters, 2006]) 17-36. Dimant writes: "Si le 'pays de Damas' était vraiment la région de Qoumrân, le texte signifierait que les 'convertis d'Israël' sont partis de Judée pour s'installer en Judée, ce qui est illogique" (24).

[25] *Archaeology and the Dead Sea Scrolls*, 114.

[26] *Ancient Library of Qumran*, 109, 116.

reer must have been spent at a location other than Qumran. Neither D nor
the archaeological data support Cross' interpretation.

Murphy-O'Connor's interpretation develops a suggestion made by
Rabinowitz in 1969. "Damascus," Rabinowitz had argued, was actually a
reference to Babylon. This follows from Rabinowitz's reading of the
phrase שָׁבֵי יִשְׂרָאל, which could be vocalized either שָׁבֵי, "penitents/ returnees," or שְׁבִי, "captivity" of Israel. Rabinowitz opts for the latter reading
and draws parallels with Ezra 2:1 and Neh 7:6, where the phrase הַגּוֹלָה
שְׁבִי, "the captivity of the exile" occurs. On the basis of this alleged parallel Rabinowitz argues that CD's phrase, שְׁבִי יִשְׂרָאל, refers to those who
were held captive in Babylon.[27] Rabinowitz concludes, "The land of 'Damascus,' then, is merely the author's way of designating the place to which
the saved remnant of Israel, the Captivity, was exiled ...," that is, Babylon.
Without going into any detail to try to disprove Rabinowitz's suggestion,
we may simply note that his vocalization of שׁבי is not the one that most
scholars have opted to follow.[28] Even though Murphy-O'Connor himself
does not adopt the vocalization of שׁבי that Rabinowitz had proposed, he
did agree with the thesis that "Damascus" referred to Babylon.

Murphy-O'Connor relies also on the argument of S. Iwry. Iwry, although he translates שׁבי יִשְׂרָאל as "returnees of Israel," also understands
the phrase as referring to the return of Jewish refugees following the
Babylonian captivity. Like Rabinowitz, Iwry draws a parallel between CD
6:5 and passages from Ezra and Nehemiah. Included among these references is Ezra 6:21, with its reference to "the sons of Israel who returned
(הַשָּׁבִים) from the exile."

Like Rabinowitz and Iwry, Murphy-O'Connor argues that the beginnings of the Association (which Murphy-O'Connor identifies with the
Essenes) are to be located during the "exilic period." Murphy-O'Connor's
argument relies on the standard periodization of history that is utilized by
modern historians when referring to the history of Israel. In this scheme,
the "exilic period" lasts from 586 BCE, when Jerusalem was destroyed by
the Babylonians, until 539 BCE, when the Persians captured Babylon and
allowed peoples from various regions to return to their homelands. Successive waves of Jews subsequently returned to Judea during the latter sixth
and fifth centuries BCE. This period is known to modern historians as the
"postexilic" period. Murphy-O'Connor, relying on this scheme of perio-

---

[27] "A Reconsideration of 'Damascus' and '390 Years' in the 'Damascus' ('Zadokite')
Fragments," *JBL* 73 (1954) 11–35. The arguments cited appear in notes 20 and 38.

[28] See, for example, Knibb, "Exile in the Damascus Document," 105; S. Iwry, "Was
There a Migration to Damascus? The Problem of שׁבי יִשְׂרָאל," *Eretz-Israel* 9 (1969) 86;
cp. Baumgarten's translation, "penitents," in CD 6:9 (*PTSDSSP* 2:23).

dizing the sixth – fifth centuries BCE, is forced to place the origin of the Essene sect very early – during the sixth-century "exilic period."

However, as Michael Knibb has shown, many Jews did not share the periodization of history that is employed by modern biblical scholars. For many Jews living in the Hellenistic period, the "exile" referred not to a past epoch, but rather was a lived reality. As long as there was a Jewish diaspora, the Jews remained in exile. Many Jews looked forward to a time in which foreign oppressors would be defeated in a decisive, eschatological battle, and Jews would come streaming from all parts of the globe to return to their homeland. Until these decisive events occurred Israel remained, for all intents and purposes, in captivity.[29]

As we have already seen, D relies on this view of history. According to the schematization of history that was employed by the author of D, the present was a time of exile. Only when the messiahs of Aaron and Israel arose, the eschatological battle was waged against Israel's oppressors, and the temple was restored to the Essene Zadokites would the present time of exile end.

Knibb's criticism does not in itself disprove the possibility that the sectarian Association arose during the sixth century BCE in Babylon, but it raises a fundamental issue: the references to "exile" in D need not be read in light of the periodization of history according to which the "exile" ended during the sixth century BCE. Rather, the author of D relied on a scheme in which the exile was initiated during the sixth century BCE, but which continued until the author's own time. This effectively widens the period in which the Essene sect may have had its origins from the sixth century BCE until some time prior to D's composition, the latest portions of which may have been added early in the first century BCE. Knibb has not disproven Murphy-O'Connor's contention, but he has effectively demonstrated that the period of "exile" during which the Essene sect arose included the Hellenistic period, in which the majority of scholars today would locate the origin of the Essene sect.

If Knibb's critique did not finally succeed in disproving Murphy O'Connor's contention that "Damascus" may refer to Babylon, we may add a few of our own observations regarding Murphy O'Connor's thesis. In my judgment, two factors weigh heavily against Murphy O'Connor's thesis. The first is that the phrase "ארץ *x*" ("the land of *x*") is not elsewhere used in the DSS as a coded reference. Elsewhere the term ארץ is used in a straightforward geographical sense. If we take the phrase ארץ דמשק, "the

---

[29] James M. Scott has edited two books that bear on Jewish constructions of exile and restoration during the Second Temple Period which are appropriately entitled, *Exile: Old Testament, Jewish, and Christian Conceptions* (Leiden: Brill, 1997) and *Restoration: Old Testament, Jewish, and Christian Perspectives* (Leiden: Brill, 2001).

land of Damascus" in D as a coded reference to Babylon, this would represent an anomalous usage in the DSS.

Secondly, and more importantly, any proponent of the hypothesis that the phrase "the land of Damascus" represents a coded reference to a locale other than Damascus must be able to provide a motivation for the substitution. Why would the author of CD have chosen to "encode" his reference to Babylon or, for that matter, Qumran?

The phenomenon of using "coded language" in the DSS to refer to persons and groups is well known. The pesharim refer to the Pharisees as "Ephraim," to the Sadducees as "Manasseh," and to Alexander Jannaeus as the "angry lion." However, the motivation for the use of such coded speech is evident in each case: the members of the sect were unwilling openly to criticize powerful groups who opposed them. Such open criticism may have resulted in retaliation. Clearly, the motive for the use of coded speech was to protect the members of the sect from reprisal by powerful groups who opposed the sect. However, one is at a loss to explain why the location of the group's formative period should have required such protection through the use of coded speech. Neither the theory that the "land of Damascus" refers to Qumran, nor the theory that it refers to Babylon can withstand this criticism. It certainly would not have been necessary to have protected the location of the Essene headquarters at Qumran, since by most accounts this was the most famous of all the Essene meeting-places. It is generally agreed that not only Pliny the Elder,[30] but even Dio of Prusa were aware of the Essene habitation at Qumran.[31] It seems unlikely that the author of D would have felt the need to have concealed the location of the most famous of all Essene habitations through the use of coded language. One cannot conceal what is common knowledge.

Likewise, the theory that "the land of Damascus" refers to Babylon also falls prey to this criticism. If, as Murphy O'Connor argued, the sect had its origins in sixth century BCE Babylon, it would have been futile to have attempted to "protect" such knowledge by hiding the fact under a cryptonym. On the contrary, if the sect had in fact been able to claim such origins, this would have supported their claim to have been the "remnant" of Israel. Scriptural traditions indicated that a remnant in exile in Babylon would return triumphantly to Jerusalem (cf. Jer 23:3; 31:7–8). Had the sect

---

[30] See the article of T. S. Beall, "Pliny the Elder," *EDSS* 2:677–679. Pliny's mention of an Essene settlement occurs in *Nat. Hist.* 5.17, and is cited in Alfred Adam, *Antike Berichte über die Essener* (KIT 182; Berlin: Verlag Walter de Gruyter & Co., 1961) 38.

[31] The testimony of Dio of Prusa is cited in Synesius of Cyrene's biography of Dio (*Dio* 3.2). The text is cited in G. Vermes and M. D. Goodman, *The Essenes According to the Classical Sources* (Sheffield: JSOT Press, 1989) 58–59.

in fact been able to trace its origins to Babylon, this fact would have been emphasized, not hidden. Murphy O'Connor's thesis of Babylonian origins fails to provide a plausible reason for the use of "coded language" in referring to Babylon under a cryptonym. Murphy O'Connor's theory in fact involves a fatal contradiction: the very Babylonian origins which would have legitimated so well the "remnant theology" that was central to the sect's identity, rather than being duly emphasized, were in fact submerged, hidden under a cryptonym. Even the most casual reader of the first sections of D would be forced to credit the author of D with more rhetorical finesse than to have committed so gross an ideological blunder.

Murphy O'Connor appeals to CD 7:14–15 to support his argument that "Damascus" refers to Babylon. These verses paraphrase Amos 5:26–27, but with an important modification. The text in Amos condemns Israel for sacrificing to סכות and כיון and (probably vocalized Sakkuth[32] and Kaiwān[33]), followed by a pronouncement of Yahweh's judgment on Israel for failing to abide by its covenantal obligations. The clause in which the divine judgment is pronounced reads, והגליתי אתכם מהלאה לדמשק, "therefore I will send you into exile beyond Damascus." D however, paraphrases the whole sentence, so that it becomes והגליתי את סכות מלככם ואת כיון צלמיכם מאהלי דמשק, "therefore I will send into exile the booths (*sukkoth*) of your king and Kiyyun of your images from my tent to Damascus."[34] The text as it stands in CD represents a significant modification and reinterpretation of the text as it appears in MT and LXX.[35]

Accounting for the differences between the MT of Amos 5:26–27 and D's paraphrase of those verses could probably constitute a study of its own. Luckily, for our purposes the significant variant between the two texts can be reduced to the single change from Amos' והגליתי אתכם מהלאה לדמשק, "I will send you into exile beyond Damascus" to D's read-

---

[32] M. Stol, *DDD*, 722-723.

[33] M. Stol, *DDD*, 478.

[34] The translation of the phrase, מאהלי דמשק, is problematic. It may be rendered either, "from the tents of Damascus" or "from my tent to Damascus." Tigchelaar and García-Martínez (*DSSSE* 1:561), Baumgarten (*PTSDSSP* 1:27), and Vermes (*The Complete Dead Sea Scrolls in English*, 133) choose the latter alternative. Wise, Abegg, and Cook translate "beyond the tents of Damascus" (*The Dead Sea Scrolls: A New Translation*, 57). The absence of the *lamedh* before "Damascus" in D's paraphrase of Amos might lead one to conclude that אהלי דמשק was a construct phrase, and to adopt a translation similar to Wise, Abegg, and Cook's. However, as CD 7:18–19 (הוא דורש והתורה הבא הבא דמשק) shows, the syntax of the Amos midrash is such that motion towards a place is indicated by means of the unmarked accusative (on this category, see Joüon-Muroaka, §125n), which favors the translation, "from my tent to Damascus."

[35] LXX appears to translated substantially the same Heb. *Vorlage* as that preserved in MT, with the exception that כיון was read Ραιφαν (ריפן), מלכבם was read Μολοχ, and צלמיכם was translated, τοὺς τύπους αὐτῶν (= צלמיהם).

ing, מאהלי דמשׂק ...וְהִגְלֵיתִי, "I will send into exile ... from my tent to Damascus." It is on the basis of this change that much of the weight of Murphy-O'Connor's argument rests. Since D substitutes Amos' reference to Babylon (i.e., the region "beyond Damascus") with a reference simply to "Damascus," therefore "Damascus" must be equivalent to Babylon. Although this simple logic has appealed to many scholars, it suffers from a fatal flaw.

Leaving aside the obvious objection that the change from Amos' מהלאה לדמשׂק to D's מאהלי דמשׂק can be accounted for on the basis of scribal error (מאהלי for מהלאה due to metathesis, although this leaves the *yod* unaccounted for), and so may not represent a motivated substitution, a more serious objection may be raised. Murphy-O'Connor's position in-volves an inherent contradiction. On the one hand, Murphy-O'Connor argues that D is interested in presenting the sectarian Association as trac-ing its origins to Babylon at the time of the exile there. On the other hand, we are asked to believe, D alters its clear proof-text for this Babylonian origin, Amos 5:27, by removing the clear reference to Babylon (מהלאה לדמשׂק) and replacing it with a hidden code, whereby Babylon is referred to, not by a clear reference, but by the name of a city that at the time when D was composed had no obvious connection to Babylon.

According to Murphy O'Connor, Acts 7:43, which cites Amos 5:27, constitutes a further example in which Damascus is equivalent to Baby-lon.[36] In the Acts text, Amos 5:25–27 is quoted in a speech delivered by Stephen in which the history of Israel is briefly surveyed. The phrase which in LXX reads, καὶ μετοικιῶ ὑμᾶς ἐπέκεινα Δαμασκοῦ, "and I will send you into exile beyond Damascus" in Stephen's speech is cited as, καὶ μετοικιῶ ὑμᾶς ἐπέκεινα Βαβυλῶνος, "and I will send you into exile beyond Babylon." From this change Murphy-O'Connor infers a simple equivalence, Damascus=Babylon. However, we should draw from this evidence the opposite conclusion. If the simple equivalence Damas-cus=Babylon had been a commonplace in the Roman period, then the author of Acts would not have needed to substitute the somewhat vague "beyond Damascus" with the more specific "Babylon," as the reference to Damascus would have in itself been enough to connote Babylon in the mind of the reader/hearer. It was only because LXX's "exile beyond Da-mascus" would not have been heard as a straightforward reference to Babylon that the biblically-literate author of Acts decided to substitute Babylon for Damascus. The author of Acts clarified a passage that may

---

[36] *RB* 81 (1974) 221, n. 39. See also Murphy O'Connor's article, "Damascus," *EDSS* 1:165–166, although there the reference to Acts 7:43 is miscited as Acts 7:23. Murphy-O'Connor's argument is cited with approval in P. R. Davies, "The Birthplace of the Essenes: Where is 'Damascus'?" *RQ* 56 (1990) 511-513.

have been a source of confusion for the work's audience. Rather than supporting the notion that in antiquity, one could assume a well-known equivalence between Babylon and Damascus, Acts 7:42 argues against it.

On Murphy-O'Connor's reading of CD 7, the text subverts its own narrative interest (i.e., to present the Essene sect as having arisen in Babylon during the exile) by effectively destroying the very proof text that would have supported D's claims. To say the least, this seems to be a strange way for D to have supported its claim that the sect had its origins in Babylon. Murphy-O'Connor's argument is self-contradictory. Rather than altering the text of Amos 5:27 in order to assert Babylonian origins, as Murphy-O'Connor has argued, D altered its biblical proof text in order to make it prove exactly what the "literal sense" of the altered text of Amos stated: the Teacher and his first followers resided in Damascus in Syria.

4. An Account of Essene Origins in the "Land of Damascus"

The proper context within which to locate the references to the beginnings of the Essene sect is not sixth century BCE Babylon, but the politically volatile eastern Mediterranean region during the mid-second century BCE. As we shall see, the "exile" to which the Righteous Teacher was relegated did not correspond to the Babylonian exile, but was rather a matter of political survival at a period when the Teacher had powerful and perhaps homicidal enemies. The Teacher's exile was an attempt to escape political enemies in Jerusalem.

In order to understand D's references to the beginnings of the Essene sect in Damascus, we will do well to recall some of the salient aspects of the political situation in Judea during the first half of the second century BCE. The high priesthood of the old Zadokite Oniad house had come to an end when the Tobiad Menelaus offered the Seleucid king, Antiochus IV Epiphanes, a large sum for the right to serve as high priest in place of the Oniad Jason (2 Macc 4:23–50). Onias III, whom many must have considered to have been the last "legitimate" Oniad to have held the office of high priest, was murdered by an agent of Menelaus in 170 BCE. Onias III had fled north to Daphne, which was about 5 miles northwest of Antioch, the capital of the Seleucid empire. Onias sought refuge there in a place of sanctuary (ἄσυλον; 2 Macc 4:33) that was sacred to Apollo and Artemis. Onias was enticed to leave his place of sanctuary on the pretence that he would not be harmed, but upon leaving his place of refuge, he was quickly dispatched. Onias IV, the son of Onias III, fled to Egypt. He would later establish a Jewish temple at the site of an abandoned pagan temple in Heliopolis (*Ant* 13.62-73).

These stories of the effective end of the high priesthood of the Oniad line demonstrate two points: 1) once deposed, the Oniads were still viewed as a threat by rival factions in Jerusalem and so were forced into exile to escape the danger posed by these rival factions; and 2) the deposition of the Oniads raised the issue of the legitimacy of subsequent high priests at the Jerusalem temple, as witnessed by the formation of a substitute temple in Heliopolis. Yet as we will see, the Oniads were not the only figures who were forced into political exile during the second century BCE.

From the middle of the second century BCE until the destruction of the second temple, the factions of the Pharisees and the Sadducees engaged in bitter rivalry, apparently even to the point of forcing members of the opposing party into exile.[37] John Hyrcanus I had supported the Pharisees during part of his reign, implementing their halakhic rulings among the populace. However, at some point during his reign, he broke with the Pharisees and began to support instead the Sadducees (cf. *Ant* 13.293–298). This situation persisted until 76 BCE, when Salome Alexandra reversed Hyrcanus' decision. At that time the Pharisees again fell under the good graces of the Hasmoneans. According to *Ant* 13.409 the Pharisees, after regaining a position of political power, "even recalled exiles and freed prisoners" (καὶ γὰρ φυγάδας οὗτοι κατῆγον καὶ δεσμώτας ἔλυον). Many of these exiles (φυγάδας) undoubtedly had been associated with the attempted coup against Alexander Jannaeus in 88 BCE. When this attempt failed, Jannaeus retaliated against the instigators with brutal force. After 800 of those responsible for the uprising had been captured and executed, others fled into the safety of exile. According to Josephus (*BJ* 1.98),

τοσαύτη δὲ κατάπληξις ἔσχεν τὸν δῆμον, ὥστε τῶν ἀντιστασιαστῶν κατὰ τὴν ἐπιοῦσαν νύκτα φυγεῖν ὀκτακισχιλίους ἔξω Ἰουδαίας ὅλης, οἷς ὅρος τῆς φυγῆς ὁ Ἀλεξάνδρου θάνατος κατέστη.

Such great consternation took hold of the people that 8,000 of the insurrectionists fled out of the whole region of Judea during the following night, for whom the death of Alexander (Jannaeus) established the terminus of their exile (φυγή).

---

[37] Josephus, *Ant* 13.16.2, §409 states that, upon coming to power under Salome Alexandra, the Pharisees "recalled exiles, set prisoners free ... and differed in no way from despots." We may infer from this passage that some Pharisaic leaders had been exiled or imprisoned during the reign of Jannaeus. Jannaeus' crucifixion of his political enemies, some of whom were probably Pharisees, is well known. This event is alluded to in Pesher Nahum, frags. 3–4, col. 1:6–11. For an overview, see J. Charlesworth, *The Pesharim and Qumran History: Chaos or Consensus?* (Grand Rapids, MI and Cambridge, UK: Eerdmans, 2002) 99–106.

But the Pharisees did not stop at recalling exiled compatriots. They also initiated a brutal series of retaliatory strikes against those who had sided with Jannaeus against the Pharisees and their supporters in the coup attempt of 88 BCE. In light of Josephus' description of these supporters of Alexander as "the preeminent" (οἱ προὔχειν δοκοῦντες; *BJ* 1.114) or "the powerful" (οἱ δυνατοί; *Ant* 13.411), at least some of them must have been Sadducees, with whom the Judean nobility were closely allied. After many of these powerful citizens had already been assassinated, Salome granted them control of several of the fortresses that were then under Jewish control (*Ant* 13.410-418), to which they quickly withdrew.

Since they were implicated within a political context that inevitably involved taking sides for or against the Hasmoneans, the struggles between the Jewish sects of the Maccabean period could occasionally lead to political assassinations, imprisonments, or flight into exile by the members of the party which, as fortune might have it, had lost their position of power within the Judean political system.

We do not know the reason why, but the founder of the Essene movement appears to have been forced into exile. According to Pesher Habakkuk 11:6, the Teacher was confronted by the "Wicked Priest" (probably one of the Hasmoneans), in "his place of exile" (בית גלותו). The third person singular possessive suffix indicates that this is a personal exile and not the national exile of the Babylonian period. As we have seen, flight into exile was the most common and effective way of escaping one's political enemies. Even this remedy however, had limits to its effectiveness, as the case of Onias III clearly illustrates.

The precipitating factor that led to the Teacher's exile is impossible to discern. However, we may make some hypotheses about the general issues that were involved. Pesher Habakkuk 11:4-8, commenting on Hab 2:15, states:

Its interpretation concerns the Wicked Priest, who pursued the Righteous Teacher to his place of exile, to consume him in his angry wrath. And at the time of the festival, the rest of the Day of Atonement, he appeared to them to consume them and to cause them to stumble on the day of the fast, their Sabbath of rest.

The hyperbolic language used in this text does not provide many of the details that we would like to have known about this episode. However, we may draw attention to several important details. Firstly, the Wicked Priest, whom we take here to have been one of the Hasmoneans, "pursued the Teacher to his place of exile." Since the Hasmoneans resided in Jerusalem, clearly the Teacher at that point resided outside of Jerusalem. Where then was the location of the Teacher's "place of exile"? Pesher Habakkuk does not tell us. However, as CD 19:33–20:1 associates the activity of the

Teacher with Damascus, it seems likely that Damascus was the "place of exile" referred to in Pesher Habakkuk.

As Shemaryahu Talmon pointed out at a very early stage in the study of the Dead Sea scrolls, the Teacher and his group are depicted as celebrating the Day of Atonement according to the sectarian solar calendar.[38] The Association's calendar did not correspond with the lunar calendar that was in use at the temple regarding festal days. It is only this calendrical discrepancy that can account for Jonathan's presence at the Teacher's "place of exile" on the Day of Atonement – a day on which travel was forbidden. In addition, since the Hasmoneans assumed the high priesthood, any Hasmonean "Wicked Priest"[39] would have been required in the temple to officiate in the Day of Atonement ceremony there. The Teacher and his group then, were engaged in a sectarian observance of the festival. It does not appear that the Wicked Priest's visit represented an assassination attempt against the Teacher, but rather an attempt to disrupt the festal proceedings and perhaps to intimidate the group to abandon their practices, which according to the standard of the Jerusalem temple were deviant.

The inference that the intention of the Wicked Priest's visit to the Teacher was to persuade or threaten him and his group into abandoning their practices is supported by the verb used in the Habakkuk pesher regarding the reason for this visit. According to the pesher, the Wicked Priest appeared in order to "cause them to stumble" (לכשילם). This verb is one that would appropriately be used when a matter of orthopraxy was in question (cf. CD 2:17; 1QS 11:12; 1QH^a 4:23; 4Q184 1:14). As an aside, we may note that 4QPsalms Pesher^a (4Q171), col. 2:14–20 presents a more ominous picture; it appears to describe to an attempt on the life of the Righteous Teacher, who is referred to simply as "the Priest." The comments in col. 4, lines 7–10a seem to indicate that the attempt to kill the Teacher involved having him indicted on capital charges.

Whereas the Habakkuk pesher merely taunted us with its reference to the "place" of the teacher's exile, D is very specific in the matter. According to D, the teacher and his earliest followers resided in Damascus.

Before we turn to a brief examination of each of the passages in D which mention Damascus, let us review the conclusions that we have reached up to this point. Regarding the referent of the term "Damascus" three main positions have been advocated during the period since the discovery of the Cairo Genizah version of CD. Scholars have argued that

---

[38] "Yom Hakippurim in the Habakkuk Scroll," reprinted in Talmon, *The World of Qumran from Within: Collected Studies* (Jerusalem: Magnes and Leiden: Brill, 1989) 186–199.

[39] It is generally assumed that that epithet, "Wicked Priest" (הכוהן הרשע) puns on the title, "High Priest" (הכוהן הראש), assumed by the Hasmoneans.

Damascus refers to 1) a city in Syria, 2) Qumran, and 3) Babylon. We have seen that option #2, at least in the form in which it was propounded by Cross, is untenable due to chronological difficulties. If the Righteous Teacher's floruit is placed in the mid-second century BCE, then most or all of his life had been spent in locations other than Qumran, which was inhabited by members of the Essene sect ca. 100 BCE. Since D associates the activity of the Teacher with Damascus, Damascus cannot be a coded name for Qumran. Option #3 is untenable because it involves the self-contradictory assertion that the author of D, although he wished to present the Essene sect as having originated in Babylon, removed the clear reference to Babylon in Amos 5:27, a proof text that supported the very claim that the author wished to make. The most likely solution is that "Damascus" refers to the well-known city in Syria.

5. Ancient Damascus, Cradle of the Association

Ancient Damascus, situated on a fertile basin between the Anti-Lebanon Mountains and the Syrian desert and watered by the Barada River, was a major trading center. LaMoine DeVries describes it in this way:

> With the development of trade routes Damascus became a major caravan center and perhaps the most vital link in the whole trade route system. It was at Damascus that the major trade routes of the ancient Near East converged. Damascus entertained caravans and merchants from Egypt and Arabia to the south, Anatolia and Syria to the north, and Mesopotamia to the east.[40]

During the second century BCE Damascus was controlled by the Seleucids. When Syria was divided by civil war between the brothers Antiochus VIII Grypus and Antiochus IX Cyzicenus in 111 BCE, the latter may have established his capital in Damascus.[41] Excluding D, the earliest evidence for a Jewish community in Damascus comes from the New Testament (Acts 9:2; 2 Cor 11:32). According to Josephus 10,500 (*BJ* 2.561) or alternately 18,000 (*BJ* 7.368) Jews were killed in the city at the outbreak of the Jewish rebellion of 66–70 BCE.

Just how early a Jewish community was established in Damascus is difficult to say. *Megillat Ta'anit* 12 mentions an uprising against the "scholars" in Chalcis,[42] which according to the scholiast occurred during

---

[40] *Cities of the Biblical World* (Peabody, MA: Hendrickson, 1997) 60.

[41] Schürer-Vermes, *The History of the Jewish People in the Age of Jesus Christ (175 B.C. –A.D. 135)*, 4 vols. (Edinburgh: T&T Clark, 1973) 2:128.

[42] בשובעת עשׂר ביה קמו עממיא על פלטת ספריא במדינת בלקים בבית זבדי ופרק, והוה פרקן, "On the seventeenth of it (i.e., of the month of Adar) the Gentiles rose against the remnant of the scholars in the city of Chalcis in Beth-Zavdai, but there was

the reign of Alexander Jannaeus.[43]   Chalcis was about 25 miles northwest of Damascus. This mention of a Jewish presence in Syria during the Hasmonean period, in what was a much less important city than Damascus, allows one to infer that there may have been a Jewish presence in Damascus already at the beginning of the first century BCE. This view may receive support from D, as we will see.

According to the Habakkuk pesher, the Teacher celebrated a sectarian version of the Yom Hakkippur service in "the place of his exile." CD 19:33b–20:1a associates the activity of the Teacher with Damascus. Why would the Teacher have been in exile in Damascus? We have seen that political exile among Jews was a common phenomenon throughout the politically turbulent second century BCE. Beginning with the exile of Onias III and his murder at Daphne, five miles from Antioch, down to the time of John Hyrcanus and onward into the reigns of Salome Alexandra and Aristobulus II, struggles for power within the Judean political system often left those who had been ousted from power in danger of being assassinated by those who had recently acquired power. Whereas Onias III had fled deep into Seleucid territory in an effort to escape his enemies, his son Onias IV chose to flee to Egypt. Although there was no single "preferred location" to which political exiles could flee, the common element that binds each of these examples is that the parties who had recently been ousted from power fled Judea in an effort to escape being killed by their political enemies.

The information that we possess about the Righteous Teacher conforms to this general pattern. According to the Habakkuk pesher, the Teacher resided in exile, although the location of that exile is not stated. The Damascus Document associates the activity of the Teacher with Damascus (19:33b–21:1a; 6:3–11). The obvious conclusion to be drawn is that the Teacher had fled to Damascus to escape some perceived political threat. That political threat is likely to have been constituted by one of the Hasmoneans, each of whom the Essenes opposed. However, it does not seem that the Teacher's fears of assassination were wholly founded: when the Wicked Priest had his chance to kill the Teacher, he did not take it. The Wicked Priest, although concerned by the heteropraxy of the Teacher and his group, seems to have considered the Essenes neither a serious threat to

---

deliverance." The text and a translation are given in J. A. Fitzmyer and D. J. Harrington, *A Manual of Palestinian Aramaic Texts* (Rome: Biblical Pontifical Institute; 2nd reprint, 1994) 185-187. My translation is based on Fitzmyer and Harrington's.

[43]H. Lichtenstein, "Die Fastenrolle, eine Untersuchung zur jüdisch-hellenistischen Geschichte," *HUCA* 8–9 (1931–32) 257–351. The seventeenth of Adar is discussed on p. 293.

his own power, nor to the hegemony of the Jerusalem temple in matters of religious practice.

This sketch is both confirmed and filled out by the various references to Damascus in the Damascus Document, to which we now turn. The term Damascus occurs in CD first in 6:5. This line occurs in the "well midrash," a comment on Num 21:18, "the princes dug a well, the nobles of the people dug it with a staff" (במחוקק). CD 6:4–5 interprets the line as follows: "the 'well' is the Torah and those who dug it are those of Israel who have repented, who came out of the land of Judah and dwelt in the land of Damascus." This line presents a clear reference to an emigration from Judah to Damascus. This line has typically been a stumbling block for the theory that "Damascus" referred to Qumran, since here Damascus clearly lies outside of Judah.

The phrase שבי ישראל, which I have translated, "those of Israel who have repented" is susceptible of several interpretations. It could be pointed שֶׁבִי and translated "captivity," as advocated by Rabinowitz, or it could be taken as a *qal* active participle, masculine plural construct form derived from the root שׁוּב, "to turn, return" or in a religious or ethical sense, "to repent." Depending on which of these two senses of the root שׁוּב is imputed to the verb here, it might be translated either "the returnees of Israel" with Murphy-O'Connor[44] or, as it is more commonly translated, "the penitents of Israel."

In order to rule out Murphy-O'Connor's reading however, we may simply note that the direction of movement that is depicted here is that of departure from Judah, not return to it. The verbal noun היוצאים, literally, "those who have come out" (of Judah) and the subsequent act of "sojourning" or "dwelling" (ויגורו) in the land of Damascus clearly indicate that the subjects of these verbs are thought of as residing in Damascus – and not in Judah, as the translation of שבי as "returnees" would imply. It is not a "return" of exiles that is envisioned in CD 6:4–5, but rather the opposite. It is the act of going into exile that is envisioned, an exile in the land of Damascus.

Previous commentators such as Knibb have been right to point out that the term שׁוּב is used here in the sense of "turning" from sin in CD 6:5. However, these commentators have overlooked the fact that the use of this seemingly innocent term masks a highly charged religio-political context in which the very act of "turning" or "repenting" implicates the penitent within a series of legal judgments which constituted contested territory during the Hasmonean period, as we shall see.

The act of "turning" from sin for the members of the Association constituted not merely an ethical category, but involved turning away from the

---

[44] "An Essene Missionary Document: CD II,14–VI,1," *RB* 77 (1970) 211–215.

temple and the legal precepts that were advocated by those in charge of it. The Associates held that all Israel had been led astray by Belial into accepting false interpretations of the Torah. The result of this misrepresentation of the Torah, according to the ideology of D, was that acts which God found abhorrent had come to be viewed as acts of righteousness (cf. CD 4:12–21 esp. ll. 16–17). All who were ensnared by the "three nets of Belial" had unwittingly constituted themselves as enemies of God, and those who associated with them would merit God's wrath (CD 5:14–16).

In an age in which the interpretation of the Torah had become a highly contentious endeavor, with competing groups whose identity was in part constructed on the basis of particular legal positions, the term שוב became charged with a political as well as a more specifically "religious" significance. During the Hasmonean period, the sects of the Pharisees, Sadducees, and the Association each vied to influence the masses to submit to the particular set of halakhic rulings in accordance with which each sect constructed its own particular identity. In this context the act of תשובה, "repentance" (from the root שוב) was a matter that carried a great political, as well as "religious" significance.

Repentance involved "turning" from one set of practices in order to embrace another. Inasmuch as several of these practices constituted points on which the various sects disagreed among themselves, and which these sects used as a means of distinguishing themselves from other sects which they construed as rivals, "repentance" involved committing oneself to the practical as well as ideological positions of one of the sects.[45] The use of the term שוב in CD 6:5 refers to those who had turned away from a set of cultic and halakhic practices that were advocated by the temple establishment, but which were construed by the Associates as transgressive. According to the ideology of the Association, repentance involved renouncing the halakhot of other groups, particularly those of the Pharisees, and committing oneself to the halakhic practices of the Association, such as are detailed in CD 9–16, MMT, and the Temple Scroll.

The act of repentance which is referred to in the phrase שבי ישראל, "the penitents of Israel," used not only in CD 6:5 but also in 4:2–3, involves a "turning" away from those practices which, according to the halakhic precepts of the Association, were deemed transgressive. As we have seen,

---

[45] This generalization holds true into the Roman period, during which the "repentance" that was associated with John the Baptist involved participation in John's ritual of ablution in the Jordan River (Mt 3:1–6), and perhaps entailed some continuing sense of loyalty to John (cf. R. Brown, *The Gospel According to John I–XII* [AB 29; New York: Doubleday, 1966] 46–50), whereas the repentance that was associated with the early Jesus movement involved "believing the gospel" (i.e., that the eschaton was imminent and that Jesus would play a role in the last judgment; cf. Mk 1:15).

this involves a concomitant "turning away" not only from such groups as the Pharisees, but from the temple and its personnel as well. The path that these groups had chosen to follow, as far as the Associates were concerned, was a path of transgression against the Torah and open rebellion against God's covenant.

That which was implicit in the use of the verb שׁוב in CD 6:5 is made explicit in CD 8:16 and its parallel in 19:29: "the penitents of Israel departed from the way of the people" (שׁבי ישׂראל סרו מדרך העם). "The way of the people" was held to have been a transgressive way of life, not only because "the people" had been led astray by a "guilty inclination" (יצר אשׁמה; 2:16), but also because they had chosen to follow interpretations of the Torah whereby transgressive acts were deemed to have been righteous ones (4:16–17). The problem with "the people," as far as D was concerned, was that they did not adhere to the Association's halakhot.

The passage in CD 6:11–20a yields some important information about the early history of the Essene sect. Lines 18–19 concern "keep(ing) the day of the Sabbath in accordance with its exact interpretation, and (keeping) the festivals and the day of fasting in accordance with the findings of those who entered the new covenant in the land of Damascus." These two lines illuminate the Habakkuk pesher's brief narrative concerning the "Wicked Priest's" visit to the Teacher in "his place of exile," Damascus. CD 6:18–19 corroborates the inference that Talmon made on the basis of the Habakkuk pesher: that the Teacher and his group followed a different calendar than did the temple. D refers to the Essene calendrical system as corresponding to "the findings of those who entered the new covenant in the land of Damascus." These "findings" were the product of the exegetical labors of the Teacher and his followers. These labors, however, centered not only on the works that now form the Hebrew scriptures, but also on such works as 1 Enoch and Jubilees. Fragments of both of these works have been found in the Qumran caves. Both of these works were held in high regard by members of the sect, and both works advocate the use of a solar calendar, such as the Essenes did actually adopt.

There is scant evidence that a solar calendar was ever actually employed to order the festal year in the Jerusalem temple. Ben Sira 43:6–7 and 50:6 would seem to indicate that immediately prior to the turmoil that precipitated in the Maccabean revolt, the temple followed a lunar calendar, such as is known to have been followed during the Roman period. The Teacher and his followers, however, had access to texts in which the solar calendar was presented as the one that was used to order all creation (1 Enoch 72–82), and according to which God and the angels conducted their own heavenly festal cycle (cf. Jub 6:32–38).[46] According to the book of Jubilees, the solar calendar had been used by the patriarchs, but had only been abandoned in the Hellenistic period. While this was probably a case of revisionist history, the Teacher and his followers appear to have given credence to Jubilees' account. The rejection of the temple's lunar calendar in favor of the solar calendar, in the view of the Associates, represented a departure from the calendrical reckonings of a corrupt temple regime, and represented a return to the purity of an ancient scheme that had wrongfully been abandoned. If Talmon[47] is correct in asserting that the calendrical systems described in 1 Enoch and Jubilees were theoretical constructs which had never actually been implemented, then it would seem that the Essenes had become unwitting innovators in the matter of calendrical practice, even as they held their calendrical system to have been grounded in the very order of creation.

But in addition to the important information that it provides about the Essene calendar, CD 6:19 also contains a phrase that is especially relevant to our study: "those who entered the new covenant in the land of Damascus" (באי הברית החדשה בארץ דמשק). The term "new covenant" is used only three times in D, each time only in connection with the geographical tag "in the land of Damascus" (CD 6:19; 8:21; 20:12). Whereas the term ברית referred to the "covenant" that was constituted by the sect's halakhic rulings, the term "new covenant" had much more specific connotations. The term "covenant" and the phrase "new covenant" are not interchangeable in D. The "new covenant" is something that was established (or "entered into," using a form of the verb בוא) in Damascus.

It is striking that D does not use the phrase "new covenant" to refer to the set of halakhic precepts that it espouses per se, but reserves the term to refer to a covenant that was ratified in the past, in Damascus. As CD 20:13–15 indicates, the temporal perspective of the author of that section is one according to which the Teacher was no longer living. If the hortatory sections of D were written during the reign of Alexander Jannaeus, then the Teacher had probably died some years before the final stages of the text's composition. From the perspective of the author(s) of D's hortatory sections, the "new covenant" was something that was ratified in the past, during the Teacher's lifetime, in the land of Damascus.

The temporal perspective of the author(s) of the exhortations is expressed nicely in CD 7:11–21: the exhortations were composed between the time of the "star" and the time of the "staff." Likening the exile of the Teacher to the time when "the two houses of Israel separated" (i.e., during

---

[46] The idea that Israel should celebrate the Sabbath on the same day on which the angels in heaven celebrated the Sabbath is found in Jub 2:17-22.

[47] Art. "Calendars and Mishmarot," *EDSS* 1:114.

the time of the divided monarchy that began with Jeroboam I in the tenth century BCE),[48] the text states that the "backsliders were handed over to the sword," while "those who held firmly (to the covenant) escaped to the land of the north." This "escape" refers to the Teacher's flight from Judea during the second century BCE. Here once again D dovetails nicely with the account in the Habakkuk pesher, which mentions the Teacher's "exile" (גלות). While D does not use the same term as the Habakkuk pesher, in light of the other examples that we have seen from the same period and due to the narrative of the Wicked Priest's "pursuit" of the Teacher to the "place of his exile" in the Habakkuk pesher, we may surmise that the Teacher's was a political exile. The "escape to the land of the north" refers to the Teacher's flight to Damascus, which is north of Jerusalem. One of the terms that Josephus uses to refer to political exile, φυγή, which may be translated either "flight" or "exile," nicely captures the connection between exile and escape from one's enemies.[49]

We may also mention once again D's use of Amos 5:27. As we have already mentioned, whereas the text in Amos places Israel's exile, מהלאה לדמשק, "beyond Damascus," (i.e., in Babylon) D alters the text so as to depict an exile, מאהלי דמשק, "from my tent to Damascus."[50] In order to appreciate the subtle polemic that is developed in this passage, we return to the text of CD 7:14b-21a:

כאשר אמר והגליתי את סכות מלככם

ואת כיון צלמיכם מאהלי דמשק   ספרי התורה הם סוכת

המלך כאשר אמר והקימותי את סוכת דוד הנפלת   המלך

הוא הקהל וכיניי הצלמים וכיום הצלמים הם ספרי הנביאים

אשר בזה ישראל את דבריהם   והכוכב הוא דורש התורה

הבא דמשק כאשר כתוב דרך כוכב מיעקב וקם שבט

מישראל השבט הוא נשיא כל העדה ובעמדו וקרקר

את כל בני שת

As he said, "And I will send into exile Sakkuth (סכות) your king and Kaiwan of your images from my tent to Damascus" (Amos 5:27). The books of the Torah are "the booth

---

[48] For an outline of the history of this period, see Miller and Hayes, *A History of Ancient Israel and Judah*, 218–249.

[49] We may distinguish between at least three types of exile: 1) the type such as that which was imposed on many Judeans by the Babylonians, which involves the capture and forcible removal of people from one land to another, in which they are forced to remain; 2) the type which results from banishment; and 3) the type which involves fleeing from a powerful enemy. The Teacher's exile was of the third type.

[50] The noun דמשק here and in line 19 represents an unmarked accusative of direction or motion towards a place (cf. Joüon-Muraoka, *A Grammar of Biblical Hebrew*, 449, §125, for some biblical examples). In view of the location of the action in l. 19 in Damascus, the translation of מאהלי דמשק as "from the tents of Damascus" (which would imply an exile from, rather than to Damascus) seems inappropriate.

of (סוכה) the king," as he said, "I will set up the fallen booth (סוכה) of David" (Amos 9:11). "The king" is the assembly and "the kiyyun of the images"[51] are the books of the prophets, the words of which Israel despised. And "the star" is the interpreter of the Torah who has come (or, "is coming") to Damascus. As it is written, "A star stepped forth from Jacob, and a scepter[52] will arise (or, "arose") from Israel" (Num 24:17). "The scepter" is the prince of the whole congregation, and when he arises, he will tear down all the sons of Seth.

This passage has received intense scrutiny regarding the identity of the figure referred to as the "interpreter of the Torah." We will return to examine this problem momentarily. First, however, let us draw attention to a couple of aspects of this text that have received less attention. CD 19:33–20:1 associates the activity of the Teacher with Damascus, while 7:17 informs us that there was also an "assembly" (קהל) that was associated with Damascus. The Teacher was not alone in Damascus, but was associated with a group of Jews who either had fled with him or who constituted an established community there. Such a community is presupposed by the Habakkuk pesher's notice that the Teacher was holding services on the Day of Atonement (according to a solar calendar). As Damascus was a major trading center in antiquity, it seems likely that there would have been a Jewish community, comprised in part of merchants, resident in the city during the second century BCE. When the Teacher fled into exile, he may have turned to this Jewish community for support.

We should also notice the *objects* that are said to have accompanied the assembly into exile. These include the "books of the Torah" and the "books of the prophets." Here we have a reference to an important distinction between the Associates and Jews who were not members of the sectarian Association. Jews who did not belong to the Association, referred to here as "Israel," are said to have "despised" the books of the prophets. This statement is of course not historically accurate. "Israel" preserved the words of the prophets and revered the prophetic books as holy writings. CD's polemical statement is illuminated once again by the Habakkuk pesher, 2:5–10:

Likewise: *Blank* The interpretation of the word [concerns the trai]tors in the last days. They are violator[s of the coven]ant who do not believe when they hear all that is going [to happen t]o the final generation, from the mouth of the priest whom God has placed wi[thin the Commun]ity to foretell the fulfillment of all the words of his servants, the

---

[51] This phase is written twice in CD-A, the first time incorrectly. No attempt was made to erase or otherwise indicate the mistake.

[52] Unfortunately Baumgarten's edition in *PTSDSSP* 2 mistakenly reads בנכט at this point. The photograph of CD-A published in M. Broshi's, *The Damascus Document Reconsidered* (Jerusalem: Israel Exploration Society, 1992) 22, clearly reads שבט, and this reading is also reflected in Baumgarten's translation.

prophets, [by] means of whom God has declared all that is going to happen to his people Is[rael].[53]

It was not the prophets that "Israel" despised, but the Teacher's interpretation of them. According to the Habakkuk pesher, the Teacher applied a hermeneutical technique whereby the course of future events was to be uncovered through the interpretation of the prophetic books. The lasting influence of the Teacher's hermeneutical methods is seen not only in the pesharim, but also in the hortatory sections of D. Both the pesharim and D employ primarily the prophets as proof-texts in their eschatological predictions.

6. Interpreter of the Law

As promised, we now return to the matter of identifying the דורש התורה, or "interpreter of the law" in CD 7:14–21. We need not discuss here the theories that various scholars have put forth positing a dying and rising Teacher of Righteousness.[54] However, there is a legitimate question as to whether the "interpreter of the law" referred to in CD 7 is a figure of the past (i.e., the Teacher) or whether he corresponds with a messianic priest who is to arrive at the end of the age. The figure referred to in lines 19b–21 is clearly a figure that is expected to come in the future. He is the "prince of the congregation" who is otherwise identified as the "messiah of Israel" (CD 19:10–11; cf. 1QSb 5:20; 1QM 5:1) and who is associated with the destruction of the sect's enemies.

The reason that it is so difficult to determine whether the "interpreter of the law" refers to a past or a future figure lies in the fact that the two key verbs in the passage, הבא and ובעמדו ("who is coming/has come" and "and when he arises/arose," respectively), both involve Hebrew atemporal forms; the participle and infinitive construct, respectively. With regard to each of these verbal forms, the temporal reference must be supplied from the context. Usually this is a simple matter, but in CD 7:19–21, since it is unknown whether the referent is a past figure or one who is expected to come in the future, assigning a temporal value to these verbs becomes problematic.

The problem then, is one that must be decided on the basis of exegesis and not grammar. However, this does not make matters any clearer. On the one hand, the designation "interpreter of the law" is applied to the Righteous Teacher in CD 6:7. Furthermore, D associates the activity of the

---

[53] Trans. of García Martínez and Tigchelaar, *DSSSE* 1:13.

[54] For a refutation of this idea, see J. J. Collins, *The Scepter and the Star*, 102–112.

Righteous Teacher with Damascus (CD 19:33b–20:1). The reference to the "interpreter of the Torah who came/is coming to Damascus" might therefore seem like a straightforward reference to the Righteous Teacher. On the other hand however, 7:19–21 clearly refers to a future figure, the "prince of the congregation." This fact, combined with the probability that the authors of D did look forward to the coming of a priestly as well as a kingly messianic figure, as were expected in 1QS 9:11; 1QSb 2:11–14, may indicate that the dyad constituted by the "interpreter of the law" and the "prince of the congregation" refers to these two expected messiahs. The phrase משיח אהרן וישראל, "the messiah(s) of Aaron and Israel," which occurs repeatedly in D (CD 12:23–13:1; 14:19; 19:10–11; 20:1) is unfortunately equivocal on the point of whether one or two messiahs are expected.[55] I prefer to take the *nomen regens* in this construct as functioning distributively, and thus referring to two messiahs, although the singular remains a grammatical possibility.

If neither the grammar of CD 7:18–21 nor the broader discursive context of D is sufficient to demonstrate unequivocally whether the "interpreter of the law" of 7:18 refers to a past or a future figure, perhaps the verbal parallelism demonstrated in the Numbers quotation, "A star stepped forth from Jacob, and a scepter arose from Israel," may help to decide the question. Since the known entity in the quotation is, according to D's interpretation, a future messianic figure, in order to preserve the parallelism involved in the biblical quotation, the "interpreter of the law" must also refer to a future figure. If so, then D falls into the pattern of dual messianism that is (arguably) present elsewhere in D and which is demonstrably present in other sectarian texts from among the DSS (most notably, 1QS and 1QSa).

Even if CD 7:18–21 does not refer to the activity of the Righteous Teacher in Damascus, however, we may still glean some interesting information regarding the early history of the sectarian Association from this text. Firstly, we may notice that the priestly messiah is to some extent modeled on the activity of the sect's own Righteous Teacher. Both the Teacher and the expected priestly messiah are referred to as "interpreter(s) of the law." As the Teacher had instructed the community in the authoritative interpretation of the law in the past, so the priestly messiah would do in the future (cf. CD 14:27–34, in conjunction with 7:18–19).[56]

---

[55] John Collins has effectively demonstrated that dual messianism was the "norm" in the sectarian texts from among the Dead Sea scrolls. This dual messianism, he argues, was formed as a reaction against the combination of the roles of high priest and king by the Hasmoneans. Collins' argument appears in *The Scepter and the Star*, 74–101.

[56] For the teaching role of the eschatological high priest, see also 4Q541 9.1.3, and Collins, *The Scepter and the Star*, 114–115.

Before we leave this section of D, we may make one last observation. The priestly messiah is expected to arrive, not in Jerusalem nor even in Judea, but in Damascus. Here Gunkel's dictum that "Endzeit gleicht Urzeit"[57] is apropos. Although for Gunkel the dictum applied to the homology between the pre-lapsarian perfection in Eden and the bliss to be achieved in the eschatological age, in D the homology is between the time of the formation of the sect and the beginning of the eschatological period, when the messiahs of Aaron and Israel arrive. In accordance with D's homology, if the activity of the Teacher had taken place in Damascus, it is only appropriate that the activity of the eschatological high priest should take place there also.

We may recall that in CD 7:14–18, both the sectarian "assembly" (קהל) and the "books of the prophets" are said to have departed מאהלי דמשק, "from my tent to Damascus." In the context of the oracular speech quoted in this passage (the source of which is Amos 5:27), the antecedent of the first person singular possessive pronoun ("*my* tent") is Yahweh. D has transformed what was in Amos an innocuous prepositional phrase, "beyond (Damascus)," into a polemical statement asserting the departure of the divine presence from the temple (here referred to as the tent, אהל) at Jerusalem. The identification of the Jerusalem temple as a "tent" relies on Scriptural traditions in which a portable tent, in which the deity was said to have appeared, accompanied the Hebrews in their wilderness wanderings (cf. Ex 33:7–11; Num 11:16–17; Ex 26:1–37).[58] Later, the temple would replace the tent as the locale of God's habitation (cf. 1 Chron 17:1–27). The idea that God had abandoned the temple due to Israel's sin is expressed in Ezek 10:18–19; 11:22–25. By transforming Amos' prepositional phrase into a polemical statement asserting the removal of the divine presence from Jerusalem, D indirectly lodges its complaint not only against the Hasmonean high priests who served in the Jerusalem temple, but against the entire temple cultus. The Hasmoneans may have held the title of high priest, but they officiated in a temple that was bereft of God's presence. God had abandoned Jerusalem.

The consequences of D's rereading of Amos 5:27 are highly significant. By asserting that the divine presence had left Jerusalem, D effectively demoted Jerusalem as God's "holy city." According to D, until the end of the present "age of Belial," the locus of God's salvific activity was not Jerusalem, but Damascus. It is in Damascus that the author of D expected

---

[57] *Schöpfung und Chaos in Urzeit und Endzeit: Eine religionsgeschichtliche Untersuchung über Gen. 1 und Ap. Joh. 12* (Göttingen: Vandenhoeck & Ruprecht, 1921). Gunkel's dictum was borrowed from the Epistle of Barnabas 6:13, ἰδοὺ ποιῶ τὰ ἔσχατα ὡς τὰ πρῶτα.

[58] See also Cross, *Canaanite Myth and Hebrew Epic*, 298–300.

Israel's two messiahs, the scepter and the star, to arise. In light of the significant role that Damascus plays in D's version of Israel's *Heilsgeschichte*, a role that is unparalleled either in biblical or in post-biblical literature, it is possible that parts of D, including the well-midrash, were composed by a member (or members) of the sectarian assembly (קהל) that was located in Damascus.

7. Restricted Semantic Range of "New Covenant" Phrase

The last occurrence of the phrase "new covenant" that we will explore is in CD 20:11–12. These lines, as Murphy-O'Connor has argued,[59] come from a section of CD that is concerned to discourage "backsliding" (that is, the failure to follow faithfully sectarian halakhot) among members of the Association. Members of the sect are discouraged from acting like the "men of mockery," who דברו תועה על חקי הצדק ומאסו בברית ואמנה אשר קימו באֶרץ דמשֶק והוא ברית החדשה, "spoke error against the righteous statutes and they rejected the trustworthy covenant which they established in the land of Damascus, that is, the new covenant."

Several aspects of this passage are highly significant for D's construction of the "new covenant." It seems likely that, as Baumgarten notes, the phrase the "'men of mockery' refers to the rulers in Jerusalem."[60] As we have already seen, the Hasmonean "Wicked Priest" is known to have opposed the practices of the Association; consequently it is not difficult to imagine why D might have wished to label the Hasmoneans as "mockers." This point, at any rate, is less important presently than the information that 20:11–12 contains regarding D's view of the Association's "new covenant."

Line 11 refers to those who "spoke error against the righteous statutes." D's reference to "righteous statutes" of course constitutes a characterization of the Association's legal precepts. These "statutes" would have included calendrical as well as other halakhic material that was deemed to have been "found" in the Torah as well as in the prophets. We may recall here CD 6:17–7:6, in which "the findings of those who entered the new covenant in the land of Damascus" were listed as including calendrical matters as well as matters of conduct within the community. CD 20:11–13 also hints at the contention that the Teacher and his group engendered when they began to implement their halakhic "findings" in Damascus. The

---

[59] "A Literary Analysis of Damascus Document XIX,33–XX,34," *RB* 79 (1972) 544–564.

[60] Baumgarten notes that Isa 28:14 refers to the rulers of Jerusalem as "men of mockery" (*PTSDSSP* 2:35, n. 116).

"men of mockery," who are probably to be regarded as including the Hasmoneans, did not share D's evaluation of the Association's halakhot. According to the Hasmoneans, as well as the priestly apparatus of the Jerusalem temple which the Hasmoneans controlled, the Association's legal interpretations were to be characterized as "error" (תועה).

Not only did the Jerusalem establishment "speak error" against the Association's legal interpretations, but they also "rejected the trustworthy covenant" that had been established in Damascus. The phrase, "trustworthy covenant" (בברית ואמנה)[61] characterizes the Association's covenant as one that is grounded in the faithfulness of God; it is a covenant to which God will maintain fidelity. The characterization of the covenant as "trustworthy" heightens the "error" into which the sect's opponents have fallen in their efforts to oppose the Association's covenant.

The "trustworthy covenant" is subsequently defined: הוא ברית החדשה, "that is, the new covenant." Significantly, CD does not use the term "new covenant" to apply to the covenantal oath that was sworn by those who were admitted into the sect during the yearly covenant renewal ceremony. D is consistent in limiting the semantic range of the phrase, "new covenant." For D, the "new covenant" refers only to the foundational act of ratification of the covenant between God and the original group of Associates, accomplished by the Righteous Teacher in Damascus. The "new covenant" is one that was ratified in the past; for the author of D it has passed into the realm of sacred history. Even though the members of the Association recapitulated the oaths made at that foundational act of covenant ratification, accomplished by the Teacher in Damascus, the yearly "covenant renewal" is never referred to as the "new covenant." The "new covenant" occupies a moment in past history, one that was accomplished during the time of the Righteous Teacher.

Why does D reserve the phrase "new covenant" for the time of the sect's founding, refusing to apply it to the contemporary (relative to the composition of CD) covenant that was renewed yearly during the Feast of Weeks? D reserves the phrase ברית חדשה to refer to the foundational act of "covenant renewal" that was accomplished in Damascus. The use of the verb קום, here translated "established," corresponds to the use of the same verb to refer to "establishing" or "ratifying" a covenant with Yahweh that

---

[61] I take the terms בברית ואמנה as hendyadic, as is reflected in my translation. The latter term, אֲמָנָה, is used to denote reliability in adhering to an agreement, and may be glossed as "trust, faith." The term is used in Neh 10:1, apparently as a substitute for ברית (so J. Meyers, *Ezra-Nehemiah*; Anchor Bible Commentary Series; Garden City, NY: Doubleday & Co., 1965; 173, note to Neh 10:1). As J. VanderKam notes ("Covenant and Biblical Interpretation in Jubilees 6," 97), the אֲמָנָה involves swearing an oath (cf. Neh 10:29).

is found in P and Ezekiel (Gen 6:18; 9:9; Ezek 16:60).[62] The covenant had been "ratified/established" by the sect only once – by "those who had entered the new covenant in the land of Damascus." After this initial act of covenant ratification, the members of the sect entered the "covenant" – and in these instances the noun is not qualified by any adjective. D's use of "new covenant" is thus restricted to the act of "covenant renewal" that was accomplished in the past, by the group that had initially constituted the sectarian Association under the leadership of the Righteous Teacher.

In light of D's reservation of the phrase "new covenant" to refer exclusively to the foundational act of covenantal ratification that was accomplished by the earliest members of the sectarian Association, Talmon's observation that the phrase ברית חדשה should be understood to signify a "renewed covenant" are relevant.[63] Our investigation supports Talmon's contention. In addition to the reasons that Talmon adduced, based on the ideology of D, we may now observe that understanding D's ברית חדשה as a "renewed covenant" has a basis in the ritual practice of the Association: it rests on the sect's foundational act of establishing (cf. קימו) a covenant on the basis of an oath that was taken in the land of Damascus. This covenant renewed, as Talmon noted, the ancient covenant that Yahweh had established with Abraham, Isaac, and Jacob, and which was later deepened by the addition of specific stipulations at Sinai. According to D's construction of "salvation history," a third act in the drama of God's covenant with his people was accomplished in Damascus, around the middle of the second century BCE. The ancient Mosaic covenant, which had been broken in the seventh century BCE, the result of which was a protracted period of exile for the Jewish people, was at last renewed by a group which, with God's help, was able overcome the blindness that had descended upon Israel through the agency of Belial, in order to discern God's "true ways and his just statutes"; that is, the sect's own, inspired interpretation of the Torah. It was on the basis of this new legal construct, the interpretation of the Torah that was based on the "findings" of the original members of the Association in Damascus, that God was able once again to renew the covenant between himself and his people.

---

[62] This usage of קום came to replace the archaic term כרת that had been used by J and E (cf. *BDB*, s.v.).

[63] "The Community of the Renewed Covenant: Between Judaism and Christianity" in E. Ulrich and J. VanderKam, eds., *The Community of the Renewed Covenant: The Notre Dame Symposium on the Dead Sea Scrolls* (Notre Dame, IN: Notre Dame, 1994) 3–24, esp. 12–15.

8. Summary and Brief Analysis

In chapters 2 and 3, we have outlined the ways in which "covenant" and "new covenant" are construed in the Damascus Document. To summarize, these terms served to legitimate Essene claims to priestly authority, in opposition to the Hasmonean high priesthood, and to legitimate Essene claims to authority in legal interpretation, in opposition to similar claims made by representatives of the Pharisaic sect. The Essene "new covenant" signified an act of covenant renewal that the sect viewed as accomplished in Damascus during the time of the Righteous Teacher. This act of covenant renewal was made possible only by the Teacher's reception of divine inspiration in matters of legal interpretation. According to the sect's interpretation, the Teacher had been appointed by God to lead Israel – or at least those Jews who would adhere to his teachings – out of a period of "blindness," in which the true interpretation of the Torah had been obscured by Israel's stubborn refusal to accept the terms of the covenant that had been mandated at Sinai. The sect's delimitation of the phrase to apply only to this act of covenant renewal in Damascus had an important implication: only those who accepted the sect's interpretation of the Torah, much of which was attributed to the Righteous Teacher, could legitimately claim to be parties to the "new covenant" that God had re-established with his people. According to the logic of D, being a party to God's "new covenant" meant accepting the contentious interpretation of the Torah that was advocated by the Essene sect.

In terms of the programmatic questions raised in chapter 1, two points may be made. Firstly, the essentialist construction of Judaism, which supposes that the new covenant in D was "legalistic" because it was Jewish is insufficiently nuanced to describe the social and ideological functions played by the "new covenant" in D. D's claims about the new covenant arise, not as the result of its participation in the reified entity, Judaism, but as the result of inner-Jewish rivalries. In D, the new covenant is construed so as to serve an ideological function: that of delegitimating the claims of rival sects to authority in legal interpretation, while legitimating only those claims that could plausibly be linked with the authoritative halakhic interpretations of the Righteous Teacher (i.e., the sect's own tradition of halakhic interpretation).

We may also make an observation about the sociological role played by the Essene construction of the new covenant. This role was not limited to narrowing the covenant between God and Israel to a covenant between God and the Essene sect, as per Christiansen. The function was more specific: it served to delegitimate the halakhic positions of the Pharisees, while valorizing Essene legal rulings as the sole means of mediating the covenant between God and humans. Rather than simply narrowing the focus of the covenant, D's ideology served to differentiate one possible construal of covenantal stipulations (i.e., halakhic rulings) from rival construals. Sociological explanations that focus on the constriction of a generalized covenant with Israel to a particular covenant with the Essene sect are too simplistic; they ignore the primary function of Essene formulations of covenant as inter-sectarian polemic. The narrowing of the focus of the Essene new covenant was not accomplished in a vacuum, but in response to the claims of rival groups to possess authority in halakhic matters, and thus to serve as legitimate mediators of the covenant between God and humans. Sociological interpretations that fail to recognize the Essene construction of the new covenant as a form of inter-sectarian polemic are insufficiently contextualized within the Second Temple Jewish society that gave rise to that construction.

9. Transition from the Damascus Document to 2 Corinthians

In chapter 1, I claimed that comparisons of early Jewish and early Christian discourses should not be carried out until those themes were sufficiently contextualized by examining the local interests that those discourses served. I hope to have contextualized D's discourse on the new covenant, and shown the local interests that it served. In the next section, we will examine Paul's very different construal of the new covenant. D's discourse defined the new covenant in terms of the legal interpretations of the Righteous Teacher, interpretations that enabled the teacher and the group of which he was a part to renew the Sinai covenant, probably in the city of Damascus. We will see that Paul's construal of the new covenant is very different. Far from advocating a sectarian interpretation of Jewish law, Paul championed the position that Gentile converts to the Christian movement had no need to follow the law at all. We will also see that this position was developed in conversation with rival groups, in response to the contingencies raised by a particular local situation. We will find that a divergence in ideological viewpoint existed, not only between Paul's view of the new covenant and D's, but also between Paul's view and that of other members of the early Christian movement with whom Paul was in contact.

Chapter 4

Rival Missionaries in Corinth

1. Prolegomenon: Partition Theories of 2 Corinthians

Frank Matera, after surveying various theories regarding the literary integrity of II Corinthians, made the following observation, "When it is all said and done, it is probably impossible to present a conclusive argument that will convince everyone of a particular partition theory or of the literary integrity of 2 Corinthians."[1] We could restate this candid comment as a matter of historical fact: to date no theory concerning the literary partitioning or unity of 2 Corinthians has proven acceptable to all scholars. However, some general trends in scholars' solutions to the problem may be discerned.

Two eras in the views on the partitioning of 2 Corinthians are represented by the commentaries of H. D. Betz[2] and V. P. Furnish.[3] Although the two commentaries were published within a year of each other, they stand as representatives of two epochs in the history of the interpretation of 2 Corinthians. H. D. Betz wrote his commentary on 2 Corinthians 8 and 9 for the Hermeneia series in 1985, and his work presented the view that was dominant in the academy at that time. Betz viewed 2 Corinthians as a composite document, consisting of six originally distinct letters of letter fragments. Betz was largely in agreement with the dominant view that six, originally distinct documents were combined by an editor of Paul's letters. The documents are identified as follows:

1) 2 Corinthians 1:1–2:13; 7:5–16 and perhaps also 13:11–13, often referred to as the "letter of reconciliation;"
2) 2:14–7:4, the first defense of Paul's ministry; excluding
3) the section in 6:14–7:2, which was often taken as a non-pauline or, according to Betz, an anti-pauline interpolation;
4) chap. 8, the collection letter to Corinth;

---

[1] F. J. Matera, *II Corinthians: A Commentary* (New Testament Library series; Louisville, KY and London: Westminster John Knox Press, 2003) 32, n. 26.

[2] *2 Corinthians 8 and 9: A Commentary on Two Administrative Letters of the Apostle Paul* (Hermeneia series; Philadelphia, PA: Fortress Press, 1985).

[3] *II Corinthians* (Anchor Bible series; New York, NY and London, UK: Doubleday, 1984).

5) chap. 9, the collection letter to Achaia, directed toward the communities outside Corinth; and

6) chaps. 10:1–13:10, Paul's self-comparison with rival missionaries.

The consensus view was critiqued by Victor Paul Furnish in his influential 1984 commentary on 2 Corinthians. Furnish denied that there were adequate grounds to distinguish six separate letters within 2 Corinthians. Instead, Furnish distinguished only two: 2 Cor 1–9 and 10–13. These two sections alone, according to Furnish, exhibit the kinds of thematic and stylistic discontinuity that would warrant their being considered originally separate letters. Furnish's arguments have proven influential enough to forge a new consensus. At present, most scholars tend to argue in favor of this two-source hypothesis. Margaret Thrall presents a history of research in her own 1994 commentary on 2 Corinthians, to which I refer the reader for a discussion and bibliography.[4]

My own view, which I will not attempt to defend here, largely coheres with the older consensus as it existed when Betz wrote his commentary on 2 Cor 8 and 9. However, I leave open the question whether chapters 8 and 9 were originally distinct, or formed a single letter. I would distinguish the following, originally independent letters within 2 Corinthians:

Letter #1: 2 Cor 1:1–2:13; 7:5–16; 13:11–13: The Letter of Reconciliation
Letter #2: 2:14–6:13; 7:2–4: First Apology
Early Letter Fragment(?): 6:14–7:1: Exhortation to Avoid Defilement (cp. 1 Cor 5:9–13)
Letter #3: 8:1–9:15 Collection letter(s) to Corinth/Achaia
Letter #4: 10:1–13:10: Second Apology

The analysis of Paul's discursive strategies that constitutes the substance of this and the following chapter largely center on the argument that Paul presents in 2:14–4:6. I view this as a section of an originally independent letter that extends from 2:14 to 6:13 and includes also 13:11–13. I view the Second Apology as a letter written later than the First Apology, but addressing problems raised in Corinth by the presence of an identical group. However, the results of my study are not dependant on my particular solution to the problem of the literary partitioning of 2 Corinthians. Furnish and others who adopt his position regard 2:14–6:13 as a literary subunit within the larger unit of 2 Cor 1–9. Therefore, my delimitation of the particular material is justifiable regardless of the view that one adopts regarding the literary history of the material that now constitutes 2 Corinthians. Since my study focuses on the discursive strategies that Paul employs within a particular section of 2 Corinthians, the conclusions that I reach are not dependent on a particular view of the epistolary history of the letters – be there two, or five, or six – that have been combined to form the

---

[4] *The Second Epistle to the Corinthians* (ICC; Edinburgh, Scotland: T&T Clark, 1994).

text of 2 Corinthians in its canonical form. However, because the arguments that I make in chapters 5 and 6 presuppose a solution to the problem of the epistolary history of the sections that now constitute 2 Corinthians, it is important that I state my own position on the issue.

2. Paul's Rivals: An Overview of Research

Both the first and second apologies mention missionaries who had come to Corinth, setting themselves in opposition to Paul's ministry. The precise identification of both the ideology and identity of these missionaries have been subjects of debate. Some studies from the late 19th and early 20th centuries were misled by a false dichotomy in which the Greek "spirit" was equated with freedom, universalism, spontaneity, and ecstasy, whereas the Jewish "spirit" was identified with legalism and nationalistic exclusiveness. As a result of this dichotomy, some scholars felt the need to choose between either a "pneumatic" (read here "Greek") or nomistic (read "Judaizing") orientation for Paul's rivals. Some scholars, following the heresiologists of the early church, have labeled Paul's rivals in Corinth as "Judaizers" who "falsified" the pure gospel that is the essence of Christianity. That is, the "Judaizers" attempted to import "legalism" into early Christianity, which was defined as "essentially" a religion of grace, in which legal precepts were held to be inimical to the freedom from law entailed by the "gospel." Such perspectives serve as veiled attempts to assert the supremacy of Christianity over Judaism, on the one hand, or as attempts to assert the supremacy of Protestant Christianity (construed as Lutheran in orientation) over Catholicism, on the other. The image of Paul's opponents, as well as the story of Paul's dealings with them, that will be developed in this and the following chapter is both more interesting and more complex than the caricatures of the 19th and early 20th centuries would suggest.

In light of the history of research into the question of Paul's opponents in 2 Corinthians, an important methodological caveat is in order from the outset. When comparing Paul with the rival missionaries in 2 Corinthians, it must be made clear that we are not comparing two religions, Christianity and Judaism. At the time in which 2 Corinthians was written, "Christianity" had not yet evolved as a religion separate from Judaism. The Book of Acts, written perhaps early in the second century CE, attests that "Christianity" was at that point still conceived as a sect (αἵρεσις) within Judaism (Acts 24:5, 28:22). Although the term *"Christianoi"* had been used of followers of Jesus as early as 40–44 CE in Antioch, this term seems to have been coined by outsiders to the movement,[5] and was not used regularly as a self-designation until the mid-second century CE,[6] by which time Christianity had evolved into a distinct religion that could define itself in relation to other "religions," including Judaism. During Paul's lifetime, and at least until the first decades of the second century, the term "Christians" did not refer to the group as a "religion" that was to be distinguished from Judaism, but rather designated an identifiable political-religious group within Judaism. Therefore, the use of the term "Christian" as it appears in this study should be taken as referring to a sect within Judaism, and not as a "religion" that was separate from and defined in opposition to Judaism. Rather than reading 2 Corinthians as encapsulating an argument between the "patterns of religion" of Christianity and Judaism, this study will view the dispute between Paul and the rival missionaries in Corinth as an internal matter, an inner-sectarian dispute within the early Christian movement, itself constituted as a Jewish sect.

In order to prepare the way for my own reconstruction of Paul's rivals and his relationship to them, it will be necessary to outline some of the positions that have shaped the present state of the discussion. Most of the articles and books that will be discussed were written since the 1950s, although the influence of F. C. Baur's late 19th century reconstruction of Paul's opponents is still palpably present today. Baur therefore, will serve as the starting point for this discussion.

2.1. F. C. Baur

In his classic reconstruction of the life and theology of Paul, F.C. Baur interpreted the NT and later Christian sources through the lens of Hegel:[7] Judaism and Christianity were viewed as two combating "principles" or "spirits." Due to the intrinsic superiority of the latter, the former was doomed to die, while Christianity was destined to become "the great spiritual power which determines all the belief and thought of the present age."[8] Judaism represented nationalistic particularism; Christianity uni-

---

[5] M. J. Wilkins, art. "Christian," *ABD* 1:925-926.

[6] Wilkins, *ABD* 1:926. See also Jan Bremmer, *The Rise and Fall of the Afterlife* (London and New York: Routledge, 2002); Appendix 1: "Why did Jesus' Followers Call Themselves 'Christians'?" 103–108, who argues that the term became prominent only as a result of Roman persecutions, in which the accused was asked, "Are you a Christian?"

[7] See W. Baird, *History of New Testament Research, Vol. 1: From Deism to Tübingen* (Minneapolis, MN: Fortress Press, 1992) 258–269, for an overview of Baur's life and work.

[8] *Paul, the Apostle of Jesus Christ* (2 vols., London and Edinburgh: Williams and Norgate, 1875), vol. 1:2. Originally published as *Paulus, der Apostel Jesu Christi. Sein Leben, sein Wirken, seine Briefe und seine Lehre. Ein Beitrag zu einer kritischen Geschichte des Urchristenthums* (Leipzig: Fues's Verlag, 1866).

versalism. Since universalism as a principle was intrinsically stronger than particularism, Christianity necessarily overcame and replaced Judaism. The story of early Christianity was thus the story of universalism struggling to extricate itself from particularistic Judaism. Baur summarizes, "The relation of Christianity to heathenism and Judaism is, as we have seen, defined as that between the absolute religion and the preparatory and subordinate forms of religion. We have here the progress from servitude to freedom, from nonage to majority, from the age of childhood to maturity, from the flesh to the spirit."[9]

Even if few today would accept Baur's interpretative framework, nonetheless many of the positions that he advocated are still defended. For example, Baur argued that there were two main "principles" that were at odds in the early church: those of nationalism and legalism, on the one hand, and those of "spirit" and universalism, on the other. These principles were embodied historically within Petrine and Pauline Christianity, respectively. Petrine and Pauline Christianity related to one another as thesis to antithesis, and were finally replaced by a synthesis of the opposing principles in Catholic Christianity, accomplished by the mid-second century.[10] For Baur, this reconstruction entailed the view that, throughout Paul's letters there was a single, unified opposition: Petrine Christianity, with its headquarters in Jerusalem. The view that there was a unified opposition to Paul, evident throughout his letters, is still debated.[11] Although it is beyond the scope of this study to evaluate the thesis that there is a unified opposition to Paul that is manifested throughout his letters, there is enough data in 2 Corinthians to enable us to draw some conclusions about the relationship of the missionaries mentioned in the first and second apologies to the Jerusalem church.

2.2. E. Käsemann

Ernst Käsemann, in an influential article entitled, "Die Legitimität des Apostels: Eine Untersuchung zu II Korinther 10–13,"[12] developed the thesis that Paul's legitimacy as an apostle was questioned by his opponents in Corinth, and defended in 2 Cor 10–13. This approach is now universally

---

[9] *Paul, the Apostle*, 2:212.

[10] So Baird, *History of New Testament Research*, 266–267.

[11] G. Lüdemann, for example, in his *Opposition to Paul in Jewish Christianity* (Minneapolis, MN: Fortress, 1989; translation of *Paulus, der Heidenapostel*, vol. 2: *Antipaulinismus im frühen Christentum*), develops the idea of a unified opposition to Paul and Paulinism both during and after Paul's lifetime.

[12] First published in *ZNW* 41 (1942) 33–71. Subsequently published as an independent monograph in Darmstadt by Wissenschaftliche Buchgesellschaft, 1956. In the citations that follow, the page numbers from the reprinted version will appear first, followed by the page numbers as they appeared in the original article in parentheses.

recognized as correct. In regard to the identity of Paul's opponents, Käsemann finds himself in substantial agreement with the thesis of Baur, for
whom "Paul resisted in II Cor., as in his other letters, a 'Judaistic', thus
nomistic falsification of the gospel."[13] The source of this "Judaistic falsification of the gospel" was, as Baur had posited, a delegation from the Jerusalem church. Käsemann takes the 2 Cor 11:3 as a point of departure:
Paul's mention of ὁ ἐρχόμενος designates "one or more arbitrators sent
from Jerusalem, who were to pronounce a final verdict in the present conflict"[14] whose apostolic authority had come into question. Käsemann's
construal of the situation is reminiscent of the affairs that had taken place
earlier in Antioch, described in Gal 2 and Acts 15, in which the Jerusalem
church had sent a delegation to the Antioch church with a ruling regarding
dietary purity regulations to be followed by Jewish members of the community there.[15]

Käsemann is able to draw a connection between 2 Corinthians and the
Jerusalem church on the basis of his reading of 10:12–18. He views this
section as Paul's response to criticisms by his opponents that he lacks
"well-defined authority and a clear mandate"[16] to preach as an apostle,
such as his opponents had by virtue of their connections with the Jerusalem church. Paul's response is that, since he is a pneumatic, he is subject
to no one's judgment (cf. 1 Cor 2:15–16). Furthermore, his mandate comes
from heaven, from the Lord himself, rather than from any earthly authority, such as the connections of which Paul's opponents boast.

These opponents were able to prove their authority by producing letters
of recommendation written by the Jerusalem church. References to the
Jerusalem apostles themselves appear in 2 Cor 11:4–5, where they are
referred to as ὑπερλίαν ἀπόστολοι, "super-apostles."[17] The "super-
apostles" are distinguished from the emissaries whom they had sent, whom

---

[13] "Paulus erwehre sich im II Cor ebenso wie in seinen anderen Briefen
'judaistischer', also nomistischer Verfälschung des Evangeliums" 7 (33).

[14] Käsemann: "einem oder mehreren von Jerusalem her erwarteten Schiedsrichtern,
die im vorliegenden Konflikt ein abschliessendes Urteil sprechen sollen" 14–15 (38).

[15] This summary corresponds with Paul's view of the matter. In Acts, the delegation
arrives with a statement that the Gentiles should follow the Noachic laws: they should
abstain from fornication, from animals that had been killed by strangling, and from
consuming meat with blood in it. The Acts narrative may represent a mediating position
that was formulated only after c. 51 CE, when the Antioch delegation was sent. Paul does
not mention anything of the Noachic laws that were purportedly recommended for the
Gentiles.

[16] "eindeutig Autorität und ein klares mandatum" 43 (56).

[17] The term is a compound of the preposition ὑπέρ, "above, over" and the intensify-
ing adverb, λίαν. Although formally an adverb, the term ὑπερλίαν is used here as an
adjective. The translation "super-apostles" is suggested by DBAG, s. ὑπερλίαν (cf. also
BDF §§12.3; 116.3; 230).

Paul referred to derisively as "servants of Satan." Out of respect for the former group, when Paul compares himself with them he claims only "I no less than they" am an apostle. However, in comparison with the latter group, Paul's claim is bolder: "I still more" than they am an apostle (or, as NRSV translates, "I am a better one"). Käsemann argues that there is a "hidden cleavage" within Paul's discourse: his writing concerns the Jerusalem apostles in such passages as 11:5 and 12:11, in which Paul's tone is moderated; however, in passages in which his tone is more severe, Paul has the "gate crashing" emissaries in mind (11:3–5, 13–15). We will return to examine each of these points of Käsemann's reconstruction later in this chapter.

2.3. W. Schmithals

Schmithals developed his teacher Rudolf Bultmann's thesis that Paul's rivals in Corinth were gnostics. Both Schmithals and Bultmann wrote at a time when historians of religion routinely argued that there existed a pre-Christian Gnosticism which may have influenced early Christianity. However, this position has now been abandoned, since all of the "gnostic" sources appear to have been composed during the second century CE, at the earliest. It is illustrative of the problem that the sources that Schmithals cites in his reconstruction of pre-Christian Gnosticism (Irenaeus, Tertullian, Hippolytus, Epiphanius of Salamis, and the Coptic Nag Hammadi documents) date from the second to fourth centuries CE.[18]

However, Schmithals' methodological problems do not preclude an examination of some of the salient points in his reconstruction of Paul's opponents. Schmithals asserts that "not a single word" in 2 Corinthians suggests that Paul's opponents were "Judaizers,"[19] by which he refers to those who advocate following Jewish law. Schmithals takes the position that, while Paul's opponents were indeed Jews, they were not "Judaizers": they did not advocate the observance of Jewish law. "A 'judaizing Gnosticism' or a 'Gnostic *Judaismus*' is an absurdity and never existed," Schmithals opines. This is because, in his view, "Pure Gnosticism rules out

---

[18] For an overview of the sources and their contents see H.-J. Klauck, *The Religious Context of Early Christianity: A Guide to Greco-Roman Religions* (Minneapolis, MN: Fortress Press, 2003; first published as *Die religiöse Umwelt des Urchristentums;* Stuttgart: Kohlhammer, 1995). Edwin Yamauchi has evaluated the evidence for pre-Christian Gnosticism and found it wanting in *Pre-Christian Gnosticism: A Survey of the Proposed Evidences* (Grand Rapids, MI: Eerdmans, 1973) and the article "Pre-Christian Gnosticism in the Nag Hammadi Texts?" in *Church History* 48 (1979) 129–141.

[19] *Gnosticism in Corinth: An Investigation of the Letters to the Corinthians* (Nashville, TN and New York, NY: Abingdon Press, 1971; originally published in Göttingen by Vandenhoeck & Ruprecht under the title, *Die Gnosis in Korinth; eine Untersuchung zu den Korintherbriefen*, 1956). The quote appears on p. 118.

the way of the law as a way of salvation in any form."[20] The means of salvation in Gnosticism was the realization of certain metaphysical propositions about the origin and nature of the soul and its kinship with the divine, and not in one's adherence to legal precepts. We may readily agree with Schmithals that Paul's opponents were Jews, and we will return to the proposition at a later point to examine the evidence pertaining to their attitude toward Jewish law.

2.4. D. Georgi

Dieter Georgi[21] is to be credited for having devised a novel hypothesis in the history of scholarship on Paul's opponents in 2 Corinthians. Rejecting both the thesis that Paul's opponents were primarily concerned to advocate Jewish law among Paul's Gentile churches and the thesis that Paul's opponents were gnostics, Georgi argued that they were Greek θεῖοι ἄνθρωποι, divine men who possessed superhuman traits such as a seemingly infinite store of knowledge and the ability to work miracles. The θεῖος ἀνήρ *par excellence* was Apollonius of Tyana, but others were known and satirized by Lucian.[22] Itinerant Jewish missionaries assimilated the characteristics of the *theioi andres*, and used ecstatic displays and works of miraculous power to legitimate their own missionary activities. In so doing, these Jewish missionaries believed themselves to be recapitulating the performances of Moses, who was taken as the ideal θεῖος ἀνήρ.

Georgi's thesis met with criticism on several fronts. It was widely denied that there was a Jewish mission in Second Temple times, a thesis that formed a cornerstone of Georgi's reconstruction. On another front, Carl Holladay, in a study entitled, *Theios Aner in Hellenistic Judaism: A Critique of the Use of This Category in New Testament Christology*,[23] found that, contrary to Georgi's assumption that there was a blurring of the line of demarcation between the human and the divine in Hellenistic Judaism, an examination of the sources reveals that just the opposite was the case: "Hellenization among Jews, rather than bridging the gap, only widened it."[24] Holladay also criticized the indiscriminate use by Georgi and others of diverse sources to arrive at a composite picture of "the Hellenistic divine man." Holladay insisted that the disparity in the way in which the concept was used among various sources precluded any attempt to

---

[20] *Gnosticism in Corinth*, 294.

[21] *The Opponents of Paul in Second Corinthians* (Philadelphia: Fortress Press, 1986; translation of *Die Gegner des Paulus im 2. Korintherbrief: Studien zur religiösen Propaganda in der Spätantike*; Neukirchen-Vluyn: Neukirchener Verlag, 1964).

[22] *Opponents*, 155–164.

[23] Published in Missoula, Montana by Scholars Press, 1977.

[24] *Theios Aner*, 235.

synthesize a single θεῖος ἀνήρ figure which could be of any use in comparisons with early Christian literature (as Holladay's subtitle suggests, his main interest was the use of the *theios anēr* figure in comparisons with depictions of Jesus as miracle worker).

2.5. C. K. Barrett

Whether or not one agrees with all of the details of C. K. Barrett's analysis, his work on the missionary rivals to Paul in 2 Corinthians provides a host of insights. Barrett sifts carefully through the literature on the subject, judiciously evaluating the positions advocated by various scholars. Barrett raises many of the issues that must be confronted if one is to arrive at a coherent picture of the rival missionaries in Corinth.

We will deal in detail with the positions that Barrett holds on various points in a later section. At present, however, we may simply outline the main points of his reconstruction. Barrett argues that Paul's missionary opponents in 2 Corinthians are "Judaizing" Jews who arrived in Corinth with letters of recommendation from officials of the Jerusalem church. These emissaries were "unsatisfactory agents who misrepresented their principals"[25] in the Jerusalem church, namely James and Cephas. In 2 Corinthians 11, the ὑπερλίαν ἀπόστολοι are to be distinguished from the ψευδαπόστολοι. The former designation refers to the "pillar apostles" in Jerusalem, James and Cephas/Peter, the latter to the missionaries who had arrived in Corinth claiming to represent the Jerusalem church (cf. Käsemann). The missionaries were not themselves pneumatics; rather it was the Corinthians themselves to whom Paul responds in passages such as 12:5–7a and 12:12. The Corinthians demanded pneumatism as a proof of apostolic status.[26]

In response to the objections of Lütgert and Friedrich that the Corinthians missionaries could not have been "nomists" or "Judaizers" because there is no evidence that they advocated Sabbath observance, circumcision, or "cultic purity," Barrett adduces Cephas as an example of an early missionary who, although he advocated that the Gentiles follow some aspects of Jewish law, did not advocate that they be circumcised.[27]

Barrett's essays also reveal a very interesting contradiction. Although he is certainly referring to circumstances that are addressed in 1 Corinthians, presumably he also means to include the preaching of rival missionaries that is contested in 2 Corinthians when he writes:

---

[25] "Paul's Opponents in 2 Corinthians," in C.K. Barrett, *Essays on Paul* (Philadelphia, Penn.: Westminster Press, 1992) 81.

[26] "Paul's Opponents ," 73.

[27] "Christianity at Corinth," 21; citing the Apostolic Decree of Acts 15:20, 29.

There is no epistle (apart from Philemon) in which Paul does not deal with some deviation from or perversion of the Christian faith, but nowhere else [than in the Corinthian correspondence] is so great a variety of deviations and perversions so fully displayed ...

and later adds,

Alexandrian Judaism, Jewish Christianity, Hellenism, all seem to have played upon the already inflammatory material assembled at Corinth. It is no wonder that there was a blaze; no wonder the city could add to its trade fairs as fine an exhibition of Christian deviation as could be seen anywhere in the world.[28]

However in a later essay, Barrett is able to write what may be seen either as a contradiction of or a corrective to his earlier statements:

Paul's rivals [in 2 Corinthians] proclaimed 'another Jesus' and a 'different gospel' (2 Cor 11.4). Doubtless they would have brought the same charge against him. This means that theological conflict runs back into the origins of Christianity, for Paul's adversaries claimed ultimate authority for their beliefs. Historically, topographically, and perhaps traditionally they may well have stood nearer than Paul to the historical Jesus.[29]

In a footnote Barrett adds, "we probably owe to them [i.e., Paul's rivals] part at least of the synoptic tradition." Barrett is one of the few scholars here surveyed who raises the issue of the rival missionaries', as well as Paul's own, relationship to the earlier traditions that were current within the early Jesus movement. Any position that would characterize the teaching of Paul's missionary rivals in Corinth as "deviation," "perversion," "heresy," or the like must first deal with this fundamental issue.

2.6. D. W. Oostendorp

Derk William Oostendorp, in his 1967 Free University of Amsterdam dissertation, argues that the missionary opponents of Paul in 2 Corinthians were Jews who were closely associated with the Palestinian church. These missionaries were convinced that prophecies from the Book of Isaiah had been fulfilled, in which it is stated that in the eschatological age, Israel would become preeminent among the nations and many Gentiles would begin to worship Israel's God (cp. Isa 41:2–16; 56:1–8). These missionaries attempted to impress upon the Gentiles in Corinth the need to study the Torah, for it is only in this way that one may receive the "spirit."[30] The fact that these missionaries boasted in their Jewishness (cp. 2 Cor 11:21–22) was meant "to impress upon the Corinthians that they [i.e., the missionaries] have a superior position as members of the nation of Israel and heirs of the Old Testament promises."[31] Oostendorp offers an inter-

---

[28] "Christianity at Corinth." The first quotation appears on p. 1, the second on p. 3.

[29] "Paul's Opponents," 60.

[30] *Another Jesus: A Gospel of Jewish-Christian Superiority in II Corinthians* (Amsterdam: Kampen, 1967) 45–46.

[31] *Another Jesus*, 12.

pretation of the triad "another Jesus, another spirit, another gospel" mentioned in 2 Cor 11:4 which coheres with this understanding of the missionaries' goals. The missionaries preached Jesus from the perspective of "the Jewish nationalistic conception of the messiah." This conception consists of the belief that Israel, and concomitantly its messiah, has a "divinely promised prerogative to rule the world."[32] The missionaries argue that there is an indissoluble bond between the reception of the spirit and following the law of Moses.[33] The gospel preached by this group is related to the use of the term in Isaiah, in which Israel was expected to become the world's preeminent nation during the eschatological age.[34]

On the basis of his analysis of 2 Cor 10:1–6 and 12:19–13:10, Oostendorp argues that Paul's opponents "were disturbed by the sins committed at Corinth and thought that Paul should have punished them at the earliest opportunity." These sins may have been a continuation of those already mentioned in 1 Corinthians, and are referred to in 2 Cor 12:21. The rival missionaries, calling themselves "servants of righteousness," claim that "they were truly promoters of righteousness whereas Paul was not."[35] The missionaries thought that Paul should have dealt more forcefully with the sinners at the time of his second visit. The fact that he did not cast Paul's apostolic authority into grave doubt (noting especially the emphasis placed on δόκιμος cognates in 13:5–10). This emphasis on "righteousness" coheres with the missionaries' understanding that the Torah must play a central role in the messianic era. We will evaluate some of Oostendorp's contributions in a later section.

2.7. J. Murphy-O'Connor

Murphy-O'Connor's reconstruction is somewhat more complex than many of the other theories regarding Paul's opponents in 2 Corinthians. He traces the origin of the rival missionaries, not to Jerusalem, but to Antioch, which at the time of the Jerusalem conference in 51 CE had come under the influence of the Jerusalem church. The Jerusalem church had taken the position that Jews within the Jesus movement should observe purity regulations at their meals (which prevented them from dining with Gentiles) and that Gentiles within the movement should be circumcised. Paul's Antiochene mentor, Barnabas, accepted the ruling of the Jerusalem church, while Paul rejected it. Marginalized and disillusioned by the Antioch church's acceptance of these rulings, in the spring of 52 CE, Paul left Antioch in search of fresh missionary fields in which to propound his

---

[32] *Another Jesus*, 55.

[33] *Another Jesus*, 45.

[34] *Another Jesus*, 9–10.

[35] *Another Jesus*, 20.

particular version of the gospel. The Antioch church, however, sends emissaries who, in Paul's wake, attempt to persuade the members of the Pauline churches to accept the rulings of the mother church in Jerusalem.

In 2 Corinthians, Paul must deal not with one, but two groups of enemies, who had joined forces in their opposition to Paul. The first group consists of representatives of the Antiochene church who advocated following the law of Moses, who was viewed as "the great Lawgiver, whose words had enduring value."[36] The second group Murphy-O'Connor designates "the Spirit people." These people were residents of Corinth, and had already been addressed derisively in 1 Corinthians. This group formed a cabal, from which Paul received continued opposition. On the principle that the enemy of one's enemy is one's friend, Murphy-O'Connor reasons that these two groups formed an alliance of convenience in opposition to Paul. In 2 Corinthians, which Murphy-O'Connor takes to consist of two separate letters, the first in chapters 1–9 and the second in 10–13,[37] Paul attempts to refute the positions advocated by both groups.

2.8. M. Thrall

In her two-volume commentary on 2 Corinthians, Margaret Thrall develops a picture of the missionaries who were rivals to Paul. According to Thrall, Paul's rivals were emissaries of the Jerusalem church, some of whom had some competence in sophistic rhetoric, while others may have spoken Aramaic as a first language and been versed in the tradition of the sayings of Jesus. These missionaries claimed apostolic status, worked miracles, and most likely were visionaries who boasted of their visions.[38] These missionaries preached a Jesus who appeared as "a splendid figure of post-resurrection glory by contrast with the Pauline gospel of the crucified Christ." In addition, their message stressed "obedience to the teaching of the earthly Jesus, including some measure of Torah-observance."[39]

Thrall rejects the identification, argued by Käsemann and Barrett, of the ὑπερλίαν ἀπόστολοι mentioned in 2 Cor 10–13 with the Jerusalem apostles. Instead she applies the term to the missionaries who had arrived in Corinth.[40] She does, however, see a relationship between the missionaries and the Jerusalem church. This relationship is suggested by Paul's discussion of the division of missionary territory in 10:12–18. In the background of this discussion, Thrall argues, lies the agreement that was reached be-

---

[36] *Paul: A Critical Life* (Oxford and New York: Oxford University Press, 1996) 303.

[37] *Paul: A Critical Life*, 254-256.

[38] *II Corinthians* (ICC; 2 vols., Edinburgh: T&T Clark, 1994, 2000) 2:941.

[39] The first quote appears in 2:940, the second on the page following.

[40] *II Corinthians* 2:671-676.

tween Paul and the "pillar apostles" James and Peter, in which Peter was to preach to the Jews, Paul to the Gentiles.

On the basis of her analysis of 2 Cor 3, Thrall concludes that "judaizing opponents of the Galatian type" are not combated in this section. "The total absence of any reference to circumcision throughout 2 Corinthians makes the identification of the opponents as troublemakers of the Galatian type highly problematic."[41] Because the structure of Paul's argument in 2 Cor 3 takes for granted the postulate that the law brings death, Paul cannot be arguing against "opponents who themselves claim to be agents of a new covenant but who saw it as including, still, the observance of the law of Moses."[42]

There seems, however, to be a tension within Thrall's position as she expresses it at various points in her two-volume work. Whereas she is able to claim that "judaizing opponents of the Galatian type" are not refuted in 2 Cor 3, nevertheless she does liken the position of these opponents to that espoused in the Gospel of Matthew. In Mt 5:17–19, Jesus is presented as teaching that the law of Moses must be fulfilled perfectly. This leads Thrall to make the following comment:

Paul's opponents in Corinth preach an 'alternative gospel.' The phrase εὐαγγέλιον ἕτερον suggests a partial parallel with the Galatian situation (Gal 1.6), and this, in turn, would mean that the opponents' gospel involves some measure of Torah observance.[43]

The tension in Thrall's treatment of this issue is illuminating. While she argues that the opponents are not of the "Galatian type," by which she presumably means that they did not advocate circumcision, nevertheless the "opponents' gospel involves some measure of Torah observance." Yet in the Matthean quote that Thrall adduces, Jesus states that "not a jot nor a tittle will pass away from the law" until the consummation of the end of the age. The position espoused in this Matthean passage does not refer to "some measure of Torah observance," but to the observance of the Torah in its entirety. This would certainly have included circumcision, even though it is not explicitly mentioned in Matthew's gospel. We will explore the possible ideological links between the missionaries in Corinth and the Gospel of Matthew later in this chapter. We will explore more fully Thrall's interesting observation that Paul takes for granted the postulate that the law brings death in chapter 5.

---

[41] *II Corinthians* 2:939–940.

[42] *II Corinthians* 1:236, 296–297; 2:939.

[43] *II Corinthians* 2:667–670. The quote appears on p. 670.

2.9. J. Sumney

Jerry Sumney, both in the revision of his 1987 doctoral dissertation[44] under the direction of Victor Paul Furnish and in his more recent work, *'Servants of Satan', 'False Brothers' and Other Opponents of Paul*,[45] has pointed out methodological flaws in earlier works on Paul's opponents in 2 Corinthians, and has developed his own methodological approach to the material. Sumney's approach identifies several different types of material from which we may expect to extract information regarding the identity and ideology of Paul's opponents. Sumney's own approach is somewhat more complicated, although it may be stated simply as follows: four different types of material in 2 Corinthians yield information regarding Paul's opponents which vary in the "level of certainty" that we may presume regarding the factuality of the information contained in them. The four types of material are identified as follows:

1) Explicit statements in various contexts yield the most certain information about Paul's opponents.

2) Allusions in polemical and apologetic contexts yield information which ranks second to explicit statements in terms of their reliability.

3) Presumed allusions in polemical contexts, in which material concerning the position of Paul's opponents may be extracted only if it is assumed that the opponents' position is exactly counter to what Paul asserts in a given passage (a process of inference known as the "mirror technique"), rank third in terms of the certainty of the information that they yield.

4) A fourth level of certainty is provided by major themes within 2 Corinthians, as these may "indicate a major focus of the author's response to the opponents."[46] (Here it must be supposed that Paul's major themes counter major themes of his opponents – another version of the "mirror technique.") This last category, however, only serves a corroborative function; it must be supported by information derived from one of the previous three categories in order to be considered valid.

In addition to these four criteria for determining the "level of certainty" of the information extracted from specific passages in 2 Corinthians, Sumney introduces another methodological constraint which he considers to be of fundamental importance: each of Paul's letters must be interpreted individually, without presupposing that the opponents of Paul who were addressed in one letter were the same as those addressed in another. In this regard, Sumney attempts to correct the perceived methodological deficiencies of earlier scholars, and in particular Baur, whose reconstruction of early Christian history led him to posit that the Petrine mission constituted a unified front in opposition to Paul.

---

[44] *Identifying Paul's Opponents: The Question of Method in 2 Corinthians* (JSOTSupp 40; Sheffield: Sheffield Academic Press, 1990).

[45] JSOTSupp 188; Sheffield: Sheffield Academic Press, 1999.

[46] *Identifying Paul's Opponents*, 111.

Sumney's method for identifying the "level of certainty" of information extracted from references or allusions to opponents in Paul's letters is salutary. In our own reconstruction of Paul's opponents, Sumney's analysis of individual passages will often constitute a useful starting point. We may, however, identify two weakness in Sumney's method. Firstly, his insistence that each letter must be interpreted without regard to Paul's other letters may, in the case of 2 Corinthians, lead to a neglect of points of continuity between the First and Second Corinthians. Clearly, Paul is addressing the same group in both letters: the Corinthian congregation. Just as clearly, many of the problems that had plagued the church in the former letter are still evident in the latter. (On the other hand, virtually all scholars today would agree with Sumney that the missionary opposition to Paul in 2 Corinthians represented a development in the situation vis-à-vis 1 Corinthians, in which these missionaries played no part.) The second weakness in Sumney's approach is that he does not follow through with his own methodological dictum that roughly contemporary sources may be used as an aid to historical reconstruction.[47] In fact, Sumney limits himself almost entirely to the text of 2 Corinthians when discussing the identity of Paul's missionary opponents,[48] neglecting any discussion of historical trends within Judaism or the early Christian sect. I will argue that a contextualizing approach is essential to establishing certain characteristics of the preaching of Paul's missionary opponents.

Sumney's method proves very useful, and indeed a solid starting-point, in questions pertaining to the use and assessment of particular passages in which Paul refers or alludes to the position of his opponents. However, the weakness of Sumney's method lies in its inability to contextualize sufficiently Paul's opposition; we are left with a series of opponents in Paul's letters who have neither background nor relation to the contemporary environment in which the letters were written. Therefore, we may view Sumney's results as a useful beginning point, yielding the raw data from which we may construct a more comprehensive picture, which insofar as possible contextualizes Paul's opponents within the Greco-Roman world of the mid-first century of the common era.

---

[47] *Identifying Paul's Opponents*, 77–94.

[48] In *'Servants of Satan'*, 132–133, Sumney does devote three paragraphs to the social milieu in which he perceives the debate between Paul and his missionary opponents to have been conducted (i.e., popular philosophy). However, these ruminations are undeveloped and do not include any reference to the early Christian movement.

3. Reconstructing the Identity and Ideology of Paul's Opponents

3.1. Navigating the Contentious Issues

In view of the positions regarding Paul's opponents that we have outlined, it may from the outset be useful to identify a set of contentious issues that must be settled in order to establish a profile of this group. These issues are summed up in the following set of questions:

1. Were Paul's missionary rivals in Corinth Jews? What is the significance of the terms "Hebrews," "Israelites," and "Abraham's descendants"?
2. Were the missionaries in Corinth emissaries of the Jerusalem church?
3. Did the missionaries in Corinth preach, in contradistinction to Paul, that Gentile converts should follow the Torah?
4. Did the missionary rivals in Corinth use "pneumatic" displays to establish their legitimacy? If so, how? In what ways did Paul rely on pneumatic displays to establish the legitimacy of his own mission?
5. What was the nature of the "other Jesus, other spirit, other gospel" preached by the rival missionaries in Corinth? How is this related to the same phrase in Galatians?
6. How closely were the missionary rivals related to earlier traditions that circulated within Judaism and, more narrowly, within the early Christian sect? How closely was Paul related with earlier traditions that circulated within Judaism and within the early Christian sect?

Any reconstruction of the identity and ideology of Paul's missionary rivals in Corinth must at minimum address these six issues. In the following discussion, we will address each of these.

3.2. Were Paul's missionary rivals in Corinth Jews? What is the significance of the terms "Hebrews," "Israelites," and "Abraham's descendants"?

All scholars today would agree with the minimal assertion that Paul's missionary rivals in Corinth were Jews. All would probably agree that these missionaries represented an ideology that found its home within the early messianic movement that revered Jesus as its founder. That these missionaries were Jews is guaranteed by 2 Cor 11:22–23a:

"Are they Hebrews? I am, too. Are they Israelites? I am, too. Are they descendants of Abraham? I am, too. Are they emissaries of Christ? I am speaking foolishly – I am a better one!"

The precise significance of the terms Ἑβραῖοι, Ἰσραηλίται, and σπέρμα Ἀβραάμ however, has been debated. The first of these terms may designate 1) a person whose lineage is Israelite, 2) a person of Israelite descent who is fluent in Hebrew,[49] Aramaic,[50] or both, or 3) a Jew who lives in

---

[49] On the first two definitions, cf. DBAG, s.v., Ἑβραῖος.

[50] So K. G. Kuhn in *TDNT* 3:369.

Palestine.[51] The minimum that may be indicated by the use of the term Ἑβραῖος is indicated by definition #1: a person who traces his ancestry to Israel, construed as God's chosen nation. In light of usages of the term such as one in Philo in which Ἑβραῖοι are designated in specifically linguistic terms,[52] it is possible that the use of the term by Paul's missionary rivals may have included this connotation.[53] However, two facts would seem to mitigate against this interpretation in the case of 2 Cor 11:22. Firstly, a synagogue inscription in which was inscribed – in Greek, not Hebrew – [ΣΥΝ]ΑΓΩΓΗ ΕΒΡ[ΑΙΩΝ] has been found in Corinth.[54]   If the term Ἑβραῖοι was used primarily in a linguistic sense, the inscription should have appeared in Hebrew, not Greek! Also, Paul's own usage of the term elsewhere implies not that he spoke Hebrew, but that he traced his genealogy back to one of the twelve tribes of Israel (Phil 3:5). It is possible that either Paul or his opponents meant to include the connotation that they spoke Hebrew when they used the term Ἑβραῖος, but it is more likely that the term referred simply to the ability of Paul, and his opponents, to claim that their ancestors were Ἑβραῖοι.

It has been popular since Walter Gutbrod's 1938 *TWNT* article[55] to argue that the term Ἑβραῖος refers to an individual of Palestinian extraction. While this is sometimes the case, this seems to be a function of contextual association, and not itself constitutive of the semantic import of the "naked" term.[56] That is, in cases where the term Ἑβραῖος appears without a concomitant reference to Palestine, we may not assume that such a con-

---

[51] Thrall's discussion (*II Corinthians* 2:723–730) provides a detailed examination of the various positions advocated along with some citations of the use of the term in primary sources.

[52] *Conf Ling* 129: ὡς μὲν Ἑβραῖοι λέγουσι Φανουήλ, ὡς δὲ ἡμεῖς ἀποστροφὴ θεοῦ. ("As Hebrews say, 'Phanuel," but as we (say), "turning from God.") Cited in Thrall, *II Corinthians* 2:724; here following her translation.

[53] As Matera, *II Corinthians*, 263-264 observes, Paul's usage of the term Ἑβραῖος in Phil 3:4-5 strongly suggests that his own use of the term points to "ethnic purity." However, the opponents may have used the term to evoke different connotations than those suggested by Pauline usage.

[54] The inscription derives from perhaps as late as the fourth century CE, which however detracts from its ability to shed light on the first century usage of the term "Hebrew" in Corinth. The inscription is pictured in Furnish, *II Corinthians*, pl. VIb.

[55] S.v. Ἰσραήλ, vol. 3:374–375 in the ET: *Theological Dictionary of the New Testament* (G. Kittel, W. Bromily, G. Friedrich, eds., Grand Rapids, MI: Eerdmans, 1964–1976); trans. of the German original *Theologisches Wörterbuch zum Neuen Testament* (G. Kittel, ed., Stuttgart: Kohlhammer, 1938).

[56] The relevant inscriptions have been edited recently by David Noy, *Jewish Inscriptions of Western Europe* (2 vols., Cambridge, New York, and Melbourne: Cambridge University Press, 1995). The Roman inscriptions in vol. 2 are central to the discussion, esp. nos. 112 and 561, but also nos. 2, 33, and 44.

notation is present. We need not argue here whether Paul had lived in Jerusalem during his young adulthood[57] – a point which I am, however, inclined to doubt. Paul's own usage of the term seems to point, as noted above, to a hereditary link with ancient Israel, for in Phil 3:5, Paul associates being a "Hebrew" with his descent from one of the twelve tribes of Israel.

The use of the term Ἰσραηλίται by Paul's missionary opponents as a self designation parallels the connotation of definition #1 of Ἐβραῖοι: they traced their ancestry to the Israel of Scripture, construed as God's chosen nation. The use of the third designation, σπέρμα Ἀβραάμ, recalls God's promise to Abram/Abraham, recounted in Gen 12–13 and 17, that God would give to Abraham and to his descendants the land of Canaan – which would later be called Israel, and that Abraham's posterity would be numerous: πᾶσαν τὴν γῆν, ἣν σὺ ὁρᾷς, σοὶ δώσω αὐτὴν καὶ τῷ σπέρματί σου ἕως τοῦ αἰῶνος. καὶ ποιήσω τὸ σπέρμα σου ὡς τὴν ἄμμον τῆς γῆς... "All the land which you see, I will give to you and to your offspring forever. And I will make your offspring like the sand of the sea ..." (Gen 13:15–16a). The promise to Abraham is recalled also in Lk 1:55, 73; Acts 3:25; Heb 11:12. As Oostendorp has suggested, the use of the phrase σπέρμα Ἀβραάμ – as well as the other two terms – probably served to distinguish the missionaries, who used these terms to refer to themselves, from the Gentile converts in the church at Corinth.[58] Such a distinction was probably drawn as part of a claim to authority on the part of these missionaries. Since they had a hereditary link to Israel's sacred traditions, these missionaries could claim to be bearers of authentic traditions, and therefore could feasibly wield this authority as they sought to institute a particular regime of praxis among the converts in Corinth.

The fact that in Acts 13:26, the descendants of Abraham[59] are distinguished from Gentile proselytes ("fearers of God") lends support to Oostendorp's view that the "two terms, Ἰσραηλίται and σπέρμα Ἀβραάμ, distinguish the apostles, not from Paul, but from the Gentile Christians at

---

[57] As argued by J. Murphy-O'Connor in *Paul: A Critical Life*, 52–70, and repeated in *Paul: His Story* (Oxford and New York: Oxford University Press, 2004) 7–16.

[58] "If the opponents were convinced that Jesus as the Christ had established the priority of Israel, then it is in the power of this Messiah that they must treat the Gentiles harshly for their former sinfulness or at least remind the Gentiles of their second-rate position in the kingdom of Christ as far as righteousness is concerned because of their ignorance of the law" (*Another Jesus*, 56). Oostendorp's view may seem to impute to Paul's opponents a less than salutary evangelistic approach toward the Gentiles! The "Jewish priority" claimed by Paul's opponents may, however, have served the purpose of legitimating their claims to authority over the Gentile converts.

[59] Υἱοὶ γένους Ἀβραάμ, lit. "sons of the family of Abraham" is synonymous with the more common designation, σπέρμα Ἀβραάμ, "seed" or "offspring" of Abraham.

Corinth."[60] We may add that the use of the term Ἑβραῖοι serves the same function. Oostendorp draws attention to the connection of 11:22–23 with the preceding section, in which Paul appears to be caricaturing the activities of his rivals with the following comment: "You put up with it if someone enslaves you, if someone devours you, if someone grasps, if someone is presumptuous, if someone slaps you in the face." It is not necessary to delineate precisely the significance of each of these phrases here; it is enough to indicate that the terms καταδουλοῦν ("to enslave") and ἐπαίρεσθαι ("to be presumptuous, to put on airs") alone suggest that Paul's rivals have claimed some sort of authority over the Corinthians. The link between v. 20 and the following claims in vv. 22–23 is provided by 21b: ἐν ᾧ ἄν τις τολμᾷ, ἐν ἀφροσύνῃ λέγω, τολμῶ κἀγώ ("In whatever someone is bold – I speak foolishly – I, too, am bold"). Verse 21b indicates that what follows constitutes the ground for the missionaries' boldness in their claims: they are Hebrews, Israelites, and descendants of Abraham. It is these qualities that provide them with the ideological basis for the authority over the Corinthians to which they are able to lay claim. Oostendorp refers to this claim to legitimacy as a "misuse of Jewish privileges,"[61] although he provides no rationale that would explain why the missionaries would emphasize these claims. In light of the progression that is evident between v. 20 and vv. 22–23, it seems likely that these claims were invoked in order to undergird the missionaries' status as authoritative emissaries (διάκονοι) of Christ. Paul accepts the thesis that one's status as a Hebrew, Israelite, and offspring of Abraham does indeed legitimate one's claim to be an emissary of Christ (cf. the repeated use of κἀγώ), although he proceeds to argue, on the basis of the hardships that he has endured in the service of Christ, that he, as an emissary of Christ, provides a service that is superior to that of his opponents (11:13b–33).

On the basis of their claim to be Hebrews, Israelites, and Abraham's descendants, it appears that the missionaries had proposed to institute some regime of praxis upon the Corinthians – a regime which Paul brands as a form of enslavement (εἴ τις ὑμᾶς καταδουλοῖ)! We will query the form that this regime of praxis may have taken later in this chapter.

---

[60] The quote continues, "The main thrust of their Jewish claims is not to prove that they are legitimate apostles of Christ ... but to impress upon the Corinthians that they have a superior position as members of the nation of Israel and heirs of the Old Testament promises" (*Another Jesus*, 12–13). Oostendorp's general thesis that Paul's opponents promote a gospel that involves "Jewish Christian superiority" is lacking in that he can produce no compelling reason that would explain why the missionaries would have emphasized this superiority.

[61] *Another Jesus*, 13.

3.2.1. Were the missionaries in Corinth emissaries of the Jerusalem church?

The thesis that Paul's opponents in Corinth were emissaries of the Jerusalem church was propounded by Baur and later advocated by Käsemann. It was accepted in a slightly modified form by Barrett, who reasoned that any emissary who was beyond the reach of the authority who sent him was free to misrepresent that authority. According to Barrett, this is exactly what happened in the case of the missionaries in Corinth: by accepting "a veneer of non-Jewish practice ... [and by] adopting a gnostic framework of thought and the ecstatic accompaniments of pagan religion," they misrepresented the actual position of the Jerusalem church, which taught that Gentile converts must accept "at least certain basic legal requirements."[62] The basic thesis of Baur and Käsemann that Paul's missionary opponents had some institutional ties with the Jerusalem church has been held in some form by most recent commentaries.

Four main arguments are regularly adduced in support of the thesis that Paul's missionary opponents had institutional ties with the Jerusalem church. These arguments concern the issue of letters of recommendation that arises in 2 Cor 3; the discussion of missionary territory that arises in 10:12–18; Paul's discussion of the ὑπερλίαν ἀπόστολοι ("super-apostles") in chapters 11–12; and the issue of apostolic maintenance that arises in 2 Cor 12.

3.2.2. Argument #1: Letters of Recommendation

Paul's missionary rivals had apparently produced letters of recommendation when they arrived in Corinth.[63] Paul creates an argument in 2 Cor 3 in which he attempts to persuade the Corinthian congregation to avoid making the natural inference that, since Paul at the time of his introduction to the Corinthians had produced no letter of recommendation, he was inferior as an apostle to the newly-arrived missionaries, who had been able to produce such letters.

Both Käsemann and Barrett have followed the thesis of Baur, who used the fact that the missionaries produced letters of recommendation to argue that these missionaries had been commissioned by the authorities of the Jerusalem church. Who else, these scholars have argued, would have been able to produce a letter endowed with such authority as to cause the Corinthians to question their loyalty to Paul?

However, letters of recommendation were commonly written on behalf of members of the early Christian movement. Such letters were written not

---

[62] "Paul's Opponents," 82.

[63] So Sumney, on the basis of 3:1b (*'Servants of Satan'*, 83–84).

only by the Jerusalem church (cf. Acts 15:23–29), but also quite commonly, outside of it. Acts 18:27 indicates that the church at Ephesus provided a letter of recommendation for Apollos when he planned to travel to Achaia. Second Corinthians 3:1 indicates that the Corinthians both received and wrote letters of recommendation on behalf of traveling missionaries. Paul included within his own letters recommendations on behalf of his "fellow workers" in the gospel. In Rom 16:1–3, Paul recommends Phoebe, his own patroness from Cenchrae, to the church at Rome. Jerry Sumney draws the correct conclusion from these data:

[T]here is no indication in [2 Cor 3:1] that the letters were from authorities, much less from Jerusalem ... So, we cannot say who wrote these letters, only that they gave these preachers a favorable hearing upon their arrival.[64]

3.2.3. Argument #2: The Discussion of Missionary Territory in 10:12–18

C. K. Barrett has argued that 2 Cor 10:12–18 alludes to the results of the Jerusalem council, in which Paul and the "pillar apostles" in Jerusalem agreed that Peter would be concerned with the apostolic mission to the Jews, Paul with that to the Gentiles (cf. Gal 2:6–9). Barrett correctly identifies the major theme in 10:12–18 as that of apostolic territory: who is able to lay claim to a particular area as his own missionary sphere. Barrett points to language that indicates Paul's interest in indicating a geographical boundary for his ministry, as well as that of others:

The words ἐφικέσθαι ἄχρι καὶ ὑμῶν point clearly to the extension of Paul's mission in space ... In view of these facts it is better to take κανών in the sense of limit or boundary, and thus of measured space ... [T]he geographical bounds of [Paul's] apostleship are such as to include Corinth ...[65]

Subsequently Barrett outlines the main questions that Paul addresses in the section, and proceeds to assert the existence of a link between 2 Cor 10:12–18 and Gal 2:1–10:

Within whose area of apostolic ministry does Corinth fall? Whose work has justified itself (in Corinth, for example) in the creation of new churches, and not in a mere facade of boasting about the achievements of others? Whose ministry shows the true marks of apostleship? It is impossible to state these questions without calling to mind Gal 2.1–10, where there is not only a mutual recognition of apostolic ministries but also an agreed division of apostolic labour. Paul is to go to the Gentiles, Cephas to the Jews. This was an agreement the practice of which was bound to cause difficulty because there were few places that were purely Jewish or purely Gentile in population, and there is no reason to be surprised that trouble of precisely this kind arose in Corinth.[66]

---

[64] *'Servants of Satan'*, 83-84.
[65] "Christianity at Corinth," 18; cf. also "Paul's Opponents," 65.
[66] "Christianity at Corinth," 18–19.

At this point, Barrett introduces a plausible, but subtly misleading link between 2 Cor 10:12–18 and Gal 2:1–10. After Barrett had correctly pointed out the geographical import of Paul's language in 10:12–18, he then proceeds to undermine this interpretation by introducing a very different (i.e., non-geographical) mode of apportioning apostolic territory, the ethnic division between Jew and Gentile. Perhaps Barrett failed to see the contradiction inherent in implying that the Jerusalem agreement included a geographical component, even when "there were few places that were purely Jewish or purely Gentile in population." There is no indication that the Jerusalem agreement, as Paul formulates in Gal 2:1–10, included any geographical component; the division of apostolic labor described there consists entirely of an ethnic division between Jew and Gentile.

Barrett's exegesis was partially correct; he correctly pointed out the geographical component involved in the section. However, there is no evidence in this section that would validate his construction of a link between 2 Cor 10:12–18 and Gal 2:1–10, the latter of which makes no mention of, and may perhaps even logically exclude, any geographical division. Barrett's faulty linkage of the section with the Jerusalem agreement resulted in his failure to recognize an important aspect of Paul's discussion: the temporal element. By including this element in our discussion, we can arrive at a clearer picture of Paul's intention in writing the section, which will in turn aid us in our reconstruction of the profile of Paul's missionary opponents.

Barrett correctly pointed to the geographical element involved in Paul's assignation of responsibility for missionary territory. In 10:13, Paul clearly claims Corinth within the geographical sphere which God had assigned to him: ἡμεῖς δὲ οὐκ εἰς τὰ ἄμετρα καυχησόμεθα ἀλλὰ κατὰ τὸ μέτρον τοῦ κανόνος οὗ ἐμέρισεν ἡμῖν ὁ θεὸς μέτρου, ἐφίκεσθαι ἄχρι καὶ ὑμῶν ("But we will not boast without limits; nevertheless (we will boast) in accordance with the measure of the assignment,[67] which measure[68] God had appor-

---

[67] So *BDAG* glosses κανών (category #2). Incidentally, *DBAG* appears to have miscited the reference in Anacleto de Oliveira, *Die Diakonie der Gerechtigkeit und der Versöhnung in der Apologie des 2. Korintherbriefes* (Münster: Aschendorff; 1990). The reference should be corrected to n. 294, pp. 139–140. De Oliviera argues that the term κανών should not be understood as a reference to the "geographische Umgrenzung des apostolischen Missionsgebiets ("geographical boundary of the territory of the apostolic mission"). Even if we agree, however, that lexically, κανών does not itself refer to a geographical boundary, this certainly does not imply that the context does not otherwise indicate one. The comments of E. A. Judge regarding the use of the term κανών in a bilingual inscription from Burdur are apropos: "The κανών in itself is not a geographical concept, but the services it formulates are in this case geographically partitioned" (G. H. R. Horsley, ed., *New Docs* 1:45).

tioned to us, so that we reached as far even as you." Paul refers to the spatial boundaries of his ministry again in Rom 15:19 and 24. Paul avers that he has preached through the areas from Jerusalem to Illyricum (modern Albania) and declares his wish to proceed westward to Spain. In antiquity, the Straits of Gibraltar were thought to have marked the westernmost point of the known world.[69] Clearly, Paul had an expansive view of what constituted his missionary territory. His "assignment" (κανών), as he refers to the extent of his missionary territory here, includes the entire region north of the Mediterranean, extending west to the edge of the known world!

In addition to the geographical component of Paul's missionary mandate, as he saw it, Paul also emphasized an ideology in which temporal priority played a crucial role. Paul view of missionary activity was that it should be conducted in regions which had not previously received exposure to the "gospel." Paul clearly espouses this view in Rom 15:20–21, which states in part: "Thus I make it my ambition to proclaim the good news, not where Christ has already been named, so that I do not build on someone else's foundation ..." (NRSV). In Paul's view, the missionary who first introduced the gospel within a given locale maintained a primary claim to authority there. Paul uses the metaphor of "laying a foundation" to refer to the preaching activity of the first missionary to arrive in a given location (1 Cor 3:10-15; Rom 15:20b). In 1 Cor 4:14–15, Paul uses a different metaphor. Here he constructs his relationship to the members of the Corinthian church as that of a father to his children. In light of the contrast between "father" and "caretakers" (παιδαγωγοί), it is evident that here, too, Paul is concerned with the issue of apostolic priority. By implication Apollos, who arrived after Paul in Corinth, is reduced to the level of "caretaker," while Paul retains the privileged role as "father" of the Corinthians.

The two issues of geographic extent and temporal priority in respect to missionary activity assume an important role in 2 Cor 10:12–18. In v. 13b, as we have seen, Paul alludes to the geographical extent of his missionary activity. In the phrases, τὸ μέτρον τοῦ κανόνος οὗ ἐμέρισεν ἡμῖν ὁ θεὸς

---

[68] The syntax of this phrase is difficult. This translation assumes that οὗ refers to μέτρον as its antecedent, but has been attracted to the case of the immediately preceding κανόνος; at the end of the phrase Paul added μέτρου in an attempt to clarify the antecedent of the relative pronoun. This explanation is offered by *BDF* 294.5.

[69] Cf. P. S. Alexander, art. "Geography and the Bible (Early Jewish Geography)," *ABD* 2:977-988. Hanno the Carthaginian's account of the circumnavigation of Africa was significant in part because he explored the regions "beyond the Pillars of Hercules" (i.e., the Straits of Gibraltar). Hanno's account appears in *Periplus: or, Circumnavigation (of Africa): Greek text with facing English translation, commentary, notes and facsimile of Codex palatinus Gr. 398*; Al. N. Oikonomides, ed. (Chicago, IL: Ares Publishers, 1995).

μέτρου, ἐφικέσθαι ἄχρι καὶ ὑμῶν ("the measure of the assignment, which assignment God has apportioned, so that we have reached as far as even you"), Paul alludes to the spatial dimension of his missionary "assignment," as is evident both from the verb of motion ἐφικέσθαι ("to reach, come upon") as well as the preposition ἄχρι, which is a "marker of extension up to a certain point" (and glossed "as far as").[70] Paul continues his apology: οὐ γὰρ ὡς μὴ ἐφικνούμενοι εἰς ὑμᾶς ὑπερεκτείνομεν ἑαυτούς, ἄχρι γὰρ ὑμῶν ἐφθάσαμεν ἐν τῷ εὐαγγελίῳ τοῦ Χριστοῦ ("for we did not overextend ourselves as though we had not reached you; for we reached as far as you with the gospel of Christ"). In this passage, Paul continues to employ spatial language (ἐφικέσθαι εἰς ὑμᾶς: "to reach you"; ὑπερεκτείνειν ἑαυτός: "to overextend oneself"; φθάνειν ἄχρι ὑμῶν: "to reach as far as you"), but also introduces a temporal distinction. Paul introduces the temporal distinction subtly, almost slyly. In stating that Paul had not "overextended himself as though he had not reached" Corinth, Paul implies his criterion of temporal priority in apostolic mission: the apostle who reaches an area first, claims the right of authority over those whom he evangelizes there. The implication in this passage is that Paul's missionary rivals,[71] who had not reached the Corinthians (the ordinal "first" is implied!), had "overextended" themselves; that is, by intruding in a missionary area that Paul, by virtue of having been the first to evangelize, claimed as his own.[72] Also, Paul's use of the verb φθάνειν in v. 14 introduces an ambiguity: did Paul intend this verb to be read as a synonym of ἐφικέσθαι ("to reach" a point in space), or did he instead refer to the act of reaching Corinth prior to his opponents ("to precede")? Either of these two senses is possible for the verb φθάνειν, and both positions have their defenders.[73] It may be, however, that Paul intentionally chose this term precisely because of its ambiguity: with it, Paul is able at once to hint at both the spatial and temporal aspects of his ideology of missionary territorial claims.

Paul continues in vv. 15–16:

---

[70] *DBAG*, s.v., #2.

[71] Note that the contrast between Paul and his rivals, which had been stated in 10:12, continues in vv. 13–18, as the contrastive use of the personal pronoun and conjunction in the phrase ἡμεῖς δέ indicates.

[72] Paul makes this claim even though there were members of the Jesus movement in Corinth prior to Paul's arrival, notably Priska and Aquila. According to Acts 18, Paul's innovation was that he persuaded the believers in Christ to organize regularly outside of their wonted synagogue venue.

[73] In favor of the connotation, "to reach": Furnish, *II Corinthians*, 472; in favor of "to precede": Martin, *2 Corinthians*, 322; Klauck, *2. Korintherbrief*, 81; Matera, *II Corinthians*, 228–229; Lambrecht, *Second Corinthians*, 166; Thrall, *II Corinthians* 2:648–649.

... not boasting beyond limits in the labors of others, but having hope, if your faith is increasing,[74] that we will be magnified[75] by you, to preach[76] abundantly in the lands[77] that lie beyond you, in accordance with our assignment,[78] so as not to boast[79] of things that have been accomplished in an assignment belonging to another.

οὐκ εἰς τὰ ἄμετρα καυχώμενοι ἐν ἀλλοτρίοις κόποις, ἐλπίδα δὲ ἔχοντες αὐξανο-μένης τῆς πίστεως ὑμῶν ἐν ὑμῖν μεγαλυνθῆναι κατὰ τὸν κανόνα ἡμῶν εἰς περισ-σείαν εἰς τὰ ὑπερέκεινα ὑμῶν εὐαγγελίσασθαι, οὐκ ἐν ἀλλοτρίῳ κανόνι εἰς τὰ ἕτοιμα καυχήσασθαι.

Paul states that he will not "boast in the labor of others," which very thing, by implication, Paul's rivals have done. The "labor" referred to here connotes activity in spreading the missionary message (cp. 1 Cor 3:8; 1 Thess 3:5).[80] Paul hopes to be "magnified" by the Corinthians. This phrase, like the earlier use of φθάνειν, involves a double entendre. The verb μεγαλύνω may involve the act of praising or speaking highly of someone – which, in light of the charges that Paul reports had been made against him,[81] is just the opposite of how Paul was being talked about in Corinth – or it may involve the enlargement of some physical entity,[82] namely, his missionary territory. By using this term, Paul implies two things at once: his hope that the Corinthians will praise, rather than slander[83] him, and his hope that

---

[74] The semantic import of the genitive absolute (αὐξανομένης τῆς πίστεως ὑμῶν) is difficult to interpret. While genitive absolute phrases usually carry a temporal nuance, they may also be used to convey any of the other adverbial nuances that may be conveyed by the circumstantial participle (Wallace, *GGBB* 655). Here it could indicate either cause, "because/since your faith is increasing," time, "while/as your faith ..." or even condition "if your faith ..." Both the causal and the temporal sense may be contraindicated by the fact that Paul is writing an apology here, and it is precisely the quality of the Corinthians' faith that is being questioned (cp. 13:5). The imputation of a conditional sense to the genitive absolute here could be taken as a challenge to indicate, by aiding Paul on further missionary journeys, that their faith – including their fidelity to Paul's authority and teaching – was in fact increasing.

[75] The infin. μεγαλυνθῆναι serves as the object of the phrase ἐλπίδα δὲ ἔχοντες in an indirect discourse construction.

[76] The translation assumes that εὐαγγελίσασθαι is an infin. of purpose.

[77] Supplying μέρη after the phrase τὰ ὑπερέκεινα ὑμῶν, with *DBAG*, s. ὑπερέκεινα.

[78] Understanding the phrase κατὰ τὸν κανόνα ἡμῶν as adverbial, modifying εὐαγγελίσασθαι.

[79] The verb καυχήσασθαι could be either an infin. of purpose or result.

[80] These passages are cited by Thrall, *II Corinthians* 2:649, n. 387, who in turn cites Hans Windisch.

[81] These charges included vacillation in his travel plans, the charge that Paul "walked according to the flesh" (both in 2 Cor. 1:17), and financial misconduct in the collection affair (7:2; 12:17–18), for example.

[82] Cp. *DBAG*, s.v.

[83] Cf. Paul's use of the terms καταλαλία ("slander") and ψιθυρισμός ("gossip") in 12:20.

they will help him to increase the limit of his missionary activity. The desired increase in Paul's missionary territory is mentioned in the following clause, κατὰ τὸν κανόνα ἡμῶν εἰς περισσείαν εἰς τὰ ὑπερέκεινα ὑμῶν εὐαγγελίσασθαι ("to preach abundantly in the regions beyond you in accordance with our assignment"). The infinitive εὐαγγελίσασθαι is subordinate to μεγαλυνθῆναι: Paul hopes to be "magnified" for the purpose of preaching the gospel (or with the result that he may preach the gospel) "in the regions beyond" Corinth. There is only the faintest hint here that Paul might rely on the Corinthians to fund this endeavor. It was in fact Paul's standard practice to receive financial support when he took leave of a given church in search of new missionary territory. After he had left Macedonia, Paul had received financial support from Philippi (2 Cor 11:8–9), and he intended to enlist the church at Rome in support of his effort to travel to Spain (Rom 15:24).[84]

Finally, Paul alludes again to the temporal aspect of his construction of missionary territory in v. 16b: οὐκ ἐν ἀλλοτρίῳ κανόνι εἰς τὰ ἕτοιμα καυχήσασθαι ("so as not to boast of things that have been accomplished in an assignment belonging to another"). Here Paul again mentions his own territorial "assignment," while at the same time demoting the work of missionaries who arrived in Corinth subsequent to Paul: these missionaries are able to boast only in "things that have been accomplished," in this instance by Paul himself. To this passage we may compare 1 Cor 3:5–15, in which Paul had dealt with the issue of his own priority to Apollos as a missionary to Corinth. In the latter passage Paul is very temperate, constructing his and Apollos' relationship as that of planter and waterer, foundation-layer and subsequent builder, respectively. Paul's temperance here is politic; he continued to have good relations with Apollos (cf. 1 Cor 16:12). In 1 Cor 4:15, however, Paul is less restrained: by virtue of his priority in Corinth, Paul is able to claim parental authority over the Corinthians (NRSV: "For though you might have ten thousand guardians in Christ, you do not have many fathers. Indeed, in Christ Jesus I became your father through the gospel.").

This exposition of 2 Cor 10:12–18 has been pursued, not so much to show that Paul was a master of insinuation and the double entendre, as to belie Barrett's assertion that "It is impossible to state [certain questions raised by this passage] without calling to mind Gal 2.1–10." As we have seen, it is quite possible to interpret 2 Cor 10:12–18 without recourse to Galatians or to the Jerusalem agreement. There are reasons to deny any

---

[84] Paul similarly conceals a financial request that the Romans fund his westward journey; he asks only that the Romans "send him on his way" (προπέμπω; Rom 15:24). "Sending someone on their way" according to *DBAG*, s.v., #2, involves providing "food, money ... means of travel, etc."

connection between the present passage and Gal 2:1–10. As Furnish notes, "The key word, *kanōn*, however, does not appear in Paul's account of the Jerusalem agreement (Gal 2:1–10), nor does anything here in 2 Cor 10 require us to think that Paul has that meeting specifically in mind."[85] We may add to Furnish's observations another: if Paul had meant to make reference to the Jerusalem agreement, it seems highly likely that he would have made reference to the foundational opposition upon which the agreement was made, that between Jew and Gentile (the agreement had been that Paul would preach to Gentiles, Peter to Jews). Yet nowhere does this opposition appear in 2 Cor 10:12–18. Rather than referring to any ethnic distinction, as we would have expected if Paul had been referring to the Jerusalem agreement, we encounter instead the geographical and temporal aspects of Paul's construal of a missionary's right to claim authority within a given area. The best parallels to this idea occur not in Gal 2:1–10, but in 1 Cor 3:5–15, in which Paul's authority vis-à-vis Apollos is outlined (Paul claims temporal priority) and Rom 15:17–29, in which Paul "boasts" about the extent of his missionary activity (including both geographical and temporal aspects). The parallels in 1 Cor 3 and Rom 15 constitute the necessary and sufficient "background" for a proper understanding of Paul's construction of missionary authority in 2 Cor 10:12–18. Barrett's suggestion that Paul in this passage refers to the Jerusalem agreement therefore must be rejected as groundless. If there is no reason to read 2 Cor 10:12–18 as though it referred to the Jerusalem agreement, this removes yet another plank in the argument that Paul's missionary opponents in 2 Corinthians stemmed from Jerusalem.

3.2.4. Argument #3: Concerning the "super-apostles"

Another argument that has been used to link Paul's missionary rivals in Corinth with the Jerusalem church is one first associated with the name of F. C. Baur, but which subsequently was championed by Käsemann and then by Barrett. Baur's thesis was that Paul's missionary rivals claimed the authority of Peter, and in fact had been sent to Corinth as a deputation of the Jerusalem church. Baur, Käsemann, and Barrett are able even to find references to the Jerusalem apostles in 2 Corinthians. The Jerusalem apostles are referred to as ὑπερλίαν ἀπόστολοι, "super-apostles." The designation "super-apostles," the argument goes, sounds a lot like Paul's designation for the Jerusalem apostles in Galatians, where he calls them "pillar apostles" and "those of repute," although with a tinge of sarcasm. In Paul's argument in 2 Corinthians, the "super-apostles" must be distinguished from the missionaries who have been sent to Corinth; these Paul refers to derisively as "servants of Satan." There are then two groups referred to in

---

[85] Furnish, *II Corinthians*, 472.

2 Corinthians 10–12: the Jerusalem apostles, whom Paul treats with respect, and the missionaries whom the Jerusalem apostles have sent to represent them in Corinth: these Paul refers to derisively.

The argument that the "super-apostles" and the 'Servants of Satan' should be distinguished in 2 Cor 10–13 has received criticism from R. Bultmann, in an article which responded to E. Käsemann's formulation of the thesis. In Bultmann's view, the difference between Paul's protests that he is not inferior to his opponents in 11:5 and 12:11, on the one hand, and his protest in 11:23 that he is in fact superior as an apostle of Christ, on the other, is to be attributed not to the thesis that Paul is describing his relationship with two distinct groups, but rather to "rhetorical intensification" ("rhetorische Steigerung").[86] In the sections preceding 11:23, Paul had asserted that he could boast of credentials equal to those of his opponents, arguing, "Are my opponents such-and-such? So am I" (κἀγώ; cf. 11:21b, 22). Bultmann agrees with Käsemann that in 11:21b, Paul is writing about the missionaries who had come to Corinth. In 11:23, however, Paul takes off his rhetorical gloves; here he asserts, "I am more so" (ὑπὲρ ἐγώ). In 11:23, Paul is not writing about a group different from that which he had been characterizing in 11:21b; rather it is at this point that Paul finally asserts his supremacy over them. The repeated use of κἀγώ ... κἀγώ ("So am I ... So am I") followed by ὑπὲρ ἐγώ ("I am more so") is a case of rhetorical intensification. Käsemann's hypothesis that Paul replies to two different groups here results in his failure to grasp Paul's rhetorical strategy.[87]

Whereas Käsemann had argued that there was an abrupt ("sprunghaft") transition between 11:4, which on Käsemann's reading concerns the rival missionaries in Corinth, and 11:5, which according to Käsemann concerns the Jerusalem apostles, Bultmann shows that both passages in fact refer to the same group. According to Bultmann, 11:1–4 concerns the rival missionaries (so Käsemann), as does v. 6. (Here Bultmann assumes without stating it that the Jerusalem apostles could not have been compared favorably with Paul on the basis of λόγος, public speech.) The intervening verse (verse 5) must also concern the rival missionaries. In this way, v. 6 may serve indirectly to explicate the identity of the ὑπερλίαν ἀπόστολοι in v. 5: they must have been impressive public speakers. Bultmann adduces a

---

[86] Bultmann, *Exegetische Probleme des zweiten Korintherbriefes* (Darmstadt: Wissenschaftliche Buchgesellschaft, 1963) 26.

[87] Christopher Forbes has also argued that only one group is alluded to under the titles "false apostles" and "super-apostles." Forbes claims that the recognition that Paul is speaking ironically when referring to the "super-apostles" "removes any necessity" for the distinction between the two designations ("Comparison, Self-Praise, and Irony: Paul's Boasting and the Conventions of Hellenistic Rhetoric," *NTS* 32 [1986] 1–30, esp. p. 17).

second argument: "12:11 shows that [in] the μηδὲν ὑστερηκέναι τῶν ὑπερλίαν ἀποστόλων of 11:5, the effectiveness of Paul is not affirmed in the abstract, but in view of the developments and actions in Corinth." The aorist tense of the verbs in 12:11 and 12 (ὑστέρησα, κατειργάσθη) indicate that Paul's past actions are being compared unfavorably with those of the group which had already been active in Corinth: the missionaries who had arrived in the city. One of the points of comparison was Paul's refusal to accept financial support from Corinth vis-à-vis the missionaries' willingness to accept it. Paul alludes to his refusal to accept support in a passage that concerns the ὑπερλίαν ἀπόστολοι in 12:11–13;[88] the same failure to accept support that he had mentioned earlier in connection with the ψευδαπόστολοι in 11:7–11, 12–13. This proves that the ὑπερλίαν ἀπόστολοι are identical with the ψευδαπόστολοι, who live at the expense of the community.

We may agree with Bultmann that it seems unlikely in the extreme that Paul would have mentioned the preaching activity of the arriving missionaries in 11:4, only to switch the referent of v. 5 without warning to the Jerusalem apostles, and then equally without warning revert to describing the missionary arrivals in v. 6. If v. 5 is to be understood within its present context, it can only be understood as a reference to the missionaries who had begun to preach in Corinth. Bultmann is also correct to point out the importance of the theme of apostolic support in this discussion. With the phrase, ἡμεῖς δὲ οὐκ εἰς τὰ ἄμετρα καυχησόμεθα, Paul contrasts his own boasting with that of a group introduced in 10:12 as those who ἐγκρῖναι ἢ συγκρῖναι ἑαυτούς τισιν τῶν ἑαυτοὺς συνιστανόντων (10:12). In 10:13–18, Paul insinuates that this group had "boasted beyond limits" by laying claim to evangelistic work that Paul had already done in Corinth. Implicit in this insinuation is an important point: the group referred to in the passage has arrived at Corinth subsequent to Paul's founding visit. They were boasting therefore in ἐν ἀλλοτρίοις κόποις; that is, in the work that had been done by Paul and (perhaps) his associates (v. 15). The element of Paul's temporal priority over the missionaries who had arrived subsequently is alluded to again in 11:4: εἰ μὲν γὰρ ὁ ἐρχόμενος ἄλλον Ἰησοῦν κηρύσσει ὃν οὐκ ἐκηρύξαμεν, ἢ πνεῦμα ἕτερον λαμβάνετε ὃ οὐκ ἐλάβετε, κτλ. Paul contrasts his aboriginal preaching with the subsequent preaching of the same group who in 10:12 had been characterized as engaging in self-comparisons, and who in v. 13, by insinuation, had been characterized as boasting beyond limits. These missionaries take Paul's unwillingness to accept financial support from the Corinthians (11:7–11) as an opportunity (ἀφορμή) for boasting (11:12); boasting that in receiving

---

[88] This seems to be the force of Bultmann's argument, even though he does not mention 12:13 specifically.

support from the Corinthians they fulfilled a long-standing missionary mandate that was reputed to have been established by Jesus himself. These boasters are in fact, according to Paul, ψευδαπόστολοι, ἐργάται δόλιοι, μετασχηματιζόμενοι εἰς ἀποστόλους Χριστοῦ (11:13). The practice of boasting, attributed by insinuation to those who engage in self-comparison in 10:12–13 and said to characterize the missionaries who had arrived in Corinth subsequent (11:4) to Paul in 11:12, brackets the mention of the ὑπερλίαν ἀπόστολοι in 11:5–6, in comparison with whom Paul appears to be ἰδιώτης τῷ λόγῳ. The fact that the mention of the ὑπερλίαν ἀπόστολοι is bracketed by discussions of the missionaries who had arrived in Corinth subsequent to Paul supports the thesis that the ὑπερλίαν ἀπόστολοι and the missionary arrivals were one and the same group. The fact that, in the same passage, Paul appears to be defending himself from a comparison (σύγκρισις) in which he fared badly (λογίζομαι γὰρ μηδὲν ὑστερηκέναι τῶν ὑπερλίαν ἀποστόλων), which is precisely the thrust of the bracketing material, in which the missionary arrivals employ comparison (10:12: ἐγκρῖναι, συγκρῖναι), and in particular comparisons of themselves with Paul on the basis of his refusal to accept support from Corinth (11:12), one can hardly see any reason to deny that the ὑπερλίαν ἀπόστολοι are indeed identical with the missionaries who had arrived in Corinth subsequent to Paul.

This conclusion receives some support from the grammar of 11:5. The verse reads, λογίζομαι γὰρ μηδὲν ὑστερηκέναι τῶν ὑπερλίαν ἀποστόλων. The NRSV translates this verse, "I think that I am not in the least inferior to *these* apostles," taking the definite article to be anaphoric. In Hellenistic as in classical Greek, it is standard practice that, when characters are first introduced in a narrative, they are introduced either with an indefinite pronoun, so for example, ἀνήρ τις ἦλθεν, "a certain man came," or through the omission of the article, ἀνὴρ ἦλθεν, "a man came." In light of this practice, it is unlikely that οἱ ὑπερλίαν ἀπόστολοι (with the article) in 11:5 is a group that is being newly introduced at this point in the narrative. The NRSV is probably right in taking the article as anaphoric. If so, then οἱ ὑπερλίαν ἀπόστολοι must be identical with the group that had introduced the "other Jesus, spirit, and gospel" in Corinth; they are "*these* apostles," who had already been introduced within the narrative prior to v. 5.

In light of these considerations, the assessment of Christopher Forbes, who argued that the epithet ὑπερλίαν ἀπόστολοι is to be taken ironically, commends itself. If one were to listen to that which Paul characterizes as their boasting, one would surely believe that these missionary arrivals were ὑπερλίαν ἀπόστολοι! Paul's intent in designating the incoming missionaries as ὑπερλίαν ἀπόστολοι is surely both ironic, inasmuch as Paul thinks that they are really not apostles at all, but emissaries of Satan who are disguised as such (11:13–15), and parodic, inasmuch as the designation parodies claims that these missionaries appear to have made about themselves. These missionaries had probably claimed that they were superior as apostles to Paul, who refused to accept support from the congregation – and the ability to demand support was, according to tradition, the "sign of an apostle." Other bases of comparison were certainly found: compared to the missionaries, Paul appeared to be ἰδιώτης τῷ λόγῳ ("untrained in public speaking"). Also, it is possible that the missionaries felt that they would do a better job than Paul in dealing with certain cases of immoral behavior in Corinth (so Oostendorp). In each of these cases, Paul fares worse in the comparison between himself and the rival apostles, so that he must defend himself by countering, "I am not less than they" – despite apparent evidence to the contrary. In the eyes both of the rival missionaries and of the Corinthian church, Paul was in fact the inferior apostle (if he was to be considered an apostle at all; cf. 1 Cor 9:2), while his missionary rivals were superior – ὑπερλίαν ἀπόστολοι.

Bultmann certainly has the better part of the argument with Käsemann. Not only does Käsemann's thesis that two distinct groups are referred to in the designations "false apostles" and "super-apostles" render a contextual interpretation of the passages in which the latter appear impossible, it fails to recognize the genius of Paul's discourse: using irony and parody, Paul attempts to ridicule not only his rivals' claims about their status and authority, but also the Corinthians' perception of the status of these missionaries vis-à-vis Paul. In the eyes of the Corinthians, Paul had not fared well in the comparison between him and his missionary opponents, either in terms of rhetorical presence or in terms of claims to apostolic authority. In these respects, Paul is the lesser, and his rivals the superior apostles. Paul's discourse, not only in 11:1–15, on which we have concentrated, but also through the end of the "Fool's Speech" in 12:13, attempts to persuade the Corinthians to reverse this assessment.

3.2.5. Argument #4: Apostolic support

The fact however, that the Paul's opponents adhered to the rule whereby missionaries were expected to receive room and board from the communities to which they preached, does indicate a link in terms of practice with the first disciples of Jesus (Mt 10:9–10). Does this then indicate a link between the Corinthian missionaries and Jerusalem? There is certainly a link in terms of missionary practice, for Paul attests that Cephas also followed the customary practice of accepting support from the communities that he visited (1 Cor 9:3–14). However, this practical link does not necessarily indicate that Paul's rivals in Corinth either came from Jerusalem or had any direct institutional ties with the church there. The practice of supporting missionaries was not in fact confined to Jerusalem; in 1 Cor 9:3–14 Paul seems to suppose that the Corinthians were already aware that other "apostles," including Cephas, received support from the communities that they visited.[89] The practice is attested also in the gospels of Mark and Matthew; the former written perhaps in Rome or more likely in Syria,[90] the latter perhaps in Syria, more specifically, in Antioch.[91] The practice is attested also in Luke, but the geographical origin of this gospel is even more problematic to establish than that of Mark and Matthew.[92] The practice remained alive at least until the end of the first century CE, as attested by the Didache (11:3–12), written in Syria or Palestine.[93] The practice of supporting missionaries was then known at least in Corinth and Syria, in addition to Palestine. Although the practice of supporting itinerant preachers probably originated with Jesus and was propagated by his first followers; the geographical distribution and early dissemination of this practice renders it dubious as a criterion for proving that the Corinthian missionaries either originated specifically from Jerusalem or claimed to act as representatives of that church. The practice seems rather to have been a common inheritance within the Christian movement from its earliest period.

3.2.6. Conclusion

We have now surveyed the evidence that has been used by scholars from Baur to Käsemann to Barrett (and beyond) in order to link Paul's missionary opponents in 2 Corinthians with the Jerusalem church. We have found that no such link is suggested in Paul's discussion of apostolic territory in 2 Cor 10:12–18, nor by the mention of "super-apostles" in chapters 10–13. The designation "super-apostles," contrary to the claims of Käsemann and others, does not refer to the Jerusalem "pillar apostles," but rather constitutes an ironic reference to the missionaries who had arrived in Corinth

---

[89] C. K. Barrett argues that Cephas had visited Corinth prior to Paul ("Cephas and Corinth" in *Essays on Paul*, 28–39). This is unlikely; otherwise Paul would have been unable to make his claim to having been the first "apostle" to visit the city.

[90] So Joel Marcus, *Mark 1–8: A New Translation with Introduction and Commentary* (AB 27; New York, NY and London, UK: Doubleday, 1999) 36.

[91] W. D. Davies and D. Allison hesitantly adopt this hypothesis in *The Gospel According to Saint Matthew*, Vol. 1 (ICC; Edinburgh: T&T Clark, 1988) 138–147.

[92] J. Fitzmyer writes: "As for the place of composition of the Lukan Gospel, it is really anyone's guess. The only thing that seems certain is that it was not written in Palestine" (*The Gospel According to Luke I–IX*; AB 28; Garden City, NY: Doubleday, 1981).

[93] So H. van de Sandt and D. Flusser, *The Didache: Its Jewish Sources and its Place in Early Judaism and Christianity* (Minneapolis, MN: Fortress and Assen, Netherlands: Royal Van Gorcum, 2002) 48–52.

subsequent to Paul, preaching "another Jesus, another spirit, and another gospel." We must conclude therefore that the evidence that has been adduced in support of the thesis that Paul's missionary opponents in Corinth had institutional ties with Jerusalem is insufficient to support such a claim.

3.3. Did the missionaries in Corinth preach, in contradistinction to Paul, that Gentile converts should follow the Torah?

In order to address this question cogently, three related issues must be addressed. Firstly, we must examine the connection, if any, between the preaching of Paul's rival missionaries in 2 Corinthians and the preaching of Paul's opponents who were addressed in Galatians. Secondly, we must ask whether Paul's language in 2 Corinthians suggests that Jewish law (here defined as the Torah) is a concern in 2 Corinthians. Thirdly, we must address the issue whether 2 Cor 3 may be used to draw any conclusions about the position of Paul's missionary opponents regarding the status of Jewish law.

3.3.1. Connections with Galatia?

As we have seen, Baur construed Paul's rivals in 2 Corinthians as emissaries of the Jerusalem church, similar to the ones whom Paul was supposed to have encountered in Galatia. These emissaries were representatives of the "Petrine wing" of early Christianity, which opposed Paul regarding the matter of whether converts should follow the Torah. Käsemann follows Baur in construing Paul's Corinthian opponents as espousing the necessity of adherence to the Torah. For Käsemann, the opponents' preaching amounted to a "nomistic falsification of the gospel." As we have seen, Käsemann believed, as Baur had, that Paul's opponents in 2 Corinthians had originated from Jerusalem. However, we have already demonstrated in the previous section that there is in fact no evidence that would allow us to assert the existence of any administrative links between Jerusalem and Paul's missionary opponents in Corinth.

Wilhelm Lütgert[94] argued against the Galatian connection by pointing out that the central issues of the debate, circumcision and observance of the law, were lacking in Corinth. This observation is apropos. None of the terms that were central to the Galatian controversy – ἀκροβυστία, νόμος, σάββατον – are present in 2 Corinthians. The issues that were at stake in Galatia were not those that were at stake in Corinth. If we are to assume that Paul's opposition in Galatia were emissaries of the Jerusalem

---

[94] *Freiheitspredigt und Schwarmgeister in Korinth: Ein Beitrag zur Charakteristik der Christuspartei* (BFCT 12.3; Gütersloh: Bertelsmann, 1908) 58–62.

church – although this point has recently been criticized[95] – then because there is no evidence that Paul's missionary opponents in Corinth were connected with Jerusalem, and because the concerns of Paul's Galatian opponents were distinct from those of his opponents in Corinth, we must reject the hypothesis of Baur, Käsemann and others that Paul's Corinthian opponents were identical with those whom he had encountered in Galatia. There is insufficient evidence to support such a hypothesis.

3.3.2. Did Paul's missionary opponents in Corinth advocate Torah observance?

The main evidence pertaining to this question comes from 2 Cor 3:1–4:6. However, there are different views as to the way in which the information contained in this section ought to be handled. Scholars typically have argued that Paul in this section is arguing in response to the preaching of his missionary opponents in Corinth, so that information pertaining to these opponents may be extracted (so Käsemann, Oostendorp). Jerry Sumney recently has argued that on methodological grounds, this section may not be used to extract information regarding Paul's opponents. We will recall that, according to Sumney, explicit statements yield the most certain information about Paul's opponents, while allusions in polemical and apologetic contexts yield a secondary source of data on Paul's opponents. Thus Sumney's first task is to determine whether a given passage may be labeled as polemical or apologetic, for it is primarily these contexts that yield data about Paul's opponents.

Sumney delineates 2 Cor 3:7–18 as a section that deserves special attention. Noting that Baur, Oostendorp, Georgi, and Friedrich identify the section as polemical, whereas other scholars have identified it as apologetic, Sumney defies this trend by asserting that the section is neither polemical nor apologetic, but didactic. Sumney makes the following argument regarding 3:7–18:

[The section] is clearly an explication of what it means to be a *minister* of the new covenant [which Paul had mentioned in 3:6]. Therefore it is best to identify this passage as didactic. It springs from comments of Paul rather than accusations or teachings of opponents. Paul is explaining the significance of the claim he makes for himself in 3:6.

---

[95] M. D. Nanos, *The Irony of Galatians: Paul's Letter in First-Century Context* (Minneapolis, MN: Fortress Press, 2002). Nanos argues that "the influencers are from Galatia too, that they are indigenous to the addressees' social world, and that they represent the interests and norms of the majority or dominant Jewish communities ... within which the addressees' Christ-believing groups function as Jewish subgroups" (p. 183). However, Nanos cannot be correct if Murphy-O'Connor's contention, that there were no Jews in northern Galatia at the time, holds true (*Paul: His Story*, 59).

We may note that R. P. Martin seems to share a similar evaluation of the significance of the passage when he states that "it is legitimate to see Paul's thought [in 3:7–18] soaring to embrace this far-reaching disquisition before returning to the local scene at Corinth ..."[96]

Is it true that 3:7–18 serves neither a polemical nor an apologetic function? Has Paul's soaring disquisition really taken wing so as to rise above the local scene at Corinth? Or has Paul crafted his discourse in such a way that the polemical and apologetic interests are veiled in this passage? Without going into any detail about the procedures involved in Paul's formulation of this discourse (which we reserve for chap. 5), we may point out that there are some indications that, contrary to the supposition of Sumney and Martin, Paul indeed intended for his audience to relate his disquisition on the two covenants to the "local scene at Corinth."

The first and most obvious argument is not probative, but suggestive: 3:7–18 is bracketed at the beginning by 3:1–6, in which Paul clearly defends himself against the charges that he lacks the sufficiency (ἱκανότης) to conduct a ministry (διακονία) which represents Christ (vv. 4–6), in part because he could not produce letters of recommendation (3:1–2) that would have offered some legitimation for his missionary activity. The passage in 3:7–18 is bracketed at the end by 4:1–4, where Paul admits that he preaches a "veiled gospel," but denies that this implies that he has "falsified the word of God." Because the section is bracketed by material in which Paul defends his ministry vis-à-vis that of rival missionaries, we may at least suspect that the intervening material may in some way relate to the local scene at Corinth, and that Paul may be responding to criticism in this passage.

The second argument is grammatical. In 4:1, Paul begins, "For this reason, because we have *this* ministry as we have received it as a gift ..." (διὰ τοῦτο, ἔχοντες τὴν διακονίαν ταύτην ...). The use of the demonstrative pronoun/adjective "this" (acc. ταύτην) is often used in Greek narrative to refer to a character – or here, the abstract concept διακονία – that was mentioned in a preceding section of the narrative,[97] and is sometimes referred to as "back-reference." L. Neeley notes that "back-reference often occurs at the beginning of a new paragraph,"[98] in order to link the paragraph with the discussion that has preceded. On this point, M. Thrall correctly points out that "'this ministry' refers to what has gone before"

---

[96] *2 Corinthians*, 61.

[97] See *DBAG*, οὗτος, for examples. The example of 2 Cor. 4:1 is listed in 2b, "pert. to an entity perceived as present or near in the discourse."

[98] Cited in S. H. Levinsohn, *Discourse Features of New Testament Greek* (2nd ed., Dallas: SIL International, 2000) 280.

within the narrative.[99] Far from constituting a departure from the theme of
the text that brackets it, 3:7–18 concerns Paul's ministry, the same ministry that Paul must defend in 4:1–4, as the use of the demonstrative adjective in 4:1 shows.

A third argument is suggested by Paul's statement in 3:12 that, in the
exercise of his ministry, he acted with complete candor (πολλῇ
παρρησίᾳ χρώμεθα).[100] That this statement serves as a response to criticism that Paul had received is confirmed by 4:1–3, in which Paul resumes
his denial: he did not act cunningly nor did he falsify the word of God.
This verse problematizes Sumney's labeling of the section in 3:7–18 as
didactic and his denial that it has an apologetic purpose. Clearly, there is a
demonstrable element of apology involved in this section.

A fourth argument is suggested by the fact that Paul's opponents apparently refer to themselves as διάκονοι (cf. 2 Cor 11:15). The use of this
term implies that they claimed to represent a διακονία – a term that appears in juxtaposition to Paul's "ministry of the spirit" in 3:7, and again in
v. 9. This suggests that Paul's comparison between his διακονία and that of
Moses may conceal within itself a comparison between Paul's ministry and
that of the rival missionaries in Corinth.

A fifth and final argument is suggested by the statement in 3:17,
οὗ δὲ τὸ πνεῦμα κυρίου, ἐλευθερία, "where the spirit of the lord (is), (is)
freedom." The use of the term ἐλευθερία suggests an opposition to the
actions of Paul's missionary rivals, who according to Paul had attempted
to enslave (καταδουλοῦν) the Corinthians (2 Cor 11:20).

In light of these five arguments, it becomes very difficult to dissociate
3:7–18 from its immediate context. Paul's statement in 3:12 suggests that
he is using his discussion of the "two ministries" in order to respond to
criticism and to establish his own "sufficiency" to serve as a minister of
the new covenant" (3:5–6). His use of the term διακονία – a term that is
also associated with his missionary opponents – suggests that his narrative
is not innocent of polemical intent. Paul's attempt to associate his own
"ministry of spirit" with "freedom" suggests a polemical formulation in
response to the ministry of his opponents, whom he will characterize in
11:20 as attempting to "enslave" the Corinthians. The strong likelihood
that this section is formulated to serve both apologetic and polemical interests opens the door for us to employ 3:7–18 in a reconstruction of the
position of Paul's missionary opponents. The question remains, however,
as to the best methodology to use in order to extract such information.

---

[99] *II Corinthians*, 1:298.
[100] Once again, the first person plural inflectional ending probably refers solely to
Paul.

Firstly, we must limit ourselves to information that may be gleaned without resorting to the method of "mirror exegesis," that is, assuming that Paul's opponents must have held a position diametrically opposed to that which Paul espouses in a particular section. In the absence of direct data regarding the position of Paul's opponents, it is difficult to know when Paul might be agreeing with, modifying, suppressing, mischaracterizing, or directly contradicting particular elements of his opponents' position. For this reason, the use of "mirror exegesis" has justly been avoided in recent scholarship on Paul. We may arrive at some data, however, based on Paul's own characterization of his opponents in other sections of 2 Corinthians. The data derived in this way may be filled out with reference to parallels from within the early Christian movement and other groups within early Judaism.

We have already seen that Paul's opponents referred to themselves as "Hebrews," "Israelites," and "descendants of Abraham." Each of these designations indicates an attempt to define themselves in terms of their links with the traditions of Israel's past. Based on this consideration, we would expect that such persons would have given some role to the Sinai tradition, which played a foundational role within the various theologies of Second Temple Judaism.

Paul's opponents referred to themselves as "ministers of righteousness" (διάκονοι δικαιωσύνης) in 11:15. "Righteousness" in Second Temple literature is often conceived as a legal construct: it consisted of acting in accordance with the Torah (Wis 2:11; Pss Sol 8:6–10). The use of this self-designation by Paul's missionary opponents may suggest that they advocated Torah-observance for Gentile converts to the early Christian movement.

Paul's statement that his missionary opponents had attempted to "enslave" (καταδουλοῦν) the Corinthians (11:20) implies that they had attempted to institute some regime of praxis within the community there. This verb occurs only twice in the entire NT; both usages are Paul's. The term appears also in Gal 2:4, where it refers to an attempt that had been made to "enslave" the Gentile converts to the Christian community at Antioch by compelling them to adhere to the precepts of the Torah, including circumcision. This usage suggests that the regime of praxis that Paul's missionary opponents had attempted to institute in Corinth may have included adherence to the Torah.

Further evidence that the missionaries had attempted to institute a regime of praxis in Corinth may be found in Paul's use of the term ἐλευθερία in 2 Cor 3:17. Paul uses the same term in the context of a discussion of whether Gentile converts to the early Christian sect should follow the Torah in Gal 5:1 and 13. In Gal 2:4, the two terms ἐλευθερία and καταδουλοῦν are juxtaposed; this is the only time that these terms occur together in the Pauline corpus. The fact that both of these terms occur in 2 Corinthians suggests that Paul has a similar situation in mind there. Probably, the regime of praxis with which, in Paul's terms, the rival missionaries had attempted to "enslave" the Corinthian converts, and with respect to which Paul recommended "freedom" as an alternative, was an attempt to institute Torah observance among the converts.

These examples exhaust the obvious data from 2 Corinthians. However, there is still comparative data to be considered. The comparative data falls into two categories: firstly, we may compare texts from the early Christian sect in which themes are dealt with which are similar to those broached in 2 Cor 3. In this way, we may hope to find some common ideological trends that may help us to make inferences about the position of Paul's opponents. Secondly, we may examine the ways in which similar themes are treated in other Jewish texts that are roughly contemporary with Paul's discussion. This may also help us to identify some common trends within Judaism that may allow us to make some inferences about the position of Paul's opponents.

3.3.3. The Law and Covenant Restoration in the NT and Early Judaism

We do not have to look far in the history of religions to find a close parallel to the profile that emerges of Paul's missionary opponents in Corinth. In the Gospel of Matthew we find "apostles," such as Paul's missionary opponents designated themselves (cf. 2 Cor 11:13), who were concerned to promote "righteousness," that is, behavior that corresponds with the precepts of the Torah (Mt 5:20; 6:1; 12:37; 21:32). These apostles preach a gospel (εὐαγγέλιον) concerning Jesus. Their proclamation will be empowered by the spirit (πνεῦμα; cf. Mt 10:20; 12:18). Here we may refer to Paul's notice that his opponents have preached a "gospel, Jesus, and spirit" that differed from that which Paul had preached (2 Cor 11:4). The Matthean missionaries are enjoined to "instruct all the Gentiles" (or "nations"; Mt 28:19), which very thing Paul's missionary opponents at Corinth were doing, just indeed as Paul was. The Matthean missionary mandate includes also the injunction to "teach them to adhere to everything that [Jesus] has commanded"; which would certainly have included Jesus' instructions in the Sermon on the Mount (Mt 5–7) that his followers should be obedient to the law of Moses, not only in action, but also in thought and intention. In an important passage in Matthew's gospel, Jesus states (5:17–20):

Do not think that I have come to abolish (καταλῦσαι) the law or the prophets; I have not come to abolish but to fulfill. Truly I say to you, neither a single *yod* nor a single serif will pass away from the law, until all things have taken place. Therefore whoever loosens one of the least of these commandments and teaches others to do so, will be designated least in the kingdom of the heavens; but whoever does and teaches (the law) will be designated great in the kingdom of the heavens. Indeed, I say to you that if your right-eousness does not abound more than that of the scribes and Pharisees, you will by no means enter the kingdom of the heavens.

The Gospel of Matthew here teaches that members of the Jesus movement are to follow Pharisaic halakhah – but they are to do so even better than the Pharisees themselves do! In Matthew's gospel, Jesus is to a certain extent presented as a new Moses, preaching a radicalized version of the Mosaic law (chaps. 5–7) from a mountainside, reminiscent of Moses' delivery of the Torah to Israel.[101] In the series of antitheses in Mt 5:21–48, Jesus proclaims time after time, "You have heard it said ... but I say to you ..." In several of these antithesis, Jesus recites commandments from the law of Moses, and then asserts that it is not only the commission of the prohibited act, but even the desire to engage in such an act, that renders one liable to divine punishment. Matthew's gospel includes a missionary mandate that missionaries should go and "instruct all the Gentiles (πάντα τὰ ἔθνη), teaching them to observe all that I have commanded them" (διδάσκοντες αὐτοὺς τηρεῖν πάντα ὅσα ἐνετειλάμην ὑμῖν). The lan-guage used in this formulation is legal: even the Gentiles here are in-structed "to observe" (τηρεῖν) that which Jesus has "commanded" (ἐντέλλομαι), including his injunction to follow the Torah even more scru-pulously than the Pharisees.

Margaret Thrall has already suggested a link between the preaching of the missionaries whom Paul opposed in Corinth and the theology propa-gated in the Gospel of Matthew. The verbal parallels between the language which Paul associates with his missionary rivals in Corinth and that in the Gospel of Matthew are certainly strong. As Thrall notes, this does not mean that Paul's opponents in Corinth espoused a fully developed Matthean theology. However, it may support the thesis that Paul's mis-sionary opponents advocated that Gentile converts adhere to the precepts of the Torah, and it may support the thesis that those same missionaries included favorable references to Moses in their preaching.

A second example from within the early Christian movement is offered by the Letter to the Hebrews. Here we have a sustained discussion of some of the same themes that Paul discusses in 2 Corinthians 3. Like 2 Cor 3, Hebrews comments on the glory of Moses, comparing it unfavorably with the glory of Jesus. Like 2 Cor 3, Hebrews offers a reflection on the char-acter of the new covenant. Unlike 2 Corinthians, however, Hebrews does not attempt to dissociate the new covenant from its legal basis; the cove-nant in Hebrews, as in Israel's scripture, is predicated upon the fulfillment

---

[101] Dale Allison, *The New Moses: A Matthean Typology* (Minneapolis, MN: Augsburg Fortress, 1993).

of the law. Hebrews' treatment of the law however, is nuanced, and requires discussion.

The central text on the new covenant is in Hebrews 8. Below I quote verses 8–13, according to the translation of C. Koester.[102] In the quotation, the italicized words are themselves a quotation from Jer 31:31–34, which constitutes the central scriptural locus from which the idea of the new covenant was derived.

> But now [Jesus] has received a ministry that is superior to the same extent that he is also a mediator of a superior covenant, which has been lawfully established upon superior promises.
>
> Now if that first [covenant] were faultless, no place would be sought for a second. For finding fault with them, he says, *Behold, the days are coming, says the Lord, when I will complete with the house of Israel and with the house of Judah a new covenant, not like the covenant that I made with their forebears in the day when I took hold of their hand to bring them out of the land of Egypt, because they did not remain in my covenant, and I paid no attention to them, says the Lord. For this is the covenant that I will establish with the house of Israel after those days, says the Lord: Putting my laws into their mind, I will even write them on their hearts, and I will be their God and they shall be my people, and no one shall teach his fellow citizen and no one his brother, saying, "Know the Lord," because they shall all know me, from the least to the greatest of them, for I will be merciful toward their unrighteous deeds and I will not remember their sins anymore.* In speaking of a new covenant, he has made the first one obsolete. And what is becoming obsolete is also old and near obliteration.

It is striking that Hebrews quotes the Jeremianic oracle in full. We will remember that, although the Damascus Document mentions the "new covenant," it does not quote the Jeremianic text from which it was probably derived. The Dead Sea sect would have had good reason to omit a large portion of the oracle: one of the oracle's central contentions is that, when the new covenant is established, it will be "written on the hearts" of the people, so that they will have no further need to study the Torah. According to the oracle, when the new covenant is established, everyone will know and follow the Torah without being taught or exhorted to do so ("no one shall teach his fellow citizen ... because they shall all know me"). In the parlance of Jeremiah, "knowing the Lord" is actualized by knowing the Torah. The intensive study of the Torah with which the members of the sect were engaged contradicted the oracle's contention that such activity would no longer be necessary when the new covenant was established.

Of course the addressees of the Letter to the Hebrews had their own problems in actualizing Jeremiah's Torah-based, utopian vision. According to the oracle, God will write the Torah upon the minds and hearts of his

---

[102] *Hebrews: A New Translation with Introduction and Commentary* (Anchor Bible commentary series 36; New York and London: Doubleday, 2001) 8. I will cite Hebrews according to Koester's translation in the following discussion.

people; the result is that they will thereafter conduct themselves according to the precepts of the Torah unfailingly. Thereupon God forgives the people's former transgressions ("I will not remember their sins anymore"). Since the Jeremianic new covenant is inscribed upon the very will of the people, there is no question of its being disobeyed. This poses an interesting problem for the audience of Hebrews, for whom sin – transgression of the Torah – continued to pose a problem. Hebrews warns (6:4–6):

> For it is impossible to restore to repentance those who have once been enlightened, who have tasted the heavenly gift and become partakers of the Holy Spirit, who have tasted the good word of God and the powers of the age to come, but who then fall away, since they crucify the Son of God to themselves and make a spectacle of him.

"Repentance" in Hebrews retains its traditional Jewish connotations: it involves eschewing conduct that is construed as not corresponding to the law, and a concomitant adoption of practices that are set forth in the Torah. This is confirmed by the use of agricultural metaphors that follow in 6:7–8, which constitutes traditional imagery associated with conduct befitting God's people (Mt 3:10; 13:24–30 and 36–43). In 6:1, repentance is said to take place "from dead works" (ἀπὸ νεκρῶν ἔργων). The use of the preposition ἀπό, "from" here probably encodes a directional metaphor – one turns "away from" dead works, and at the same time, adopts a perspective of "faith toward God" (πίστις ἐπὶ θεόν). The "dead works" from which one is instructed to repent are constituted by sins,[103] actions in violation of the Torah, for which one will be held responsible at the last judgment (cf. 10:26–30). Those who repent from "dead works" however, become "enlightened" (φωτισθέντες), and "become partakers of the holy spirit ... and taste ... the powers of the age to come." The connection between repentance from actions in violation of the Torah and the reception of the holy spirit takes us into an ideological complex that is familiar from the Hebrew Bible as well as Second Temple Judaism.

3.3.4. Spirit and Covenant Renewal: Traditional Associations

The connection between "spirit/holy spirit" and the restoration of the covenant had already been firmly established within Judaism, and even earlier within the Hebrew Bible itself. We have already discussed Jeremiah's oracle on the new covenant, but a brief summary is in order here. According to Jeremiah, the "new covenant" that God promises to establish with Israel is one which, unlike the Mosaic covenant, will have no possibility of being broken. This is because, under the conditions of the new covenant, God will "put [his] law within them, and [he] will write it upon their hearts" (Jer 31:33). That is, the law will be inscribed within

---

[103] So convincingly Koester, *Hebrews*, 304.

human intentionality, such that God's will becomes that of his people. The result will be that God's people become characterized by perfect obedience to the law, which is inscribed within their very being. Consequently there will be no need even to teach the law; it will have become an intrinsic part of the psyche of God's people (31:34). At the time at which the covenant is renewed, God forgives past transgressions (v. 34). The Jeremianic construction of the "new covenant" became the foundational narrative for later Jewish and Christian understandings of the phenomenon.

Like the Book of Jeremiah, Ezekiel relies on covenantal theology in construing the exile that ensued after the Babylonians sacked Jerusalem and carried away captives in 586 BCE as the result of the people's failure to adhere to the stipulations of the Mosaic covenant. The prophet imagines a remedy to this problem which is similar to that found in Jeremiah (Ezek 36:26–27):

A new heart I will give you, and a new spirit (רוח חדשה) I will put within you; and I will remove from your body the heart of stone and give you a heart of flesh. I will put my spirit (רוחי) within you, and make you follow my statutes (ועשיתי את אשר תלכו בחקי) and be careful to observe my ordinances (NRSV).

In this passage, a remedy for covenantal transgression is provided: God provides a new spirit for the people, by putting his own spirit within them. The "spirit" and "heart" that had formerly allowed the people to disobey the precepts of the law will be replaced by a new spirit and heart; in this way God will see to it that the people obey the Torah (NRSV's "I will ... make you follow my statutes").[104]

The connection between spirit and covenant renewal is also affirmed by the Book of Jubilees, which states (1:22–25a):

The Lord said to Moses: 'I know their contrary nature, their way of thinking, and their stubbornness. They will not listen until they acknowledge their sins and the sins of their ancestors. After this they will return to me in a fully upright manner and with all (their) minds and all (their) souls. I will cut away the foreskins of their minds and the foreskins of their descendants' minds. I will create a holy spirit for them (*wa-'efaṭṭer lomu manfasa qeddusa*) and will purify them in order that they may not turn away from me from that time forever. Their souls will adhere to me and to all my commandments. They will perform my commandments. I will become their father and they will become my children. All of them will be called children of the living God.'[105]

As the context makes clear, this was an oracle that was expected to be fulfilled during the eschatological age (cf. 1:27–29). Although covenant

---

[104] This example as well as those that follow are suggested by Lars Hartman in his excellent study, *'Into the Name of the Lord Jesus': Baptism in the Early Church* (Edinburgh: T&T Clark, 1997) 11–12.

[105] Translation of J. VanderKam, *The Book of Jubilees*, 5. VanderKam's critical text appears in the companion volume, *The Book of Jubilees: A Critical Text*.

renewal is not mentioned per se, it is clearly implied: the people are to "acknowledge their sins" and return to God, so that they "adhere to [God] and to all [God's] commandments." At that time, the people are adopted once again as God's children, signaling that the covenant is reestablished. As in Ezekiel, God is the active agent in bringing about a reordering of human intention so that God's people might obey the Torah. God circumcises the "minds" of his people, creates a "holy spirit" for them and purifies them. The result of this transformation is similar to that envisioned in Ezekiel and Jeremiah: perfect obedience to the Torah.

The Community Rule from among the Dead Sea scrolls also links the spirit with the capacity of humans to adhere perfectly to the Torah during the eschatological age. The following quote from 1QS 4:18b–23a makes predictions about the purification of humans that will take place at the time of the פקודה, or "visitation": the time when God will judge the wicked and reward the faithful.

But God, in his mysterious understanding and his glorious wisdom, has set an end for the existence of deceit (עולה). At the appointed time of visitation he will destroy it forever. Then truth will appear forever (in) the world, which has polluted itself by the ways of ungodliness during the dominion of deceit until the appointed time for judgment which has been decided. Then God will purify (יברר) by his truth all the works of man and purge (יזקק) for himself the sons of man. He will utterly destroy the spirit of deceit from the veins of his flesh. He will purify him by the Holy Spirit (ברוח קודש) from all ungodly acts and sprinkle upon him the Spirit of Truth like waters of purification, (to purity him) from all the abominations of falsehood and from being polluted by a spirit of impurity, so that upright ones may have insight into the knowledge of the Most High and the wisdom of the sons of heaven, and the perfect in the Way may receive understanding. For those God has chosen for an eternal covenant (ברית עולמים), and all the glory of Adam (כול כבוד אדם) shall be theirs without deceit.[106]

The term "deceit" refers to all manner of halakhic transgressions: "slackness in righteous activity ... unclean worship ... blasphemy, ... [and] walking in all the ways of darkness" (1QS 4:9–11). As was the case in Ezekiel, the Community Rule speaks of a transformation of humans that is to take place at the time of the "visitation." At this time, humans will either be destroyed or purified "from all ungodly acts ... [and] from all the abominations of falsehood"; acts that would include the violation of civic as well as cultic legal precepts. The instrument of the purification is described as the "holy spirit."[107] The "holy spirit" in 1QS however, has a dual signifi-

---

[106] This translation as well as that those that follow are by J. Charlesworth, *PTSDSSP* 1. The passage cited appears on p. 19.

[107] Depending on how the text is vocalized, one could translate the phrase ברוח קודש either as "by a spirit of holiness" or "by the spirit of holiness." Charlesworth's translation understands the genitive as attributive, and assumes the determinate vocalization, *bāruăḥ kōdesh*, "by the Holy Spirit." In light of the phrase ברוח קדושה, "by the/a

cation: it refers at once to a spiritual or angelic presence who inspires humans to conduct themselves in accordance with the Torah (cf. 3:24–4:8), but at the same time to the set of beliefs and dispositions that manifest themselves within the practices of the community.[108] The two significations however, are complementary: an angelic presence empowers the members of the community to embody the righteous practices envisioned in its halakhic precepts.

In comparison with Paul's discourse in 2 Cor 3, we should only point out here that 1QS presents a scenario in which, during the eschatological age, God will enable people to act in accordance with the Torah, empowering them to do so by means of the holy spirit. At that time, they will regain the "glory" that had been Adam's at the time of his creation.[109] The holy spirit will "purge" people of their unrighteous deeds. All of this is possible because God has chosen the members of the sect to inherit the promise established in an "eternal covenant."

3.3.5. Hebrews and Covenant Renewal

The discussion of the role of the spirit in the Hebrew Bible and Second Temple Judaism brings us back again to the passage from Jeremiah quoted in Hebrews. Hebrews 8:10 quotes Jeremiah 31:33: "For this is the covenant that I will establish with the house of Israel after those days, says the Lord: Putting my laws into their mind, I will even write them on their hearts ..." The fact that the central affirmation of this oracle (i.e., that at the time of his renewal of the covenant, God would "write [his laws] upon their hearts") is repeated in 10:16–17 indicates the importance that the author of Hebrews attaches to this passage. As in Jeremiah, the author of Hebrews conceives of the new covenant as an internalization of the Torah. Hebrews thus follows a solid tradition within Judaism that links the restoration of the Mosaic covenant with a future time of renewal, in which God causes his people to maintain faithful adherence to the stipulations of the covenant.

As we have seen, the text of the Jeremianic new covenant oracle seemed to contradict the sect's practice of Torah study, which is probably the reason that the Dead Sea scrolls do not quote the oracle in full, but rather allude to it when they make mention of the new covenant. Hebrews' adoption of the full text of the Jeremianic oracle likewise causes problems.

---

holy spirit" in 3:7, Charlesworth is probably correct to take the genitive as attributive, and in light of the parallel in function between the "holy spirit" and God's "angel of truth" in 3:24, he is probably correct in attributing determinacy to the phrase: "*the* holy spirit."

[108] Note the role of the "community's holy spirit" in 3:7–12.

[109] On this theme, see chap. 2, §3.10; pp. 60-61.

If, as the text of Jeremiah asserts, when God inaugurates the new covenant, he "puts his laws into the people's minds, and writes them on their hearts," it would seem that, after the new covenant had been inaugurated, it would be impossible for such a person to sin again. Of course, this utopian vision was contradicted by the actual practice of the intended audience of Hebrews, some of whom must certainly be addressed by the warnings in 2:1–4; 6:4–8; 10:26–31. In each of these sections, the author of Hebrews warns that those who sin after having "become partakers of the holy spirit" (6:4) face the prospect of a harsh judgment. The problem is that, whereas under the "old" cultic system, there existed mechanisms for the periodic removal of guilt and impurity, under the "new covenant" there existed only a single offering for sin: Jesus' atoning death (9:25–28). If there is but one sin-offering, the author of Hebrews reasons, then there is but one opportunity for each individual to have his or her sin removed. After this, there "no longer remains an offering for sin" (10:18, 26).

Even if Hebrews assigns the law a constitutive function within the "new covenant," nevertheless the role of the law is at the same time relativized. The law, and the cultic apparatus associated with the Jerusalem temple, were able to purify only the flesh (σάρξ; 9:13), but they did not "perfect" (τελειῶσαι) the individual "with regard to his conscience" (κατὰ συν–είδησιν). Although humans were able to have impurity removed from their flesh by means of ablutions and the sprinkling of blood, they retained the capacity to disobey the law. Hebrews employs an inner/outer dichotomy in order to facilitate the argument: the "old" cultic apparatus was efficacious for the "flesh," but was unable to transform human intention (cp. συνείδησις). The sacrifice accomplished by Christ inaugurates the new covenant, according to which human intentionality is transformed, so that sin no longer remains, either in intention or in practice (cf. 8:7–12; 9:14, 26, 10:10, 14, 16–17). The result of the inauguration of the new covenant through Christ's sacrifice for sins is that "when he mentions the 'new' [covenant, God implies that] the first has become old; and that which is old and decrepit is near to disappearing" (8:13). The "first" covenant is "old and decrepit" and is replaced by a new, eternal covenant (cf. 9:15).

A corollary to the idea that the "first" covenant is old and "near to disappearing" is that Moses, the mediator of the "first" covenant was inferior to Christ, the mediator of a superior covenant (8:7). Moses is characterized as a servant, and contrasted unfavorably with Christ, characterized as God's son. Similarly, Christ's "glory" is said to be greater than that of Moses (3:1–6). The comparison between Christ and Moses, new covenant and old – even though Hebrews does not use the term "old covenant," the language is not far from such a formulation – recalls 2 Cor 3.

3.3.6. Missionary Apostles in Corinth: A Hypotheses Based on the Parallels

In light of the material that we have assembled from Hebrews, Matthew, Ezekiel, Jubilees, and 1QS, we may make some inferences about the teaching of Paul's missionary opponents in Corinth. Firstly, it seems likely that these missionaries maintained a positive view about the role of the law. In Jeremiah and Ezekiel, as well as in Jubilees and 1QS, the law remains in full effect when the covenant is renewed. Also in Matthew and Hebrews, the law is thought to retain its force, even though in different ways, both texts relativize its importance: in comparison with the ministry (for Matthew, the legal pronouncements) of Jesus, that of Moses was inferior. Between the Jewish and in the early Christian texts, there is common ground: covenant renewal was predicated on the fulfillment of the law. In the early Christian texts, the law is still viewed as the basis of civil life, and the transgression of the civil law is still regarded as "sin."[110] In view of these commonalities, it seems likely that Paul's missionary opponents would have shared this common perception.

The second aspect of the missionaries' preaching that we may infer concerns the role of the spirit in connection with covenant renewal. In Jeremiah and Ezekiel, one of the hallmarks of the "new" or restored covenant was that God would in some way transform individuals so that they would be able to fulfill the Torah perfectly. In Jeremiah's formulation: God "will write [his] laws upon their minds." This tradition is continued in Jubilees and 1QS, in which God's spirit is identified as the effective agent through which the transformation of humans is accomplished. The same idea is found in Hebrews, which connects the holy spirit with repentance from sin and the concomitant life lived in accordance with the Torah, in which there is no longer any consciousness of sin, precisely because no sin is committed – although this is true only of some (!) of Hebrews' addressees (cf. 9:14, 26; 10:14–17, 22). Again, both Jewish and Christian texts are in agreement: it is the spirit that empowers individuals to fulfill the Torah

---

[110] This formulation involves an oversimplification. There is a difference between Matthew and Hebrews in this regard. Whereas Matthew follows Pharisaic halakhah, in which the laws of purity and cultic practice – according to Pharisaic interpretation – were held to be legally binding, in Hebrews, only the civil law seems to be viewed as legally binding; cultic law is demoted as a Platonic "shadow" of Jesus' cultic service, while the laws of purity and kashrut are held to be of no importance. However, we must not conclude from this that Hebrews had abandoned the law of Moses: it was a perfectly legitimate legal position to hold that purity laws were irrelevant outside of the temple cultus. It seems in fact to have been an innovation of the second century BCE that the purity laws began to be practiced by non-priestly Jews. Jesus' own position in this regard seems to have had some affinity with that of Hebrews, although it is beyond the scope of this study to develop this argument.

during the age of the renewed covenant. In light of this broad agreement, we may probably infer that Paul's missionary opponents shared this common theological idea.

Thirdly, we may infer that Paul's missionary opponents compared Moses and Jesus, to the disadvantage of the former. Such a comparison is stated or implied in Matthew and Hebrews. Such a position does not imply a rejection of the law; on the contrary it implies a belief that Jesus had inaugurated an era in which God's spirit enabled individuals properly to fulfill the law. This "outpouring of spirit" enabled an obedience to the law which was not possible in former ages.

3.3.7. Testing the Inferences

An examination of Jewish and early Christian texts reveals some interesting and significant agreements regarding issues of covenant renewal: there is broad agreement that the proper fulfillment of the law forms the basis of covenant renewal, that the spirit or holy spirit enables individuals to fulfill the law when the covenant is renewed, and within the early Christian texts, when Moses is compared with Jesus, the former is compared unfavorably.[111] In light of these broad agreements, we may hypothesize that Paul's missionary opponents in Corinth also espoused some version of these three common theological tenets. In order to test this hypothesis, we may proceed in two steps: firstly, we should review the data that we have gathered from 2 Corinthians regarding these missionaries, in order to see if what we have already found coheres with our hypothesis based on literary parallels. Secondly, we may examine Paul's argument in 2 Cor 3–4, to see whether this hypothesis illuminates aspects of Paul's argument.

We have already seen that Paul's missionary opponents referred to themselves as "ministers of righteousness" (διάκονοι δικαιοσύνης; 2 Cor 11:5), and that they had attempted to institute some regime of praxis in Corinth that Paul referred to as a form of enslavement (καταδουλοῦν; 11:20). We have already noted that the only other instance in which Paul uses the verb καταδουλοῦν, "to enslave" is in Gal 2:4, where he refers to an attempt to promote Torah observance among the Gentile converts of Galatia. All of this follows quite nicely if our first hypothesis, that Paul's missionary opponents advocated the observance of Torah, is correct. The Gospel of Matthew places an emphasis on following Torah without connecting this to covenant renewal; however in light of Paul's discussion of the two covenants in 2 Cor 3, it seems likely that Paul's opponents linked covenant renewal with the proper performance of the law, as had Jeremiah, Ezekiel, Jubilees, 1QS, and Hebrews. The hypotheses that Paul's mission-

---

[111] The Gospel of John could also be added to the list of texts which compare Moses and Jesus, with Jesus compared advantageously (cf. Jn 1:17; 6:30–40; 9:24–41).

ary opponents in 2 Corinthians promoted Torah observance strongly coheres with the information that we have otherwise gathered regarding
Paul's opponents.

There is no information in 2 Corinthians outside of chapter 3 that bears
on the question of whether Paul's missionary opponents were preaching
about covenant renewal. However, we may note that this theme was important within Judaism as well as early Christianity. Paul adverts to the
idea of two covenants in Gal 3–4 as well as in 2 Cor 4, but at these points
he is not inventing this distinction; it was already present within Judaism
and early Christianity. We may only conclude at this point that it is possible that Paul's missionary opponents were preaching about two covenants.
However, some more data that bear on this question is forthcoming on the
basis of an examination of the role of the spirit, a question to which we
now turn.

3.3.8. The Role of Spirit in the Missionaries' Preaching

We have scant information outside of 2 Cor 3 concerning the role that the
spirit played in the preaching of Paul's missionary opponents in Corinth.
According to Paul, their preaching involved the reception of a spirit other
than the one that was entailed in Paul's preaching (ἢ πνεῦμα ἕτερον
λαμβάνετε ὃ οὐκ ἐλάβετε; 11:4). The reception of the spirit that was associated with Paul's ministry had inspired ecstatic speech[112] and prophecy
among the Corinthian congregants, and was purported to impart healing
capabilities (1 Cor 12:4–11; 14:13–40) – even Paul himself produced
ecstatic utterances (1 Cor 14:18). Paul's missionary opponents apparently
criticized this manifestation of spirit within Paul's ministry, charging that
Paul was "out of his mind" (ἐξιστάναι), probably as the result of speaking
in tongues (2 Cor 5:13). To this charge, Paul responds by invoking a distinction that he had used in 1 Corinthians. In 1 Corinthians, Paul had tried
to harness the Corinthians' enthusiasm for charismatic gifts by arguing
that, by itself ecstatic speech was little more than noise. It was only intelligible speech that could benefit the church (1 Cor 14:6–12), for it is only
intelligible speech that is able to affect the mind (νοῦς; 1 Cor 14:14–15,
19). Paul probably intends the same distinction in his phrase, εἴτε γὰρ
ἐξέστημεν, θεῷ· εἴτε σοφρονοῦμεν, ὑμῖν (2 Cor 5:13; "For if we were out of

---

[112] For an examination of the phenomenon of glossolalia within Greek religion, see
H.-J. Klauck, "Von Kassandra bis zur Gnosis. Im Umfeld der frühchristlichen
Glossolalie." Regarding the situation at Corinth, see Klauck's essay, "Mit Engelszungen?
Von Charisma der verständlichen Rede in 1 Kor 14." Both essays appear in Klauck,
Religion und Gesellschaft im frühen Christentum: Neutestamentliche Studien (WUNT
152; Tübingen: J.C.B. Mohr, 2003), pp. 119–144 and 145–167, respectively.

our minds, it was for God's benefit;[113] if we are in our right mind, it is for your benefit").

What position could Paul's missionary opponents have held that resulted in Paul's characterization of it as entailing "another spirit" and which allowed these missionaries to criticize Paul's own characteristic portrayal of spirit as that which manifests itself in ecstatic displays? The hypothesis that Paul's missionary opponents held a view of the role of spirit as that which empowers individuals to adhere to the law suggests an explanation. Such a view, held by Paul's opponents, would certainly have allowed Paul to characterize it as "another spirit" than that which was entailed in his ministry. Such a position on the part of Paul's rivals would also have allowed them to disparage the "spirit" that Paul imparted as ostentatious display. The role of spirit within the Christian community, they would have argued, is that it empowers individuals to adhere to the Torah – an idea also found in Hebrews, 1QS, and Jubilees. Such a position would cohere with what we have already established as a probability: that the Corinthian missionaries advocated adherence to the law of Moses.

Finally, we have hypothesized that Paul's missionary opponents compared Jesus and Moses, to the detriment of the latter. This comparison may imply a corollary comparison between two covenants, such as that which we encounter in Hebrews. There is no evidence in 2 Corinthians outside of chapter 3 however, that could substantiate this hypothesis. The comparative data constitutes the sole support for this hypothesis. However, this hypothesis receives indirect support from the second: according to the comparative texts that we have examined, the transformation of individuals at the time when the covenant is renewed is accomplished by the holy spirit. If Paul's opponents were in fact preaching about the law and the role of the spirit in enabling individuals to fulfill it, these elements point toward the complex of ideas that we have seen are associated with narratives of covenant renewal in Judaism and early Christianity. In these narratives, it is only at the time of the restoration of the covenant that God enables humans, through the agency of the spirit, perfectly to fulfill the law. Stated more simply, in light of the comparative material, the conjunction of the themes of law and spirit may imply the corollary theme of restoration of the broken covenant.

3.3.9. Objections to the "Nomist" Theory

Before we take leave of the subject of the role of the law in the preaching of Paul's missionary opponents, we should linger for a moment to address a few points that have often been raised against the idea that Paul's opponents in 2 Corinthians were "nomists." Firstly, we should note that the

---

[113] Θεῷ is a dative of advantage, as is ὑμῖν.

older discussions about Paul's opponents revolved around the question of whether the Corinthians opponents of Paul were of "the Galatian type." To this question we have answered "no." If as it is generally argued, Paul's opponents in Galatia had ties with the Jerusalem church, then because there is no evidence that Paul's opponents in Corinth had such ties, there is no reason to assume any institutional connection between the two groups. The opponents of Paul in 2 Corinthians were not of "the Galatian type" – if by that we mean that they had ties with the Jerusalem church (or correspondingly, the "Petrine mission").

In the older discussions, the corollary point was raised: because in 2 Corinthians, Paul does not mention either "the law" or circumcision, therefore his opponents were neither "nomists" nor "Judaizers." However, the structure of the two apologies provides obvious reasons for Paul's omissions. In 2 Corinthians, Paul's discourse is not framed as a point-by-point refutation of the ideology of his opponents. Rather, Paul is responding to two sets of concerns: firstly, that Paul's sufficiency (ἱκανότης) as a minister of Christ had been called into question, and secondly, that the members of the Corinthian congregation, spurred on in part by Paul's missionary rivals, had entered Paul into a contest of comparison (σύγκρισις) with his missionary rivals. At the point at which Paul wrote his second apology (2 Cor 10–13), Paul appears to have been judged as inferior in quality to his missionary rivals. In response, Paul crafts an apology in which he calls into question the criteria by which the Corinthians judged Paul wanting. Paul agrees that his own qualifications may seem inferior to that of his missionary rivals, but that is only because they were judging according to "fleshly" categories. Paul argues that paradoxically, it is his very "weakness," or lack of external qualifications, that renders him most fit to serve as Christ's apostle! This approach had been adumbrated, but without bringing the paradox to the forefront, in the first apology (i.e., 2 Cor 2:14–6:13; 7:2–4). When Paul cites aspects of his rivals' theological formulation, it is only in passing. More specifically, Paul does so only when he is able to modify his opponents' theological position so as to turn it into an argument for the supremacy of his own ministry vis-à-vis theirs (2 Cor 3). When we properly appreciate the rhetorical function of Paul's arguments in 2 Corinthians (i.e., that Paul is pleading for the sufficiency of his own ministry, in competition with rivals) then the old objection that because Paul does not discuss circumcision or law, therefore his opponents must not have advocated adherence to the Torah, is seen to be what it was all along – a red herring!

3.4. Did the missionary rivals in Corinth use "pneumatic" displays to establish their legitimacy? If so, how? In what ways did Paul rely on pneumatic displays to establish the legitimacy of his own mission?

Dieter Georgi argued that Paul's missionary opponents in 2 Corinthians were representative of an apologetic phenomenon that Georgi claimed to have identified within the Judaism of the Hellenistic period. According to Georgi, certain groups within Judaism were influenced by the common Greek idea "divine men" (θεῖοι ἄνδρες), special individuals who were thought to have special contact with the realm of divine which resulted in their ability to perform miracles, their possession of superhuman knowledge, and often culminated in an act whereby they were transformed into heavenly beings.[114] These Jewish groups modified this Greek idea so that it served the purposes of Jewish apologetic among the religions of antiquity. Famous individuals from Israel's past, such as Moses and Elijah, were portrayed as Hellenistic divine men. But ordinary individuals could also hope to participate in the divine attributes exhibited by these exemplary individuals. This was accomplished, according to Georgi, through emulating the lives of past "divine men," but above all by contemplating the Torah on the basis of allegorical interpretation. This contemplative activity results in the metamorphosis of the individual who engages in it; he was "heighten[ed in his] vital consciousness beyond human limits ... In their encounter with the text, the Apologetic exegetes could not help but experience the increasing proximity of the divine and sense themselves transformed as a result."[115] Georgi's argument is complex and far-reaching. In the discussion that follows, we will examine only one aspect of Georgi's thesis: whether Paul's opponents in 2 Corinthians legitimated their ministry through the performance of miraculous deeds and visions of the divine realm.

Georgi correctly points out the centrality of 2 Cor 12:12 to the question as to the form of legitimation that Paul's missionary opponents employed. Georgi states:[116]

Paul does not renounce the σημεῖα τοῦ ἀποστόλου (2 Cor 12:12), but even in this respect Paul seems to lag behind the opponents. Their signs and wonders must have resembled those of the Hellenistic-Jewish and Hellenistic θεῖοι ἄνδρες.

Georgi assumes that Paul's opponents were able to produce "signs and wonders," and infers that those must have been similar to those of other "divine men." However, the activities and attributes that Georgi assigns to "divine men" are of a varied assortment. They include the possession of

---

[114] Georgi, *Opponents of Paul*, 83–228.

[115] *Opponents of Paul*, 147–148.

[116] *Opponents of Paul*, 236.

notable wisdom, the ability to cast out demons, perform healings, and predict the future, the ability to peer into the heavenly realm by means of visionary experiences, and sometimes involve a transformation of the individual into a luminous or heavenly being.[117] Did Paul's missionary opponents in 2 Corinthians engage in some or all of these activities? Georgi's own arguments on this point are not very strong. Georgi proceeds in several instances by engaging in a mirror-reading of 2 Corinthians. On the assumption that the position of Paul's opponents must have been dia-metrically opposed to the position that Paul takes, Georgi is able to draw conclusions such as the following: (regarding 2:14–16) "Paul's allusions to qualities and activities of God might be easily explained if the opponents had spoken with strong assuredness about their abilities and had claimed divine qualities."[118] Regarding 12:12, we may recall Georgi's statement quoted above, "[The] signs and wonders [of Paul's opponents] must have resembled those of the Hellenistic-Jewish and Hellenistic θεῖοι ἄνδρες." But in cases such as these Georgi is not able to produce evidence to sup-port his assertions.

3.4.1. Signs and Wonders in the Acts of the Apostles

The Book of Acts constitutes a *locus classicus* for establishing the role of "signs" in early Christianity. In his Pentecost speech in Jerusalem, Peter says (Acts 2:22), "Israelites, listen to these words: Jesus the Nazorean, a man attested to you by God with acts of power and wonders and signs that God accomplished through him ..." (ἄνδρα ἀποδεδειγμένον ἀπὸ τοῦ θεοῦ εἰς ὑμᾶς δυνάμεσι καὶ τέρασι καὶ σημείοις οἷς ἐποίησεν δι᾽ αὐτοῦ ὁ θεός). These "acts of power, wonders, and signs" included the actions that the author had earlier recounted in the Gospel of Luke. In Luke's gospel, Jesus is said to have cast out demons (4:31–37) and healed people who suffered from illnesses (4:38–40). Jesus is presented as sufficiently powerful to effect a cure even when the patient was not physically present (7:1–10). Jesus is said even to have revived the dead (7:11–17). This list is sufficient to indicate the connotations of Luke's triad δυνάμεις, τέρατα, and σημεῖα. The "acts of power, wonders, and signs" performed by Jesus included miraculous acts. These acts serve in the narrative to demonstrate Jesus' legitimacy as an agent of God; Jesus is said to have been ἀποδεδειγμένον ἀπο τοῦ θεοῦ, "attested by God" on the basis of the miraculous acts, which themselves are attributed to God, but accomplished through Jesus' agency (ἅ ἐποίησεν δι᾽ αὐτοῦ ὁ θεός). Jesus is "attested" inasmuch as he is able to serve as an agent through which God can perform miracles.

---

[117] *Opponents of Paul*, 155–174; 254–264; 271–283.
[118] *Opponents of Paul*, 233.

In perfect conformity with Acts' portrayal of Jesus' "signs" is the text's portrayal of the signs performed by the apostles. According to Acts 2:43, among the community of Jesus' followers in Jerusalem, "fear (φόβος) came upon every individual; many signs and wonders came about through the apostles" (πολλά τε τέρατα καὶ σημεῖα διὰ τῶν ἀποστόλων ἐγίνετο).[119] Miraculous deeds are worked, implicitly by God, through the agency (διά + gen.) of the apostles. Like Jesus, the apostles are presented as healers (3:1–10), men endowed with prophetic abilities (5:1–11), the ability to impart the holy spirit (8:14–24), the ability to revive the dead (9:36–42), and recipients of revelatory visions (10:9–16). It is this Lukan formulation of the role of "signs and wonders" in early Christianity that has shaped the way in which Paul's opponents in 2 Corinthians have been viewed in scholarly literature. Paul's opponents are presumed to have been master thaumaturges, as are "the apostles" in Acts.

Georgi's portrait of Paul's opponents in 2 Corinthians shares many characteristics with the portrait of the wonder-working Jesus and the won-der-working apostles (including Paul) found in Luke-Acts. According to Georgi's thesis, this is because the portrayals of Jesus and the apostles in the New Testament have been influenced by the Hellenistic θεῖος ἀνήρ tradition. We have seen already that the adequacy of applying the designa-tion θεῖος ἀνήρ to the New Testament and the texts of Hellenistic Judaism has been questioned. The designation itself appears very infrequently in this literature. However, aside from this terminological problem, Georgi is undeniably correct to point out that certain individuals in Greco-Roman antiquity were described as possessing a divine quality that was demon-strated through the production of astounding feats (θαύματα) and extraor-dinary knowledge. The heroes of early Christian history were legitimated in similar ways. One may make the distinction that, in general the Greco-Roman figures were thought to have been able to produce "wonders" on the basis of their innate, godlike qualities, whereas the early Christian figures (at least according to Acts) were described as agents who accom-plished similar deeds, not on the basis of their innate divinity, but rather as instruments through which an external power, that of God or the holy spirit, was exercised. Nevertheless, the generic similarity holds.

3.4.1.1. Paul in Acts Compared with Paul in the Pauline Epistles

When we compare Paul's own accounts of the activities that took place in his churches, there is a remarkable correspondence with the "signs and wonders" that Acts employs to legitimate the preaching of "the apostles." Like the first apostles in Luke's depiction, Paul spoke in tongues (1 Cor

---

[119] An almost identical formulation appears in Acts 5:12.

14:18; cf. Acts 2:1–13) and mediated the holy spirit (cf. Acts 19:6),[120] through which some of his converts were assumed to have been endowed with the gifts of prophecy, healing abilities, glossolalia, and the ability to interpret ecstatic utterances. Paul is also able to cite occasions on which he was the recipient of revelatory experiences and visions (Gal 1:12, 16; 1 Cor 2:6–13; 2 Cor 12:1–4). Of course, Paul subordinates all of these charismatic gifts to what he considers to be the most important "spiritual gift" of all: a love that manifests itself in harmonious relationships within the community (1 Cor 13:1–14:40). The only "sign" that was said to have been performed by the apostles in Acts but which is lacking in Paul's letters is also the most extreme: the ability to raise the dead.[121]

3.4.2. Paul's Opponents and "Signs and Wonders"

The question to which we now turn is, what is the specific evidence that Paul's opponents in 2 Corinthians (more specifically, in the first and second apologies) engaged in such "wonder-working" activities? Jerry Sumney has usefully combed the data of 2 Corinthians with this question in mind. His work provides a convenient point of departure for our enquiry.

Sumney explicitly rejects Georgi's thesis: "This study finds no evidence that the opponents in the letters of 2 Corinthians are Gnostics or the type of divine men Georgi hypothesizes."[122] Nevertheless, many of Sumney's descriptions of Paul's opponents sound very similar to Georgi's: "Paul's reference to his weakness in this context [i.e., 2 Cor 12:1–10] implies that they [i.e., the opponents] claim the Spirit as the source of their powerful lives."[123] Or again: "the opponents believe that divine power shows itself in the glorious lives of apostles."[124] "The opponents argue that the Spirit enables apostles to lead powerful and obviously successful lives and lifts them above hardships and humiliations. In addition, the spirit grants visions and revelations to apostles and enables them to perform miraculous deeds ('signs, wonders, and mighty deeds')."[125]

---

[120] Although Acts states that Paul was able to mediate the presence of the holy spirit through laying his hands upon the recipient, Paul himself makes no such claim. However, as we will see in a later section, the converts in the Pauline churches were expected to have received the holy spirit. Paul may have conceived of himself as a mediator of the spirit through his preaching of the gospel.

[121] According to Acts 20:7–12, Paul himself was able to raise the dead. There is also one "gift" that Paul attests that is lacking in Acts: the ability to interpret ecstatic utterances. In Acts, such an interpretative act is unnecessary, for glossolaliacs speak in languages that are known to the bystanders who witness the activity (Acts 2:5–11).

[122] *'Servants of Satan'*, 131.

[123] *'Servants of Satan'*, 122.

[124] *'Servants of Satan'*, 123.

[125] *'Servants of Satan'*, 128.

Even though Sumney claims to have rejected Georgi's hypothesis, nevertheless his own formulations echo Georgi's. There seems to be some tension, however, between Sumney's painstaking examination of particular passages in 2 Corinthians and his own resultant descriptions of Paul's opponents. The main evidence that could be used to identify specific thaumaturgic practices in which Paul's missionary opponents may have engaged falls under two categories: ecstatic speech and visionary experience.

3.4.3. Paul's Opponents and Ecstatic Speech

Georgi adduces 2 Cor 11:6 as evidence that Paul's opponents engaged in ecstatic speech. However, Paul's admission that he is "untrained in speech" (εἰ δὲ καὶ ἰδιώτης [εἰμὶ] τῷ λόγῳ) has nothing to do with ecstatic speech. It concerns rather Paul's (admitted!) lack of training in public speaking.[126] Betz[127] has noted that at times the best orators may deny their oratorical ability as part of a rhetorical ploy to heighten their credibility by allaying the suspicion that may arise among members of the audience that the speaker sought to "seduce them with clever words." While this is certainly the case, Paul's situation is somewhat different: he is not feigning a lack of ability, but rather responding to the evaluation of the Corinthian congregation that he did lack such ability. The same charge is echoed in 2 Cor 10:10. Paul's statement in 11:6, since it concerns training in rhetoric and not ecstatic utterances, cannot be used in support the thesis that Paul's opponents engaged in glossolalia, as Sumney has correctly concluded.[128]

The support that could establish that Paul's opponents engaged in ecstatic utterances (glossolalia) is lacking. On the contrary, it is possible that Paul's opponents attacked *him* for engaging in such activity. However, this supposition rests on the interpretation of 2 Cor 5:13, a passage concerning which scholars have offered conflicting opinions. The passage reads, "For if I was beside myself,[129] it was for God's benefit; if I am in my mind, it is for your benefit" (εἴτε γὰρ ἐξέστημεν, θεῷ· εἴτε σωφρονοῦμεν, ὑμῖν). For the purposes of this investigation, the passage raises an important question: is Paul here responding to a charge that had been leveled by his opponents?

---

[126] Confer *DBAG*, s. ἰδιώτης, category 1, where 2 Cor. 11:6 is cited.

[127] Betz's thesis is that in 11:4 Paul employs a topos that stems from the Socratic tradition, whereby philosophers distinguish themselves from Sophists by denying that they are clever orators. The passage is to be taken as ironic on Betz's reading (*Der Apostel Paulus und die sokratische Tradition: Eine exegetische Untersuchung zu einer "Apologie" 2 Korinther 10–13* [Tübingen: J. C. B. Mohr, 1972] 59–69).

[128] *'Servants of Satan'*, 114.

[129] The aorist tense of ἐξέστημεν may be interpreted as a constative aorist (referring to past action), or it may be a dramatic aorist and translated as a present tense verb.

In his 1915 commentary on 2 Corinthians, Alfred Plummer reasoned that in 5:13, Paul was responding to an accusation made by his missionary opponents.[130] Plummer argues that the verb ἐξίστημι in this passage refers to "madness" or "mania," which in Paul's case was variously manifested in his speaking in tongues, his excessive self-commendation, and his visionary experiences (such as his vision on the "road to Damascus"). Here however, Plummer interpreted Paul in light of a current theory that viewed religious zeal and in particular ecstatic experience as signs of mental illness. (This was little more than a decade prior to Freud's 1928 publication of *The Future of an Illusion*.) Even if we reject Plummer's mental illness thesis, however, this does not invalidate his surmise that in 5:13 Paul may have been responding to an accusation by his opponents.

Hans Windisch[131] argued subsequently that it was hardly likely that the Corinthians, who had such a fondness for ecstatic displays, would have used such displays to discredit Paul. (Windisch does not address the possibility that this charge may have arisen from Paul's missionary rivals, and not from within the community itself.) Rather, Windisch argues, the issue pertained to Paul's use of ecstatic experiences for the purpose of self-recommendation. In particular, Paul relied on such experiences to prove his "special intimacy with God" ("besondere Intimität mit Gott").

Subsequent to Windisch, Käsemann[132] and Bultmann[133] championed an interpretation that denied that Paul used ecstatic experiences as a means of self-legitimation. This stream of interpretation is heavily represented in recent commentaries (as, for example, Klauck, Martin, Furnish). According to this line of interpretation, in 5:13 Paul is responding to his opponents' illegitimate use of charismatic experiences as a legitimating trope. Whereas it is hypothesized that Paul's opponents freely spoke, and even boasted of their own ecstatic experiences, Paul was more restrained in his own references to such activities. Paul's attitude is that ecstatic experiences have only a personal, private significance; they are "between Paul and God," whereas Paul's most important contributions are public; they served to build up the church. Hans-Josef Klauck sums up this position succinctly in his comments on 5:13:[134]

---

[130] *Second Epistle of Paul to the Corinthians* (ICC; Edinburgh: T&T Clark, 1915; reprinted 1960) 171–173.

[131] *Der zweite Korintherbrief* (Kritisch-exegetischer Kommentar über das Neue Testament; Göttingen: Vandenhoeck & Ruprecht, 1924; 9th ed.) 179–180.

[132] "Die Legitimität," 60–66 (67–71).

[133] *The Second Letter to the Corinthians* (Minneapolis, MN: Augsburg, 1985; trans. of *Der zweite Brief an die Korinther*; Göttingen: Vandenhoeck & Ruprecht, 1976) 149–150.

[134] *2. Korintherbrief*, 53; the translation is mine. Compare also Klauck, "Die Authorität des Charismas: Zehn neutestamentliche Thesen zum Thema" in his *Gemeinde-*

Ecstatic experiences pertain to external merits (12:1–4). About such experiences, which pass only between him and God and do not contribute to the upbuilding of the community, Paul himself does not speak, or only of necessity. He flatly refuses them as legitimating evidence. His work took place outwardly; more down-to-earth, less conspicuous, and more tedious.

The positions of Windisch and Plummer vis-à-vis the Käsemann-Bultmann formulation that currently holds sway call for evaluation. Did Paul legitimate himself by recourse to ecstatic experiences? Did his opponents legitimate themselves in this way?

3.4.4. Paul's Appeals to Revelation and Charisma

In each of Paul's uncontested letters save Philemon, Paul uses references to revelatory, charismatic, or ecstatic experiences to legitimate either his authority or the content of his preaching. In 1 Thess 1:5, Paul states, "because our gospel did not come to you by means of discourse alone (ἐν λόγῳ μόνον), but also with power and the holy spirit and with full conviction (ἐν δυνάμει καὶ ἐν πνεύματι ἁγίῳ καὶ πληροφορίᾳ πολλῇ).[135] Paul's discourse is legitimated here by the accompaniment of "power" and "the holy spirit." The triad of "discourse," "power," and "holy spirit" combines to effect the desired outcome: "consequently (καί) you became imitators (μιμηταί) of us and of the Lord." In this passage, the referent of the terms "power" and "holy spirit" is probably to the persuasive effect of Paul's discourse: it caused pagans to exchange their former patterns of behavior and religious ideology for new ones set forth in Paul's gospel (cf. 2:13–14).

In addition to the use of "power" and "spirit" as legitimating tropes in 1 Thessalonians, Paul offers a glimpse of some of the manifestations of spiritual "gifts" that the Thessalonians had experienced. In 5:19–21, Paul admonishes the Thessalonians, "Do not quench the spirit, do not despise prophecy, but test everything ..." Paul here attests that some of the members of the Thessalonian congregation prophesied. While this phenomenon is not used here in a legitimating function, it nevertheless indicates that

---

Amt-Sakrament: neutestamentliche Perspektiven (Würtzburg: Echter, 1989): "Charismen als Selbstzweck, als Privatvergnügen, läßt Paulus nicht gelten. Jedes Charisma verpflichtet zu aktivem Einsatz und zu unermüdlichem Eifer im Dienst der Gemeinde. Nur vor dort her gewinnt es seine Authorität" (p. 227).

[135] Nestle-Aland (27th ed.) prints καὶ [ἐν] πληροφορίᾳ πολλῇ. The ἐν does not seem to me to be original. It is omitted by Alexandrinus as well as the mid-third century papyus 65 (text in P. W. Comfort and D. P. Barrett, *The Complete Text of the Earliest New Testament Manuscripts* [Grand Rapids: Baker Books, 1999] 350). It seems more likely that scribes inserted the preposition to parallel those of the preceding phrases, rather than accounting for the shorter text as the result of an omission.

such activity was not confined to Corinth, but rather was characteristic of
Paul's congregations.

In Galatians 1:11–12, Paul famously declares that the discursive content of his "gospel" was not taught him by any human; rather it was given
to him by Jesus Christ through revelation: "For I want you to know, brothers, (about) the gospel that is preached by me, that it is not of human origin
(κατὰ ἄνθρωπον); for I neither received it from a man, nor was I taught it,
but (it came) through a revelation from Jesus Christ" (δι᾽
ἀποκαλύψεως Ἰησοῦ Χριστοῦ). In this passage, Paul wishes to assert his
independence from the Jerusalem authorities. His gospel, he argues, is not
the result of oral tradition that they had passed to him; rather its discursive
content was provided by the risen Jesus Christ himself (cf. also vv. 15–17).
In 3:1–5, Paul argues that the Galatians had not received the spirit on the
basis of adherence to the Torah, but rather on the basis of "the obedience
of faith" (ἐξ ἀκοῆς πίστεως; 3:2). Paul asks a rhetorical question: "As for
he who grants you the spirit and brings about acts of power in your midst
(ἐνεργῶν δυνάμεις ἐν ὑμῖν), (does he do so) on the basis of (ἐκ) works of
the law or on the basis of the obedience of faith?" Paul points to tangible
evidence with which he expects the Galatians to be familiar and to assess
positively. Both the "spirit" and "acts of power" therefore, were known
within the Galatian congregation. Paul adduces this dyad to legitimate his
own preaching vis-à-vis that of others who advocated adherence to the
Torah.

In Galatians 2:2, Paul asserts that a trip that he had made to Jerusalem
had occurred "in response to a revelation" (so NRSV, translating
κατὰ ἀποκάλυψιν). Paul probably includes this notice regarding the motivation for his Jerusalem visit in response to the (probably accurate) report
that Paul and Barnabas had been sent to Jerusalem as part of a delegation
sent to ask for an authoritative ruling from the founding members of the
Jerusalem church on the question of the role of the law for Gentile converts to the early Christian movement (Acts 15:1–5). Paul wishes to indicate that he is subject to no human – he takes his marching orders directly
from God. Again, Paul adverts to the theme of revelation in an effort to
legitimate his ministry.

Paul crafts a particularly poignant self-portrait as one who is a hierophant of God's mysteries in 1 Cor 2:1–4. In this passage, Paul asserts, "My
speech and my proclamation were not in plausible words of wisdom, but
with a demonstration of the Spirit and of power ..." Here, Paul returns to
the dyad that he had used in 1 Thessalonians: spirit and power. As they had
in Thessalonica, we may assume that these terms refer to the persuasive
power of Paul's discourse to effect conversion to belief in Christ among
the pagans (or God-fearers, or both) of Corinth. Paul continues in 2:7:

But we speak God's wisdom, secret and hidden, which God decreed before all ages for our glory ... But, as it is written: 'What no eye has seen, nor ear heard, nor the human heart conceived, what God has prepared for those who love him' – these things God has revealed to us through the Spirit (NRSV).

In this striking passage, Paul states that he has access to knowledge that has been hidden since the foundation of the world ("before all ages"). This knowledge is revealed to him by the spirit. In the following verses (11–16), Paul hints that if the Corinthians, too, are "spiritual" then they will accept the mysteries that Paul is able to reveal to them. In 4:1, Paul provides an appropriate label for himself in the service that he claims to be able to provide: "Think of us in this way: as servants of Christ and stewards of God's mysteries" (so NRSV, translating ὑπηρέτας τοῦ Χριστοῦ καὶ οἰκονόμους μυστηρίων θεοῦ).

In the latter half of 1 Corinthians, Paul offers some insights into his own ecstatic practices. In 14:18, Paul offers thanks to God that he "speaks in tongues more than" all the Corinthians. In 15:8, he mentions Christ's appearance (ὤφθη) to Paul, which resulted in his commission as an apostle (v. 9). Similarly in 9:1, Paul connects the vision that he had seen of the risen Jesus with his status as an apostle: "Am I not an apostle? Have I not seen (ἑόρακα) Jesus our Lord?" In both 15:8–9 and in 9:1, it is the appearance of the risen Jesus to Paul that legitimates the latter's apostolic authority.

In 2 Corinthians 12:1–4, Paul is able to boast of his ascent to the third heaven. He also includes his own estimation of the value of such experiences. Paul refers to his own revelations as having an "exceptional character" (ἡ ὑπερβολὴ τῶν ἀποκαλύψεων; 12:7). Such experiences posed a threat to Paul, that he may become "self-aggrandized" (ὑπεραίρομαι) as a result of them. Visionary experiences and charismatic gifts not only serve to authorize discursive productions, but they also elevate the status of the recipient relative to that of other members of the community (this view is also implied, and countered by the discussion in 12:1–14:40). We may also mention here that Paul makes reference to the "signs and wonders and mighty works" (σημεῖα τε καὶ τέρατα καὶ δυνάμεις) that he was able to perform in Corinth in an effort to establish his legitimacy as an apostle vis-à-vis his missionary rivals in 12:12.

In Romans 15:18–19a, Paul relies on familiar terms to establish his own legitimacy as an apostle: "For I will not be so bold as to mention anything which Christ did not bring about through me to win obedience from the Gentiles, through discourse and deed, with the power of signs and wonders, with the power of the holy spirit ... so that I have brought the gospel of Christ to completion ..." As in 2 Corinthians, Paul here adduces his "signs and wonders" to prove the efficacy of his preaching mission. As in Corinthians, however, he does not make explicit what might have constituted such. I would suggest that this was a purposeful strategy, whereby Paul was able to lay claim to the authorizing capacities of these terms, but without claiming specifically to have healed the sick, raised the dead, or the like – such deeds as these terms might connote. Despite the favorable testimony of Acts that Paul did in fact accomplish such miraculous deeds, there is no evidence in Paul's own letters that he did such things. Paul's activities were, in Klauck's words, "more down-to-earth, less conspicuous, and more tedious" than Acts would lead us to believe: at least Paul does not claim to have raised the dead!

Gathering together the data from Paul's letters, we may assert confidently the following:

1) Paul did employ the signifiers "signs" and "wonders" in efforts to legitimate his preaching and to illustrate its effectiveness. Such signifiers proved useful to Paul because they invoked connotations of miraculous activities such as healing the sick and raising the dead. Paul however, does not specify the content of these signifiers, preferring instead to draw upon the persuasive power of such terms. Probably, Paul did not engage in many of the miraculous activities that could be connoted by these terms.

2) The communities in which Paul preached did, however, engage in ecstatic phenomena such as prophecy and glossolalia. Paul even intimates that the "gift of healing" was evidenced among the congregation in Corinth.

3) Paul prided himself on the frequency with which he engaged in glossolalia.

4) Paul asserted that the "power of the spirit" was evident in his preaching; the evidence for this assertion consisted in the conversions that he was able to effect.

5) Paul boasted of visions and revelations that he had experienced and referred to these in contexts in which he wished to legitimate the content of his preaching.

6) Paul's statements imply that visions, revelations, and charismatic endowments conferred upon their recipients a privileged status within the communities in which Paul preached. Paul himself enjoyed a privileged status as the result of his own spiritual endowments: his very status as an apostle was legitimated by a visionary experience.

3.4.5. Early Christian Portrayals of Paul as Legitimated by Spiritual Display and Revelation

If Paul viewed himself as a powerful missionary preacher, the content of whose preaching was vouchsafed by revelatory experiences, the early Christian tradition viewed him similarly. We may instructively adduce Acts 18–19 and the Pseudo-Clementine Homilies 13 in support of this point.

Acts 18:24–19:7 describes the activities of one Apollos of Alexandria, who is described as an "eloquent man, well-versed in the scriptures" (NRSV; ἀνὴρ λόγιος ... δυνατὸς ὢν ἐν ταῖς γραφαῖς). This Apollos, although he had received instruction concerning the "way of the Lord" (ἦν κατηχήμενος τὴν ὁδὸν τοῦ κυρίου) and taught accurately about Jesus (ἐδίδασκεν ἀκριβῶς τὰ περὶ τοῦ Ἰησοῦ), nevertheless exhibited one important defect: he knew only the "baptism of John." John's baptism was one of repentance for the forgiveness of sins (19:4; cf. Mt 3:1–12). We need not assume here that Apollos was baptized by John himself; this baptism was mediated by John's – and apparently also Jesus' – followers. After Apollos had preached in Ephesus and subsequently traveled to Corinth, Paul arrived and began to preach in Ephesus. To those Ephesians to whom Apollos had preached, and to whom Apollos had apparently administered John's baptism of repentance (19:1–4), Paul was able to grant an important boon: the holy spirit. Paul baptized the group of Ephesians "in the name of Jesus" and "when Paul laid his hands upon them, the holy spirit came upon them; they both spoke in tongues and prophesied" (καὶ ἐπιθέντος αὐτοῖς τοῦ Παύλου τὰς χεῖρας ἦλθε τὸ πνεῦμα τὸ ἅγιον ἐπ᾽ αὐτούς, ἐλάλουν τε γλώσσαις καὶ ἐπροφήτευον). According to the presentation of the author of Acts, Apollos, although a skilled orator and conversant with the traditions about Jesus' teaching, was unable to mediate the presence of the holy spirit. This Paul was able to do, through baptizing and laying his hands upon the recipient. According to Acts, this ritual imparted the spirit, the presence of which was manifested in the behavior of the recipients: they spoke in tongues and prophesied. Acts' narrative recapitulates data that we have already encountered in Paul's own letters: Paul's congregations both at Thessalonica and Corinth engaged in prophecy, and in Corinth they also practiced glossolalia. It seems likely, though not demonstrable, that such activities may have taken place within some or all of Paul's other congregations as well. For our purposes, it is not necessary that the author of Acts must have presented solid historical tradition based on reliable evidence in the case of Acts 18:24–19:7. What is more important is that this author conceived of Paul as distinctive from some other traveling missionaries based on Paul's ability to impart the holy spirit, the presence of which was manifested in glossolalia and prophetic speech.

Another early Christian author who conceived of Paul as legitimating his ministry on the basis of his purportedly exceptional spiritual abilities is the author of the Pseudo-Clementine Homilies 18.13–19. In this section, Peter debates with Simon – a figure who is generally acknowledged to represent Paul[136] – about which man has the stronger claim to legitimacy in his preaching. Peter, for his part, can claim to have been directly taught by Jesus, whereas Paul claims that Jesus communicated with him through revelatory experiences. Peter asks "Simon" pointedly (17.19.1):

---

[136] So for example G. Strecker in *NTApoc*, 490–491. An English translation of parts of the Homilies appears in the same work; see esp. pp. 535–537. Strecker developed the argument that Simon Magus appears as a guise for Paul in certain parts of the Homilies in *Das Judenchristentum in den Pseudoklementinen* (Berlin: Akademie-Verlag, 1981) 187–196.

If, then, our Jesus became known to you also by appearing through a vision and spoke as one who is angry with an adversary, therefore he spoke through visions and dreams or again through revelations which come from without. But can anyone be instructed for teaching by a vision?

εἰ μὲν οὖν καὶ σοὶ ὁ Ἰησοῦς ἡμῶν δι᾽ ὁράματος ὀφθεὶς ἐγνώσθη καὶ ὡμίλησεν ὡς ἀντικειμένῳ ὀργιζόμενος, διὸ δι᾽ ὁραμάτων καὶ ἐνυπνίων ἢ καὶ δι᾽ ἀποκαλύψεων ἔξωθεν οὐσῶν ἐλάλησεν. εἰ τις δὲ ὀπτασίαν πρὸς διδασκαλίαν σοφισθῆναι δύναται;[137]

The distinction that the author of this section of the Homilies relies upon in the passage is that direct, personal communication best serves to guarantee the authenticity of the information that is conveyed. Direct personal communication enables communication to take place ἐναργείᾳ, "with clear and distinct perception"[138] (13:1; 14:1), as opposed to revelatory experience, which is ἐπισφαλής, "misleading" (14:3). Direct personal communication is presented as unmediated, whereas revelatory experience is, interestingly enough, derogated as originating "outside" of the perception of the recipient (ἔξωθεν οὐσῶν). In the Pseudo-Clementine Homilies Paul, under the guise of the arch-heretic "Simon (Magus)," is attacked for legitimating his teaching activity, and even his status as an apostle (19:4),[139] on the basis of revelatory experiences. This view corresponds both with Paul's own self-presentation and that of the Book of Acts.

In light of the evidence from Paul's own letters as well as the way in which he was portrayed by later authors, it is difficult to escape the conclusion that Paul was known for adducing both revelatory experiences and charismatic endowments in an effort to legitimate both his authority and the content of his preaching.[140]

3.4.6. Paul's Opponents and Visionary Experience: 2 Cor 12:1–10

Paul's discussion of his own visionary experience in 2 Cor 12:1–10 is taken as a crucial bit of evidence that Paul's opponents legitimated themselves through appeal to visionary experience. The argument (as developed by Sumney) runs as follows:

---

[137] The Greek text appears in B. Rehm, *Die Pseudoklementinen, Bd. I: Homilien* (3. Aufl., ed. G. Strecker, 1992) 239.

[138] So LSJ, s.v., I. 2.

[139] εἰ δὲ ὑπ᾽ ἐκείνου μιᾶς ὥρας ὀφθεὶς καὶ μαθητευθεὶς ἀπόστολος ἐγένου ... "And if, by being visited by him [i.e., Jesus] for an hour and being instructed by him, you became an apostle ..."

[140] One could also adduce the Apocalypse of Paul in NHC 5.2, as well as the Acts of Paul to the same effect. H.-J. Klauck outlines the contents and significance of NHC 5.2 in "Die Himmelfahrt des Paulus (2 Kor 12,2–4) in der koptischen Paulusapokalypse aus Nag Hammadi (NHC V/2)" in his *Gemeinde-Amt-Sakrament*, 391–429.

Paul apparently agrees to match his opponents' claims to 'visions and revelations of the Lord' in 12.1. This is the first clear evidence that spiritual experiences are important for the opponents; the polemical context allows us to infer that they claim to receive visions and revelations.[141]

Sumney here follows the standard line of argumentation with respect to this passage. Apropos of this passage, Furnish (to whom Sumney refers) writes the following:

Paul's reiteration that *boasting is necessary*, v. 1 (cf. 11:30) is perhaps a concession to his competitors in Corinth, who may be faulting him for not having displayed the kinds of apostolic credentials of which they themselves boast. Among these, apparently, are accounts of ecstatic experiences they claim to have had.[142]

We should note the careful way in both Sumney and Furnish introduce an element of tentativeness with their conclusions: "Paul *apparently* agrees" (Sumney); Paul's comment about boasting "*is perhaps* a concession" to competitors "who *may be* faulting him" (Furnish). Sumney has become overconfident when he asserts that 12:1–4 provides "the first *clear evidence* that spiritual experiences are important for [Paul's] opponents."

Far from providing "clear evidence" that Paul's opponents claim to have had ecstatic experiences, 12:1–4 in fact indicates only that Paul had such experiences. It is only the assumption that Paul must here be responding directly to a similar claim made by his opponents that this passage may be turned into evidence related to Paul's opponents. Sumney has elsewhere lambasted such an approach as "mirror exegesis" and rightly rejected the method as inadequate and misleading. Sumney's own espoused methodological procedure is that mirror exegesis should never be used unless the specific attribute to be proven by such exegesis can be regarded as already established by another passage.[143] That is, mirror exegesis can only be used as supporting evidence for facts that have already been established on the basis of explicit statements or allusions. Unfortunately, Sumney has abandoned his usual methodological rigor in this case. Sumney states: "This is the first *clear evidence* that spiritual experiences are important for the opponents; the polemical context allows us *to infer* that they claim to receive visions and revelations." In his methodological statement, Sumney explicitly – and rightly – rejects inferences based on mirror exegesis, unless these are supported by other material. Sumney forecloses the possibility that supporting material may be adduced

---

[141] *'Servants of Satan'*, 121.

[142] Furnish, *II Corinthians*, 543 (emphasis Furnish's).

[143] *Identifying Paul's Opponents*, 98–100. "Such information [i.e., that gained through the application of mirror exegesis] must be coherent with what we already know about the opponents and can only clarify their position on a previously identified issue. Mirror exegesis cannot, with any certainty, add a topic to the discussion" (p. 100).

in this case, asserting that 12:1–4 constitutes "the first clear evidence ..."
Sumney's methodological slip may be forgivable – he is after all following
the majority of interpreters on this point – but it is also something that
must be pointed out and corrected.[144] I do agree with Sumney, however, in
his assessment that nowhere outside of 12:1–4 do we have any clear evidence that Paul's missionary opponents legitimated themselves on the
basis of visionary activity.

As we have already seen, in his letters, Paul often referred to ec-
static/charismatic activity (glossolalia) or to visionary/revelatory experience in contexts in which he wished to provide legitimation for his ministry and message. Since this is one of Paul's favored modes of legitimation,
and since it is stated or implied that these were *Paul's own experiences*, it
is methodologically indefensible to propose that 2 Cor 11:6 or 12:1–4 refer
to the supposed behavior of Paul's opponents. In fact, nowhere in 2 Corinthians does Paul ever refer to "visions and revelations" that were claimed
by his missionary opponents. To assume that Paul's boast concerning his
own visions and revelations appears only as a response to the similar activities of his rivals runs the clear risk of falsely imputing Paul's own
characteristic method of self-legitimation to his opponents, although there
is in fact no evidence to support this view in 2 Corinthians.

3.4.7. The "Foolishness" of Boasting in the Second Apology

An obvious objection may be raised against the view advocated here, that
Paul uses visions and revelations to legitimate his ministry. That is, why
does Paul make such statements as "there is nothing to be gained" by
boasting of visions and revelations, if he believed that there was something
to be gained by it? Why does he refer to 11:22–12:10, in which he adduces his visions and revelations, as a "foolish" speech (cf. 11:16; 12:11)?
The answer lies in the rhetorical scheme of the second apology. Paul
makes these statements not because he actually devalues ecstatic, visionary, or revelatory experiences. On the contrary, as we have seen, throughout his letters, Paul – in harmony with other early Christian sources, such
as Acts – assumes that visions and revelations play a large part in legitimating one's authority. Paul certainly has no trouble in boasting of his
accomplishments when he feels it serves his purpose (cf. Rom. 15:17–19)!
Rather, Paul refers to his boastful discourse as "foolish" because he is
parodying the activity of comparison (σύγκρισις) among apostles. Paul has

---

[144] In Sumney's defense, we may note that he does list 12:1 in a section that appears
under the heading "allusions," and he does state that the section occurs in a polemical
context. However, even though Paul did accuse his opponents of boasting (cf. 10:13), the
boast in 12:1 is Paul's own, and does not refer in any obvious way to a specific boast
made by his opponents. Therefore, it is misleading to categorize 12:1–4 as an allusion.

argued that his opponents should not engage in comparison between themselves and him (10:12), while ironically his own second apology in 2 Corinthians also takes the form of a comparison. Paul does what he denies should be done; he boasts of his own merits (constituted in part by a series of humiliations!), all the while insisting that boasting in one's own accomplishments is foolish. In the second apology, Paul crafts an ironic discourse in which he highlights his own particular ground for boasting, while at the same time claiming that boasting on one's own behalf – as his opponents had done! – was of no value. Such activity constitutes "foolish" speech. For the purposes of the ironic discourse, Paul characterizes himself as a "fool," boasting in an effort to combat the effect of his rivals' own foolish boasting. By boasting in this way – boasting "foolishly" – Paul hopes to recover the status and authority that he had lost in Corinth as the result of the boasting of his missionary rivals there.

3.4.8. Two Models of Comparison: Direct Analogy and Implied Antithesis

We should also distinguish between two types of comparison in 2 Corinthians. Paul directly compares himself with his opponents in some regards, while in other respects he describes only his own experience, adducing no analog from the claims of his missionary rivals. In the σύγκρισις, when Paul is comparing himself on points that his opponents also boast about, he does so directly: "Are my opponents such-and-such? So am I" (11:22). In this section, we may be certain that Paul is responding directly to a claim that was made by his opponents. But in the immediately following section (11:23–29), Paul abandons a point-by-point comparison and begins to adduce evidence in respect to which he apparently assumes that there is no analog in the experience of his opponents.

> Are they ministers of Christ? I speak foolishly: I am a better one (ὑπὲρ ἐγώ) – with more troubles, more imprisonments, with many more wounds (ἐν πληγαῖς ὑπερβαλλόντως), many times near death.

By the use of the preposition ὑπέρ, Paul appears to be introducing a topic in regard to which he expects that he will clearly best his opponents, an area in which he is "better" than they. Paul has suffered more hardships during the course of his ministry than he expects his opponents will be able to adduce. Whereas Paul paints his opponents as preaching for payment (2:17; 11:7–12), employing sophistic arguments only to deceive their audience (11:1–6), and documenting their success in letters of recommendation (cf. 3:1), Paul presents himself by way of contrast. Rather than enjoying obvious success in his missionary endeavors, he endures troubles, beatings, and imprisonments. Paul assumes that his audience will understand that the comparison is antithetical: Paul's opponents enjoy external advantage, rather than suffering hardship in their service of the gospel.

In the case of visions and revelations similarly Paul does not attempt to make a point by point comparison, such as we would expect if his opponents had claimed to have had similar experiences. Rather, as in the case of the hardship lists, Paul simply adduces his own experiences, assuming that his audience will agree that Paul far outshines his missionary opponents in this respect. Is it because such experiences have no known analogy in the lives of his opponents – or at the least, that the frequency of such experiences was less in the opponents' case – that Paul can assert that he is "superior" to them in these respects.

Paul significantly employs the preposition ὑπέρ in contexts where he expects that his ground for boasting is not something that his opponents share: in 11:23, Paul is a "better" minister of Christ (ὑπὲρ ἐγώ) because he has suffered more in his service of the gospel; in 11:23 he claims "many more beatings" (ἐν πληγαῖς ὑπερβαλλόντως). In 12:7, Paul mentions the "exceptional nature of the revelations" (ἡ ὑπερβολὴ τῶν ἀποκαλύψεων) to which he had been privy. Because of these revelations, Paul runs the risk of being "self-aggrandized" (ὑπεραίρομαι). When he adduces his list of hardships and his visionary and revelatory experiences, Paul expects that his audiences will agree with him that they boost his legitimacy "above" (ὑπέρ) that of his opponents whom, we will recall, Paul referred to ironically as "super-apostles" (ὑπερλίαν ἀπόστολοι). Paul employs his own characteristic legitimating devices (visions, revelations, and here also hardships) in order to deal what he expects will be the *coup de grace* to his opponents, with respect to whom Paul expects that his Corinthian audience will be able to adduce no parallel experiences, or for whom such experiences are less characteristic.

3.4.9. Conclusion

There is no evidence in 2 Corinthians that Paul's missionary opponents boasted of revelations, visions, or ecstatic experiences such as glossolalia to legitimate their missionary enterprise. Arguments to this effect have been based on a mirror exegesis of 2 Corinthians. Because Paul makes reference to his own visions and revelations, it is assumed, he therefore must be responding in kind to similar boasts made by his opponents. However, we have seen that in most of Paul's undisputed letters, he does point to revelations, visions, and ecstatic experience (glossolalia) as evidence that legitimates his own message and ministry. Because of this, it is methodologically improper to use mirror exegesis in an effort to impute revelatory/visionary/glossolaliac activity to Paul's opponents. Such a method runs the risk of falsely imputing Paul's own characteristic mode of self-legitimation to his missionary rivals. Paul assumes, on the contrary, that his rivals will be able to adduce no experiences that can parallel Paul's own claims to revelatory/visionary/ecstatic phenomena. By using this argument, Paul assumes that he will be able to prove that he is "superior" (ὑπέρ) to the "super-apostles" (ὑπερλίαν ἀπόστολοι).

3.5. What was the nature of the "other Jesus, other spirit, other gospel" preached by the rival missionaries in Corinth? How is this related to the same phrase in Galatians?

The issues in 2 Corinthians are not debates over theological issues, per se. Rather, at issue in 2 Corinthians is Paul's legitimacy as an apostle. Central to Paul's concerns in 2 Corinthians was the comparison that the Corinthians had made between Paul and his opponents, in which Paul – prior to his writing of the second apology – appears to have fared very badly. For this reason, Paul does not engage in heated polemic over specific theological topics, as he does in Galatians and Romans. In 2 Corinthians, Paul's references to the theology of his missionary opponents are few and provide scant data. When he does refer to the theology of his opponents most extensively in 2 Cor 3, it is only as part of an effort to show that Paul's own ministry was superior to that of his opponents. In 2 Cor 11:4, Paul does offer one tantalizing glimpse into three issues over which Paul and his opponents disagreed: the nature of "Jesus," "spirit," and "gospel."

After an introduction in which Paul refers to his worry that the Corinthians had been deceived, as Eve was deceived by the serpent in the Garden of Eden (Gen 3), Paul writes (11:4):

> For if the one who comes preaches another Jesus whom we did not preach, or you receive another spirit which you did not receive, or another gospel which you did not receive, you tolerate it readily.

> εἰ μὲν γὰρ ὁ ἐρχόμενος ἄλλον Ἰησοῦν κηρύσσει ὃν οὐκ ἐκηρύξαμεν, ἢ πνεῦμα ἕτερον λαμβάνετε ὁ οὐκ ἐλάβετε, ἢ εὐαγγέλιον ἕτερον ὁ οὐκ ἐδέξασθε, καλῶς ἀνέχεσθε.

The way in which Paul formulates his objection indicates an inner-sectarian discussion: the opponents preach in the same terms as Paul ("Jesus," "spirit," "gospel"), but interpret these terms differently. Because Paul is concerned to defend himself and the integrity of his ministry against the apparent superiority of his opponents' preaching, and not over theological issues, per se, in the first and second apologies, Paul does not elaborate on the ways in which his opponents interpret "Jesus," "spirit," and "gospel." However, we may make a few informed guesses, based on our knowledge of Paul's religious environment.

The nature of the "spirit" that Paul's opponents may have preached has already been suggested in our examination of their attitude toward the Torah. We have seen that in the Hebrew Bible, in Second Temple Judaism, and within the early Christian movement, the eschatological period is often

marked 1) by the restoration of the covenant between God and his people;
and 2) by the irruption of God's spirit, which enables people to fulfill the
Torah perfectly. Most likely, Paul's missionary opponents espoused a
variant of this prominent ideological formulation. These missionaries
probably preached that the spirit enabled believers to fulfill the law. This
position on the part of Paul's opponents would account for Paul's characterization of them as trying to "enslave" (καταδουλοῦν) the Corinthians (2
Cor 11:20). Paul uses this term in only one other instance, in Gal 2:4,
where he also uses it to refer to an attempt to impose the observance of
Torah on the Galatian congregation. This supposition also explains Paul's
phrase in 2 Cor 3:17: "where the spirit of the Lord is, is freedom"
(ἐλευθερία). Although the range of Paul's usage with respect to ἐλευθερία
is less restricted than that of "enslavement," he does use this term, too, in
contexts in which he discusses whether or not his converts should follow
the Torah. In Gal 2:4, Paul mentions the "false brothers who crept in to spy
out our freedom (ἐλευθερία) which we have in Christ Jesus, in order to
enslave us" (ἵνα ἡμᾶς καταδουλώσουσιν; cp. also Gal 5:1, 13). Since Paul
uses the language and ideology of "slavery" and "freedom" in a clear
context in which the issue of Torah observance is being discussed, it seems
likely that the same holds true for 2 Corinthians: Paul's opponents probably preached that the "spirit" empowered believers to live lives that ac-
corded with the precepts of the Torah. This in turn reflected the conditions
of a restored covenant between God and his people; a people expanded by
the inclusion of Gentile converts.

The issue of what "Jesus" Paul's missionary opponents preached is
more difficult to answer. For the issue of spirit, there is at least Paul's
polemical discussion in 2 Cor 3 that offers some guidance as to what the
rival missionaries may have preached. In the case of the Jesus which these
missionaries preached however, there are no data in 2 Corinthians. Perhaps
the best way to proceed here is to point out the peculiarities of the Pauline
Jesus. Whereas stories about the life and teaching of Jesus circulated and
were constitutive elements in the "gospel" preached by some early Christians (as for example, in the canonical gospels), Paul's own preaching
focused on a particular theme with regard to Jesus: his death. In a telling
statement in 1 Cor 2:2, Paul avers that "I resolved to know nothing among
you except Jesus Christ, that is,[145] him crucified" (οὐ γὰρ ἔκρινά τι
εἰδέναι ἐν ὑμῖν εἰ μὴ Ἰησοῦν Χριστὸν καὶ τοῦτον ἐσταυρωμένον). One of
the defining characteristics of Paul's preaching about Jesus was his con-
centration on Jesus' death and resurrection. Paul redeploys these two ideas
in several instances in contexts in which he wishes to make ethical points
relevant to the practice of his communities (cf. Phil 2:1–11; 2 Cor 4:7–11;

---

[145] Taking the καί as epexegetical.

Rom 6:1–11). In contrast, Paul seldom refers to stories from the life of Jesus in support of his ethical arguments – even though he was familiar with some traditions about Jesus' life and teaching (1 Cor 7:10; 11:23–26; cf. also Gal 1:18). Even though Paul did not characteristically refer to incidents from Jesus' life or aspects of his teaching to authenticate his own preaching, it does not seem that Paul would have maligned rival apostles' teaching about Jesus as constituting "another Jesus" unless that teaching conflicted in some important way with Paul's own.

We may suggest – and this suggestion, in the absence of supporting evidence from 2 Corinthians, must be taken as tentative – that Paul's missionary opponents may have preached a Jesus similar to that in the Gospel of Matthew; that is, one who espoused adherence to the Torah. This suggestion has in fact already been offered by Margaret Thrall, who argues that, in Mt 28:16–20,

the Eleven are to teach obedience to Jesus' commands. In the Matthean context, this must include obedience to the law of Moses. According to Mt 5.17–19, Jesus has come to fulfill this law, and it is to be kept meticulously by those who would be called great in the kingdom of heaven. The phrase ἕτερον εὐαγγέλιον suggests at least a partial parallel with the Galatian situation (Gal 1.6), and this, in turn, would mean that the opponents' gospel involves some measure of Torah observance.

Thrall also points to Paul's notice in 2 Cor 11:4 that the Corinthians καλῶς ἀνέχεσθε. Thrall takes the fact that the Corinthians were described as "tolerating" the "Jesus," "spirit," and "gospel" of the missionaries who were preaching it as an indication that this preaching the Corinthians did not find particularly congenial. Responding to Georgi's thesis that Paul's missionary opponents preached about Jesus as a "divine man," Thrall comments: "The proclamation of a glorious Christ would have been highly congenial to [the Corinthians]: not something that would require toleration."[146] However, we may surmise that an attempt to impose Torah observance among the Corinthians would have been such as to require "toleration."

As for "gospel," we need only mention that the usage of this term in earliest Christianity was as a general designation for the content of one's preaching. The "gospel" could include such elements as the imminent arrival of the kingdom of God (Mk 1:14–15), stories about the life of Jesus (Mt 26:19), or about Jesus' death and resurrection (1 Cor 15:1–8). It seems likely that the "gospel" of the missionaries whose influence Paul addresses in the first and second apologies included mention of the law of Moses, "engraved on stone tablets" (2 Cor 3:7), and included reference to the eschatological "spirit" that enabled believers to fulfill this law. Paul may have chosen to malign the "Jesus," "spirit," and "gospel" preached by his

---

[146] This and the previous quotation are from Thrall, *II Corinthians* 2:669.

opponents as a Satanic deception (11:3) not because their preaching had a different emphasis than Paul's own preaching, itself centered almost exclusively on the death and resurrection of Jesus, but because the preaching of these individuals differed importantly with regard to the praxis that it entailed: fulfillment of the law of Moses through the aid of the spirit. It may have been this aspect of the missionaries' preaching that most unsettled Paul, for it undercut his own insistence that Gentile converts need not follow the Torah. For Paul, a community-based ethic, inspired by love of one's neighbor – which to be sure was according to some contemporary or nearly contemporary Jews, the "fulfillment" of the Torah – was the necessary and sufficient basis for ordering the praxis of the communities that he had founded (1 Thess 4:9–12; 1 Cor 13; Rom 15:1–6).

To recapitulate: the significance of the triad, "Jesus," "spirit," and "gospel," within the preaching of the Paul's missionary rivals is difficult to ascertain due to a lack of evidence in 2 Corinthians. However, in Second Temple Judaism and in earliest Christianity, the connection between spirit and renewed covenant is stereotypical: God's spirit empowers individuals perfectly to fulfill the law under the conditions of a renewed covenant. It seems likely that Paul's missionary rivals espoused some variant of this general theological narrative. The other two terms may be interpreted in a way that coheres with this understanding of the opponents' use of "spirit": both "Jesus" and "gospel" may have connoted adherence to the Torah. We do in fact have a close parallel for such an understanding of the significance of "Jesus" and "gospel" in the Gospel of Matthew, in which Jesus is presented as radicalizing the precepts of the Torah, and asks for his disciples to adhere to this radicalized version of the Torah, and to teach it "to all the Gentiles."

3.6. How closely were the missionary rivals related to earlier traditions that circulated within Judaism? within the early Jesus movement?

We may recall Barrett's observations, cited earlier in this chapter, regarding the alleged "deviance" of Corinthian belief and practice:

Alexandrian Judaism, Jewish Christianity, Hellenism, all seem to have played upon the already inflammatory material assembled at Corinth. It is no wonder that there was a blaze; no wonder the city could add to its trade fairs as fine an exhibition of Christian deviation as could be seen anywhere in the world.[147]

It is unclear from Barrett's statement whether he considered the belief and practice advocated by Paul's missionary opponents in Corinth as falling into the category of "as fine an exhibition of Christian deviation as could be seen anywhere in the world." In a more recent essay, Barrett made the

---

[147] "Christianity at Corinth," 3.

following pregnant remark: "Historically, topographically, and perhaps traditionally [Paul's missionary opponents in 2 Corinthians] may well have stood nearer than Paul to the historical Jesus."[148] Are we to see the preaching of Paul's missionary opponents in Corinth as – in Käsemann's formulation – a "Judaistic falsification of the gospel," or did these missionaries indeed display a greater affinity with the earlier traditions the Christian movement, some of which originated with Jesus himself, than did Paul, as Barrett suggests? In order to answer the question, we will examine the relationship of these missionaries to earlier traditions in several areas, most of which we have already discussed in other contexts earlier in this chapter: 1) apostolic support; 2) traditions of ancient Israel; 3) Torah and covenant; 4) covenant renewal and spirit; 5) Jesus. We will conclude the section with a brief look at the modes of legitimation employed by the missionaries.

As we have seen earlier, Paul's missionary opponents accepted support from Corinth during their stay in that city. This practice corresponded with a mandate instituted by Jesus (Lk 10:7) – as Paul himself was aware (1 Cor 9:14) – and was practiced by Jesus' earliest followers, notably Cephas (1 Cor 9:3–6). The missionaries who opposed Paul in Corinth had a strong claim to represent traditional practice in this regard. It was Paul whose mode of financial support represented a "deviation" from established practice within the early Christian communities.

The claim by the missionaries in Corinth to the designations "Hebrews," "Israelites," and "descendants of Abraham" indicates the importance that they attached to a genealogical descent from Israelite ancestors, and indicates a link with scriptural traditions in which Israelites, Hebrews, and descendants of Abraham played a part. However, since one may claim to represent tradition while in fact differing in important ideological and practical respects from one's predecessors, the use of these titles indicates little except that these missionaries used their genetic ties to Israelite ancestors as a means of self-legitimation.

An important aspect of the missionaries' teaching concerned the law of Moses (2 Cor 3). In this respect, it may be hypothesized that these missionaries espoused some variant of the view held by both the gospel of Matthew and the Letter to the Hebrews, that Jesus' teaching and/or death inaugurated a period in which the law of Moses was at once relativized and radicalized. According to the Gospel of Matthew, Jesus, as a "new Moses," espoused a rigorous interpretation of the Torah, which involved perfect obedience to the Torah, not only with respect to overt actions, but also with respect to one's very intention to fulfill the law. According to the Letter to the Hebrews, Jesus relativized the law because his death provided

---

[148] "Paul's Opponents," 60.

a single remedy for the problem of disobedience to the mandates of the Torah. As Hebrews reasons, under the "old covenant" disobedience to the Torah constituted an ongoing problem, which was solved through periodic sacrifices. Jesus' death made possible a "new covenant" in which a single sacrifice (Jesus') achieved atonement for individuals who were expected to be empowered by the spirit to conform fully to the precepts of the Torah. There is not enough data in 2 Cor 3 to reconstruct the specifics of the missionaries' teaching with regard to their position on the law of Moses, but it likely entailed some variant of the view that the law was still in full effect, although under the changed circumstances brought about by Jesus' teaching and/or death. This probably entailed some idea that the law was relativized by Jesus' ministry, without thereby negating the idea that it constituted the basis of the covenant between God and humans.

If indeed these missionaries held some variant of the early Christian view that the law was still in force, but under a new set of conditions inaugurated by Jesus' teaching/death (those conditions constituting the "new covenant"), then we are faced with a complicated question as to these missionaries' relationship with tradition. It seems likely that they were in continuity with early Christian traditions that both assumed the continuing function of the Torah as a legal and practical norm, while asserting that the conditions under which the Torah was fulfilled were different than they had been under the "old," Mosaic, covenant. This would indicate a continuity of tradition with early Christian views, but attests to a complex relationship to earlier scriptural traditions. There was certainly a tension with the foundational documents on the role of the law, such as that in Deut 32, but also a continuity with later scriptural traditions, such as the exilic views espoused in the books of Ezekiel and Jeremiah. In early Christian tradition, the scriptural promise of the "new covenant" had been fulfilled; the problem of disobedience to the Torah had been solved through the teaching and death of Jesus of Nazareth. In this respect also, Paul's opponents stood closer to early Christian tradition and scriptural traditions than did Paul, who did not advocate that converts should view the Torah as a normative guide to behavior.

Related to the topic of Torah and covenant is the role that the spirit played in the preaching of the missionaries in Corinth. We have argued that these missionaries probably viewed the spirit as a force that enabled converts to follow the Torah perfectly, a view that corresponds with scriptural traditions in Ezekiel and Jeremiah, and is also found in Second Temple Jewish texts such as Jubilees and the Community Rule. Again, it was Paul who deviated from earlier, established tradition: it was he who suggested that "where the spirit of the Lord is, is freedom." Paul's freedom is a freedom from the law.

3.6.1. Issues of Legitimation

Lastly, issues of legitimation distinguished Paul from the rival missionaries in Corinth. Whereas Paul legitimated himself on the basis of the "surpassing nature" of the revelatory experiences and visions that he had witnessed, as well as his own charismatic abilities, such as glossolalia, Paul's opponents – at least in the eyes of the Corinthians – were legitimated by letters of recommendation and their powerful rhetorical skills. It appears to have been a commonplace for early Christian communities to provide letters of recommendation for traveling missionaries. In terms of their relationship to tradition, however, this practice does not reveal a great deal. On the other hand, when we turn to the issue of rhetorical skills, we encounter an interesting link to early Christian tradition. In contradistinction to the view of the church fathers that the earliest Christians were plain-spoken and lacked rhetorical sophistication, the earliest Christian documents attest a somewhat different attitude toward rhetorical ability. Apollos of Alexandria was well known for his eloquence (Acts 18:24). The Book of Acts indicates how such oratorical skill functioned: Apollos "refuted the Jews in public, showing from the scriptures that Jesus was the messiah" (18:28). Within the rhetorical and propagandistic program of earliest Christianity, rhetorical skill was highly valued. First Corinthians 1:17–3:3 indicates the value that the Corinthians placed upon Apollos' rhetorical abilities; Paul is forced to counter such abilities by denigrating them as "worldly wisdom," while attempting to inculcate within his audience a preference for revealed knowledge. Paul presents himself as a hierophant who is able to lead his initiates through graded stages of esoteric knowledge, to which he had access by revelation (2:6–13). In Second Corinthians, Paul encounters missionaries whose rhetorical ability was perhaps on a par with that of Apollos; only in the case of the former the threat posed to Paul's authority was much greater. These missionaries apparently employed their considerable rhetorical prowess in an effort to discredit Paul's teaching, labeling him a "deceiver" who preached a "veiled gospel" (12:16; 4:3). By contrast, the preaching of the missionaries was straightforward: they did not present themselves as hierophants of sacred mysteries, who could dangle the tantalizing lure of progressive revelation before their hearers. Their message, they may have argued, was simple and scripturally based, and in the eyes of the Corinthians it was presented persuasively.

3.7. Summary of Conclusions

This study has argued that Paul's missionary opponents were Jews who had no institutional ties with the Jerusalem church. There is no evidence that these missionaries were from Palestine; more likely they originated from elsewhere in the Mediterranean region. The missionaries stood in continuity with traditions that are likely to have originated with Jesus, inasmuch as they accepted support from the churches to which they preached. The fact that Paul did not do so was taken as a tacit admission that he was not truly an "apostle." The missionaries preached that Gentile converts to the early Christian movement should follow the legal precepts of the Torah. The missionaries probably espoused an ideology familiar from the Hebrew Bible as well as early Jewish and Christian texts, according to which, under the conditions of the new covenant, the spirit enabled individuals to maintain perfect obedience to the Torah. The oft-raised objection that, unlike Galatians, 2 Corinthians does not have any explicit polemic against Torah observance is shown to be misleading. The first and second apologies of 2 Corinthians were written, not to argue the relative merits and weaknesses of adherence to the law, but to assure the Corinthians that Paul was a better apostle than his rivals were. That is, the apologies defend Paul and his ministry; they do not purport to be a refutation of the theological tenets held by the opposition.

It was also argued that, contrary to the view that is sometimes taken, Paul validated himself and his ministry through repeated appeals to visions and revelatory experiences, as well as his exemplary glossolaliac ability. This is evident in Paul's letters and in the portrayals of him in the Book of Acts and the Pseudo-Clementine Homilies. The evidence that Paul's missionary opponents legitimated themselves through appeals to ecstatic and visionary experiences rests entirely on the assumption that, because Paul adduces such experiences of his own in 2 Corinthians, he must therefore be doing so in an effort to counter similar claims made by his opponents. Such an assumption runs the risk of imputing Paul's favored legitimating themes to his opponents, with regard to whom there is no evidence that they legitimated themselves in this way. The missionaries in Corinth instead legitimated themselves on the basis of their letters of recommendation and their exceptional rhetorical capabilities.

Chapter 5

The New Covenant According to Paul

In the last chapter, we made some observations and suggested some hypotheses about the nature of the preaching of the missionaries who had arrived in Corinth some time after Paul had left the city in the early 50s of the common era. This information will play a central role in our understanding of the pressures to which Paul responded in the first and second apologies in 2 Corinthians. In this chapter, we will begin by delineating some important incidents in Paul's own prior missionary experience that also played a formative role in the situation to which Paul was forced to respond in his two apologies in 2 Corinthians. After that, we will examine the particular charges that Paul's missionary opponents brought against him in Corinth. Lastly, we will examine the way in which Paul crafted his discourse on the new covenant in 2 Cor 3:1–4:6 in response to these charges.

1. Before Paul Arrived in Corinth:
Experiences in Antioch and Philippi

1.1. Paul and Antioch[1]

Paul's first experiences as a missionary for the early Christian movement occurred under the tutelage of Barnabas who, like Paul, was a Jew from the diaspora. Barnabas hailed from Cyprus. During ca. 46–48 CE, Paul accompanied Barnabas on a missionary trip that began in Antioch, proceeded westward to Cyprus and then northwest to Pamphylia and Pisidia,

---

[1] As was made clear in chapter 4, I see no institutional connection between the missionaries against whom Paul argues in 2 Corinthians and the Jerusalem church. My purpose in introducing the events in Antioch here is very different: it helps to explain why Paul brought no letter of recommendation to Corinth. It also helps to explain Paul's mode of self-legitimation – visionary and revelatory experience – which served in lieu of institutional legitimation. In addition, the practices and ideology to which Paul was introduced in Antioch continued to inform his own practice and ideology throughout his subsequent career.

ending again in Syrian Antioch.[2] During and after this time, Paul served as a representative of the Antioch church. However, in 51 CE, events would transpire that would result in Paul severing ties with this church, as well as with Barnabas his mentor, and journeying alone westward in search of fresh missionary territory.

The events that transpired in 51 CE are notoriously difficult to reconstruct. The two sources that purport to describe the situation, Acts 15 and Gal 2:1–10, differ in some important respects. Both accounts serve apologetic functions, and both have distorted the events that they purport to describe. The account developed here largely follows the outline suggested by Betz in his commentary on Galatians.[3]

According to Acts 15:1–2,

> Then certain individuals came down from Judea [to Antioch] and were teaching the brothers, 'Unless you are circumcised according to the custom of Moses, you cannot be saved.' And after Paul and Barnabas had no small dissention with them, Paul and Barnabas and some of the others were appointed to go up to Jerusalem to discuss this question with the apostles and the elders (NRSV).

This résumé probably serves as an accurate portrayal of the situation as it arose in Antioch.[4] In Jerusalem, a "council" was convened, which included James (Jesus' brother), Peter, the elders of the Jerusalem church, and some Pharisaic members of the Christian community, in addition to the delegation from Antioch. In Betz' view, three positions were represented at the council: that of Paul and Barnabas, in which Gentiles were not expected to adhere to Jewish law, that of the Pharisaic Christians, who advocated that Gentile converts should follow Jewish law, and the mediating position of James and Peter, who advocated that Jewish members of the Christian movement could freely associate with Gentile members, because they did not need to follow the "Jewish way of life, especially the part of separation from the unclean."[5] Under pressure from the Pharisaic group, the Jerusalem apostles eventually capitulated to the demand that Jewish members of the Christian sect follow the laws of purity. As a result of this pressure,

---

[2] Acts 13-14. See also *Collins Atlas of the Bible* (J. Pritchard, ed., Ann Arbor, MI: Borders Press, 2003) 172–173.

[3] *Galatians: A Commentary on Paul's Letter to the Churches in Galatia* (Hermeneia commentary series; Philadelphia, PA: Fortress Press, 1979); esp. pp. 81–83, 103–104. Other reconstructions include those of J. Murphy-O'Connor, *Paul: A Critical Life*, 93–95; 130–146; G. Luedemann, *Opposition to Paul in Jewish Christianity* (Minneapolis, MN: Fortress, 1989; trans. of *Paulus, der Heidenapostel*, vol. 2: *Antipaualinismus im frühen Christentum*) 35–39; R. N. Longnecker, *Galatians* (Word Biblical Commentary, vol. 41; Dallas, TX: Word Books, 1990) lxxiii–lxxxviii; J. Taylor, *Les Actes des Deux Apôtres*, vol. 5: *Commentaire Historique* (Paris: J. Gabalda, 1994) 197–225.

[4] So Murphy-O'Connor, *Paul: A Critical Life*, 132–133.

[5] *Galatians*, 104.

Peter, who after the council had taken temporary residence in Antioch, withdrew from table fellowship with Paul and the Gentile converts for whom Paul was responsible.[6]

When Peter withdrew from table fellowship with the Gentiles in Antioch, Barnabas joined him. This move was not an act of hypocrisy, as Paul presents it, but rather an acceptance of the authority of James, who had come to accept that the Pharisaic position with regard to purity laws was the correct one. (The Pharisees may have derided the position of the Jerusalem apostles as lacking in legal sophistication, regarding the provincial apostles as "unlearned in the law.") The position adopted by James, and subsequently by the leadership at Antioch (Paul excluded), Paul viewed as untenable because it introduced an element of internal division within the Christian community. This division implied a devaluation of the status of Gentile converts as potential sources of impurity, and would almost certainly have introduced a pressure among Gentiles to conform to Pharisaic legal prescriptions.

Marginalized by his refusal to accept the decision of James, Peter, Barnabas – and, we may assume, the rest of the Antioch church – Paul dissociated himself from Antioch and set off in search of "fresh" territory, in which he could promulgate his own version of the gospel. According to Paul's version of the gospel, Gentile converts were accepted as members of the "Israel of God" in full standing on the basis of their confession that "Jesus is lord" and their adherence to the standards of Hellenistic morality. Paul's position represented the practice that was followed in the Antioch church prior to the Jerusalem council in 51 CE – a practice subsequently repudiated by that church.

---

[6] Betz's summary of the events in Antioch and the Jerusalem council seem to me to represent a judicious evaluation of the sources. I would only like to nuance the understanding of Jewish law as it played a role in the situation. It seems that the mediating position originally adopted by the Jerusalem apostles represented, not a rejection of the "Jewish way of life," but rather a rejection only of the thesis that the laws of purity applied outside the Jerusalem temple. The Pharisaic position, which viewed the laws of purity as applicable to some or all meals eaten outside of the temple precincts, seems to have been an innovation of the mid-second century BCE. The position of the Jerusalem apostles then does not represent a rejection of Jewish law, but of the Pharisaic interpretation of the law. This rejection of the Pharisaic position seems to be in keeping with Jesus' own attitude toward purity laws. In other respects, we may probably assume that both Jesus and the Jerusalem apostles fully endorsed following the Torah – at least for Jewish members of the Christian sect (which leads us to a position not dissimilar from Paul's as expressed in 1 Corinthians). The issue of Gentile inclusion within the new Jewish movement, however, does not seem to have been as important an issue for Jesus, Cephas, and the original core of the Jesus group as it later became for Paul and the Antioch church.

Murphy-O'Connor evokes the pathos of Paul's situation in the following passage:

> Even if he was no longer the emissary of a church, the divine commission ... would validate his subsequent career. He was 'an apostle, not from men or through a man, but through Jesus Christ and God the Father' (Gal 1:1).
>
> Sometime in the spring of AD 52, therefore, when the gorge through the Taurus mountains known as the Cilician Gates was passable, and most of the snow had melted on the plateau, Paul left Antioch. He was never to return.[7]

Murphy-O'Connor is probably correct in inferring that, after Paul left Antioch, he no longer functioned as "the emissary of a church." At that point, Paul can only legitimate himself through his claims to revelation and the appearance of Jesus to him in a vision, which Paul subsequently recalled in an effort to legitimate his (disputed) status as an apostle (Gal 1:1; 1 Cor 9:1). These circumstances are probably largely responsible for Paul's choice of visionary and revelatory experiences as his main mode of self-legitimation (as we have seen in the previous chapter). Paul's lack of a "home church" that he could use to provide him with letters of recommendation, and which he could rely on to vouch for his authority, stood in stark contrast to the missionary rivals whom Paul encountered in Corinth. These missionaries, we will remember, were able to produce letters of recommendation from another church – letters which augmented their claims to authority. Paul would, after leaving Antioch and prior to arriving in Corinth, develop relationships with groups in other cities – Philippi, Thessalonica, Ephesus – but it is striking that he did not rely on any of these groups to provide him with commendatory letters. It was not that Paul was opposed to the practice, because he himself provides commendations for his "fellow workers" in the gospel (e.g., Phoebe in Rom 16). Perhaps it was due to Paul's painful memory of being marginalized within a church for which he had served as an emissary for some years that he did not rely on any specific church to legitimate his claims to authority. Paul's experiences had taught him how quickly a relationship with a particular community could degenerate (cp. also Gal 1:6, not to mention the second apology of 2 Corinthians!).

1.2. Paul's Model of Economic Support

Unlike the missionary "servants of righteousness" who had received support from the Corinthians while they were in the city, Paul chose to work at a trade and so to support himself. We will remember that the "servants of righteousness" were following a missionary mandate that is likely to have been propounded by Jesus. What was at stake in the difference between Paul's mode of support in Corinth and that of his missionary com-

---

[7] *Paul: A Critical Life*, 158.

petitors? In order to answer this question, a little background information is necessary.

In *The Social Context of Paul's Ministry*,[8] Ronald Hock outlines four modes of support that were available to Greco-Roman philosophers and public speakers, whom Hock takes as a model for understanding Paul. The four modes included the following:

1) a philosopher or orator could charge fees of his students, such as was common practice among sophists;
2) a philosopher or public speaker could become a retainer at the house of a wealthy statesman or merchant;
3) he could beg for his sustenance, such as many Cynic philosophers did, or
4) he could work to earn a living.[9]

Each mode of support however, had some drawbacks. As Hock points out, those who charged fees opened themselves to the charge that they were greedy, and taught only for the sake of financial gain. They could easily be described as "merchants," "hawking" their wares. Entering into the house of a wealthy patron could be even more dangerous to one's image. Lucian describes how demeaning this profession could be: one had to sit at the least honored seat during banquets, and had to line up with the servants at the end of every month in order to receive his pay.[10] Begging, of course, had its own drawbacks. One was never certain whether or how much one would eat. Also, begging was regarded as shameful behavior. Lastly, working for a living often put one in the company of slaves, and the hunched postures required for some professions were regarded as demeaning and "slavish." Also, the long hours of work required to sustain oneself detracted from the amount of philosophizing in which one could engage![11]

Why did Paul choose then to work to support himself, in view of the various options? In light of Paul's statement in 1 Cor 9:6, "Or is it only I and Barnabas who do not have the right not to work?" it seems likely that even during his stint at Antioch, Paul labored at a profession to support himself.[12] As was the case with his practice of accepting Gentiles into fellowship without requiring them to adhere to the precepts of the Torah, Paul seems also to have followed the early practice of the Antioch church in his mode of support. Both Paul's attitude toward the Gentiles and his

---

[8] Subtitled *Tentmaking and Apostleship* (Philadelphia, PA: Fortress Press, 1980).

[9] *The Social Context,* 50–59.

[10] Hock (p. 55) cites Lucian's *De Mercede conductis* 23.

[11] Hock, *The Social Context*, 50–59.

[12] So G. Fee, "In this case Paul and Barnabas in particular were known to have worked at a trade when they evangelized" (*The First Epistle to the Corinthians*; NICNT: Grand Rapids, MI: Eerdmans, 1987) 404.

practice of self-support represent the practice that Paul followed during his time at Antioch.

It was not that Paul did not have the option of receiving support during his stay in Corinth. Indeed, he received harsh criticism for refusing to accept support from the congregation there. In 1 Cor 9:1–18, Paul asserts that he does have the right, as an apostle – a designation which however, some denied to Paul (cf. 9:1–2) – to receive support from the community. However, Paul is able to turn his failure to receive support into a boast: he preaches the gospel "free of charge" (ἀδάπανον; 9:18). When Paul is faced with missionary rivals who live at the expense of the community in 2 Corinthians, he is able to make use of the standard criticism that was leveled against the Sophists: they operated only for the sake of financial gain.[13] According to Paul, his missionary opponents "hawked the word of God" (καπηλεύοντες τὸν λόγον τοῦ θεοῦ; 2 Cor 2:17). Paul is thus able to portray his opponents as unscrupulous preachers, motivated by the prospect of financial gain. Of course, both Paul and his opponents had a mutual interest in portraying the motives of the opposing party in as negative a light as possible.

2. Charges Levied against Paul in Corinth by the Missionaries

Many of the criticisms to which Paul responds in the first and second apologies stemmed from within the Corinthian congregation. Such charges arose in part from the comparison to which the community had subjected Paul, a comparison in which he fared poorly when juxtaposed to his missionary rivals in Corinth. The charges that Paul "recommended himself" (3:1) and that he lacked "sufficiency" (ἱκανότης) to carry on an effective ministry (3:5) probably were raised internally by the Corinthians. The issue of sufficiency had already been touched on in 1 Cor 15:9, where Paul claims to be the "least of the apostles" and that he was "unfit (οὐκ ... ἱκανός) to be called an apostle." However, Paul also responds to a cluster of charges in 4:2–3 that likely were first suggested by the missionaries who had come to Corinth. In these verses, Paul states,

We have renounced shameful, hidden things, not behaving craftily nor falsifying the word of God ... But even if our gospel is veiled, it is veiled only to those who are perishing ...

---

[13] So Betz, *Der Apostel Paulus*, 100–118, esp. 117: The fact that Paul was self-supporting, "gibt Paulus die Gelegenheit, einen antisophistischen Topos zu verwenden, der ihn entlastet und seinen Gegnern die Rolle geldgieriger Betrüger zuschiebt" ("gives Paul the opportunity to employ an antisophistic topos, which exculpates him and shifts to his opponents the role of money-grubbing swindlers").

ἀπειπάμεθα τὰ κρυπτὰ τῆς αἰσχύνης, μὴ περιπατοῦντες ἐν πανουργίᾳ μηδὲ δολοῦντες τὸν λόγον τοῦ θεοῦ ... εἰ δὲ καὶ ἔστιν κεκαλυμμένον τὸ εὐαγγέλιον ἡμῶν, ἐν τοῖς ἀπολλυμένιος ἔστιν κεκαλυμμένον ...

This passage serves a dual function within the context of the first apology. On the one hand, it serves an apologetic function. The expression εἰ δὲ καί here serves a concessive function, "But even if our gospel is veiled ..." This formulation indicates that someone has alleged that Paul's gospel is veiled. The reference in v. 2 to τὰ κρυπτά, "hidden things" links this verse with the following one. In v. 3, Paul avers that his gospel is indeed "veiled"; that is, that it occludes, it "hides." We may recall that, in 1 Corinthians (2:6–10), Paul had described his gospel as

a wisdom not of this age ... but we speak God's wisdom which is hidden away in mystery ... but God revealed it to us by the spirit.

σοφίαν δὲ οὐ τοῦ αἰῶνος τούτου ... ἀλλὰ λαλοῦμεν θεοῦ σοφίαν ἐν μυστηρίῳ τὴν ἀποκεκρυμμένην ... ἡμῖν δὲ ἀπεκάλυψεν ὁ θεὸς διὰ τοῦ πνεύματος.

In 2 Cor 4, Paul is attacked for presenting himself as a hierophant of secret and hidden wisdom, which had been revealed to him by the spirit. The corollary to the charge that Paul preached a "veiled gospel" was that he had "behaved craftily" and "falsified the word of God." The charge of "craftiness" emerges again in the second apology (12:16), although there it is connected with Paul's handling of the collection for the Jerusalem church. The charge that Paul had "falsified the word of God" of course implies a construal of the "word of God" that is at odds with Paul's own. Later in the second apology, Paul accuses the "ministers of righteousness" of preaching a gospel that differs from Paul's own (11:4). The content of this gospel probably served as the basis from which the missionary "ministers of righteousness" in Corinth were able to claim that, in his preaching, Paul "falsified the word of God."

C. K. Barrett has suggested that the charge of "falsifying the word of God" arose because he did not require "all, Gentile converts included, to observe the law of Moses."[14] This suggestion has not been followed, based on the common view that "the law" is not an issue of debate in 2 Corinthians. We have already seen in chapter 4 that the role of the law under the conditions of the new covenant was in fact a point of theological and practical difference between Paul and his missionary rivals in Corinth. Barrett was probably correct in his surmise, but in light of the traditional discourse on the role of the spirit in the inauguration of the new covenant, there was more to the story than he realized.

---

[14] *The Second Epistle to the Corinthians* (New York, NY: Harper and Row, 1973) 128.

In the last chapter, we argued that the missionary "ministers of right-eousness" were probably preaching a variant of the idea, first encountered in scriptural texts such as Ezekiel and Jeremiah and later adopted by vari-ous groups within Judaism (as represented by Jubilees, 1QS) and the early Christian movement (as represented by Hebrews), that under the condi-tions of the new or restored covenant God would, by means of his spirit, transform the minds of individuals so that they would be able perfectly to fulfill the Torah (with the caveat that, as is the case with the U. S. Consti-tution, defining rules for the contemporary application of the Torah was an area of contention!). It was God's spirit, according to these missionaries, that enabled the Gentile convert to adhere to the law. The spirit was thought of as removing past impurity and transforming the intention of the individual so that he would be able to live in accord with God's will – a will defined by the Torah (cp. Heb 6:4–8; 8:10–12; 10:14–18, 19–22).

For Paul, the spirit played quite a different role: it guaranteed that Gentiles were "adopted" into the family of God (cf. Gal 4:5–6) without adhering to the precepts of the Torah. Paul's succinct formulation for this concept runs as follows: "Where the spirit of the Lord is, is freedom." Paul's "freedom" is a freedom from the law (cf. Gal 5:1–5). Since Paul, in his own formulation of the "gospel" consciously excluded any role for the Torah, he left himself open to the charge that he had occluded what should have been a major component of the "word of God." The connection be-tween new covenant, spirit, and Torah was clearly laid out in scripture (Ezekiel and Jeremiah). It was accepted in Jewish tradition (Jubilees, 1QS) and even within the early Christian sect (Hebrews). It was with some justi-fication then, that Paul's opponents concluded that he had "falsified the word of God."

3. It Takes One to Know One: Paul's Anti-Sophistic Rhetoric

Betz first pointed out Paul's use of anti-Sophistic rhetoric in 2 Corinthi-ans.[15] Bruce Winter has elaborated on Betz's fundamental insight.[16] More recently, Mark Given has argued that, even though he employs anti-sophistic rhetoric against his opponents, he himself also relies on a sophis-tic mode of argumentation at key points in his own arguments.[17] When the

---

[15] *Der Apostel Paulus und die Sokratische Tradition: Eine exegetische Untersuchung zu seiner „Apologie" 2 Korinther 10–13* (Tübingen: J. C. B. Mohr-Paul Siebeck, 1972).

[16] *Philo and Paul Among the Sophists.*

[17] *Paul's True Rhetoric: Ambiguity, Cunning, and Deception in Greece and Rome* (Harrisburg, PA: Trinity Press International, 2001). I cannot agree however, with Given's

orator Favorinus (80–150 CE)[18] argued publicly with the sophist Polemo in Rome, according to Philostratus, people viewed this as an inner-sophistic dispute. Philostratus who, according to a dichotomous classificatory scheme constituted by "philosophers" and "sophists," labels Favorinus as a "philosopher," writes, "And so when people called Favorinus a sophist, the mere fact that he had quarreled with a sophist was evidence enough; for that spirit of rivalry ... is always directed against one's competitors in the same craft" (ἐπὶ τοὺς ἀντιτέχνους).[19] By the same coin, if Paul engaged in a quarrel with people whom he insinuated used sophistic techniques, this raises the possibility that Paul himself may be subject to the same charge. In fact, an examination of some of the sophistic devices that Paul employs will help to clarify the procedures whereby Paul crafted his discourse.

Several charges were often leveled against sophists: they charged fees for their instruction (and so they could be portrayed negatively as prostitutes[20] or "hucksters"); they had little regard for the "truth" of the matters in regard to which they declaimed (privileging probability over absolute truth);[21] their craft was "eristic," or combatative (as each strove to best his competition in debate);[22] they did little to promote the moral integrity ("virtue") of the youth whom they instructed.[23] Aristotle, in his treatises, *On Sophistical Refutations* and *The "Art" of Rhetoric*, helpfully identifies several discursive "tricks" that sophists often employed: they juxtapose elements that are similar only in incidental respects, but not in essential matters;[24] they employ arguments based on homonymy or equivocation, in which a word carries a double meaning;[25] they "combine what is divided or divide what is combined," adopting the discursively "more convenient"

---

assertion that Paul's use of "cunning" rhetoric stems from his apocalyptic worldview. It stems rather from the same desire that motivated the sophists, the desire to persuade.

[18] B. Winter, *Philo and Paul Among the Sophists*, 129–134.

[19] Philostratus, *Lives of the Sophists* 491; trans. is that of W. C. Wright, *Philostratus and Eunapius* (Loeb Classical Library; London: William Heinemann and New York: Putnam, 1922).

[20] Cf. Socrates' comments to Antiphon along these lines, in a humorous passage from Xenophon's *Memoirs of Socrates* 1.6, cited in J. Dillon and T. Gergel, *The Greek Sophists* (Penguin Classics series; London: Penguin Books, 2000) 142–144.

[21] Plato, *Phaedrus* 267A–B.

[22] Aristotle refers to an argument of the sophist Bryson as a ἐριστικός λόγος in *On Sophistical Refutations* 172 A, 2–7, cited in C. J. Classen, "Aristotle's Picture of the Sophists" in Kerferd, *The Sophists and Their Legacy*, 8–9 and n. 15.

[23] Plato, *Gorgias* 455A.

[24] *On Sophistical Refutations* 5.1.

[25] *The "Art" of Rhetoric* 2.24.2. An English translation is given by J. H. Freese in the Loeb Classical Library edition, Aristotle, vol. 12: *Art of Rhetoric* (Cambridge, MA and London, UK: Harvard University Press, reprinted 1994).

element from which to base an argument;[26] and they employ syllogisms that rely on paradox.[27] Sophists use such techniques to "make the worse appear the better argument."[28] As we will see, in refuting the criticism that he acts as a sophist, Paul uses some of these sophistic techniques.

4. The Corinthians' Comparison Between Paul and the "Ministers of Righteousness"

Not only had Paul's missionary opponents initiated a contest of comparison (σύγκρισις) between Paul and themselves (cp. 2 Cor 10:12), but they persuaded the Corinthian congregations that such a comparison was appropriate. On the terms in which the comparison took place, Paul came out the worse. Paul was judged "unfit" (cf. 2:16; 3:5–6) to serve as an apostle. Paul lacked an impressive presence such was expected of public declaimers (10:10b). He was viewed as "weak," a term that connoted Paul's noted (and admitted) lack of "stage presence" (1 Cor 2:3; 2 Cor 10:10b). In comparison, his missionary rivals were probably, like Apollos before them, rhetors of some accomplishment. We have seen in the last chapter how the Acts of the Apostles placed a premium on powerful public declamation in support of the claims of the Christian sect.[29] The public performance of persuasive declamations and the ability to engage effectively in public debate elevated the status of those who were able effectively to engage in such activities. The Christian sect, as did Hellenistic culture more generally, valued its oratorical champions. Paul himself claims some success as an orator. In 1 Thessalonians he refers to the power of his oratory to bring about conversion to the Christian sect: "our message of the gospel came to you not in word only, but also in power and in the Holy Spirit ..." (1:5; NRSV). However, in comparison to that of the "ministers of righteousness," Paul's own rhetorical "power" was limited. Like Isocrates, Paul's skill appears to have resided more in composing written works than in oral delivery.[30]

To compound the problem of his inferiority to the "ministers of righteousness" with regard to the status endowed by impressive rhetorical

---

[26] *The "Art" of Rhetoric* 2.24.2.

[27] *On Sophistical Refutations* 12.

[28] *The "Art" of Rhetoric* 2.24.11.

[29] Chap. 4, §3.6.1; p. 175.

[30] The work by Alcidamas of Elaea entitled *On Those Who Compose Written Works* appears to have been directed at Isocrates. In it, spoken oratory – especially impromptu oratory – is vaunted above the carefully crafted, written speech. A translation appears in Dillon and Gergel, *The Greek Sophists*, 294–302.

performance, Paul suffered from the blight to his social status that was entailed in his choice to earn his living as a craftsman. Paul was a leather-worker, who made articles such as sandals and tents. We have already seen how, in antiquity, such a profession was associated with low social status. Workers such as Paul often labored alongside slaves, and the hunched-over postures involved in this sort of labor were themselves viewed as "slav-ish." If, as we have seen in the last chapter, Paul's rivals adhered to Jesus' mandate that missionaries should accept room and board from the commu-nities which they visited, it is likely that these "ministers of righteousness" took residence with the more affluent among the Corinthian Christians.[31] By associating themselves with such eminent patrons, Paul's missionary rivals probably benefited from status transference, whereby they were evaluated as participating to an extent in the social status of their patrons. These factors constitute important aspects of the social situation to which Paul responds as he constructs his first apology. Such factors are likely to have influenced Paul's portrayal of his missionary opponents as sophists eager for financial gain, and himself as a philosopher, eschewing "bodily" concerns. We will return to explore Paul's characterizations of himself and his rivals later in this chapter.

5. Paul and the New Covenant

As indicated briefly in chapter 4 (section 1), this study adopts as a working hypothesis the view that 2 Corinthians 2:14–7:4 (excepting the interpolated section in 6:14–7:1) represents an originally independent literary unit. We have referred to this unit as the first apology. The first apology is appro-priately structured according to the basic pattern of the forensic speech: *exordium, narratio, argumentatio,* and *peroratio*.[32] This conventional

---

[31] More affluent members would have included Titius Justus and Crispus (Acts 18:7–8) and Stephanas (1 Cor 16:15–16). Phoebe was Paul's notable patroness at Cor-inth's port city of Cenchreae (Rom 16:1–2).

[32] There is no real consensus on the literary analysis of the first apology. Margareta Gruber (*Herrlichkeit in Schwachheit: Eine Auslegung der Apologie des Zweiten Korintherbriefes 2 Kor 2, 14–6, 13*; Würzburg: Echter Verlag, 2004; 58–81) identifies 3 main sections: 2:14–4:6; 4:7–5:10; 5:11–6:13. Each section displays a concentric (A B A' or A B B' A') structure, on her analysis. J. Lambrecht also notes concentric patterns in "Structure and Line of Thought in 2 Cor 2, 14–4,6" in *Biblica* 64 (1983) 344–380 (reprinted in R. Bieringer and J. Lambrecht, *Studies on 2 Corinthians* [Leuven: Univer-sity Press, 1994] 257–294). Lambrecht divides the section as follows: Proem: thanks-giving (2:14–16a); theme (2:16b–17); transition (3:1–3); Main part: I (3:4–4:15); II (4:16–5:10); concluding part (5:11–7:4). I find Lambrecht's identification of the proem and transition convincing, and have adopted this view in my own analysis. Anacleto de

structure was easily adaptable into the characteristic form exhibited by the Pauline letters.

Paul's typical opening thanksgiving serves in the first apology as an *exordium* or προοίμιον. This section typically serves the function of gaining the attention[33] of the audience, at times through the use of a vivid metaphor, as in 2:14–17. Another function of the προοίμιον is to win the sympathy of the audience[34] through the evocation of some strong emotion. Paul's use of the metaphor of being led captive to his death serves this function.

Following the προοίμιον, Paul includes a short transitional section (*transitio*; 3:1–3), in which Paul makes mention of the issue of letters of recommendation, only to shift the focus in v. 3 to the "stone tablets" of the Mosaic covenant. This serves to introduce the topic of the "new covenant" that Paul will address in 3:4–4:6.

After this short transition, Paul introduces the main theme of his letter: his "sufficiency" or "fitness" as a minister of the new covenant. This is accomplished in the *narratio* of 3:4–6, which consists entirely of Paul's thesis statement (πρόθεσις or *propositio*).

The following section in 3:7–6:10 constitutes Paul's *argumentatio* (*probatio*) or πίστις, in which he presents a series of arguments (3:7–4:6; 4:7–5:10; 5:11–19; 6:3–10) designed to prove his thesis that God has ren-

---

Oliviera (*Die Diakonie der Gerechtigkeit*) offers the following analysis: 2:14–17: thanksgiving; serves function of prooemium; 3:1–4:6: microstructure of exordium, narratio, argumentatio, peroratio; 4:7–5:10: same microstructure as previous section; 5:11–6:10: recapitulation; 6:11–13; 7:2–4: conquestio (a bid to gain sympathy through recalling one's misfortune); 6:14–7:1 indignatio. It is difficult to accept de Oliviera's division of the microstructural units into exordium, narratio, etc. However, my own analysis does agree with de Oliveira's in a few respects. H.-J. Klauck (*2. Korintherbrief*) offers the following analysis: 2:14–16a (thanksgiving); 2:16b–17 (statement of theme); 3:4–4:6; 4:7–5:10; 5:11–6:10; 6:11–13 (personal appeal); 7:2–4. R. Bultmann (*The Second Letter to the Corinthians*) finds three main sections: 2:14–4:6; 4:7–6:10 (composed of 4:7–5:10; 5:11–6:10); 6:11–7:4. Thrall (*The Second Epistle to the Corinthians*, vol. 1) also finds three main sections, but divides them differently: 2:14–4:6; 4:7–5:10; 5:11–7:4. F. Matera (*II Corinthians*) finds four main sections: 2:14–4:6; 4:7–5:10; 5:11–6:10; 6:11–7:4. E. Gräßer (*Der zweite Brief an die Korinther, Kapitel 1,1–7,16*) analyzes the section as follows: 2:14–17 (statement of thesis); 3:1–6; 3:7–18; 4:1–6; 4:7–15; 4:16–5:10; 5:11–6:10; 6:11–7:4 (peroratio). This short list is enough to indicate the variety of positions that have been advocated regarding the literary division of the first apology.

[33] H. Lausberg, *Handbook of Literary Rhetoric: A Foundation for Literary Study* (Leiden, Boston, Köln: Brill, 1998; trans. by M. Bliss, A. Jansen, and D. Orton of *Handbuch der literarischen Rhetorik. Eine Grundlegung der Literaturwissenschaft* [2nd ed., Ismaning bei München: Max Hueber Verlag, 1973; 1st ed. 1960) §271.

[34] Lausberg, *Handbook*, §275.

dered him sufficient as a minister of Christ.[35] This section is briefly interrupted in 5:20–6:2 by the introduction of a deliberative element, an exhortation.

In the *peroratio* or ἐπίλογος in 6:11–7:4, Paul recapitulates his central
arguments,[36] reasserts his innocence of the charges that had been lodged
against him, and attempts for the last time to arouse the sympathy of his
audience.[37] In terms of his usual epistolary structure, 6:11–13 constitutes a
final appeal.

If 2 Cor 2:14–7:4 originally constituted an independent letter, Paul's
usual epistolary greeting and epistolary postscript have been deleted by an
editor. The letter also lacks a closing benediction.

5.1. Literary Limits of the Study

The main concern of the remainder of this chapter will be to explicate the
discursive procedures that Paul used in constructing his narrative on the
new covenant in 3:7–4:6. This section constitutes the first "proof" of his
thesis. However, since the *exordium* and *narratio* are closely related in
theme to Paul's first proof, we will extend the limits of the study to include
these sections also. In Paul's second proof, which begins in 4:7 and extends to 5:10, the argument turns away from the construction of the new
covenant and begins to deal with issues related to the Platonizing interpretation of "the gospel" which Paul had already encountered in 1 Corinthians.[38] Since this study is concerned with Paul's construction of the new
covenant, our main analytical effort will be focused on the first proof in
3:7–4:6, although it will be necessary to analyze minimally also the section
from 2:14–3:6, as this section provides an important context for the overall
interpretation of Paul's construction of the new covenant in the first proof.

It is Paul's discursive formulations in competition with these missionary rivals with which we are primarily concerned, for it is in response to
the local situation constituted by the presence of this group in Corinth that
Paul formed his discourse on the new covenant. For the remainder of this

---

[35] The first proof in 3:7-4:6 is structured according to a "lesser to greater" argument
(on which, see Lausberg, *Handbook*, §397).

[36] *Recapitulatio* or ἀνακεφαλαίωσις; Lausberg, *Handbook*, §434.

[37] For the presence of affective arguments in the peroration, see Lausberg, *Handbook*,
§436.

[38] The philosophical background of this particular interpretation of the early Christian
message is described in a series of articles by R. Horsley: "Pneumatikos vs. Psychikos:
Distinctions of Spiritual Status Among the Corinthians," *HTR* 69 (1976) 269–288; "Wisdom of Word and Words of Wisdom in Corinth," *CBQ* 39 (1977) 224–239; "'How Can
some of You Say that There is No Resurrection of the Dead?' Spiritual Elitism in Corinth," *NovT* 20 (1978) 203–231. J. Murphy-O'Connor develops Horsley's approach in
"Pneumatikoi in 2 Corinthians," *PIBA* 11 (1988) 59–66.

chapter, we will analyze the discursive procedures by which Paul constructed his discourse on the new covenant, paying attention not only to
the ideological content of Paul's formulations, but relating these also to the
specific local situation in response to which Paul penned his apology.

5.2. The Exordium/Opening Thanksgiving

The exordium, 2:14–17, functions also as an opening thanksgiving. However, the form of the thanksgiving is unusual in comparison with the
thanksgivings in Paul's other letters. Whereas he often gives thanks to God
related to some issue concerning the group to which he writes (e.g., 1 Cor
1:4: "I give thanks to my God at all times concerning you ..."), here Paul
omits mention of his audience entirely, instead thanking God that Paul is
led captive in a march that will eventually result in Paul's death. What a
strange way to open a letter! This arresting image, however, serves one of
the main functions of the typical exordium: it captures the attention of the
audience. The last verse of the exordium (v. 17) serves to establish Paul's
ethos, or character, and insinuates that the motives of his missionary opponents are purely financial.

The exordium reads as follows:

> Thanks be to God who at all times leads us in triumphal procession (θριαμβεύοντι
> ἡμᾶς) in Christ and who manifests through us in every place the scent of the knowledge
> of himself, for we are a scent pleasing to God (εὐωδία ἐσμὲν τῷ θεῷ), among those
> who are being saved and among those who are perishing (ἐν τοῖς σωζομένοις καὶ
> ἐν τοῖς ἀπολλυμένοις); to the latter a fragrance from death to death, to the former a
> fragrance from life to life. Who, then is sufficient (ἱκανός) for these things? For we are
> not like the many who hawk the word of God (οἱ πολλοὶ καπηλεύοντες τὸν λόγον
> τοῦ θεοῦ), but as from sincere motives (ἐξ εἰλικρινείας), as from God we speak before
> God in Christ.

The image presented here is one of a Roman *triumphus* (Gk. θρίαμβος), a
victory march in which a triumphant Roman general would bring captives
and the spoils of war in a procession through the streets of Rome. The
triumphus would culminate in the execution of the prisoners before the
temple of Jupiter Capitolinus, followed by sacrifices in honor of the deity.[39] Paul's olfactory terminology may have been suggested by the incense that was burned during the course of the *triumphus*,[40] or by the de-

---

[39] The standard treatment is that of H. S. Versnel, *Triumphus: An Enquiry into the
Origin, Development, and Meaning of the Roman Triumph* (Leiden: E. J. Brill, 1970).
Many of the sources are also collected in S. J. Hafemann, *Suffering and the Spirit: An
Exegetical Study of II Cor. 2:14–3:3 Within the Context of the Corinthian Correspon-
dence* (WUNT 2.19; Tübingen: Mohr, 1986) 18–39.

[40] So Barrett, *The Second Epistle to the Corinthians*, 98. Other commentators reject
this idea (as does Bultmann, *The Second Letter to the Corinthians*, 63–66). Many commentators favor linking the "odor" with the odor of sacrifice in the Hebrew Bible (so

scription of sacrifices, which in the Hebrew Bible are described as producing a ‏נ׳חׂח‎ ‏ר׳ח‎, or "soothing odor" (LXX translates ὀσμὴ εὐωδίας, a pleonastic formulation indicating a "sweet-smelling scent"), as the nutritive smoke of a burnt offering wafted up to the nostrils of God (cp. Gen 8:21, *The Epic of Gilgamesh*, tablet 11, lines 155-161).[41] Although the killing of captured prisoners at the culmination of the *triumphus* was considered an execution of enemies of the Roman empire, and not a sacrifice, Paul has interpreted this execution in sacrificial terms. By associating an aspect of the *triumphus*, i.e., the burning of incense, with the sacrificial terminology of the Hebrew Bible, Paul is able to present himself as a sacrificial victim who, as we will see later, recapitulates the death of Jesus in the νέκρωσις evident in his own ministry.

Using sacrificial language, Paul describes himself as a "sweet smell" (εὐωδία) "among those who are being saved and those who are perishing; to the latter, a scent from death to death, and to the former, a scent from life to life." As in the *triumphus*, the smell of the burning incense indicates to some a salvific message: the enemy has been defeated and thus no longer poses a threat. But to those who are being led captive, the smell of the incense presages an imminent death. Paul's preaching, in this metaphor, serves the same dual function: based on one's reception of it, one either marks oneself as one of those who "is being saved" or "is perishing." In Paul's formulation: God "makes manifests the scent of the knowledge of himself through us in every place." Paul presents himself as the agent who makes manifest the knowledge of God.[42] The unstated corollary of Paul's formulation in 2:14–16 is that the way in which one responds to Paul's own preaching, either by way of acceptance or rejection, determines that person's fate at the time of the last judgment. It is their response to Paul's preaching that becomes decisive in distinguishing "those who are

---

Klauck, *2. Korintherbrief*, 33; Matera, *II Corinthians*, 73). These images however, are not necessarily exclusive. The smell of the incense at the *triumphus* presages the execution of the captives, an act that Paul has reinterpreted as a sacrificial offering. Paul has exploited the double connotation that the group of olfactory terms could bear (εὐωδία, ὀσμή): the double association with incense and with sacrifice. As we will see later in this chapter, such "combining of what is distinct" is a typically Pauline discursive procedure.

[41] In the Gilgamesh epic Utnapishtim, after surviving a cataclysmic flood on board a great ship, offers sacrifice and states: "Then I let out (all) [the birds in the ark] to the four winds and offered a sacrifice ... / The gods smelled the savor/ The gods smelled the sweet savor/ The gods crowded like flies around the sacrificer" (*ANET*, 94).

[42] Grammatically, the pronoun αὐτοῦ could refer either to God or to Christ as antecedent. On the basis of Paul's expression, ἡ γνῶσις τῆς δόξης τοῦ θεοῦ in 4:6, many commentators take God as the antecedent. In this case, Paul has substituted the personal pronoun in place of the reflexive pronoun, a common procedure in Hellenistic Greek.

being saved" from "those who are perishing."[43] From the beginning of his first apology then, Paul asks (implicitly) for his audience to take a side in the conflict between himself and his missionary opponents. Paul's clear implication is that those who refuse to side with him, in so doing situate themselves on the side of "those who are perishing." Paul's mention of those who are being saved/those who are perishing introduces one of the main themes of the first apology: life and death. This theme resurfaces in various forms throughout the apology.

The life/death recurs not only in explicit references to life and death, but also implicitly in Paul's lists of hardships (6:3–10; also 11:24–33). Paul's statement in 4:7–12 connects the life/death theme with instances of personal hardship that occurred in Paul's life: "in every way oppressed but not distressed, perplexed but not completely at a loss, persecuted but not forsaken ..." It is personal hardship that, according to this formulation, manifests death in the experience of the life of the apostle, and at the same time allows God's transformative, life-giving power to become manifest within the apparent decay and weakness of the apostle. In using this discursive strategy, Paul is able to align himself with an image of the dying Jesus. As Jesus dies as a sacrifice, so Paul "daily dies," a formulation used as metaphor to describe his personal hardship. Paul thus becomes the bearer of the image of Jesus, who dies so that others may live (cp. 2 Cor 4:12; 5:14–15).

In fact Paul's rhetoric that he "carries about the dying of Jesus in his body" is a modification of a philosophical critique of sophists. In Plato's *Phaedo*, Socrates states, "Other people are likely not to be aware that those who pursue philosophy aright study nothing but dying and being dead" (ἀποθνῄσκειν τε καὶ τεθνάναι; 64A).[44] This is so because, as death is a separation of the soul from the body, so philosophy trains its adherents to spurn the "cares of the body" (αἱ τὸ σῶμα θεραπεῖαι; 64D) in order to concern himself with the soul. The philosopher strives to "separate the soul from communion with the body" (65A), and so, while living, adumbrates the state that will be achieved at death. Philosophers despise the cares of the body: "the possession of fine clothes and shoes and the other personal adornments" (64D).

According to Xenophon, the sophist Antiphon criticized Socrates for his lack of attention to bodily concerns:

---

[43] Barrett, *Second Epistle*, states, "By preaching the gospel he [Paul] leads some to life, and at the same time sentences others to death" (p. 102).

[44] Translations of the *Phaedo* are cited according to H. N. Fowler's edition in the Loeb Classical Library, Plato, vol. 1 (Cambridge, MA and London, UK: Harvard University Press, reprinted 2001).

Socrates, I supposed that philosophy must add to one's store of happiness. But the fruits you have reaped from philosophy are apparently very different. For example, you are living a life that would drive even a slave to desert his master. Your meat and drink are of the poorest: the cloak you wear is not only a poor thing, but is never changed summer or winter; and you never wear shoes or tunic. Besides you never take money, the mere getting of which is a joy ...[45]

To Antiphon's charges, Socrates replies in part, "You seem, Antiphon, to imagine that happiness consists in luxury and extravagance. But my belief is that to have no wants is divine; to have as few as possible comes next to the divine ..."

Philo of Alexandria develops the same Socratic logic in his argument against sophists. In *The Worse Attacks the Better* 34, Philo contrasts philosophers, whom he refers to as "lovers of virtue" with sophists, who pursue oratorical skills in the pursuit of wealth, fame, and public office. The following quotation is taken from a sophistic argument that Philo cites:

The so-called lovers of virtue are almost without exception obscure people, looked down upon, of mean estate, destitute of the necessaries of life, not enjoying the privileges of subject peoples or even of slaves, filthy, sallow, reduced to skeletons, with a hungry look from want of food, the prey of disease, in training for dying (μελετῶντες ἀποθνῄσκειν). Those, on the other hand, who take care of themselves are men of mark and wealth, holding leading positions, praised on all hands, recipients of honours, portly, healthy and robust, reveling in luxurious and riotous living, knowing nothing of labour, conversant with pleasures which carry the sweets of life to the all-welcoming soul by every channel of sense.[46]

This statement amplifies the earlier argument between Socrates and Antiphon. Philo's use of the phrase, "in training for dying" recalls Socrates' statement in Phaedo 64A that "those who pursue philosophy aright study nothing but dying and being dead." As Colson and Whitaker note, the phrase constitutes "a good example of Philo's intimate knowledge of Plato."[47] The fact that both Philo and Xenophon cite arguments in which the pursuit of (Socratic/Platonic) philosophy is characterized as unfit even for a slave indicates that this criticism constituted a topos in the sophistic critique of (Platonic) philosophy.

Paul makes use of this philosophical critique of sophists in 2 Corinthians. Like Socrates, Paul is a man who is "in training for dying." Paul's image of himself being led captive in Christ's *triumphus* adumbrates this

---

[45] *Memorabilia* 1.6.2–3. Translation is that of E. C. Marchant and O. J. Todd, Xenophon, vol. 4 (Loeb Classical Library; Cambridge, MA and London, UK: Harvard University Press, reprinted 2001).

[46] Translation of F. H. Colson and G. H. Whitaker in Philo, vol. 2 (Loeb Classical Library; Cambridge, MA and London, UK: Harvard University Press, reprinted 2001).

[47] Notes to *The Worse Attacks the Better*, §34, p. 494.

theme, but it is not until the second section of the *narratio* that Paul exploits the motif more fully. In 4:7–15, Paul portrays himself as one who is "in every way oppressed but not distressed, perplexed but not completely at a loss, persecuted but not forsaken, cast out but not perishing, at all times carrying in our bodies the dying[48] of Jesus." We may compare Philo's description of the "lover of virtue" as one who is "obscure ... looked down upon, of mean estate, destitute of the necessaries of life ... in training for dying." Paul however, is able to "Christianize" the philosopher's rhetoric by adducing Jesus as the exemplar: Paul carries about in his body the dying (νέκρωσις) of Jesus.

Not that Paul presents himself as a Platonic philosopher. Far from it! In 2 Cor 4–5, Paul is at pains to "correct" some of the errors that he perceives in the Corinthians' Platonically-informed interpretation of the gospel.[49] Rather Paul, in his attempt to brand his missionary opponents as verbal tricksters, makes use of a critique that philosophers had used already in their arguments with sophists. Paul modified these criticisms for his own use, just as he modified the sophistic critique of philosophers as people who were "in training for dying" and applied it to himself. In so doing, Paul implicitly casts his opponents in the role of sophists, and himself in the role of the philosopher. Paul however, does not use these terms per se. Rather, Paul refers to himself as an "apostle," and his opponents as "false apostles." Paul has transposed the philosophical argument into early Christian terms.

5.2.1. Apostolic Sufficiency

Paul's rhetorical question, "Who then, is sufficient for these things?" (καὶ πρὸς ταῦτα τίς ἱκανός;) signals a second major theme[50] of the first apology: apostolic "sufficiency" or "fitness." This issue had appeared

---

[48] The term νέκρωσις indicates not the death of Jesus, per se, but the process of dying; the reference is to a process and not to a state. On this point I follow J. Lambrecht, "The Nekrōsis of Jesus: Ministry and Suffering in 2 Cor 4, 7–15" first published in *BETL* 73 (1986) 120–143 and reprinted in Bieringer and Lambrecht, *Studies on 2 Corinthians*, 309–333. Lambrecht writes: "νέκρωσις in 2 Cor 4, 10 means 'dying', a process of wasting away, being put to death" (p. 309).

[49] Murphy-O'Connor opines: Paul "tries to win [his Corinthian detractors] by entering into their thought-world in order to reorientate it" ("Pneumatikoi in 2 Corinthians," 61).

[50] Both Klauck (*II. Korintherbrief*, 34) and Gräßer (*Der Zweite Brief*, 107) read 2:16–17 as a statement of Paul's theme. According to the canons of classical rhetoric, the theme would be indicated generally in the exordium, but laid out more explicitly in the *narratio* (cf. Aristotle, *Rhetoric* 3.14.8: "there is no need of an exordium, except just to make a summary statement of the subject"; trans. J. H. Freese, LCL *Aristotle*, vol. 22:435). On the more detailed statement of the topic in the narratio, see Lausberg, *Handbook*, §289.

already in 1 Corinthians, in which Paul had stated that he was "not fit to be called an apostle" (οὐκ εἰμὶ ἱκανός καλεῖσθαι ἀπόστολος; 1 Cor 15:9). The issue had arisen again by the time the first apology was written, because by then Paul had already been compared unfavorably with the "ministers of righteousness" who had come to Corinth. In comparison with those missionaries, powerful orators who spoke with the authority of tradition and scripture (cf. 11:22), Paul appeared uniquely inadequate as a spokesperson for Christ (cf. 11:5). The issue of sufficiency, though it was by no means a new one for Paul and the Corinthians, was revisited pointedly as the result of the comparison with rival missionaries to which the Corinthians had subjected Paul.

The third main theme that Paul signals in his exordium is that he speaks sincerely (cp. 2 Cor 1:12; 2:17).[51] Paul insinuates that his missionary opponents are to be included with "the many who hawk the word of God." Paul's notice that he speaks sincerely to the Corinthians responds to charges that he has "corrupted" the Corinthian congregation and has sought some financial gain in so doing. The motif of the sincerity of Paul's speech is a central concern of the first apology. Paul denies charges that he has "falsified the word of God" in 4:2. In the same verse, Paul states that he conducts himself "by manifesting the truth" (τῇ φανερώσει τῆς ἀληθείας), a formulation which corresponds to the "God who manifests the scent of the knowledge of himself though us" of 2:14. Paul does not treat again the charge of financial misdealing in the first apology. Later in the second apology however, he deals with it explicitly (12:14–18). The charges that Paul disseminated a corrupting discourse as well as that of financial misconduct are both referred to in Paul's recapitulation in 7:2, "We have corrupted no one, we have defrauded no one."

Although he does not respond to it directly in the first apology, Paul does not take the charge of financial misdealing lightly. Instead, Paul turns the same charge against his missionary opponents, whom he portrays as salesmen, "hawking the word of God." As we have seen, the missionary "ministers of righteousness" followed an early missionary mandate that traveling preachers should receive their room and board from the communities in which they preached. Here, Paul casts the practice in a negative light by employing an old anti-sophistic tactic: like the sophists, Paul implies, his missionary rivals offered their wares (i.e., "the word of God") for sale.[52] In this situation though, the charges of financial misdealing have run in both directions.

---

[51] Lausberg, *Handbook*, §275a, indicates that it is a usual tactic of the exordium that one indicates that one's motives are beyond reproach.

[52] Martin (*2 Corinthians*, 50) cites Plato, *Protagoras* 313: "the sophist is a merchant or retailer in knowledge." See also Plato's *Sophist* 223B, 224B-C.

5.3. Transitio

The section in 3:1–3 constitutes a transition from the exordium to the narratio. In this section, Paul acknowledges an issue that presented a problem for him in his relationship with the Corinthians. Whereas his missionary rivals had produced letters of recommendation upon their arrival in Corinth, Paul himself had failed to do so. Rather, he had been forced (or perhaps simply had chosen) to "recommend himself." Paul's use of the temporal adverb πάλιν, "again" in 2 Cor 3:1 probably implies that he has recommended himself prior to the time at which he penned the first apology ("Are we beginning to commend ourselves again?"; cp. also 5:12). It is difficult to be certain whether Paul is referring to a self-commendation that took place at the time of his initial visit, or one that was implied in his first letter to the Corinthians. At any rate, he would have been obliged to have introduced himself and in some way to have announced his qualifications as an apostle.[53] He may have done so by recounting the visionary and revelatory experiences to which he had been privy. Paul's statement in 1 Cor 9:1 indicates that the Corinthians were already familiar with Paul's vision of the risen Christ. Paul may have referred also to the hardships that he had suffered during the course of his ministry as a form of self-commendation, as he does in 2 Cor 6:4–10 ("commending ourselves in every way ...").

Paul's answer to his own rhetorical question of 3:1 is that he has no need of a letter of recommendation to or from the Corinthians (πρὸς ὑμᾶς ἢ ἐξ ὑμῶν). In a remarkable rhetorical move, Paul asserts that the Corinthian community itself (emphatic: ὑμεῖς ἐστε) constitutes Paul's letter of recommendation. The community is adduced as a letter "written on our[54] hearts" (i.e., on Paul's heart, characteristically using the plural pronoun to designate himself). The mention of "writing on the heart" provides Paul with a link to the first topic to be addressed in his probatio, that of the new covenant. The letter on Paul's heart he describes in more detail in 3:3b: it is "written not with ink, but with the spirit of the living God, not on stone tablets but on tablets that consist of hearts of flesh." With this half-verse, Paul effects a transition from discussing letters of recommendation to discussing the role of the spirit in the establishment of the new covenant.

---

[53] Compare Thrall, *II Corinthians* 1:218.

[54] Codex Alexandrinus reads "your heart" in 3:2, but the reading "our" is to be preferred as the more difficult. Thrall (*II Corinthians* 1:223–224) discusses the variant and opts for the reading "your," primarily because it "does fit the context better." According to the usual rules of textual criticism, that is precisely why the reading should be rejected (*lectio dificilior*).

Paul's mention of the "stone tablets" in 3:3b refer to the tablets of the law delivered to Moses on Mount Sinai. The mention of the "hearts of flesh" evokes the discussion of the spirit's role in restoring the covenant, thought to have been broken at the time of the exile in the sixth century BCE. Commentators sometimes draw attention to the way in which Paul's argument appears to jump from topic to topic with little apparent logic. Morna Hooker writes: "Paul's metaphor – typically becomes a mixed one ... Paul has jumped from one image to another; put them together, and he is clearly in a mess ..."[55] However, Paul's rhetorical technique here corresponds to one that was familiar in antiquity. It was that of the sophist who juxtaposes items on the basis of "incidentals" (τὰ συμβεβηκότα), according to Aristotle's formulation.[56] Aristotle noted how sophists were able to make spurious arguments appear to be convincing, and one of the ways that they accomplished this was to make comparisons between things that were in reality very different; they were only apparently similar. The early sophist Protagoras was referred to as the "ready mixer,"[57] perhaps because he was able adroitly to exploit the sort of "apparent similarity" that Aristotle complained about. In 2 Cor 3:3, we can see that Paul also was able to operate as a "ready mixer," juxtaposing two distinct topics on the basis of a verbal similarity. In this case, the connection is provided by the phrase "written on the heart," which Paul first suggests as a metaphor for the letter of recommendation constituted by the Corinthian community, and secondly the – as yet unspecified – message, written on "fleshy hearts" as opposed to stone tablets. This act of juxtaposition, however, brings Paul to his topic: a discussion of the new covenant.

5.4. Narratio

The section in 3:4–6 is to be characterized as Paul's *narratio*, in which he presents a more detailed statement of his thesis (*propositio*). We will re-

---

[55] Quoted in C. Stockhausen, *Moses' Veil and the Glory of the New Covenant* (Rome: Pontifical Biblical Institute, 1989) 35.

[56] See C. J. Classen's discussion of this tactic in "Aristotle's Picture of the Sophists" in G. B. Kerferd, ed., *The Sophists and Their Legacy* (Weisbaden: Franz Steiner Verlag, 1979) 1–24, esp. 12–15.

[57] So J. Dillon and T. Gergel translate the epithet provided by Diogenes Laertius in his *Lives of Eminent Philosophers* 9.52. The epithet reads as follows: Πρωταγόρης τ᾽ ἐπίμεικτος ἐριζεμέναι εὖ εἰδώς. The subst. adj. ἐπίμεικτος should be construed as having the semantic import of a passive participle, "mixed" (cf. Smyth, *Greek Grammar*, §472). Protagoras was referred to as "the mixed" because he "knew well how to engage in disputation." Diogenes Laertius in part relates Protagoras' epithet with the fact that "he disputed by relinquishing the intention in favor of the word" (καὶ τὴν διάνοιαν ἀφεὶς πρὸς τοὔνομα διελέχθη), a tactic that would include arguments based on homonymy. The translation of Dillon and Gergel is given in *The Greek Sophists*, 3.

member that the *exordium* of 2:14–17 introduced three themes for consideration: 1) life and death, salvation and perdition, 2) apostolic sufficiency (καὶ πρὸς ταῦτα τίς ἱκανός;) and 3) the sincerity of Paul's speech (ὡς ἐξ εἰλικρίνειας ... ὡς ἐκ θεοῦ). These themes are expanded in 3:4–6, but in reverse order. In 3:4, Paul revisits the issue of the frankness of his speech, although the frame is broadened; in 3:5–6a, he expands on the issue of apostolic sufficiency; and in 3:6b, Paul revisits the life/death theme, which he also uses to introduce the first proof in the *argumentatio*.

Furnish notes that Paul's term, "confidence" in 3:4 is related later in the second apology to the theme of "frankness of speech" (παρρησία) in 10:2. Furnish continues, "Closer to the thought of the present verse is the use of the perfect tense of the verb *peithein* in 1:9 ... where Paul's confidence is *before God* (in God's power ultimately to save or vindicate)."[58] Anacleto de Oliveira notes that there is a chiastic relationship between the formulation in 2:17 and 3:4–5.[59]   Phrases in 2:17 (ἐκ θεοῦ/ κατέναντι θεοῦ/ ἐν Χριστῷ) are mirrored in reverse order in 3:4-5 (διὰ τοῦ Χριστοῦ/ πρὸς τὸν θεόν/ ἐκ τοῦ θεοῦ). De Oliveira concludes, "So enthält πεποίθησις einen Hinweis auf die εἰλικρίνεια bzw. die ἱκανότης 2,14–17."[60]

In 3:5–6a, Paul expands on the theme of apostolic "sufficiency." Paul claims here that he is "sufficient," or "fit" for the ministry that he carried out. This "fitness" however, was not on the basis of any qualification that Paul may have possessed for the job (οὐχ ... ὡς ἐξ ἑαυτῶν); rather Paul's sufficiency proceeded from God (ἐκ τοῦ θεοῦ). God "made Paul fit" (ἱκάνωσεν, causative) for his ministry. We will recall that Paul had declared himself "unfit to be called an apostle" in 1 Cor 15:9. However, in view of the situation in which he was being compared with rival missionaries who seemed to be more "fit" than Paul in carrying out evangelistic work, Paul had to be much more careful in his formulation. The missionary "ministers of righteousness" displayed characteristics that Paul lacked: they were credentialed by letters of recommendation and they had good public speaking skills (perhaps extempore). In the second apology, Paul indicates that the Corinthians had judged Paul "inferior" to these missionaries (11:5). In 5:12, Paul obliquely refers to his rivals as those who "boast about appearances, and not about the heart" (οἱ ἐν προσώπῳ καυχώμενοι, καὶ μὴ ἐν καρδίᾳ). In 3:5–6a, Paul asserts that it is not on the basis of apparent credentials that one may become "fit" to serve as an administrator of God's covenant; apostolic sufficiency is rather a gift from God. With this tactic, Paul was able rhetorically to assuage some of the concern raised

---

[58] *II Corinthians*, 183.
[59] *Die Diakonie der Gerechtigkeit*, 64.
[60] *Die Diakonie der Gerechtigkeit*, 64, n. 50.

within the Corinthian congregation over Paul's own apparent lack of proper credentials.

The last clause of the *narratio*, "for the letter kills, but the spirit makes alive," recalls the life/death dichotomy that was introduced in the *exordium* (2:14–15) and which continues as a *Leitmotif* throughout the first apology (4:10–12, 16; 5:14–15; 7:3). Paul has engaged in an interesting bit of discursive manipulation in devising this formulation. A Pauline *tour de force* was however, in this case necessary, for Paul was faced with the position of arguing against the weight of the "plain sense" of Scripture and against an exegetical tradition that had firmly established itself within various early Jewish groups, including the Christian sect.

6. Paul and the New Covenant: A Discursive *Tour de Force*

It has become fashionable to deny that much can be known about the position of Paul's opponents regarding the new covenant. This is because, it is asserted, the only data that bears on the position of Paul's opponents is to be derived from Paul's own narrative. It is impossible to separate Paul's position from that of the missionary "ministers of righteousness" against whom he argues. Any attempt to do so requires an invalid "mirror reading" technique, cannot be verified by outside sources, and therefore entails a necessarily circular logic (cf. chap. 4). Although it is true that we do not have any data outside of 2 Corinthians relating to the missionary "ministers of righteousness" whom Paul opposes in the first and second apologies, we do have quite a bit of comparative data concerning the topic that constituted the point of contention between Paul and his missionary rivals: the new covenant. This data derives from Scripture (Jeremiah and Ezekiel), the Book of Jubilees, the writings of the Dead Sea sect (1Q/4QS), and the Letter to the Hebrews. With this data, we can make some inferences about the main points of the new covenant formulation that was propounded by the "ministers of righteousness" whom Paul opposed in Corinth.

We may recall that the main points of the construction of the new covenant in Jeremiah and Ezekiel were 1) that God would transform human intentionality so that humans would be able to fulfill the law perfectly; 2) as the result of this transformation, the law would be "written on the hearts" of God's people; 3) at the same time, the people's former transgressions would be forgiven. The same pattern is attested in Jubilees, 1QS (although here only "covenant" is mentioned, not "new covenant"), and Hebrews. In Ezekiel, Jubilees, 1QS, and Hebrews, the "spirit" or "holy spirit" is identified as the agency through which the people will be purified and transformed, enabling them to adhere perfectly to the precepts of the Torah. Based on this broad agreement in regard to the basic structure and function of the new covenant within Scriptural texts, two groups within early Judaism (the author of Jubilees and the Dead Sea sect), and more specifically within the early Christian sect (as per Hebrews), we may infer that Paul's missionary opponents in Corinth held a similar view.

For ease of reference, these data may be summarized in tabular form. The data offered for the missionary "ministers of righteousness" is hypothetical. Here I assume that they fall into the broad pattern that is provided by the comparative texts.

Table 1: *Constructions of the New Covenant in Comparative Overview*

	Transformation of intentionality	Spirit	Transgressions forgiven	Torah observance
Jeremiah	X		X	X
Ezekiel	X	X	X	X
Jubilees	X	X	X	X
1QS	X	X	X	X
Hebrews	X	X	X	X
"Ministers of Righteousness"	X	X	X	X
Paul	X	X	X	

There is broad agreement as to the main outlines of the new covenant among the texts that treat the theme. Jeremiah is notable in omitting reference to the spirit as the agency through which God was thought to accomplish the transformation of "hearts" in the utopian eschatological age. The subsequent Jewish tradition followed Ezekiel in pointing to the spirit as fulfilling this role. Paul is notable in his omission of Torah observance in his construction of the new covenant. If we infer that Paul's missionary opponents shared the broad outlines of the construction of the new covenant, as expressed by other texts – including Hebrews, which was produced within the early Christian sect – then we have a good indication of the position that Paul was arguing against in 2 Cor 3. If we have an idea of the position of Paul's rivals, then we are better able to appreciate the discursive strategies that Paul employed in an effort to counter their growing influence in Corinth.

6.1. Letter and Spirit

As we now have some indication of the position that the "missionaries of righteousness" took with regard to the new covenant, we may return again to the text of 2 Corinthians 3, with an eye to identifying the tactics that Paul used in an effort to counter the position of his opponents. Paul's statement in 3:6 is in fact programmatic for the discursive strategy that he pursues in 3:7–18: "[God] who also made us sufficient as ministers of a new covenant, not of letter but of spirit; for the letter kills, but the spirit makes alive." In this formulation, Paul makes a distinction that is fundamental to his entire argument, that between letter and spirit. Roman law sometimes made a distinction between the wording and the intention of laws, and patristic and medieval exegetes understood the spirit/letter distinction to indicate the opposition between the "spiritual" or allegorical meaning of a text as opposed to its "literal" meaning.[61] Neither of these understandings of the spirit/letter distinction however, is germane to the discussion of 2 Cor 3. As most exegetes now recognize, with the term γράμμα, "letter," Paul indicates the "letter" of the law of Moses, which according to v. 7 was "engraved on stones" (γράμματα ἐνετυπωμένη λίθοις).[62] Paul's letter/spirit distinction was driven, not by a literal/ figurative hermeneutical distinction, but by the context that was provided by his dispute with the "ministers of righteousness" in Corinth.

As we have seen, the "ministers of righteousness" probably preached a construction of the new covenant in which the spirit empowered individuals to lead lives in accordance with the demands of the Torah. This was the view of the new covenant that was championed by Ezekiel and subsequently adopted by Jewish tradition. To quote again Ezekiel's formulation (36:26–27):

A new heart I will give you, and a new spirit (רוח חדשה) I will put within you; and I will remove from your body the heart of stone and give you a heart of flesh. I will put my spirit (רוחי) within you, and make you follow my statutes (ועשׂיתי את אשׁר בחקי) and be careful to observe my ordinances (תלכו) (NRSV).

---

[61] The 1953 article of B. Schneider in *CBQ* 15; pp. 163–207 ("The Meaning of St. Paul's Antithesis 'The Letter and the Spirit'") is still fundamental. Schneider correctly concludes that, "Without doubt the concept behind the phrase 'on tablets of stone' to which *gramma* as opposed to *pneuma* corresponds, is that of the stone tablets of the Law, or the Decalogue given to Moses, the *plakai lithinai gegrammenai* spoken of in Exodus ... That this concept of the Decalogue continues through v. 6 is evident from its repetition in the following v. 7, where the ministry of Moses is described as one "of death, engraved upon letters of stone."

[62] So most recently M. Harris (*Second Epistle*, 272–273); J. Lambrecht (*Second Corinthians*, 43). F. Matera's formulation is muddled: "it is evident that *to gramma* is somehow related to the Mosaic law, but not simply to be equated with it" (*II Corinthians*, 81).

The presence of the spirit is associated with the ability to fulfill God's "statutes and ordinances"; i.e., the requirements of the Torah. According to this construction, during the utopian age in which God's people would no longer act in disobedience to the precepts of the Torah, spirit and Torah were inextricably linked. It is in response to this traditional and scriptural association that Paul is obliged to draw his own distinction between letter (i.e., Torah) and spirit.

Prior to the arrival of the missionary "ministers of righteousness" there is no indication that Paul's congregations felt obliged to follow the precepts of the Torah. Paul undoubtedly advocated the practice to which he had first been introduced in Antioch, according to which Gentile members of the ἐκκλησία were accepted as Gentiles, without being asked to follow the Torah. (As we have seen, even Antioch came to repudiate this practice.) Within the context of a Torah-free proclamation at Corinth, Paul certainly had preached a great deal about the "spirit," by which he indicated the power that was able to effect various ecstatic activities within the congregation's meetings: glossalalia, prophecy, and perhaps acts of healing and visionary experiences. Paul had never thought to associate "spirit" with the performance of the Torah; such an idea was foreign to the experience of his own churches. Given this context, it is easy to see why Paul begins his discussion of the new covenant by positing a fundamental distinction between γράμμα and πνεῦμα, letter and spirit. If the traditional, scriptural association between these two terms were upheld, this would threaten to upset the standard of practice that Paul had introduced within his communities. Such an event would surely necessitate the view that Paul was a crafty deceiver who had falsified the word of God, such charges as are reflected in 2 Cor 4:2.

Beyond Paul's initial formulation of γράμμα/πνεῦμα as contrasting terms (οὐ γράμματος, ἀλλὰ πνεύματος), we may draw attention to the strategy that Paul employed in formulating the following phrase, τὸ γὰρ γράμμα ἀποκτέννει, τὸ δὲ πνεῦμα ζῳοποιεῖ ("for the letter kills, but the spirit makes alive"). Traditionally, the law (to which Paul refers with his γράμμα) had been seen as accomplishing a dual function: based on one's actions, it served as the basis of either condemnation and acquittal, and thus of death or life. Before the people were set to cross the Jordan and to enter their promised land, Moses issued a series of blessings and curses that would befall the people (or not) on the basis of their obedience to the Torah. Adherence to the precepts of the Torah would result in blessing; failure to obey would result in curses. Moses sums up his oration:

Behold, I have set before you today life and death (τὴν ζωὴν καὶ τὸν θάνατον), good and evil. If you obey (ἐὰν εἰσακούσῃς) the commandments (τὰς ἐντολὰς) of the Lord your God, which I am commanding you today, to love the Lord your God, to walk in his ways, to observe his commandments (τὰ δικαιώματα) and his judgments (τὰς κρίσεις), then you will live (καὶ ζήσεσθε) and be many, and the Lord your God will bless you in all the land which you are entering, so as to inherit it (Deut 30:15-16; LXX).

In Moses' peroration, life and death are predicated on the basis of one's obedience or disobedience to the precepts of the Torah. To translate this into the terms of Paul's formulation, the law both kills and brings life. Paul, however, has suppressed the latter proposition. In Paul's polemical formulation, the law kills.

The latter half of Paul's formulation ("the spirit makes alive"), is easily explicable. Throughout the Mediterranean region in antiquity, breath and life were thought to be intertwined. "Breath" (πνεῦμα), otherwise translated "spirit," is in fact requisite to human life. In Gen 2:7, God breathes life into Adam's nostrils. In *Allegorical Interpretation* 3.161, Philo cites the verse as follows: ἐνεφύσησε γὰρ εἰς τὸ πρόσωπον αὐτοῦ πνεῦμα ζωῆς ὁ θεός, καὶ ἐγένετο ὁ ἄνθρωπος εἰς ψυχὴν ζῶσαν ("For God breathed into his face a breath [or, "spirit"] of life, and the man became a living being"). More to the point in terms of the debate in Corinth, Paul's missionary rivals are likely to have associated the "spirit" with "life" on the basis of a covenantal ideology. The "ministers of righteousness" are likely to have followed the traditional position of Deuteronomy: one is granted either life or death on the basis of one's obedience to the Torah.[63] If this is granted, then it is easy to see how this position would cohere with the ideology of the new covenant that we have seen developed in Ezekiel, Jubilees, 1QS, and Hebrews. The spirit, by enabling the individual perfectly to follow the Torah, would be associated with God's obligation under the terms of the covenant: to grant life.

Given the terms of the debate, neither of Paul's propositions (the letter kills; the spirit makes alive) was false. The former however, was predicated upon a gross act of obfuscation. That is, Paul has suppressed the traditional association of the covenant, and thus law, with life. It is with this discursive gesture that Paul introduces the first point of the *argumentatio* section of his discourse.

6.2. Moses and the Ministry of Death

Dieter Georgi argued that in 2 Cor 3:7–18, Paul "opposes a 'heretical' Moses-tradition"[64] in which Moses was presented as a θεῖος ἀνήρ, "a man who is strange and uncanny to his fellow beings because he has become divine."[65] According to Georgi, Paul's opponents taught that individuals could undergo a transformation whereby they became divine beings, simi-

---

[63] In Ben Sira 45:5, God gives to Moses the "law of life and understanding" (ἔδωκεν αὐτῷ ... νόμον ζωῆς καὶ ἐπιστήμης).

[64] *The Opponents of Paul*, 254.

[65] *The Opponents of Paul*, 255.

lar to the transformation that Moses underwent at Sinai. This transformation was facilitated by the allegorical exegesis of Scripture. It is in response to this "Moses-tradition" that Paul developed his own presentation of Moses as engaging, not in a ministry the emulation of which could result in the divinization of the individual, but instead in a ministry that mediated death. In objection to this position, Margaret Thrall has made the interesting observation that the form of Paul's conditional statements in 3:7–11 assumes an agreement between Paul and his Corinthian audience that Moses' ministry was a "ministry of death" and of "condemnation." Paul was not responding to an overly optimistic view of Moses, but rather was in fundamental agreement with his audience (who presumably had received this position from Paul's opponents) about the condemnatory role of the law of Moses.

Thrall's argument is based on the simple observation that in first class conditional statements, the protasis is assumed to be true for the sake of argument.[66] Thrall states:

> Paul, therefore, presupposes the agreement of his readers on two points: first, that they knew an exegetical tradition that magnified the glory of Moses; secondly, that the Mosaic covenant was an agency of death and condemnation, by contrast with the gospel, which brings righteousness and life ... Nor is the Jewish law the point of contention. Agreement of its negative characteristics is assumed. Paul is not, therefore, controverting Judaism of any kind, as has often been assumed in the exegesis of this passage.[67]

Thrall's grammatical argument certainly must be judged probative. It seems unlikely that Paul would have used a first class conditional statement unless there was agreement between him and his audience on the points involved. Thrall infers agreement in that Moses was viewed as a figure that was connected with glory, and that Moses' ministry brought condemnation. Thrall has not made an effort to contextualize her insights within early Christian discourse pertaining to the new covenant. Doing so will allow us to make some more detailed inferences about the position that Paul's opponents had mediated to the Corinthians.

As we have seen in the last chapter, it was a commonplace within early Christian discourse to compare Moses and Jesus, to the detriment of the former. The closest parallel to 2 Cor 3 occurs in Hebrews 8–9. In this section, the λειτουργία, "cultic service," that had been instituted in Mosaic law was contrasted with that provided by Jesus. The former was defective in that sacrifices and ablutions were performed on a periodic and continu-

---

[66] This seems to be the logic of the argument, although Thrall does not make this explicit. She states, "Paul ... presupposes the agreement of his readers ..." without specifying the logic that would render this conclusion likely. The grammatical argument does just that.

[67] *II Corinthians* 1:240.

ing basis. From the datum provided by the repetition of these cultic acts, the author of Hebrews infers that those acts were flawed. Such acts served only as "patterns" (ὑποδείγματα) and "shadows" (σκίαι) of the true cultic service (cf. αὐτὴ ἡ εἰκών; 10:1) that was provided by Jesus. Jesus' death as a sacrificial offering is superior to the cultic offerings of the "first covenant" (ἡ πρώτη διαθήκη; 8:13) in that Jesus' offering was a one time event, as opposed to the repeated sacrifices offered under the temple cultus. The singularity of Jesus' sacrificial offering is interpreted as being fully effective: those so cleansed "no longer have any consciousness of sins" (10:2). Former sins are forgiven; new ones are construed as a non-occurrence. Here the "cultic service" instituted by Moses is likened to the Platonic "shadow" of Jesus' service, which stands as Platonic "image" (εἰκών) for the former. The "first covenant" is superceded by the "new"; the first has grown old and become obsolete (παλαιούμενον καὶ γηρασκόν; 8:13). The linguistic parallels with 2 Cor 3 are not exact: Hebrews uses the term λειτουργία ("cultic service") as opposed to Paul's διακονία ("ministry"); Hebrews uses the phrase "first covenant" in place of Paul's "old" or "ancient" covenant. Both texts, however, clearly juxtapose the Mosaic covenant with the "new covenant" (using the identical phrase) inaugurated by the death of Jesus.

Thrall's observation that Paul's audience took for granted that the Mosaic covenant was compared unfavorably with the "new covenant" inaugurated by Jesus' death coheres with the formulation that we encounter in Hebrews. We need not argue for any direct line of transmission between Paul, or his opponents, and Hebrews in order to justify the comparison. Comparisons between Jesus' ministry and that of Moses are evident also in the antithesis of the Gospel of Matthew and in the Gospel of John, which states in its prologue: "The law was given through Moses; grace and truth came through Jesus Christ" (Jn 1:17). Comparisons between Jesus and Moses were commonplace in early Christianity, and we can infer that Paul's formulation in 2 Cor 3 occurred in response to a similar formulation on the part of Paul's missionary opponents.

If Thrall was correct in inferring that Paul and his audience agreed on some points, nevertheless she was wrong in the conclusion that she drew from that datum: "Nor is the Jewish law the point of contention. Agreement of its negative characteristics is assumed." It does not follow from "agreement on the negative characteristics (of the law)" that the law was not an issue in 2 Corinthians. On the contrary, this agreement ensures that the role of the law constituted a fundamental point of contention between Paul and his opponents. As we have seen in the last chapter, the "negative characteristics" of the law; i.e., the fact that breaking it results in the activation of the "curses of the covenant," including exile, forms the presupposition of each of the discussions of the "new covenant" from Jeremiah and Ezekiel, through Jubilees and 1QS, and into the Letter to the Hebrews. It is the "negative characteristic" of the law that necessitated a new covenant, one inscribed on the will and intentionality of the human being and which therefore could not be broken. Logically, any discussion of a "new covenant" assumes the "negative characteristics," more specifically the condemnatory function, of the old. The question then, is neither whether Paul's missionary opponents assumed that the law entailed negative consequences (which was at any rate a postulate of the Torah itself), nor whether the law constituted a "point of contention" between Paul and his opponents, but instead what modifications Paul introduced into the discussion in support of his own, Torah-free ministry.

Some scholars have argued that 2 Cor 3:7–18 represents a non-Pauline source that Paul has incorporated, perhaps in a revised form, into the body of his letter.[68] This approach has largely, and quite rightly, been abandoned on the grounds that it is impossible to separate the putative non-Pauline document from purported Pauline insertions and modifications.[69] Although I would not subscribe to the view that 3:7–18 represented the substance of an earlier *document*, nevertheless it demonstrably constitutes one example within the broader phenomenon of discussions of covenant renewal. Since Paul's discussion represents, as it were, a species situated within in a known genus, by comparing the other related species (Ezekiel, Jubilees, and so on) we may arrive at a view of what is specifically Pauline about this discourse. A comparison of Paul's discourse with others within the same discursive genus allows us to infer the positions taken by Paul's missionary rivals and also allows us to infer with some probability at what points in the discussion Paul has modified the "standard position" as exemplified by the other species within the genus.

In none of the other discourses that we have identified as participating in the "genus" of covenant renewal do we encounter anything analogous to Paul's expressions "ministry of death" (διακονία τοῦ θανάτου; 3:7) or "ministry of condemnation" (διακονία τῆς κατακρίσεως; v. 9). We have already noted that, in his programmatic statement in 3:6, Paul had already disassociated letter, which is said to "kill," from spirit, said to "bring life." We have seen as well how Paul has redescribed the traditional dual function of the Torah in monaxial terms. Whereas the Torah could typically be

---

[68] So for example D. Georgi, *The Opponents of Paul*, 264–271.

[69] So for example J. Lambrecht, *Second Corinthians*: "The majority of commentators, however, maintain serious reservations regarding the so-called source text and, it would seem, rightly so. The whole operation is too hypothetical: the indication of pre-Pauline elements, the exact wording and content of the document and, by means of this, the reconstruction of the opponents' theology" (p. 60).

described as the criterion according to which God dispensed life or death, based on one's obedience or disobedience to its precepts (Deut 30:15–16), Paul has reduced the role of the law to a single function: condemnation. Therefore, we may conclude that the highly polemical redescription of the law as entailing a "ministry of death/condemnation" was an ideological formulation introduced by Paul.

The second act of comparison that I will suggest involves only a subset of those discourses that pertain to covenant renewal. This comparison involves only the Letter to the Hebrews, which was produced by members of the early Christian sect. As we have already noted, the Letter to the Hebrews involves a comparison between Jesus and Moses, to the detriment of the latter. Comparisons between Jesus and Moses also occur in the gospels of Matthew and John, although these works do not include references to the "new covenant." In 2 Cor 3:7–18 however, the comparison is not between Jesus and Moses, but between Moses' *ministry* (διακονία) and the "ministry of the spirit." As 3:6 indicates, the "ministry of spirit" that Paul refers to is none other than Paul's own: [θεός,] ὃς καὶ ἱκάνωσεν ἡμᾶς διακόνους καίνης διαθήκης, οὐ γράμματος ἀλλὰ πνεύματος ("God, who also made us sufficient as ministers of a new covenant, not of letter but of spirit"). Paul's ministry is a ministry characterized by[70] spirit.

Again returning to a comparison between Paul's discourse and other discourses involving the new covenant or covenant renewal, we can point out a striking difference between Paul and the other sources regarding the role of the "spirit" in the constitution of the new covenant. From Ezekiel to Jubilees, 1QS, and Hebrews, the spirit plays an invariant role: it brings about a transformation of human intentionality so that humans are able perfectly to fulfill the law, a possibility that was not available under the conditions of the "old," Mosaic covenant. This position is exemplified by Ezek 36:27: "I will put my spirit within you, and make you follow my statutes and be careful to observe my ordinances" (NRSV). As we argued in the previous chapter, Paul's missionary opponents likely adhered to this "standard view" of the role played by the spirit under the conditions of the new covenant.

In his programmatic statement in 3:6 however, Paul discursively sundered the traditional association between law and spirit. Whereas in the parallel formulations in Ezekiel and related texts, the spirit enabled the fulfillment of the law, in Paul's formulation, the spirit is placed in opposi-

---

[70] The genitives in 3:6 may indicate content or material, or they may be epexegetical. The view that they are adjectival seems to me to be dependent on the "hermeneutical" understanding of the letter/spirit distinction, a view which we have rejected. The formulation "characterized by" assumes the that the genitive belongs to the general category, "descriptive genitive" (cf. *GGBB*, 79–81).

tion to the law, described as γράμμα, "letter": τὸ δὲ γράμμα ἀποκτέννει, τὸ δὲ πνεῦμα ζῳοποιεῖ. With this succinct formulation, Paul accomplishes at once a discursive reduction, reallocation, and division: the role of the law, as we have already noted, is denied its life-giving function, and is reduced to an agency of death; the life-giving function of the law is reallocated to the spirit; and law and spirit are set in antithesis.[71] The traditional idea that the spirit enabled the fulfillment of the law has, as the result of Paul's discursive manipulation, been transformed into an argument which implies that it is only the rejection of the law, and not the fulfillment of it, that results in "life." Any attempt to adhere to the law results in death (τὸ δὲ γράμμα ἀποκτέννει), for the law is in fact nothing short of a "ministry of death" and a "ministry of condemnation."

The implication of Paul's characterization of Moses' ministry as a "ministry of death" is that those who advocate adherence to the Torah participate in the "old" covenant which mediates death. Paul's formulation carries with it an implicit characterization of his missionary rivals in Corinth as individuals whose activities mediate death and condemnation, in contrast to Paul's "ministry of the spirit," which mediates life.

Paul concludes his attempt to sunder the traditional tie between spirit and law with an elegant formulation in 3:17b: οὗ δὲ τὸ πνεῦμα κυρίου, ἐλευθερία ("and where the spirit of the lord is, is freedom"). I wish to focus here on the conjunction of the terms πνεῦμα ("spirit") and ἐλευθερία ("freedom"). As we have seen, in his programmatic statement in 3:6, Paul accomplishes a discursive sundering of πνεῦμα from a term to which it was bound in the discourse of Paul's missionary rivals: law (γράμμα by metonymy). In 3:17b, Paul delivers what he probably deemed to be the *coup de grace* to the nomistic teaching of his rivals. In this verset, Paul constructs a link between πνεῦμα and ἐλευθερία. Having already set πνεῦμα in antithesis to law/γράμμα, and thereby denying the traditional association between law and spirit that was maintained by his missionary rivals, Paul accomplishes a second act of displacement. In place of the spirit/law association held by Paul's rivals, and espoused in Ezekiel, Jubilees, and the other texts in this discursive genus, Paul constructs another association, spirit/freedom. In this formulation, γράμμα is replaced by ἐλευθερία; "spirit" is correlated, not with law, but with "freedom."

In Hellenistic as in Attic Greek, mention of the term ἐλευθερία ("freedom") suggested another term to which it was related in binary opposition: δουλεῖα, "slavery" or "servitude." Although Paul does not make mention of "slavery" in 2 Cor 3, his discourse certainly implies it. At an earlier date, in his letter to the Galatians, Paul had repeatedly made use of the freedom/slavery dichotomy (Gal 4:21–26; 5:13). "Freedom" in Galatians

---

[71] The second occurrence of the conjunction δέ in this line is adversative.

implies non-participation in explicit requirements of the Torah: "For freedom Christ set us free; therefore stand firm and do not submit again to the yoke of slavery" (Gal 5:1). In Galatians, "slavery" is equated with law (νόμος), while the "spirit" plays the role of liberating individuals from the necessity of submitting to the law: "If you are led by the spirit, you are not subject to the law" (ὑπὸ τοῦ νόμου; 5:18). In 2 Cor 3:17b, Paul's use of the single term ἐλευθερία, "freedom" implies the same view that Paul had earlier espoused in Galatians: converts to the early Christian sect were under no obligation to adhere to the precepts of the Torah.[72]

In rejecting the traditional association between law and spirit that was first formulated in Ezekiel and which was likely espoused by the missionary "ministers of righteousness" who were active in Corinth and displacing it with another association, that between freedom and spirit, Paul has accomplished a rhetorical tour de force. Such a discursive procedure is not likely to have proven convincing to any member of the early Christian sect whose heritage was Jewish ("Israelites, Hebrews, Abraham's offspring"); but to a Gentile, for whom circumcision, kashrut, and Sabbath observance could be construed as unusual[73] or even offensive,[74] Paul's procedure almost may have held more charm. One of the tasks involved in the "invention" of a public address in antiquity was to judge the predispositions of one's audience so as to be able to craft one's discourse in the way deemed most effective in influencing those predispositions toward a posi-

---

[72] F. Stanley Jones has argued that "in der antiken Welt παρρησία Synonym von ἐλευθερία sein konnte" („Freiheit" in den Briefen des Apostles Paulus, 65). Jones suggests that Paul's use of the term ἐλευθερία in 2 Cor 3:1–17 reflects this common usage; therefore ἐλευθερία in this passage refers to the freedom of Paul's apostolic speech. However the conjunction of "spirit" and ἐλευθερ– cognates is a Pauline motif that occurs in Gal 4:21–5:1 and Rom 8:2 (πνεῦμα and δουλεία occur in Rom 8:12–17). In each of these instances in which Paul conjoins "spirit" with "freedom," as he does in 2 Cor 3:17, the latter term relates to action and behavior, and not to speech. Therefore, Jones' interpretation is unlikely to be correct. "Freedom" in Paul's usage is a term that applies to the category of deeds, not words (for this distinction, see e.g., Mt 23:3; Lk 6:46; Rom 2:17–24). For this reason, it is more likely that Paul's use of ἐλευθερία in 2 Cor 3:17 implies a critique of following the law (a category of deed and action) rather than referring to the purported candor of Paul's speech (παρρησία).

[73] So Martial, Epigrams 7.82: "This fellow I had imagined – for we often bathe together – was solicitous to spare his voice, Flaccus; but while he was exercising himself in view of the people in the middle of the exercising ground, the sheath unluckily fell off: lo, he was circumcised!" (LCL trans. of W. C. A. Ker, cited in M. Stern, Greek and Roman Authors on Jews and Judaism, vol. 1; Jerusalem: Israel Academy of Sciences and Humanities, 1974; p. 526).

[74] So for example Apion, according to Josephus: "He denounces us for sacrificing domestic animals and not eating pork, and he derides the practice of circumcision" (Against Apion 2.135; LCL trans. of H. Thackeray, cited in M. Stern, Greek and Roman Authors, 415).

tive reception of the speech. In contradistinction to that of his missionary rivals, Paul's formulation allowed the Gentile converts in Corinth largely to maintain their practices unmodified; no need, according to Paul, to adhere to the precepts of the Torah; on the contrary, to do so was to invite death and condemnation! However, judging from the probability that Paul found it necessary to craft a second apology (2 Cor 10–13) some time after the first, it appears that Paul's discursive efforts in 2:14–7:4 were not sufficient to bring about the favorable response that Paul had desired. Paul had either misjudged his audience or underestimated the persuasiveness of the preaching of the missionary "ministers of righteousness" in response to whom his discourse was composed.

6.3. Conflicting Views on the Role of the Spirit

In addition to the preference which we might expect of the Corinthian congregation to maintain the status quo with respect to their non-observance of the precepts of the Torah, we might also draw attention to the fact that, in the debate between Paul and his missionary rivals, two divergent constructions of "spirit" were at play. If we are to suppose that Paul's rivals had adopted the "standard view" of the role of the spirit in connection with the new covenant, then we would expect that the "ministers of righteousness" identified the spirit as the agency through which God forgave former sins and transformed human intentionality so that it became capable of perfect adherence to the precepts of the Torah. For Paul, the "spirit" was an entity that was associated not with the law, but with ecstatic experiences such as speaking in tongues and prophecy – the very experiences, as we know from 1 Corinthians, in which the Corinthian congregation was most interested! It certainly must have been jarring for the Corinthians first to have been exposed to the covenantal theology of the "missionaries of righteousness," in which spirit was associated with law, and not with ecstasy. The ability of the "ministers of righteousness" to produce scriptural support for their covenantal views in which the Torah held a central position is likely to have bolstered the credibility of these missionaries. Paul's way, by comparison, was more familiar to the Corinthians, and in spite of his opponents' ability to claim that scripture and tradition were on their side, Paul too, by dint of clever argumentation and ingenious biblical exegesis, was able to claim scriptural support for his own position. Paul's methods of clever argumentation however, would result in the charge, probably first lodged by his missionary rivals, that he had "falsified the word of God."

6.4. Paul's Transference of Charges to "Moses"

Paul's discussion in 3:7–18 takes as its point of departure a Biblical text: Exodus 34. The parallel narratives about "new covenant" or covenant renewal (Ezekiel, Hebrews, Jubilees, etc.) that have otherwise proven so useful for the reconstruction of the position of Paul's missionary rivals, do not mention Exodus 34. We have no direct parallel that correlates the new covenant with a discussion of the Exodus text. However, the parallel texts have already allowed us to make some inferences about the way in which Paul's rivals viewed the role of the spirit and the law. As we have argued, Paul's rivals probably preached that the new covenant entailed perfect adherence to the Torah; an adherence that was made possible by the transformation that was accomplished by the spirit. God's spirit transformed human intentionality so that it was able to perform the Torah (Ezek 36:27: "I will put my spirit within you, and make you follow my statutes ..."). With this in mind, we may infer that any reference that Paul's opponents may have made to the Sinai narrative in Exodus 34 would have been made for the purpose of emphasizing the legal basis of the new covenant: under the conditions of the new covenant, it was the Torah of Moses that formed the basis of ethical conduct.

Judging from the series of denials that Paul issues in 4:1–4, we may infer also that Paul's rivals had adduced the Exodus text in an effort to discredit Paul. The terms which Paul uses to phrase his denials echo terms or ideas that had been expressed in 3:12–18, as the following list indicates:

3:12–18	4:1–4
πολλῇ παρρησίᾳ χρώμεθα	τῇ φανερώσει τῆς ἀληθείας συνιστάνοντες ἑαυτούς
"we act with complete candor" (v. 12)	"commending ourselves by making the truth manifest" (v. 2)
κάλυμμα	ἔστιν κεκαλυμμένον
"veil" (vv. 13, 14, 15, 16)	"is veiled" (v. 3)
ἐπωρώθη τὰ νοήματα αὐτῶν	ἐτύφλωσεν τὰ νοήματα τῶν ἀπίστων
"their perceptions were hardened" (v. 14)	"blinded the perceptions of the unbelievers" (v. 4)

This list invites the suspicion that Paul crafted 3:12–18 as a response to allegations that been brought against him. The procedure whereby Paul constructed 3:12–18 is easy to discern: he transfers to "Moses" charges that had originally been brought against Paul himself. But "Moses" in 3:12–18 carries a double signification: "Moses" at once signifies a character from the Biblical narrative ("Moses put a veil upon his face ...") and (by association) the law itself: "whenever *Moses* is read ..." Whereas 4:1–4 indicate that Paul had been charged with doing (unspecified) shameful things in secret (v. 2), acting "cleverly," "falsifying the word of God" (v. 2), and preaching a "veiled gospel," Paul creates a discourse in 3:12–18 in which the substance of these charges is attributed to Moses. Moses veils his face so as to hide the fact that his (i.e., the law's) glory was being abolished (3:13). This action contrasts with Paul's own account of his behavior, which he characterizes as "acting with complete candor" (πολλῇ παρρησίᾳ χρώμεθα).

Why did Paul argue in this way? We can suggest two reasons: firstly, in so doing, Paul is able to discredit Moses/the law, and thereby to discredit his missionary rivals, whose διακονία featured the law as a central component. (These are the same individuals who referred to themselves as διάκονοι δικαιοσύνης in 11:15, and whose "end," Paul punningly suggests, will be in accordance with their [legal] "deeds"). Secondly, in invoking the image of the veiled Moses, Paul is able cleverly to turn the biblical text to his own advantage. In a display of exegetical alchemy, Paul is able to craft an argument which enlists the Exodus narrative in support of an enterprise which is diametrically opposed to Exodus' "plain meaning." Paul cunningly makes the weaker case appear the stronger.

6.5. Criticism of Paul's "Veiled Gospel"

We have suggested that Paul's opponents used the text of Exodus in an effort to point out to the Corinthian congregation the legal basis of the new covenant. The new covenant was in their view, predicated on the proper performance of the Torah with the empowerment of God's spirit. It is difficult to be certain whether Paul's missionary rivals focused any attention whatsoever on the motif of the veil in Ex 34. If they did so at all, it was probably in an effort to discredit Paul. Paul's admission in 4:3: "but even if our gospel is veiled" provides an indication that the motif of the veil was somehow applied to Paul's ministry, but nothing more can be ascertained from 2 Corinthians. However, there is some information from 1 Corinthians that may yet be brought to bear on the problem.

It is possible that the ministers of righteousness used the image of the veil to criticize Paul's self-presentation as a hierophant of sacred mysteries, as evidenced in 1 Corinthians. In 1 Corinthians, Paul often uses language that predicates hiddenness or concealment to the message that he proclaimed. Paul proclaims "the mystery of God" (1 Cor 2:1) and the "wisdom of God which is hidden in mystery" (2:7) and which "none of the rulers of this age knew" (v. 8). In 2:9–10, Paul furthers his theme of revelation, by citing a passage the origin of which is difficult to determine. It may be a citation of a lost apocryphon or apocalypse of Elijah,[75] a para-phrase and conflation of Isa 64:4 and 65:16, or a citation from a pre-existing catena of scriptural quotations:[76]

> Things which no eye has seen nor ear heard,
>   and have not occurred to man,
> which God has prepared for those who love him –

but God has revealed (ἀπεκάλυψεν) to us through the spirit; for the spirit searches all things, even God's deep things (τὰ βάθη τοῦ θεοῦ).

Paul implies that the Corinthians, since they were "like children in Christ," needed to rely on Paul to provide spiritual truths for them, since he was "spiritual"[77] (3:1–4) – that is, he was endowed with God's spirit, which "searches all things." Paul provides the category in which he wishes to be viewed: "Consider us in this way: as attendants of Christ and stewards of God's mysteries" (4:1). This insistence on the impenetrability – by "nor-mal" means – of the content of Paul's preaching, and the need to rely on Paul as the authorized interpreter of God's "mysteries" may have provided the impetus for Paul's missionary rivals to criticize him as one who preached a "veiled gospel." In response to Paul's emphasis on revelatory experiences,[78] Paul's missionary rivals could perhaps have offered the following description of the new covenant's discursive content:

> It is not in heaven, that you should say, 'Who will go up for us, and get it so that we may hear it and observe it?' No, the word is very near to you, it is in your mouth and in your heart for you to observe (Deut 30:12, 14; NRSV).[79]

The discursive content of the preaching of the "ministers of righteousness" was drawn, not from personal revelation but, at least in part, from a source that was a matter of public record – the words of the Torah.

---

[75] As suggested by M. E. Stone and J. Strugnell; *The Books of Elijah, Parts 1–2* (Missoula, Montana: Scholars Press, 1979) 42–73.

[76] So G. Fee (*The First Epistle to the Corinthians*) 108–109.

[77] In stating that the Corinthians were "still fleshly," Paul draws an implicit contrast between themselves and him. The implication is that Paul was not "fleshly," but "spiri-tual."

[78] We may recall that Paul's opponents attacked him on the grounds that he relied too heavily on ecstatic phenomena and revelatory experiences also in the second apology (cf. chap. 4, §§3.4.3–3.4.5; pp. 157–164).

[79] This is the citation that Rabbi Yehoshua purportedly invoked in a legal debate with Rabbi Eliezer, in which the latter was to have enlisted God's own heavenly voice in support of his position. The story is cited in D. Cartilage and D. Dungan, *Documents for the Study of the Gospels* (Philadelphia: PA: Fortress Press, 1980) 160–162.

6.6. Pauline Redeployment of the Motif of Moses' Veil

Paul however did not accept such criticism without mounting a defense. As we have suggested, in 3:12–18, Paul not only defends himself but launches a discursive counter-attack by transferring the charge of hiding/dissimulation, symbolized by the image of the veil, from himself to Moses/the law – and thus also to the missionary "ministers of righteousness," who advocated adherence to the law. Since in the case of Paul's treatment of Moses' veil, we are fortunate enough to have access to the text that Paul was reworking – Exodus 34:28–35, we can draw some substantive conclusions about the discursive procedures that Paul employed in crafting his own narrative.

The text of the Exodus narrative reads as follows:

And Moses was there before the Lord for forty days and forty nights; he neither ate bread nor drank water. And he wrote these words upon the tablets of the covenant, the ten sayings (ἐπὶ τῶν πλάκων τῆς διαθήκης, τοὺς δέκα λόγους). And when Moses came down from the mountain, the two tablets also were in Moses' hands. And when he came down from the mountain, Moses did not know that the appearance of the skin of his face was glorified (δεδόξασται ἡ ὄψις τοῦ χρώματος τοῦ προσώπου αὐτοῦ) because he had spoken with him [i.e., with God]. And Aaron and all the elders of Israel saw Moses, and the appearance of the skin of his face was glorified (ἦν δεδοξασμένη ἡ ὄψις τοῦ χρώματος τοῦ προσώπου αὐτοῦ), and they were afraid to draw near to him (ἐφοβήθησαν ἐγγίσαι αὐτοῦ). And Moses summoned them, and Aaron and all the leaders of the assembly turned toward him, and Moses spoke to them. And after this, all the Israelites (lit., "sons of Israel"/οἱ υἱοὶ Ἰσραήλ) approached him, and he commanded them everything that the Lord had told him on Mount Sinai. And when he had finished speaking to them, he put a veil (κάλυμμα) upon his face. And whenever Moses went in before the Lord to speak with him, he lifted the veil (περιηρεῖτο τὸ κάλυμμα) until he went out. And when he went out he spoke to all the Israelites (lit., "sons of Israel") what the Lord had commanded him, and the Israelites ("sons of Israel") saw the face of Moses, that it had been glorified (ὅτι δεδόξασται), and Moses put a veil upon his face until he went in to speak with him [i.e., God].

Occasionally, commentators will draw attention to the striking differences between the text of Exodus and Paul's interpretation of it. Considering Paul's treatment of what he considers to be the two "key terms" that Paul has taken from the Exodus text, James Dunn has observed, "Notice that in both of these key words Paul has gone beyond, if not actually contradicted, the sense of Exodus ..."[80] This statement is apropos. According to Exodus, Moses veiled his face because Aaron and the Israelite elders "were afraid to draw near" to Moses because – in somewhat tortured language – "the

---

[80] "2 Corinthians 3:17: 'The Lord is the Spirit'," originally published in *JTS* 21 (1970) 309–320; reprinted in J. G. Dunn, *The Christ and the Spirit*, vol. 1: *Christology* (Grand Rapids, MI and Cambridge, UK: Eerdmans, 1989) 115–125. The quote appears on p. 117 in the latter edition.

appearance of the skin of Moses' face had been glorified." This "glorification" consisted of a luminosity that radiated from Moses' face. Philo of Alexandria offers a contemporary interpretation of this phenomenon: After Moses had spent forty days without food on Mount Sinai, "he descended with a countenance far more beautiful than when he ascended, so that those who saw him were filled with awe and amazement; nor even could their eyes continue to stand the dazzling brightness that flashed from him like the rays of the sun."[81] According to Paul, Moses veiled his face not because the elders "were afraid to draw near to him" (Ex 34:30), but because Moses wished to hide the fact that his glory was being abolished (καταργουμένη; 2 Cor 3:7) – which probably entailed a dimming of the reflected divine radiance. Although Linda Belleville has claimed to have found a rabbinic parallel to Paul's idea that Moses' radiance diminished over time,[82] the parallel that she adduces is found in the Zohar, a product of the 13th–14th centuries CE.[83] All the data that she so carefully assembles from the Hellenistic and Roman periods indicate just the opposite, that the radiance of Moses' face remained undimmed until the end of his lifetime.

In keeping with Paul's use of "Moses" as signifying both a character in Biblical narrative as well as encoding a reference to the law, the description of the "abolition" of Moses' glory assumes the abolition of the law's glory, and thus assumes the impermanence of the law. In contradistinction to this formulation, we may note that the law was generally conceived as being effective in perpetuity. In the Wisdom of Solomon 18:4, the children of Israel are described as those "through whom the imperishable light of the law was to be given to the world" (NRSV). Fourth Ezra 9:36–37 states, "For we who have received the Law and sinned will perish ... the Law, however, will not perish but remains in its glory."[84] In Pseudo-Philo 11:2, God says to Moses, "I have given an everlasting law into your hands and by this I will judge the whole world."[85] The idea that the radiance of Moses' face, and concomitantly the legally binding status of the law, was

---

[81] Trans. of F. H. Colson, *Life of Moses*, 2.70 (*LCL*, Philo, vol. 7).

[82] *Reflections of Glory: Paul's Polemical Use of the Moses-Doxa Tradition in 2 Corinthians 3.1–18* (JSOTSupp 52; Sheffield, UK: Sheffield Academic Press, 1991). Belleville follows W. Oesterly's 1920 position that the Zohar relies largely on very old traditions (p. 73 and nn. 2–3 on that page), but this position has long since been abandoned.

[83] So G. Scholem, *Zohar: The Book of Splendor* (New York: Shocken Books, 1977; first ed., 1949) xii–xxi; D. C. Matt, *Zohar: The Book of Enlightenment* (New York, NY; Ramsey, NJ; and Toronto, Canada: Paulist Press, 1983; Classics of Western Spirituality series) 3–10; *idem*, *The Zohar*, vol. 1 (Pritzker edition; Stanford, CA: Stanford University Press, 2004) xliv.

[84] Trans. of B. Metzger in *OTP* 1:546.

[85] Trans. of D. J. Harrington in *OTP* 2:318.

"being abolished" is likely to have been a Pauline formulation,[86] and coheres with Paul's view as expressed in Gal 3:23–4:11 and Rom 10:4.[87] According to Paul, the law remained in effect until Christ "ended" it.

If Paul introduced an exegetical innovation by suggesting that Moses' glory was transient, he introduced another by suggesting that Moses' veil served to hide the fact of this transience. According to Exodus, Moses donned a veil to allay the people's fear of his radiant face. In antiquity, the appearance of luminous beings, such as Moses had become, almost always evoked a response of fear and religious awe (cf. Lk 2:8-10; 1 Enoch 14:8-25). According to Paul's innovative interpretation, however, Moses used the veil for the purpose of hiding the fact that his glory was "being abolished." In his creative reworking of the motif of Moses' glory and his veil, Paul has indeed "gone beyond, if not actually contradicted, the sense of Exodus."

6.7. Moses Turned Against Himself: A Pauline Inversion

The Exodus narrative certainly assumes that the Torah which Moses delivered at Sinai would remain in effect in perpetuity. According to the formula quoted in Ex 34:6–7, Yahweh is:

a God merciful and gracious.
slow to anger,
and abounding in steadfast love and faithfulness,
keeping steadfast love to the thousandth generation,
forgiving iniquity and transgression and sin,
yet by no means clearing the guilty,
but visiting the iniquity of the parents
upon the children,
and upon the children's children,
to the third and fourth generation (NRSV).

This passage relies on covenantal language. Yahweh is described as faithful to the stipulations of the covenant: he rewards – "even to the thousandth generation," a hyperbole meant to imply perpetuity – those who adhere to the stipulations of the covenant, but punishes, mercifully only to the "third and fourth" generation, those who transgress those stipulations. Paul however, is able to take the Exodus text and turn it, against its own implied intent, into a text that indicates that the stipulations of the cove-

---

[86] The idea of the abolition of the law should be distinguished from the proposition that Christ's glory surpassed Moses'. As we have seen, it was common in early Christian literature to compare Jesus and Moses, to the detriment of the latter. The idea that Jesus abolished the law is uniquely Pauline – a related view that *some* of the precepts of the Torah could be neglected is expressly contradicted in Mt 5:17-19.

[87] This aspect of Paul's ideology remains stable through Galatians, 2 Corinthians, and Romans.

nant (i.e., the Torah) are no longer in effect in Paul's own day. This transformation is accomplished in 3:12–18.

The veil which according to 2 Cor 3:13 lay over the face of Moses, in v. 14 is transferred to "the reading of the old covenant." As we have already seen however, "Moses" in this text serves the dual role as signifying a character from Biblical narrative as well as the text of the Torah itself ("Whenever Moses is read ..."). Therefore Paul's statement in v. 14 that "until today the same veil lies over the reading of the old covenant" involves only an application of this significative logic. The "old covenant" refers to the stipulations of the covenant that are set forth in the "ten sayings," or the Decalogue, as suggested by Ex 34:28: "And he wrote these words upon the tablets of the covenant, the ten sayings" (ἐπὶ τῶν πλάκων τῆς διαθήκης, τοὺς δέκα λόγους).[88] Like Moses' face, the "reading" of this covenant is veiled. Paul's assertion that the "reading" of the old covenant is veiled implies a noetic problem, a problem of perception. In v. 15, Paul once again translocates the veil; this time to the "hearts" (a term here referring to the locus of perception) of the "sons of Israel," who read aloud the text of "Moses" during meetings in the synagogue. Paul takes his reference to the Israelites/"sons of Israel" from the text of Exodus 34:35: "the Israelites ('sons of Israel') saw the face of Moses, that it had been glorified, and Moses put a veil upon his face ..." As Moses, the narrative character, hid the fact that the glory of his face was "being abolished" (v. 13), so "Moses" the text, is veiled. This veiling occurs as the result of a noetic problem: the "faculties of perception" (νοήματα) of the Israelites "were hardened" (ἐπωρώθη; v. 14). This passive verb, as is often noted, is a "divine passive"; God is the implicit actor involved in this "hardening."[89] This "hardening of the heart" is a metaphor for what Paul construes as a noetic failure: μὴ ἀνακαλυπτόμενον ὅτι ἐν Χριστῷ καταργεῖται ("since it is not revealed that it [i.e., the old covenant] is abolished in Christ"). As

---

[88] In light of the fact that Paul' discourse from 3:7–18 consists of an interpretation of Ex 34, in which the "covenant" is identified with the ten commandments inscribed on stone tablets, there is little reason to associate, as M. Harris (*Second Epistle to the Corinthians*, 305, no. 5) does, the "old covenant" with the entire Pentateuch, and still less reason to associate it with the entire "Old Testament." In fact, the first association of the "old covenant" with the "Old Testament" scriptures (both "testament" and "covenant" are translations of the Greek διαθήκη) occurs in the mid- to late-second century ecclesiastical writer Melito of Sardis, Frag. 3.1.16–24, in which "the books of the old covenant/testament" (τὰ τῆς παλαιᾶς διαθήκης βιβλία) are listed. These include the books of the Hebrew Bible as well as others such as the Odes and Wisdom of Solomon and 1 Esdras.

[89] Joel Marcus has offered the best treatment of which I am aware of the theme of God's hardening of the faculties of perception of the out-group in *The Mystery of the Kingdom of God* (Atlanta, GA: Scholars Press, 1986).

Moses the character hid the fact that the glory of his visage – symbolizing the legally binding force of the Torah – was "being abolished" in v. 13, so in v. 14, the "old covenant" – again a reference to the stipulations of the Torah – is said to be "abolished" by Christ. Paul here refers to his idea, familiar from Galatians, that the law functioned as legally binding from the time of Moses until the time of Christ. At the time of Christ, however, the law lost its legally binding force. Members of the early Christian movement, in Paul's view, not only need not but ought not to follow the Torah. To do so is to invite divine condemnation (Gal 3:10; 2 Cor 3:7a, 9a). By the end of v. 15, Paul has made significant progress in his effort to locate within the Torah itself a signifier that presages the Torah's own eventual nullification. The signifier of the veil allows Paul to do just that.

Paul's argument comes to a rhetorical climax in vv. 16–18. In v. 16, Paul quotes – with modification – Ex 34:34. According to the LXX text as it appears in the Göttingen Septuagint, the verse reads: ἡνίκα δ᾽ ἂν εἰσεπορεύετο Μωυσῆς ἔναντι κυρίου λαλεῖν αὐτῷ, περιηρεῖτο τὸ κάλυμμα ἕως τοῦ ἐκπορεύεσθαι ("and whenever Moses went in before the Lord to speak with him, he removed the veil until the went out").[90] Paul, however, alters the text in some significant ways. Whereas LXX reads, "whenever Moses went in before the Lord to speak with him" (that is, Moses "went in" to the tent of meeting, where the Lord appeared to him), Paul omits the reference to Moses, leaving the subject undefined, and permitting the translation: "And whenever one turns to the Lord ..." That is, the reference to the past habitual action of Moses (impf.) becomes a third class conditional (aor. subj.), capable of general applicability: "Whenever *(some)one* ..." In addition, Paul substitutes a term denoting conversion from one ideology or praxis to another (ἐπιστρέφω; "to turn")[91] for LXX's εἰσπορεύεσθαι, "to go in" (to the tent of meeting). LXX's statement about the past habitual action of Moses is transformed into a general statement about practical/ideological reform.

The goal of this reform is implied in v. 16b, in which LXX's third per. sing. impf. mid. indic. περιηρεῖτο ("he removed") is changed to a pres. pass. indic., περιαιρεῖται, "it is removed." Here the noetic problem referred to in 3:14–15, the divine "hardening" of the faculties of perception of the "sons of Israel" finds its remedy: God is once again the subject of the "divine passive." When one "turns to the Lord, the veil is removed."

---

[90] *Septuaginta*, Exodus, vol. II.1; J. W. Wevers, ed. (Göttingen: Vandenhoeck & Ruprecht, 1991). Wevers lists several minor textual variants, but none that affects the argument here. Paul's changes appear to be the result of his own editorial activity, and not because he was quoting a variant text.

[91] Bultmann (*Second Letter to the Corinthians*) cites 1 Thess. 1:9 in support of this view.

That is, one's perception is transformed. Later in 4:6, Paul refers to the same phenomenon as "enlightenment" (φωτισμός). And what does one perceive as the result of this enlightenment? The answer was implied already in v. 14: the function of the veil is to hide the fact that "in Christ" the law is nullified (καταργεῖται); therefore the removal of the veil implies the recognition of this fact. The "unveiled heart" therefore, recognizes the central affirmation that Paul wishes to make: members of the early Christian movement ought not to adhere to the stipulations of the "old covenant." In Paul's construction of the case, adherence to the Torah proves that one is, like those who listen to the reading of the "old covenant" in the synagogues, disenabled by an action of God to understand the truth entailed by Paul's "ministry of the spirit." In Paul's construction, the law no longer mediates the covenant between God and humans; rather the covenant is mediated on the basis of Christ's sacrifice, which brings about reconciliation between humans and God (2 Cor 5:18–21).

The association between Jesus' death interpreted sacrificially and the "new covenant" constitutes the earliest known covenantal theology within early Christian tradition. This association is evident in 1 Cor 11:23–26, Lk 22:14–20, and Heb 9:11–14, 15 (cp. Mt 26:26–29; Mk 14:22–25). Paul's modification is explicitly to remove from this covenantal theology any association that it may have had with the Torah.

The climax of Paul's argument occurs in v. 17: "where the spirit of the Lord is, is freedom." Here Paul takes one of the central terms in the dispute between himself and his missionary rivals, "spirit" and, by inscribing the term within a typically Pauline web of signification, denies the signification imputed to it by his missionary rivals. The missionary "ministers of righteousness," we will remember, viewed "spirit" as the active agency through which God was able to transform human intentionality with the result that humans would be able perfectly to adhere to the Torah. In the verses preceding v. 17, Paul had engaged in a discursive strategy whereby he characterized adherence to the Torah as the sign of a noetic failure, itself the result of a divinely hardened heart. Paul furthers this strategy of undermining the link between spirit and Torah by constructing his discursive coup de grace: "where the spirit of the Lord is, is freedom." For Paul, "freedom" implies a refusal to follow the precepts of the Torah (cf. Gal 4:21–5:1). Paul here constructs a means of authenticating the presence of the "spirit of the Lord": the spirit is evident only where (ὅπου) the Pauline "freedom" is manifest; that is, only where the Torah is not followed. With this discursive gesture, Paul wrests "spirit" from the association that his missionary rivals had sought to establish between spirit and Torah. Paul reinscribes "spirit" within a context more congenial to himself: the context of revelatory experience and personal transformation, such as had been evident in 1 Corinthians. This association, however, is not forged until verse 18.

In 3:18, the subject switches from "them," the "sons of Israel," to "us," the members of the congregation at Corinth – and here Paul includes himself within this group. Unlike the "sons of Israel," Paul writes of his "we"-group, "As we all with unveiled face see the glory of the Lord reflected, we are being transformed into the same image by degrees of glory (lit., "from glory to glory"), as from the lord of spirit." The "we" group that is characterized as having an "unveiled face" is thereby implied to be a group that is congenial to the Pauline law-free ministry. In vv. 14–16, Paul had already associated the veil with the belief that one should follow the precepts of the Torah, and the removal of the veil with "freedom," Pauline jargon for the refusal to base one's praxis on the precepts of the Torah. Therefore, Paul's characterization of the "we"-group as having "unveiled faces" implicitly marks them as sympathetic to Paul's law-free gospel.

Whether this characterization of the "we" group was calculated to win sympathy from the Corinthians by portraying them as being already "on Paul's side" or whether this was simply Paul's actual perception of the situation at the time is impossible to decide. Whatever Paul's motivation in portraying the situation in this way, it seems that the depiction failed to correspond to the actual situation in Corinth. Later, Paul would be forced to write another, more vehement apology (2 Cor 10–13) in an attempt to counter the influence of the same group of missionaries with whom Paul had been convened in the first apology (2:14–7:4). It seems then that the Corinthians were less in favor of Paul's law-free ministry at the time of the first apology than Paul's discursive formulation would indicate. One of the issues that Paul obliquely refers to in the second apology is the "other spirit" that his missionary rivals preached. Paul's first apology did not prove sufficient to put an end to the dispute between him and his rivals over the spirit's role in the regime of praxis to be followed under the conditions of the new covenant.

Verse 18 functions as an explanatory statement, commenting on the previous two verses (δέ is explanatory). In this verse, the "we" group functions in a role analogous to that of Moses, who "when he went in, removed the veil" so as to address God face-to-face, as it were (God is depicted in Exodus more as a bright light than as a human figure). Like Moses, the "we" group "beholds the glory of the Lord" with an unveiled face. The reason for Paul's suppression of the original subject (Moses) in his modified quotation of Ex 34:34, leaving open the possibility that the verse should be understood to refer to an indefinite subject, "When someone turns ..." is manifested in v. 18: the "someone" who is understood as the subject of v. 16 is revealed as being the "us" of v. 18. It is "we" who have turned to the Lord so as to have our faces unveiled by God, according to Paul's formulation. Like Moses, the "we" group beholds the glory of the Lord with an unveiled face, and like Moses, this group is transformed so as to reflect God's luminescence ("glory"). "So we all, since[92] we see the glory of the Lord reflected as in a mirror,[93] are being transformed into the same image, by degrees of glory, as from the Lord's spirit"[94] (3:18). As Furnish correctly notes,[95] Paul here modifies a standard eschatological motif, that of the transformation of the righteous into a luminous being like an angel (cp. 2 Bar 51:3, 10: "Also, for the glory of those who proved to be righteous on account of my law ... their splendor will then be glorified by transformations ...").[96] According to the Pauline modification, this transformation no longer awaits the eschatological day of resurrection, but rather is viewed as a process currently underway.

Paul's formulation in 3:18, τὴν δόξαν τοῦ κυρίου κατοπτριζόμενοι, "seeing the glory of the Lord reflected as in a mirror," introduces an ambiguity. Paul does not indicate what it is that "reflects as in a mirror" God's glory. The question is not resolved until 4:6: ὁ θεός ... ἔλαμψεν ἐν ταῖς καρδίαις ἡμῶν πρὸς φωτισμὸν τῆς γνώσεως τῆς δόξης τοῦ θεοῦ ἐν προσώπῳ Ἰησοῦ Χριστοῦ, "God ... shone in our hearts in order to enlighten us with the knowledge of the glory of God in the face of Jesus Christ." The "we" group discerns the "glory of God" in the "face of Jesus Christ." This face displays a glory that is – referring back to 3:10–11 – a "surpassing glory" which "remains" forever. This face is implicitly contrasted with the

---

[92] The nuance of the adverbial participle is difficult to ascertain; this translation takes it as causal.

[93] The semantics of the verb κατοπτρίζομαι are a subject of debate. According to LSJ, the verb in the active voice may be glossed, "to reflect" and in the middle voice normally means, "to look at one's reflection in a mirror." Apart from 2 Cor 3:18, the lexica cite one instance (Philo, *Leg.* 3.101) in which the verb carries a different nuance: "to behold (something, acc.) as in a mirror." Most commentators currently favor the latter option, and I see no reason to disagree.

[94] Καθάπερ ἀπὸ κυρίου πνεύματος. I take the word order to reflect an inversion of the normal head-noun+genitival qualifying noun sequence for the purpose of highlighting the first term, κύριος. The emphasis is that the spirit either comes from or belongs to *the Lord*, i.e., God. The identification of the κύριος in vv. 16, 17 (twice), and 18 is rendered probable by several factors: the κύριος in the LXX of Ex 34:34, which Paul has modified in v. 16, refers to Yahweh, the God of Israel; the phrase πνεῦμα κυρίου/הוה׳ רוח was standard in the OT (where of course ὁ κύριος=Yahweh; e.g., Judg 3:10; Isa 11:2); according to Ezek 36:27, it was God's spirit (רוחי; with God as speaker) that accomplished the transformation of human intentionality under the conditions of the new covenant.

[95] *II Corinthians*, 241.

[96] Trans. of A. F. J. Klijn in *OTP* 1:638. See also chap. 2, §3.10; pp. 60–61 for the use of this motif in the Dead Sea scrolls.

face of Moses – which the "they" group (the Israelites) views – a face the glory of which was "being annulled." It is "in Christ," who is represented by Paul's "ministry of the spirit" (3:8), that the glory of the Mosaic covenant, given a symbolic form by the glory of Moses' face, is annulled (ἐν Χριστῷ καταργεῖται; 3:14).

The comparison between the glory of the old and new covenants that Paul introduced in 3:7–11 is paralleled in Paul's narrative by an implicit comparison that runs through 3:12–4:6. In the latter section, the fading glory of Moses' face is bested by the "glory of God (which is) in the face of Christ" (3:6). Paul's Jesus bests Moses in that, beyond reflecting God's glory, Jesus is presented as the very "image of God" (4:4). At best, Moses could only display a glory that was destined to be abolished by the surpassingly luminous Jesus (cf. 3:7–11).

In terms of the correspondence of Paul's discursive formulation to the local situation to which Paul was responding, we may point out the contrasting characterizations of the "we" and the "they" groups. Paul's "they" group is referred to as "those who are perishing" (4:3), "the faithless" (οἱ ἄπιστοι; 4:4), who have been blinded by Satan so as to be unable to receive "enlightenment" pertaining to "the gospel of the glory of Christ" (4:4). This group fills a role analogous to the Israelites who lived during the time of Moses, whose "perceptions were hardened" (3:14) by God so that they could not perceive that Moses' glory was but transient. The apperceptions of both groups suffer(ed) from the occlusive effect of an act of veiling; the former group as the result of Moses' veiling of his face; the latter group as the result of a veil lying over their hearts.

The fundamental distinction between the two groups rests in their disparate attitudes toward the law: those who are perishing/the Israelites (both past and present) fail to perceive, when the law is read, what the "we" group knows: that the law is no longer binding; it was "nullified in Christ." It is precisely this distinction that Paul emphasizes in his use of the veil motif: the veil hid from the Israelites of a bygone age the fact that Moses' glory – symbolizing the glory of the law – was transitory, to be surpassed by that of the glory of the "ministry of spirit" (3:7–8). According to the Pauline slogan, "Where the spirit of the Lord is, is freedom" – that is, the freedom to order one's praxis without reference to the precepts of the Torah.[97] The "ministry of spirit" which is contrasted with Moses' ministry of condemnation is in fact a reference to Paul's own law-free ministry. The primary problem with the "they" group, who listen to the law read in the synagogue, is that they have not properly "turned to the Lord" (3:16) – who, according to Paul, "is the spirit": "and where the spirit of the Lord is,

---

[97] Paul probably viewed "the law" in correspondence with the prevailing Pharisaic interpretation of it, which would have included laws of purity and kashrut.

is freedom." With this formulation, Paul is able to imply that one is unable to "turn to the Lord" unless one grants the legitimacy of the Pauline law-free ministry. Access to the God of Israel,[98] in Paul's formulation, is granted through Paul's "ministry of the spirit."

It is striking that Paul does not mention his missionary rivals directly in 3:7–18. This fact, as we saw in the last chapter, has led some exegetes to deny that Paul's discourse is at all related to "the local scene at Corinth." Paul's discursive strategy proceeds on the basis of innuendo and implication. He attempts to delegitimate the ideology and praxis of those "missionaries of righteousness" who preached that, under the new covenant, the law was to be fulfilled perfectly under the guidance of God's spirit. Paul does not attack his rivals directly, however. He attacks the ideological underpinning of their entire project: the validity of the Mosaic code. By imputing a novel signification to Moses' veil, Paul is able not only to read in the law a prediction of its own demise, but in addition he is able to enlist the law as a vehicle for the legitimation of the Pauline ministry itself: "*When one turns to the Lord, the veil is removed* (Ex 34:34). Now, 'the Lord' is the spirit, and where the spirit of the Lord is, is freedom."

We may also note that the Paul's entire formulation in 3:7–18 recapitulates the practical and ideological development that many of the Corinthian congregants experienced as the result of Paul's arrival in Corinth. According to Acts 18, Priska, Aquila, and other members of the early Jesus movement, prior to Paul's arrival regularly attended services in a Corinthian synagogue. Upon his arrival, Paul convinced them to separate themselves from the synagogue's services – at which time they began to meet in a building, owned by one Crispus, which adjoined the synagogue! Subsequently they met in other locations, including the households of the wealthier members of the group such as Titius Justus (Acts 18:7–8) and Stephanas (1 Cor 1:16; 16:15–18). Thus the progression from the participation in the synagogue, in which "until this day ... Moses is read" (3:15), to participation in smaller house-churches in which "the surpassing glory" of Christ was preached – most notably by Paul (cp. 1 Cor 15:1–57, esp. v. 42) – was a progression that the members of the Corinthian congregation had themselves embodied. Paul's narrative in which the time of ascendancy of Moses as representative of the law ("whenever Moses is read ...") was superceded by the ascendancy of Christ – the embodiment of the glory and image of God – recapitulates the physical reordering that Paul accomplished among the "faithful" in Corinth: out of the synagogue and into the house-church, which was not ordered according to the precepts of the

---

[98] Here I assume that "the Lord" referred to in this section refers to Israel's God, as in Exodus 34. This is a contested point however, as κύριος in Paul may refer either to the God of Israel or to Jesus. I am influenced by the article of Dunn, "The Lord is the Spirit."

Torah. Paul's narrative in 3:7–18 thus represents the mystification, that is, the presentation in the form of a theological narrative, of the physical and ideological translocation that Paul himself had encouraged the Corinthian Christians to enact. Paul's narrative recapitulates the Corinthian Christians' movement from synagogue preaching to the Pauline gospel.[99]

Even though he does not mention his missionary rivals, per se, in 3:7–18, in his treatment of the "they" group, Paul constructs his narrative in such a way that the Israelites of old parallel the "faithless" of the present day, who "still" believe that Mosaic law should remain in effect. Although Paul's use of οἱ ἄπιστοι, "the faithless" applies only to outsiders to the early Christian movement (i.e., pagans or non-Christian Jews; cf. 1 Cor 6:6; 7:12–15), the implication of Paul's argument is clear: Paul's missionary opponents, who advocate adherence to the Torah as a constitutive element of the new covenant, participate in the Mosaic "ministry of death" (3:7) and "condemnation" (v. 9). It is Paul's missionary rivals who, in failing to respond positively to Paul's law-free "ministry of reconciliation," thereby constitute themselves as "those who are perishing" (4:3; cp. 2:15). Paul insinuates that his missionary opponents should be classified amongst the ἄπιστοι, those outsiders to the Christian movement who "lack faith." Only those who agree with Paul's law-free gospel, in this formulation, may be classified as amongst "those who are being saved," who are being transformed slowly into the radiant image of the risen Christ; for "where the spirit of the Lord is, is freedom."

In 3:18, Paul states that "we are being transformed, by degrees of glory, into the same image ..." The expression "the same image," introduces a proleptic use of the "identical pronoun." The term "image" (εἰκών) had not occurred in the narrative prior to its use in 3:18, so that its referent when Paul introduced it at that point was obscure. However, in 4:4, Paul unveils the "image" into which "we" are being transformed: it is the image of

---

[99] The oft-repeated assertion that 3:7–18 encodes a dispute between "Christianity" and "Judaism" is therefore untenable. Windisch's view is typical (*Der zweite Korintherbrief*, 112): "Christentum und Judentum, nicht Paulinismus und Judaismus, sind die grossen Gegensätze." Bultmann (*Second Letter to the Corinthians*, 84) concurs. The contrast is rather between (law-free) house-church and (law abiding) synagogue. Many of the members of the Pauline church in Corinth, as Acts 18 attests, had been active at different times both within the synagogue and the house-church. The "Jewish"/"Christian" dichotomy therefore, is false. Adherents to the early Christian movement often met in synagogues (cf. James 2:2; Rev 2:9)! Furthermore, the law/no law dichotomy that Paul constructs here does not correspond with a distinction between Christianity and Judaism, as is often thought. The dominant *Christian* position in Paul's day was that converts must adhere to the law. As we have seen, this position was adopted in Antioch, and was held by Paul's missionary rivals in Corinth.

Christ who, in turn, is an image of God (Χριστός ... ὅς ἐστιν εἰκὼν τοῦ θεοῦ).

Paul's Corinthian congregants were already familiar with the idea that Christ had been transformed at the time of his resurrection, obtaining an imperishable and glorious "spiritual" body (1 Cor 15:42–44).[100] And yet, clearly the Corinthians did not perceive themselves as possessing a luminous body analogous to that of the risen Christ! Rather, as in Paul's formulation in Rom 12:2, "be transformed (μεταμορφοῦσθε) by the renewal of your minds," the transformation that Paul has in mind is internal, and therefore not readily visible. This transformation took place in the "inner man,"[101] which could fruitfully be contrasted with the outer man, who was "wasting away daily" (4:16).

With this inner/outer dichotomy, Paul is able to invoke the shade of a standard philosophical critique of sophists, in which the sophists were described as enjoying every external advantage, including wealth, luxurious clothing, and a noble demeanor. The "true philosopher," by contrast, sustained himself on only the meager necessities: a little food, a simple robe. He was concerned with the soul. The philosopher's neglect of bodily needs led to the view that he was "in training for dying." It is with this theme that Paul inaugurates the second main section of his *narratio*: "We have this treasure in earthen pots ..." (4:7) and later, "our outer man is wasting away ..." (v. 16). And with this theme we are drawn back again to Paul's exordium: "Thanks be to God who at all times leads us in a triumphal procession," a procession that culminates in the apostle's death.

We have come full circle in our analysis, from Paul's exordium and through his narrative construction pertaining to the new covenant, and through 4:7 back again to the theme introduced in the exordium. This marks a suitable ending point for our analysis of Paul's narrative. All that remains is to make a few short comments on what was at stake, what was accomplished, and how, in Paul's narrative on the new covenant in 2 Cor 3:7–18.

In response to charges leveled by his missionary opponents that he had "falsified the word of God," and preached a "veiled gospel," Paul con-

---

[100] Paul's positing of a "spiritual body" (σῶμα πνευματικόν) illustrates how removed he was from the philosophical presuppositions of Platonism. Paul did not operate with a material/immaterial dichotomy. One could call to mind the example of the "all-devouring spirit" of TAbraham 4:9–10, who was sent into the angel Michael to enable him to consume food. This "spirit" was able to interact with the material world readily enough!

[101] See the article of C. Markschies et al., "Innerer Mensch," *RGG*⁴ 4:154-157 as well as H. D. Betz, "The Delphic Maxim ΓΝΩΘΙ ΣΑΥΤΟΝ in Hermetic Interpretation" (*HTR* 63 [1970] 464–484) and more recently Betz, "The Concept of the 'Inner Human Being' (ὁ ἔσω ἄνθρωπος) in the Anthropology of Paul," *NTS* 46 (2000) 315–341.

structs a discourse that imputes the substance of these charges to Moses, and by implication, to those missionaries who advocated adherence to Mosaic law. Paul boldly does this on the basis of an interpretation of Exodus that turns the text against itself, making the Torah foretell its own nullification in the sign of Moses' veil. It is ironic that Paul defends himself against the charge of "falsifying the word of God" by imputing to the Biblical text a meaning that runs exactly counter to its "plain sense." Paul defends himself against the charge of sophistry by employing sophistic tactics: he sunders traditional pairings (spirit and letter/law), plays on the ambiguities inherent in the use of certain terms (again, "spirit"), and relies on innuendo and implication in the development of his arguments. In terms of his relationship to scripture and tradition, Paul indeed "makes the worse case appear the better."

In reacting to charges leveled by his opponents, Paul attempts to turn the tables by portraying himself in the role, albeit "Christianized," of the philosopher who, in training for dying, eschews bodily needs, in contradistinction to his opponents, portrayed as rapacious orators who "hawk the word of God." Paul does not refer to himself as a philosopher nor to his opponents as sophists, but his characterizations are clearly drawn from typical depictions of these two groups. Rather, Paul refers to himself as an apostle, and to his opponents as "hawkers of the word of God" or, later in the second apology, "false apostles." Paul's use of topoi from debates between philosophers and sophists are modified for use in the context of a rivalry between early Christian missionaries, each group advocating an opposing viewpoint.

Paul's discourse on the new covenant amply demonstrates the substance behind the claims that he possessed the rhetorical wherewithal to "corrupt" his audience (7:2). We may also recall the related charge that Paul behaved "craftily" (4:2; cp. 12:16) and therefore could not be trusted. Matters appear to have gotten worse for Paul (cf. 2 Cor 10–13) before they got better. Yet somehow, even after his vitriolic dispute with the missionary "ministers of righteousness," Paul seems to have in the end come to an amicable understanding with the communities that he had founded in Corinth, since he seems later to have written his letter to the Romans from there (cf. Rom 16:21–23). The outcome of Paul's disputes in Corinth testifies both to his unwillingness to cede the authority to which he laid claim as the community's founder, and the community's willingness to endow Paul with the authority that he both sought and claimed. This willingness however was both partial and subject to re-evaluation. It was in part due to the discursive resources which Paul was able to marshal that he was able to negotiate his reinstatement into the good graces of the Corinthian community.

Chapter 6

Conclusions

At the beginning of this study, I suggested that the old essentialist mode of comparison between "Judaism" and "Christianity" did not apply in comparisons involving the earliest Christian literature and early Jewish material. Rather than viewing early Christianity as a "religion" that was separate and distinct from Judaism, I have chosen to categorize earliest Christianity as a Jewish sect. According to this view, earliest Christianity is a species of Judaism, and not a religion that is to be distinguished from it. I offered a schematic that represented Christianity as one of a number of Jewish sects that existed prior to the destruction of the Second Temple, which I reproduce below.

Figure 3: *Jewish Sects in the Late Second Temple Period*

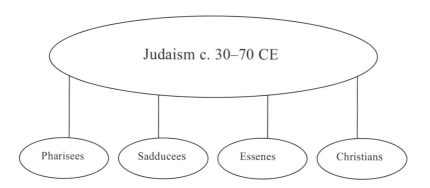

The reconstruction of the local situation to which Paul responded in writing his discourse on the new covenant in 2 Corinthians 3–4 allows us to introduce a specification into our schematic. Early Christianity, as we have seen, cannot be viewed as a unitary entity. Rather it was characterized by internal division, as Paul and other individuals and groups struggled to promote their own, often mutually exclusive ideological views. Paul formulated his discourse on the new covenant in response to the formulations of rival missionaries who apparently referred to themselves as "ministers of righteousness." Paul and the "ministers of righteousness" held views in regard to the role of the Torah in the praxis of the early Christian communities that were difficult to reconcile. In fact, no reconciliation was even attempted, as Paul and the ministers of righteousness mutually maligned the other. Based on these results, we can specify our schematic of early Christianity as composed of competing groups as follows:

Figure 4: *Two Competing Groups Within Early Christianity*

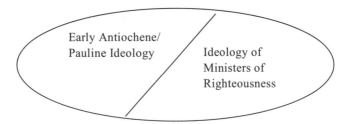

Of course this schematic does not have any pretension to representing all of the groups that comprised earliest Christianity. Rather, the schematic includes only those two groups that were included within the purview of this study. However, even this simple formulation has important implications for the classification of earliest Christianity vis-à-vis other Jewish groups. According to the essentialist classificatory scheme, Judaism is construed as a religion in which individuals earn divine favor through legal observance, whereas Christianity is construed as a religion in which law plays little part; divine favor is achieved only as the result of a gift from God. However, in the schematic presented above, early Christianity is internally divided over the matter of observance of the Torah. Paul argued that his Gentile converts need not observe it; the missionary ministers of righteousness argued that converts were obligated to do so. Earliest Christianity was not "essentially" a religion that eschewed Torah observance. Rather, it was a social entity in within which the role of the law was a contested topic. As we have seen, Paul's position was probably a minority one in the first century CE. This position was repudiated by the congregation at Antioch, where Paul was first introduced to it. The influential church at Jerusalem had also taken the position that converts should adhere to the Torah. In comparative terms, within early Christianity after the time of the Jerusalem conference, Paul's view was anomalous.

The endeavor of classifying Paul's position vis-à-vis others thus raises, but cannot answer, the question of why Paul argued in the way that he did.

Classification must be supplemented by methods that provide explanation. This study has attempted to develop a methodological framework within which some explanatory factors can be identified. That is, the study hypothesizes that the local situation provides the necessary data from which explanatory theories may be derived. It is hypothesized that particular discourses are formulated largely in response to some particular local situation, itself constituted by a particular set of ideologies, relationships involving the exercise of power and authority, and the allocation of economic and social resources. It is further hypothesized that authors, whether individuals of groups, create discourses for the purpose of influencing the ideologies, power relationships, and allocation of resources that constitute the local situation. Such discourses operate presumably by attempting to inculcate a set of ideological and practical dispositions within those individuals who constitute a discourse's target audience. Regardless of their literary genre, according to this view, all discourses participate to some degree, whether overtly or covertly, in an attempt to persuade its hearers/readers to accept some set of ideological or practical commitments. In this way, the manipulation of discourse constitutes an attempt to influence the circumstances constitutive of a particular local situation. To modify a popular phrase, "All religion is local."

In this study, I have juxtaposed discourses on the new covenant produced by representatives of two Jewish sects, the Essenes and early Christianity. In each case, I have attempted to delineate aspects of the local situation that I take to have had a significant impact on the ways in which these discourses were formulated.

With respect to the Damascus Document's use of the phrase "new covenant," we have seen that its significance was restricted. In the Damascus Document, the phrase "new covenant" is used only to refer to the originary act of covenant renewal that was inaugurated by the Righteous Teacher in Damascus. This act of covenant renewal was predicated on the belief that Israel had broken its covenant with God, a state of affairs in response to which God had enacted a series of curses, the most serious of which constituted Israel's exile from the land to which it laid claim. The members of the Essene Association believed that, prior to Israel's rebellion in breaking its covenant with God, it had been noetically disenabled by an action of God to interpret the covenantal laws, the Torah, correctly. It was not until the point at which God, in an act of divine mercy toward Israel, enlightened the Teacher with the correct interpretation of the Torah, that the broken covenant was able to be restored. The members of the Essene Association expected that the restoration of the covenant would culminate in the restoration of the land to a subset of Israelites, those who followed the sect's regime of ideology and praxis, constituted in large part by its particular interpretation of the Torah.

When correlated with salient features of the local situation, this seemingly innocuous theological narrative is seen to carry some very significant implications for the Essene Association's relations with other sects that were its contemporaries. Perhaps most importantly from the perspective of the Essenes was the idea that God had enacted a priestly covenant with the "sons of Zadok," a lineage that appears to have been represented within the sect's membership. Whereas the Hasmoneans appear to have legitimated their own seizure of the High Priesthood by appealing to the Biblical narrative of the "zeal of Phinehas" (Num 25:6–15), the Essene Zadokites lay claim to a different Biblical narrative, that of the replacement of the Elides by the Zadokites (1 Sam 2). By implicitly identifying its own Zadokite priesthood with that of the Biblical narrative and identifying the Hasmoneans with the delegitimated Elides, D was able to insinuate that the Hasmoneans would at some future point be removed from the priesthood, to be replaced by the Essene Zadokites (CD 3:18–4:4). The ideology espoused by the Essene Association included an expectation that God would destroy the Hasmoneans, thereby enabling the Zadokites to claim the high priestly "sure house" that they believed God had vouchsafed to them.

A second local interest is evident in the Damascus Document's formulation of its covenantal ideology. The Essene Association formulated its legal positions in competition with another influential sect, the Pharisees. The Pharisees appear to have espoused a body of legal interpretations at least as early as the time of John Hyrcanus (134–104 BCE). In some cases, Essene legal interpretations were formulated in conscious opposition to those of the Pharisees (e.g., niece marriage). According to the ideology of the Essene Association, any legal teaching that contradicted the sect's own was invalid and therefore constituted a breach in God's covenant with Israel. According to this construction, Pharisaic legal teaching contributed to the state of exile that Israel was construed as experiencing. From the Essene perspective, the Pharisees, as the result of their faulty legal rulings, constituted themselves as rebels against God.

Unless the Sadducees are referred to in the Damascus Document's oblique reference to the "house of Peleg," this group was spared negative characterization in the Damascus Document. Perhaps this is because the Zadokites were thought to have been included within God's priestly covenant with the "sons of Zadok" ("Sadducees" is the Graecized form of "Zadokites"), or perhaps this is an example of *Realpolitik*: the Essene Zadokites responsible for penning this section of the Damascus Document did not wish to alienate those of their kinsmen who had retained their positions within the Jerusalem Temple during the Hasmonean regime. If this is so however, the Damascus Document's somewhat sympathetic portrayal of the Sadducees contrasts with the much less sympathetic portrayal in Pesher Nahum.

Ellen Juhl Christiansen, whose work we have examined in the introduction, has interpreted the Damascus Document's construction of the covenant as doubly particularistic. That is, the Old Testament idea of covenant, limited to those who shared a particular ethnic identity, is itself particularized, such that "*identity has been narrowed down from an ethnic to a priestly covenant*, which ... creates a consciousness of narrow boundaries which ultimately creates a boundary within Israel ..."[1] According to Christiansen's theological agenda, this act of double particularization marks the Damascus Document as doubly defective, and stands in contrast to a supposed Christian universalism. If we bracket Christiansen's theological agenda, and focus on her sociological analysis, we find that while not untrue, her results are so general as to be misleading. Christiansen is correct in asserting that, in terms of the history of tradition of the covenantal idea, the Damascus Document's construal of covenant is not based on ethnic or national identity, but rather on the identity of a particular subset of this ethnic or national entity[2] (although, contrary to Christiansen, I think that the sect did accept converted Gentiles into its ranks).

Christiansen's analysis however, since it focuses exclusively on analytical acts of particularization within the text, is not sufficiently contextualized within the local situation in which the Damascus Document was written. Her analysis fails to discern the principal discursive functions of D's construal of covenant: it serves to delegitimate the Hasmonean high priesthood while at the same time legitimating the Essene Zadokite line, and to delegitimate Pharisaic legal interpretation, while legitimating Essene rulings. The Damascus Document's formulations certainly did function to delineate boundaries between groups: Hasmoneans are distin-

---

[1] *The Covenant in Judaism and Paul*, 131.

[2] Christiansen is not alone in viewing the restriction of the covenant with Israel to a covenant with the Dead Sea sect as the most salient aspect of the Dead Sea scrolls' covenantal ideology. For example, Craig Evans writes, "Simply put, the distinctive feature of the understanding of Covenant at Qumran is the reduction of the number of the elect. There is now a chosen people drawn out from among the people of Israel: a chosen from the chosen, as it were" ("Covenant in the Qumran Literature," in S. E. Porter and J. C. R. de Roo, eds., *The Concept of the Covenant in the Second Temple Period* (Leiden and Boston: Brill, 2003) 80. In the same vein, J. Vanderkam, citing J. Licht, writes, "The primary difference between the biblical covenant involving Israel and the one in the sectarian texts is that in the latter the covenantal community now embraces only those who pledged to adhere to the covenant in sectarian terms" ("Covenant and Biblical Interpretation in Jubilees 6," 101).

guished from Essene Zadokites, Pharisees from members of the Essene Association (on the basis of halakhah). Such boundaries having been indicated however, the text proceeds to legitimate and delegitimate, and so attempts both to reinforce extant boundaries, by attempting to persuade those who are already "in" to "stay in," and to reconstruct existing boundaries along lines beneficial to the sect. The latter is accomplished by the creation of a discursive structure that may have proven to be compelling to those who were not currently members of the sect, thus increasing membership and redrawing the sect's boundaries by widening them, sociologically if not ideologically.

One of Bruce Lincoln's methodological dicta is to ask of particular ideological formulations, "What would the consequences be if this project of persuasion should happen to succeed?"[3] In the case of D's construal of covenant, two effects could be postulated: the Hasmoneans would lose support in their role as high priests, and Pharisaic influence over halakhic practices would decrease. Concomitant with this loss of Hasmonean and Pharisaic influence one could posit a corresponding rise in Essene influence: the assumption of the high priesthood and control over the social practices of the Jewish populace through the dissemination of Essene halakhic precepts. The seemingly innocuous theological narrative of D masks the material interest that is was presumably formulated to serve, that of increasing the social and political influence of the Essene group within Jewish society. The politically and socially marginal Essene group deployed one of the tools at its disposal, religious discourse, in a bid to reconstruct Jewish society in manner that would further its own interest, an interest significantly shaped by a will to power.

The political interests served by D were not a salient factor in Christiansen's study. Since Christiansen's sociological method was dictated by the theological distinction which posits Judaism, construed as a particularistic religion, against Christianity, construed as a universalistic religion, Christiansen's sociological method remained at a high level of abstraction. The only sociological factor that was of interest to Christiansen was that of particularism. The specifics of the local historical situation which were so influential in the way in which the Damascus Document formulated its concerns were of no interest to Christiansen's study; both theologically and sociologically such concerns were superfluous.

Since Christiansen prescinded from applying her (limited) sociological method to the Pauline literature, preferring instead to adhere to the theological construction of an undifferentiated "Christianity" as a universal religion, we need not discuss the results of her analysis of Paul. Instead, we may draw some conclusions based on the results of our own study.

---

[3] "Theses on Method," 226.

Paul construes the new covenant as one characterized by the presence of "the spirit," construed in typical Pauline fashion as that which inspires visionary and ecstatic phenomena among the Pauline congregations. The spirit, Paul argues, implies "freedom," a freedom from adhering to the stipulations of the Torah. Paul's discourse was constructed in conscious opposition to that of rival missionaries who relied on a traditional association between spirit, construed as the agency that enabled humans to adhere with perfect fidelity to the Torah, and covenant renewal. Paul reversed the complementary associations between spirit and covenant renewal present in the ideology of his missionary rivals, constructing instead an antithesis between the two terms: "Where the spirit of the Lord is, is freedom." Thus, both the theological problem and the specific terminology in which it was expressed was dictated by the local situation in Corinth in the 50s CE.

If Paul borrowed terms and ideas from the preaching of his missionary rivals (who in turn espoused a Christian variant of an older scriptural ideology of covenant renewal), the theological position that Paul articulated was diametrically opposed to that of his rivals. Paul's own position was a development of a position that he had learned at Antioch, under the tutelage of Barnabas. Prior to Antioch's acceptance of a ruling from the Jerusalem church, Gentile converts there had been accepted as full members of the church without having to adhere to the precepts of the Torah. After Antioch repudiated this position in 51 CE, Paul became its principal advocate, carrying it westward on his missionary journeys. The local situations in which Paul participated, first defined by the situation in Antioch prior to 51 CE and later by the situation in Corinth in 56 CE, provided Paul with the ideology and the specific terms from which he crafted his discourse on the new covenant in 2 Corinthians 3–4. Paul's discourse served to legitimate the regime of ideology and praxis that he advocated, while at the same time countering the claims to legitimacy put forth by missionaries whom Paul construed, and who mutually construed Paul as adversaries.

We may also ask of the Pauline discourse in 2 Corinthians what the consequences would have been, had it succeeded. If, as the list of greetings in Rom 16 seems to indicate, this letter was written from Corinth, then it would seem that Paul's discourse did meet with some success. In his struggle with rival missionaries over the allegiance of the Corinthian congregation, Paul seems eventually to have prevailed. Paul's two apologies, which presented him as God's apostle, legitimated by charismatic and visionary experiences, like D's ideology of covenant, served a material interest. In this case, at stake were Paul's status and influence within the congregation at Corinth, both factors which bore directly on Paul's ability to draw upon the human and economic resources available to the Corinthians. As Paul likely perceived, the Corinthians' potential usefulness to him in his subsequent missionary endeavors depended in large part on the success or failure of the discursive strategies that he deployed.

In this study, we have seen that both D's discourse on the new covenant, as well as its broader constructions of covenant in general, were formulated in response to the local situation that was constituted by the Hasmoneans' assumption of the high priesthood during the middle of the second century BCE, and by the influence of Pharisaic legal interpretation during and after this same period. Paul's discourse was formulated in response to a local situation in which traditionalist Christian missionaries had assumed a position of importance within the Christian congregation at Corinth. All religious formulations – or, to confine ourselves to the results of this study, the formulations of Paul and the Damascus Document – arise in response to the concerns presented by a local situation. For this reason, comparisons between varieties of early Christianity and varieties of early Judaism cannot be predicated on essentialist constructions derived from Christian theological categories. On the contrary, such comparisons ought to be made only after each object of comparison has first been contextualized within the local situation in response to which its discursive strategies have been formulated.

Bibliography

Alexander, P. S., "Geography and the Bible (Early Jewish Geography)" *ABD* 2:977–88.

–, "A Note on the Syntax of 4Q448" *JSJ* 44:2 (1993) 301.

Allison, D., *The New Moses: A Matthean Typology* (Minneapolis: Augsburg Fortress, 1993).

Amitai, J., ed., *Biblical Archaeology Today* (Jerusalem: Ben Zvi, 1985).

Bachmann, M., *Göttliche Allmacht und theologische Vorsicht* (SBS 188; Stuttgart: Katholisches Bibelwerk, 2002).

Baird, W., *History of New Testament Research, vol. 1: From Deism to Tübingen* (Minneapolis: Fortress Press, 1992).

Baltzer, K., *The Covenant Formulary in Old Testament, Jewish, and Early Christian Writings* (Philadelphia: Fortress, 1971; trans. of *Das Bundesformular*; Neukirchen-Vluyn: Neukirchener Verlag, 1964).

Barrett, C. K., *Essays on Paul* (Philadelphia: Westminster Press, 1992).

–, *The Second Epistle to the Corinthians* (New York: Harper and Row, 1973).

Baumgarten, A. I., *The Flourishing of Jewish Sects in the Maccabean Era: An Interpretation* (Leiden: Brill, 1997).

Baumgarten, J. M., "The Essenes and the Temple: A Reappraisal" reprinted in J. M. Baumgarten, *Studies in Qumran Law* (Leiden: Brill, 1977) 57–74.

–, *Studies in Qumran Law* (Studies in Judaism in Late Antiquity 24; Leiden: Brill, 1977).

–, "Polemics in New Fragments from Qumran Cave 4" in *Biblical Archaeology Today*, J. Amitai, ed. (Jerusalem: Ben Zvi, 1985) 390–99.

–, "A New Qumran Substitute for the Divine Name and Mishnah Sukkah 4:5" *JQR* 83 (1992) 1–5.

–, "את הו הכול - אונ הו הכול": A Reply to M. Kister" *JQR* 84 (1994) 485–87.

Baumgarten, J., Chazon, E., and Pinnick, A., eds., *The Damascus Document: A Centennial of Discovery: Proceedings of the Third International Symposium of the Orion Center for the Study of the Dead Sea Scrolls and Associated Literature, February 4–8, 1998* (STDJ 34; Leiden: Brill, 2000).

Baumgarten, J. M. and Schwartz, D. R. "Damascus Document (CD)" *PTSDSSP* 2:4–79.

Baur, F. C., *Paul, the Apostle of Jesus Christ* (2 vols., London and Edinburgh: Williams and Norgate, 1875; trans. of *Paulus, der Apostel Jesu Christi. Sein Leben, sein Wirken, seine Briefe und seine Lehre. Ein Beitrag zu einer kritischen Geschichte des Urchristenthums*; Leipzig: Fues's Verlag, 1866).

Beall, T., *Josephus' Description of the Essenes Illustrated by the Dead Sea Scrolls* (SNTSMS 58; Cambridge Cambridge University Press, 1988).

–, "Essenes" *EDSS* 1:262–69.

–, "Pliny the Elder" *EDSS* 2:677–79.

Belleville, L., *Reflections of Glory: Paul's Polemical Use of the Moses–Doxa Tradition in 2 Corinthians 3.1–18* (JSOTSupp 52; Sheffield: Sheffield Academic Press, 1991).

–, *2 Corinthians* (IVP New Testament Commentary Series; Downers Grove and Leicester: InterVarsity Press, 1996).

Betz, H. D., "The Delphic Maxim ΓΝΩΘΙ ΣΑΥΤΟΝ in Hermetic Interpretation" *HTR* 63 (1970) 464–484.

–, *Der Apostel Paulus und die sokratische Tradition: Eine exegetische Untersuchung zu einer "Apologie" 2 Korinther 10–13* (Beiträge zur historischen Theologie 45; Tübingen: J. C. B. Mohr, 1972).

–, "2 Cor. 6:14–7:1: An Anti–Pauline Fragment?" *JBL* 92 (1973) 88–108.

–, *Galatians: A Commentary on Paul's Letter to the Churches in Galatia* (Hermeneia; Philadelphia: Fortress Press, 1979).

–, *2 Corinthians 8 and 9: A Commentary on Two Administrative Letters of the Apostle Paul* (Hermeneia; Philadelphia: Fortress Press, 1985).

–, "The Problem of Rhetoric and Theology According to the Apostle Paul" in A. Vanhoye, ed., *L'Apotre Paul: Personalité, Style et Conception du Ministère*; 16–48.

–, "The Concept of the 'Inner Human Being' (ὁ ἔσω ἄνθρωπος) in the Anthropology of Paul" *NTS* 46 (2000) 315–41.

Bieringer, R. and Lambrecht, J., *Studies on 2 Corinthians* (BETL 112; Leuven: University Press, 1994).

Blackman, P., ed., *Mishnayoth* (6 vols., Brooklyn: Judaica Press, 2000 [1964]).

Bonhoeffer, D., *The Way to Freedom Letters, Lectures and Notes 1935–1939*, vol. 2 (London: Collins, 1966).

Bornkamm, G., *Die Vorgeschichte des sogennanten Zweiten Korintherbriefes* (SHAW; Philosophisch–Historische Klasse 1961, Bericht 2; Heidelberg: Carl Winter Universitätsverlag, 1961).

–, "The History of the Origin of the So–Called Second Letter to the Corinthians" *NTS* 8 (1962) 258–64.

Bremmer, J., *The Rise and Fall of the Afterlife* (London and New York: Routledge, 2002).

Brin, G., *Studies in Biblical Law From the Hebrew Bible to the Dead Sea Scrolls* (JSOTSup 176; Sheffield: JSOT Press, 1994).

Broshi, M., ed., *The Damascus Document Reconsidered* (Jerusalem: Israel Exploration Society, 1992).

Brown, R. E., *The Gospel According to John I–XII* (AB 29; New York: Doubleday, 1966).

Bultmann, R., *Exegetische Probleme des zweiten Korintherbriefes* (Darmstadt: Wissenschaftliche Buchgesellschaft, 1963).

–, *The Second Letter to the Corinthians* (Minneapolis: Augsburg, 1985; trans. of *Der zweite Brief an die Korinther*; Göttingen: Vandenhoeck & Ruprecht, 1976).

Callaway, P. R., *The History of the Qumran Community: An Investigation* (JSPSup, Series 3; Sheffield: Sheffield Press, 1988).

Campbell, J. G., "Essene–Qumran Origins in the Exile: A Scriptural Basis?" *JJS* 46 (1995) 143–56.

–, *The Use of Scripture in the Damascus Document 1–8, 19–20* (BZAW 228; Berlin and New York: de Gruyter, 1995).

Carmi, I., "Radiocarbon Dating of the Dead Sea Scrolls" in L. Schiffman et al., eds., *The Dead Sea Scrolls Fifty Years After Their Discovery: 1947–1997*; 881–888).

Cartilage, D. and Dungan, D., *Documents for the Study of the Gospels* (Philadelphia: Fortress Press, 1980).

Charlesworth, J., "History of the Rechabites" *OTP* 2:443–461.

–, *The Pesharim and Qumran History: Chaos or Consensus?* (Grand Rapids and Cambridge, UK: Eerdmans, 2002).

Charlesworth, J., ed., *Old Testament Pseudepigrapha* (2 vols., New York and London: Doubleday, 1985).

Charlesworth, J., et al., eds., *The Dead Sea Scrolls: Hebrew, Aramaic, and Greek Texts with English Translations*; vol. 1: *Rule of the Community and Related Documents* (Tübingen: J. C. B. Mohr/Paul Siebeck and Louisville: Westminster John Knox Press, 1994).

Charlesworth, J., et al., eds., *The Dead Sea Scrolls: Hebrew, Aramaic, and Greek Texts with English Translations*; vol. 2: *Damascus Document, War Scroll and Related Documents* (Tübingen: J. C. B. Mohr/Paul Siebeck and Louisville: Westminster John Knox Press, 1995).

Christiansen, E. J., *The Covenant in Judaism and Paul: A Study of Ritual Boundaries as Identity Markers* (Leiden, New York, and Köln: Brill, 1995).

Classen, C. J., "Aristotle's Picture of the Sophists" in G. B. Kerferd, ed., *The Sophists and Their Legacy* (Wiesbaden: Franz Steiner Verlag, 1979).

–, "St. Paul's Epistles and Ancient Greek and Roman Rhetoric"; in S. Porter and T. Olbricht, eds., *Rhetoric and the New Testament: Essays from the 1992 Heidelberg Conference* (JSNTSup 90; Sheffield: Sheffield Academic Press, 1993) 265–91.

Collins, J. J., "The Origin of the Qumran Community: A Review of the Evidence" in *To Touch the Text: Biblical and Related Studies in Honor of Joseph A. Fitzmyer, S. J.*, M. Horgan and P. J. Kobelski, eds. (New York: Crossroad, 1989) 159–78.

–, "Was the Dead Sea Sect an Apocalyptic Community?" in *Archaeology and History in the Dead Sea Scrolls: The New York University Conference in Honor of Yigael Yadin*, L. H. Schiffman, ed. (JSPSup 8; Sheffield: JSOT Press, 1990) 25–51.

–, *The Scepter and the Star: The Messiahs of the Dead Sea Scrolls and Other Ancient Literature* (New York: Doubleday, 1995).

–, "The Expectation of the End in the Dead Sea Scrolls," in *Eschatology, Messianism, and the Dead Sea Scrolls*, C. Evans and P. Flint, eds. (Grand Rapids: Eerdmans, 1997) 74–90.

–, *The Apocalyptic Imagination: An Introduction to Jewish Apocalyptic Literature* (2nd ed., Grand Rapids: Eerdmans, 1998).

–, *Introduction to the Hebrew Bible* (Minneapolis: Fortress Press, 2004).

–, "The Time of the Teacher: An Old Debate Renewed" in P. Flint, et al., eds., *Studies in the Hebrew Bible, Qumran, and the Septuagint Presented to Eugene Ulrich*; 212–229.

Comfort, P. W. and Barrett, D., *The Complete Text of the Earliest New Testament Manuscripts* (Grand Rapids: Baker Books, 1999).

Cross, F. M., *The Ancient Library of Qumran* (3rd ed., Sheffield: Sheffield Academic Press, 1995).

–, *Canaanite Myth and Hebrew Epic: Essays in the History of the Religion of Israel* (Cambridge, MA: Harvard Press, 1997).

Davies, P. R., *The Damascus Covenant: An Interpretation of the "Damascus Document"* (JSOTSup 25; Sheffield: JSOT Press, 1982).

–, "The Ideology of the Temple in the Damascus Document" *JJS* 33 (1982) 287–301.

–, "The Birthplace of the Essenes Where is 'Damascus'?" *RQ* 56/14 (1990) 503–520.

Davies, W. D. and Allison, D., *The Gospel According to Saint Matthew*, vol. 1 (ICC; Edinburgh: T&T Clark, 1988).

Davila, J., *Liturgical Works* (Eerdmans Commentaries on the Dead Sea Scrolls; Grand Rapids and Cambridge: Eerdmans, 2000).

DeVries, L., *Cities of the Biblical World* (Peabody, MA: Hendrickson, 1997).

DiCicco, M., *Paul's Use of Ethos, Pathos, and Logos in 2 Corinthians 10–13* (Lewinston, NY and Queenston, Ontario: Edwin Mellen Press, 1995).

DiLella, A. and Skehan, P., *The Wisdom of Ben Sira* (Anchor Bible; New York: Doubleday, 1987).

Dillon, J. and Gergel, T., *The Greek Sophists* (Penguin Classics; London: Penguin Books, 2000).

Dimant, D., "The Qumran Manuscripts: Contents and Significance" in *Time to Prepare the Way in the Wilderness: Papers on the Qumran Scrolls* (Dimant, D. and Schiffman, L. H., eds.; Leiden and New York: Brill, 1994, c1995) 23–58.

–, "Non pas l'Exil au Désert mais l'Exil Spirituel: l'Interprétation d'Isaïe 40,3 dans la *Règle de la Communauté*" in A. Lemaire and S. Mimouni, eds., *Qumrân et le Judaïsme du Tournant de Notre Ère:* Actes de la Table Ronde, *Collège de France, 16 novembre 2004;* 17-36.

Dimant, D. and Schiffman, L., eds., *Time to Prepare the Way in the Wilderness: Papers on the Qumran Scrolls* (Leiden and New York: Brill, 1994, c1995).

Doudna, G., "Report and Discussion Concerning Radiocarbon Dating of Fourteen Dead Sea Scrolls," in *Methods of Investigation of the Dead Sea Scrolls and the Khirbet Qumran Site*, M. Wise, et al., eds. (New York New York Academy of Sciences, 1994) 441-53.

–, "Radiocarbon Dating of the Dead Sea Scrolls" in *The Dead Sea Scrolls Fifty Years After Their Discovery: 1947–1997* (Jerusalem: Israel Exploration Society, 2000) 881–88.

–, *4Q Pesher Nahum: A Critical Edition* (JSPSup 35; New York and London: Sheffield Academic Press, 2001).

Dunn, J. D. G., *The Christ and the Spirit*, vol. 1: *Christology* (Grand Rapids and Cambridge, UK: Eerdmans, 1989).

–, ed., *The Cambridge Companion to St. Paul* (Cambridge: Cambridge University Press, 2003).

Dupont-Sommer, A., *The Dead Sea Scrolls: A Preliminary Survey* (Oxford, UK: Basil Blackwell, 1954).

Engberg-Pederson, T., ed., *Paul Beyond the Judaism/Hellenism Divide* (Louisville: Westminster John Knox Press, 2001).

Eshel, E., Eshel, H., and Yardeni, A., "A Qumran Composition Containing Part of Ps. 154 and a Prayer for the Welfare of King Jonathan and his Kingdom" *IEJ* 42 (1992) 199–229.

Eshel, H., "Jonathan (Hasmonean)" *EDSS* 1:422–423.

Evans, C. and Flint, P., eds., *Eschatology, Messianism, and the Dead Sea Scrolls* (Grand Rapids: Eerdmans, 1997).

Falk, D., *Daily, Sabbath, and Festival Prayers in the Dead Sea Scrolls: Proceedings of the Third Meeting of the International Organization for Qumran Studies, Oslo, 1998* (STDJ 27; Leiden: Brill, 1998).

Falk, D., García Martínez, F., and Schuller, E., eds., *Sapiential, Liturgical, and Poetical Texts from Qumran: Proceedings of the Third Meeting of the International Organization for Qumran Studies, Oslo, 1998* (STDJ 35; Leiden and Boston: Brill, 2000).

Farmer, W. R., Moule, C. F. D., and Niebuhr, R. R., eds., *Christian History and Interpretation: Studies Presented to John Knox* (Cambridge: Cambridge University Press, 1967).

Fee, G., *The First Epistle to the Corinthians* (NICNT; Grand Rapids: Eerdmans, 1987).

Finegan, J., *Handbook of Biblical Chronology* (Rev. ed., Peabody, MA: Hendrickson, 1998).

Fitzmyer, J., *The Aramaic Inscriptions of Sefîre* (Rome: Biblical Pontifical Institute, 1995 [1967]).

–, "Aramaic Epistolography" *JBL* 93 (1974) 201–225, reprinted in *The Semitic Background of the New Testament* (Grand Rapids and Cambridge, UK: Eerdmans, 1997: *A Wandering Aramean* section; 183–204).

–, *The Gospel According to Luke I–IX* (AB 28; Garden City, NY: Doubleday, 1981).

–, *The Gospel According to Luke X–XXIV* (AB 28A; Garden City, NY: Doubleday, 1985).

–, *The Semitic Background of the New Testament* (Grand Rapids and Cambridge, UK: Eerdmans, 1997).

Fitzmyer, J. and Harrington, D. J., *A Manual of Palestinian Aramaic Texts* (Rome: Biblical Pontifical Institute; 2nd reprint ed., 1994).

Flint, P., Tov, E. and VanderKam, J., eds., *Studies in the Hebrew Bible, Qumran, and the Septuagint Presented to Eugene Ulrich* (Leiden and Boston: Brill, 2006).

Flint, P. and VanderKam, J., *The Dead Sea Scrolls After Fifty Years: A Comprehensive Assessment* (Leiden, Boston, and Köln: Brill, 1999).

Forbes, C., "Comparison, Self–Praise, and Irony: Paul's Boasting and the Conventions of Hellenistic Rhetoric" *NTS* 32 (1986) 1–30.

Foucart, P., *Des Associations Chez les Grecs* (New York: Arno, 1975 [1873]).

Fujita, S., "The Metaphor of Plant in Jewish Literature of the Intertestamental Period," *JSJ* 7 (1976) 30–45.

Funk, R., "The Apostolic *Parousia*: Form and Significance" in W. R. Farmer, C. F. D. Moule, and R. R. Niebuhr, eds., *Christian History and Interpretation: Studies Presented to John Knox* (Cambridge: Cambridge University Press, 1967).

Furnish, V. P., *II Corinthians* (AB 32A; New York and London: Doubleday, 1984).

García-Martínez, F. and Tigchelaar, E. J. C., *Dead Sea Scrolls Study Edition* (2 vols., Leiden: Brill and Grand Rapids: Eerdmans, 1997–1998).

Georgi, D., *The Opponents of Paul in Second Corinthians* (Philadelphia: Fortress Press, 1986; trans. of *Die Gegner des Paulus im 2. Korintherbrief; Studien zur religiösen Propaganda in der Spätantike*; Neukirchen-Vluyn: Neukirchener Verlag, 1964).

Ginzberg, L., *An Unknown Jewish Sect* (New York: Ktav, 1976).

Given, M., *Paul's True Rhetoric: Ambiguity, Cunning, and Deception in Greece and Rome* (Harrisburg: Trinity Press International, 2001).

Gräßer, E., *Der zweite Brief an die Korinther, Kapitel 1,1–7,16* (Ökumenischer Taschenbuchkommentar zum Neuen Testament; Bd. 8; Gütersloh: Gütersloher Verlagshaus and Würzburg: Echter Verlag, 2002).

Gruber, M., *Herrlichkeit in Schwachheit: Eine Auslegung der Apologie des Zweiten Korintherbriefes 2 Kor 2, 14–6, 13* (FzB 89; Würzburg: Echter Verlag, 2004).

Gunkel, H., *Schöpfung und Chaos in Urzeit und Endzeit: Eine religionsgeschichtliche Untersuchung über Gen. 1 und Ap. Joh. 12* (Göttingen: Vandenhoeck and Ruprecht, 1921).

Hafemann, S. J., *Suffering and the Spirit: An Exegetical Study of II Cor. 2:14–3:3 Within the Context of the Corinthian Correspondence* (WUNT 2.19; Tübingen: Mohr Siebeck, 1986).

Halmel, A., *Der zweite Korintherbrief des Apostels Paulus* (Halle: Niemeyer, 1904).

Harnack, A. von, *What is Christianity?* (Philadelphia: Fortress Press, 1986; trans. of *Das Wesen des Christentums*, originally published in 1900).

Harris, M. J., *The Second Epistle to the Corinthians* (NIGTC; Grand Rapids: Eerdmans and Milton Keynes, UK: Paternoster, 2005).

Hartman, L., *'Into the Name of the Lord Jesus': Baptism in the Early Church* (Edinburgh: T&T Clark, 1997).

Hatch, E. and Redpath, H., *A Concordance to the Septuagint* (2nd ed., Grand Rapids: Baker, 1998).

Hellholm, D., ed., *Apocalypticism in the Mediterranean World and the Near East: Proceedings of the International Colloquium on Apocalypticism, Uppsala, August 12–17, 1979* (Tübingen: Mohr Siebeck, 1983).

Hempel, C. *The Laws of the Damascus Document: Sources, Tradition, and Redaction* (STDJ 29; Leiden Brill, 1998).

–, *The Damascus Texts* (Companion to the Dead Sea Scrolls 1; Sheffield: Sheffield Academic Press, 2000).

Hengel, M., *Judaism and Hellenism* (2 vols., Philadelphia: Fortress, 1974; trans. by J. Bowden of *Judentum und Hellenismus* [WUNT 10; 2nd ed., Tübingen: Mohr, 1973]).

Hock, R. F., *The Social Context of Paul's Ministry: Tentmaking and Apostleship* (Philadelphia: Fortress Press, 1980).

Holladay, C., *Theios Aner in Hellenistic Judaism: A Critique of the Use of This Category in New Testament Christology* (SBLDS 40; Missoula: Scholars Press, 1977).

Holmstrand, J., *Markers and Meaning in Paul: An Analysis of 1 Thessalonians, Philippians and Galatians* (Coniectanea Biblica, New Testament Series 28; Stockholm: Almqvist & Wiksell International, 1997).

Horgan, M. and Kobelski, P. J., eds., *To Touch the Text: Biblical and Related Studies in Honor of Joseph A. Fitzmyer, S.J.* (New York: Crossroad, 1989).

Horsley, R., "'How Can some of You Say that There is No Resurrection of the Dead?': Spiritual Elitism in Corinth" *NovT* 20 (1978) 203–231.

–, "Pneumatikos vs. Psychikos: Distinctions of Spiritual Status Among the Corinthians" *HTR* 69 (1976) 269–288.

–, "Wisdom of Word and Words of Wisdom in Corinth" *CBQ* 39 (1977) 224–239.

Hübner, H., Review of H. D. Betz, *2 Corinthians 8 and 9*; *TLZ* 113 (1998) cols. 750–752.

Iwry, S., "Was There a Migration to Damascus? The Problem of ישראל שבי," *Eretz–Israel* 9 (1969) 80–88.

James, M. R., *Apocrypha Anecdota* (Texts and Studies 2.3; Cambridge: University Press, 1893).

Jastrow, M., *A Dictionary of the Targumim, Talmud Bavli, Yerushalmi and Midrashic Literature* (New York: Judaica Press, 1992 [1971]).

Jewett, R., *A Chronology of Paul's Life* (Philadelphia: Fortress Press, 1979).

Jones, F. Stanley, *„Freiheit" in den Briefen des Apostels Paulus: Eine historische, exegetische und religionsgeschichtliche Studie* (GTA 34; Göttingen: Vandenhoeck & Ruprecht, 1987).

Joüon, P. and Muraoka, T., *A Grammar of Biblical Hebrew* (2 vols., Rome: Biblical Pontifical Institute, 1996).

Käsemann, E. "Die Legitimität des Apostels: Eine Untersuchung zu II Korinther 10–13" *ZNW* 41 (1942) 33–71.

Kerferd, G.B., ed., *The Sophists and Their Legacy: Proceedings of the Fourth International Colloquium on Ancient Philosophy Held in Cooperation with Projektgruppe Altertumswissenschaften der Thyssen Stiftung at Bad Homburg, 29th August – 1st September 1979* (Hermes 44; Weisbaden: Franz Steiner Verlag, 1979).

Kister, M., "On a New Fragment of the Damascus Document" *JQR* 84 (1993–94) 249–252.

–, "Commentary to 4Q298" *JQR* 85 (1994) 237–249.

Klauck, H.-J. *2. Korintherbrief* (Die Neue Echter Bibel; Würzburg: Echter Verlag, 1986).

–, *Gemeinde-Amt-Sakrament: neutestamentliche Perspektiven* (Würtzburg: Echter, 1989).

–, "Die Authorität des Charismas: Zehn neutestamentliche Thesen zum Thema" in *Gemeinde-Amt-Sakrament: neutestamentliche Perspektiven*; 223–231.

–, "Die Himmelfahrt des Paulus (2 Kor 12,2–4) in der koptischen Paulusapokalypse aus Nag Hammadi (NHC V/2)" in *Gemeinde-Amt-Sakrament: neutestamentliche Perspektiven*; 391–429.

–, *The Religious Context of Early Christianity: A Guide to Greco–Roman Religions* (Minneapolis: Fortress Press, 2003; trans. of *Die religiöse Umwelt des Urchristentums;* Stuttgart: Kohlhammer, 1995).

–, "Do They Never Come Back? *Nero Redivivus* and the Apocalypse of John" *CBQ* 63/4 (2001) 683–698.

–, *Religion und Gesellschaft im frühen Christentum: Neutestamentliche Studien* (WUNT 152; Tübingen: J. C. B. Mohr, 2003).

–, "Mit Engelszungen? Vom Charisma der Verständlichen Rede in 1 Kor 14" in *Religion und Gesellschaft im frühen Christentum*; 145–170.

–, "Von Kassandra bis Gnosis. Im Umfeld der frühchristlichen Glossalalie" in *Religion und Gesellschaft im frühen Christentum*; 119–144.

Klauck, H.-J. and Bäbler, B., *Dio von Prusa: Olympische Rede* (SAPERE 2; Darmstadt: Wissenschaftliche Buchgesellschaft, 2000).

Klein, R., "Ezra–Nehemiah, Books of" *ABD* 2:731–742.

Knibb, M., "The Exile in the Literature of the Intertestamental Period" *Heythrop Journal* 17 (1976) 253–72.

–, "Exile in the Damascus Document" *JSOT* 25 (1983) 99–117.

–, "Teacher of Righteousness" *EDSS* 2:918–21.

Koester, C., *Hebrews: A New Translation with Introduction and Commentary* (AB 36; New York and London: Doubleday, 2001).

Kreitzer, L., *2 Corinthians* (New Testament Guides; Sheffield: Sheffield Academic Press, 1996).

Kugel, J., *The Bible as it Was* (Cambridge, MA and London: Belknap, 1977).

Lambrecht, J., "The Fragment 2 Corinthians 6,14–7,1: A Plea for its Authenticity" *NTSupp* 48 (1978) 143–161, reprinted in R. Bieringer and J. Lambrecht, *Studies on 2 Corinthians* (BETL 112; Leuven: University Press, 1994) 532–549.

–, "Structure and Line of Thought in 2 Cor 2, 14–4,6" *Biblica* 64 (1983) 344–380.

–, "The Nekrōsis of Jesus Ministry and Suffering in 2 Cor 4, 7–15" in A. Vanhoye, ed., *L'Apotre Paul: Personalité, Style et Conception du Ministère* (BETL 73; Leuven: University Press, 1986) 120–143.

–, *Second Corinthians* (Sacra Pagina 8; Collegeville: Liturgical Press, 1999).

–, "The Fool's Speech and its Context Paul's Particular Way of Arguing in 2 Cor. 10–13" *Biblica* 82 (2001) 305–324.

Lausberg, H., *Handbook of Literary Rhetoric: A Foundation for Literary Study* (Leiden, Boston, Köln: Brill, 1998; trans. of *Handbuch der literarischen Rhetorik. Eine Grundlegung der Literaturwissenschaft*, München: M. Hueber, 1960).

Lemaire, A. and Mimouni, S., eds., *Qumrân et le Judaïsme du Tournant de Notre Ère: Actes de la Table Ronde, Collège de France, 16 novembre 2004* (Paris and Louvain: Peeters, 2006).

Levinsohn, S., *Discourse Features of New Testament Greek: A Coursebook on the Information Structure of New Testament Greek* (2nd ed., Dallas: SIL International, 2000).

Lichtenstein, H., "Die Fastenrolle, eine Untersuchung zur Jüdisch–Hellenistischen Geschichte" *HUCA* 8–9 (1931–32) 257–351.

Lim, T., "Wicked Priest" *EDSS* 2:973–76.

Lincoln, B., *Discourse and the Construction of Society: Comparative Studies of Myth, Ritual, and Classification* (New York and Oxford, UK: Oxford University Press, 1989).

–, "Mortuary Ritual and Prestige Economy: The Malagan for Bukbuk" *Cultural Critique* 12 (1989) 197–225.

–, *Death, War, and Sacrifice: Studies in Ideology and Practice* (Chicago and London: University of Chicago Press, 1991).

–, *Authority: Construction and Corrosion* (Chicago and London: University of Chicago Press, 1994).

–, "Theses on Method" *Method & Theory in the Study of Religion* 8.3 (1996) 225–227.

–, *Theorizing Myth: Narrative, Ideology, and Scholarship* (Chicago and London: University of Chicago Press, 1999).

–, *Holy Terrors: Thinking About Religion After September 11* (Chicago and London: University of Chicago Press, 2003).

–, "How to Read a Religious Text: Reflections on Some Passages of the Chāndogya Upaniṣad" *History of Religions* 46.2 (2006) 127–139.

Lindenberger, J. M., *Ancient Aramaic and Hebrew Letters* (2nd ed., Writings from the Ancient World 14; Leiden and Boston: Brill, 2003).

Longnecker, R. N., *Galatians* (Word Biblical Commentary 41; Dallas: Word Books, 1990).

Lüdemann, G., *Opposition to Paul in Jewish Christianity* (Minneapolis: Fortress, 1989; trans. of *Paulus, der Heidenapostel*, vol. 2: *Antipaulinismus im frühen Christentum*, FRLANT 123; Göttingen: Vandenhoeck & Ruprecht, 1980).

Lundbom, J., "New Covenant" *ABD* 4:1088–94.

Magness, J., *The Archaeology of Qumran and the Dead Sea Scrolls* (Studies in the Dead Sea Scrolls and Related Literature; Grand Rapids: Eerdmans, 2002).

Maier, J., *The Temple Scroll: An Introduction, Translation, and Commentary* (JSOTSup 34; Sheffield: JSOT, 1985).

Main, E., "For King Jonathan or Against? The Use of the Bible in 4Q448" in M. E. Stone and E. G. Chazon, eds., *Biblical Perspectives: Early Use and Interpretation of the Bible in Light of the Dead Sea Scrolls*; 113–35.

–, "Sadducees" *EDSS* 2:812–16.

Malherbe, A. J., *Ancient Epistolary Theorists* (Atlanta: Scholars Press, 1988).

Marcus, J., *The Mystery of the Kingdom of God* (Atlanta: Scholars Press, 1986).

–, *Mark 1–8: A New Translation with Introduction and Commentary* (AB 27; New York and London: Doubleday, 1999).

Markschies, C., et al., "Innerer Mensch" *RGG⁴* 4:154–57.

Martin, D., "Paul and the Judaism/Hellenism Dichotomy: Toward a Social History of the Question" in T. Engberg–Pederson, ed., *Paul Beyond the Judaism/Hellenism Divide* (Louisville: Westminster John Knox Press, 2001) 29–61.

Martin, R. P., *2 Corinthians* (Word Biblical Commentary 40; Nashville: Thomas Nelson Publishers, 1986).

Matt, D. C., *Zohar: The Book of Enlightenment* (Classics of Western Spirituality; New York, Ramsey, NJ; and Toronto: Paulist Press, 1983).

–, *The Zohar*, vol. 1 (Pritzker edition; Stanford: Stanford University Press, 2004).

Matera, F., *II Corinthians: A Commentary* (New Testament Library; Louisville and London: Westminster John Knox Press, 2003).

Mauss, M., *The Gift: The Form and Reason for Exchange in Archaic Societies* (New York and London: W. W. Norton, 2000; trans. of *Essai sur le Don*, 1950).

McCarthy, D. J., *Treaty and Covenant: A Study in Form in the Ancient Oriental Documents and in the Old Testament* (AnBib 21A; Rome: Biblical Institute Press, 1981).

McGuire, M., *Religion: The Social Context* (5th ed., Belmont, CA: Wadsworth Thomson Learning, 2002).

Meier, J., "Is There *Halaka* (the Noun) at Qumran?" *JBL* 122 (2003) 150–155.

Meshorer, Y., *Ancient Jewish Coinage*, vol. 1: *Persian Period Through Hasmoneans* (New York: Amphora, 1982).

Metzger, B., "The Fourth Book of Ezra" *OTP* 1:516–559.

Meyer, B. and Sanders, E. P., eds., *Self-Definition in the Greco-Roman World*, vol. 3: *Jewish and Christian Self-Definition* (London: SCM Press, 1982).

Meyers, J., *Ezra-Nehemiah* (AB 14; Garden City: Doubleday & Co., 1965).

Michel, C., *Recueil d'Inscriptions Grecques Supplément* (Hildesheim and New York: G. Olms Verlag, 1976 [1912]).

Milgrom, J., "Sacrifice" *EDSS* 2:809–10.

Milik, J. T., "Milkî-ṣedeq et Milkî-reša⁽ dans les anciens écrits juifs et chretiens" *JJS* 23 (1972) 135-36.

–, *The Books of Enoch: Aramaic Fragments of Qumran Cave 4* (Oxford: Oxford Press, 1976).

Miller, J. M. and Hayes, J. H., *A History of Ancient Israel and Judah* (Philadelphia: Westminster Press, 1986).

Mitchell, M. M., *Paul and the Rhetoric of Reconciliation: An Exegetical Investigation of the Language and Composition of 1 Corinthians* (Louisville: Westminster/John Knox Press, 1991).

Murphy, C., *Wealth in the Dead Sea Scrolls and in the Qumran Community* (STDJ 40; Leiden Brill, 2002).

Murphy O'Connor, J., "Qumran and the Interpolated Paragraph in 2 Cor. 6:14–7:1" *CBQ* 23 (1961) 271–280.

–, "An Essene Missionary Document CD II,14–VI,1" *RB* 77 (1970) 211–215.

–, "Critique of the Princes of Judah (CD VIII, 3–19)" *RB* 79 (1972) 200–217.

–, "A Literary Analysis of Damascus Document XIX,33–XX,34" *RB* 79 (1972) 544–64.

–, "Pneumatikoi in 2 Corinthians" *PIBA* 11 (1988) 59–66.

–, *The Theology of the Second Letter to the Corinthians* (Cambridge: Cambridge University Press, 1991).

–, *Paul: A Critical Life* (New York and Oxford: Oxford University Press, 1996).

–, "Damascus" *EDSS* 1:165–166.

–, *St. Paul's Corinth: Texts and Archaeology* (Collegeville, MN: Liturgical Press, 2003).

–, "1 and 2 Corinthians" in J.D.G. Dunn, ed., *The Cambridge Companion to St. Paul* (Cambridge: Cambridge University Press, 2003) 74–90.

–, *Paul: His Story* (Oxford and New York: Oxford University Press, 2004).

Nanos, M., *The Irony of Galatians: Paul's Letter in First-Century Context* (Minneapolis: Fortress Press, 2002).

Nau, F., "History of the Rechabites" *Revue Sémitique* 7 (1899) 54–75.

Newsome, C., "'Sectually Explicit' Literature from Qumran" in W. H. Propp, et al., eds., *The Hebrew Bible and its Interpreters*; 167–187.

Nicklesburg, G., "Social Aspects of Palestinian Jewish Apocalypticism" in D. Hellholm, ed., *Apocalypticism in the Mediterranean World and the Near East* (Tübingen: Mohr Siebeck, 1983) 642–54.

Nitzan, B., *Qumran Prayer and Religious Poetry* (STDJ 12; Leiden: Brill, 1994).

–, "4QBerakhot (4Q286–290): A Preliminary Report" in *New Qumran Texts and Studies: Proceedings of the First Meeting of the International Organization for Qumran Studies, Paris, 1992* G. J. Brooke and F. García Martínez, eds. (Leiden: Brill, 1994) 53–71.

–, "4QBerahkot[a-e] (4Q286-290): A Covenantal Ceremony in the Light of Related Texts" *RQ* 64.16 (1995) 487-506.

–, "The Benedictions from Qumran for the Annual Covenantal Ceremony" in L. H. Schiffman, ed., *The Dead Sea Scrolls Fifty Years After Their Discovery: 1947–1997*; 263-271.

Nöldeke, T., *Compendious Syriac Grammar* (Winona Lake, IN: Eisenbrauns, 2001 [1904]).

Noy, D., *Jewish Inscriptions of Western Europe* (2 vols., Cambridge, New York, and Melbourne: Cambridge University Press, 1995).

Oikonomides, A. N., ed., *Periplus or, Circumnavigation (of Africa): Greek text with facing English translation, commentary, notes and facsimile of Codex palatinus Gr. 398* (Chicago: Ares Publishers, 1995).

Oliveira, Anacleto de, *Die Diakonie der Gerechtigkeit und der Versöhnung in der Apologie des 2. Korintherbriefes* (NTAbh 21; Münster: Aschendorffsche Verlagsbuchhandlung GmbH & Co., 1990).

Oostendorp, D. W., *Another Jesus: A Gospel of Jewish–Christian Superiority in II Corinthians* (Kampen: Kok, 1967).

Oppenheimer, A., *The 'Am ha-Aretz: A Study in the Social History of the Jewish People in the Hellenistic-Roman Period* (ALGHJ 8; Leiden: Brill, 1977).

–, "Haverim" *EDSS* 1:333–336.

Paul, S. et al., eds., *Emanuel: Studies in Hebrew Bible, Septuagint, and Dead Sea Scrolls in Honor of Emanuel Tov* (Leiden and Boston: Brill, 2003).

Pfann, S., "The Essene Yearly Renewal Ceremony and the Baptism of Repentance" in D. W. Parry and E. Ulrich (eds.), *The Provo International* Conference on the Dead Sea Scrolls: Technological Innovations, New Texts, and Reformulated Issues (STDJ 30; Leiden: Brill, 1999) 337-352.

Plummer, A., *Second Epistle of Paul to the Corinthians* (ICC; Edinburgh: T&T Clark, 1960 [1915]).

Porter, S., "The Theoretical Justification for Application of Rhetorical Categories to Pauline Epistolary Literature" in S. Porter and T. Olbricht, eds., *Rhetoric and the New Testament: Essays from the 1992 Heidelberg Conference*; 100–122.

Porter, S. and Olbricht, T., eds., *Rhetoric and the New Testament: Essays from the 1992 Heidelberg Conference* (JSNTSup 90; Sheffield: Sheffield Academic Press, 1993).

Pritchard, J., ed., *Collins Atlas of the Bible* (Ann Arbor: Borders Press, 2003).

Propp, W. H., Halpern, B., and Freedman, D. N., eds., *The Hebrew Bible and its Interpreters* (Winona Lake, IN: Eisenbrauns, 1990).

Rabinowitz, I. "A Reconsideration of 'Damascus' and '390 Years' in the 'Damascus' ('Zadokite') Fragments" *JBL* 73 (1954) 11–35.

Rasmussen, C. ed., *NIV Atlas of the Bible* (Grand Rapids: Zondervan, 1989).

Rajak, T., "Jews and Greeks: The Invention and Exploitation of Polarities in the Nineteenth Century" in T. Rajak, ed., *The Jewish Dialogue with Greece and Rome: Studies in Cultural and Social Interaction* (AGJU 48; Leiden Brill, 2001) 535–57.

Reiff, S., "Cairo Genizah" *EDSS* 1:105–108.

Sanders, E. P., *Judaism: Practice and Belief 63 BCE–66 CE* (London: SCM Press and Valley Forge: Trinity, 1992).

Sandt, H. van de and Flusser, D., *The Didache: Its Jewish Sources and its Place in Early Judaism and Christianity* (Minneapolis: Fortress and Assen, Netherlands: Royal Van Gorcum, 2002).

Schechter, S., *Documents of Jewish Sectaries*, vol. 1: *Fragments of a Zadokite Work* (Cambridge: University Press, 1910).

Shemesh, A., "Expulsion and Exclusion in the Community Rule and the Damascus Document" *DSD* 9 (2002) 44–74.

Schiffman, L., *The Halakhah at Qumran* (SJLA 16; Leiden Brill, 1975).

–, *Sectarian Law in the Dead Sea Scrolls: Courts, Testimony and the Penal Code* (BJS 33; Chico, CA: Scholars Press, 1983).

–, *The Eschatological Community of the Dead Sea Scrolls* (SBLMS 38; Atlanta: Scholars Press, 1989).

–, "Pharisaic and Sadducean Halakhah in Light of the Dead Sea Scrolls: The Case of *Ṭevul Yom*" *DSD* 1, 3 (1994) 285–299.

Schiffman, L., ed. *Archaeology and History in the Dead Sea Scrolls: The New York University Conference in Honor of Yigael Yadin* (Sheffield: JSOT Press, 1990).

Schiffman, L., Tov, E. and VanderKam, J., eds. *The Dead Sea Scrolls Fifty Years After Their Discovery: 1947–1997* (Jerusalem: Israel Exploration Society, 2000).

Schiffman, L. and VanderKam, J., *Encyclopedia of the Dead Sea Scrolls* (2 vols., Oxford and New York: Oxford University Press, 2000).

Schmithals, W., *Gnosticism in Corinth: An Investigation of the Letters to the Corinthians* (Nashville and New York: Abingdon Press, 1971; trans. of *Die Gnosis in Korinth; eine Untersuchung zu den Korintherbriefen*; Göttingen Vandenhoeck & Ruprecht, 1956).

Schneider, B., "The Meaning of St. Paul's Antithesis 'The Letter and the Spirit'" *CBQ* 15 (1953) 163–207.

Scholem, G., *Zohar: The Book of Splendor* (New York: Shocken Books, 1977 [1949]).

Schubert, P., *Form and Function of the Pauline Thanksgivings* (Berlin: Alfred Töpelmann, 1939).

Schürer, E., Vermes, G., Millar, F., et. al., eds. *The History of the Jewish People in the Age of Jesus Christ* (175 B.C.–A.D. 135) (4 vols. Edinburgh: T&T Clark, 1973).

Scott, J. M., *Exile: Old Testament, Jewish, and Christian Conceptions* (Supplements to the Journal for the Study of Judaism 56; Leiden Brill, 1997).

–, *Restoration: Old Testament, Jewish, and Christian Perspectives* (Supplements to the Journal for the Study of Judaism 72; Leiden Brill, 2001).

Seow, C. L., "The Designation of the Ark in Priestly Theology" *HAR* 8 (1984) 192–194.

Smith, J. Z., *Imagining Religion: From Babylon to Jonestown* (Chicago and London: University of Chicago Press, 1982).

–, *Divine Drudgery: On the Comparison of Early Christianities and the Religions of Late Antiquity* (Chicago: University of Chicago Press, 1990).

–, *Relating Religion: Essays in the Study of Religion* (Chicago and London: University of Chicago Press, 2004).

Stegemann, H., *The Library of Qumran: On the Essenes, Qumran, John the Baptist, and Jesus* (Grand Rapids and Cambridge, UK: Eerdmans and Leiden: Brill Academic Publishers, 1998).

–, "Identity and History of the Community" in *The Dead Sea Scrolls After Fifty Years: A Comprehensive Assessment*; P. W. Flint and J. VanderKam, eds. (Leiden, Boston, and Köln: Brill, 1999) 487–533.

–, "Towards the Physical Reconstruction of the Qumran Damascus Document Scrolls" in *The Damascus Document: A Centennial of Discovery: Proceedings of the Third International Symposium of the Orion Center for the Study of the Dead Sea Scrolls and Associated Literature, February 4–8, 1998*; J. Baumgarten, et al., eds. (STDJ 34; Leiden Brill, 2000) 177–200.

Stern, M., *Greek and Roman Authors on Jews and Judaism* (2 vols., Jerusalem: Israel Academy of Sciences and Humanities, 1974).

Steudel, A., *Der Midrasch zur Eschatologie aus der Qumrangemeinde (4QMidrEschat^{a,b}) (STDJ* 13; Leiden Brill, 1994).

Stirewalt, M. L., *Paul the Letter Writer* (Grand Rapids and Cambridge, UK: Eerdmans, 2003).

Stockhausen, C., *Moses' Veil and the Glory of the New Covenant: The Exegetical Substructure of II Cor. 3,1–4,6* (AnBib 116; Rome: Pontifical Biblical Institute, 1989).

Stone, M. E. and Hazon, E. G., eds., *Biblical Perspectives: Early Use and Interpretation of the Bible in Light of the Dead Sea Scrolls: Proceedings of the First International Symposium of the Orion Center for the Study of the Dead Sea Scrolls and Associated Literature, 12–14 May 1996 (STDJ* 28; Leiden Brill, 1998).

Stone, M. E. and Strugnell, J., *The Books of Elijah, Parts 1–2* (SBLTT Pseudepigrapha series 8; Missoula: Scholars Press, 1979).

Stowers, S., *Letter Writing in Greco–Roman Antiquity* (LEC 5; Philadelphia: Westminster Press, 1986).

–, "*Peri men gar* and the Integrity of 2 Cor. 8 and 9" *NovT* 32.4 (1990) 340–48.

Strack, H. and Stemberger, G., *Introduction to the Talmud and Midrash* (Minneapolis: Fortress, 1992).

Strecker, G., *Das Judenchristentum in den Pseudoklementinen* (TUGAL 70; Berlin: Akademie-Verlag, 1981).

Sumney, J., *Identifying Paul's Opponents: The Question of Method in 2 Corinthians* (JSOTSup 40; Sheffield: Sheffield Academic Press, 1990).

–, *'Servants of Satan', 'False Brothers' and Other Opponents of Paul* (JSOTSup 188; Sheffield: Sheffield Academic Press, 1999).

Sundermann, H.-G., *Der schwache Apostel und die Kraft der Rede. Eine rhetorische Analyse von 2 Kor. 10–13* (Europäische Hochschulschriften, Reihe 23, Theologie 575; Frankfurt am Main: Peter Lang, 1996).

Talmon, S., "Yom Hakkippurim in the Habakkuk Scroll" *Biblica* 32 (1951) 549–63.

–, *The World of Qumran from Within: Collected Studies* (Jerusalem: Magnes and Leiden: Brill, 1989).

–, "The Community of the Renewed Covenant: Between Judaism and Christianity" in E. Ulrich and J. VanderKam, eds., *The Community of the Renewed Covenant: The Notre Dame Symposium on the Dead Sea Scrolls*; 3–24.

–, "Calendars and Mishmarot" *EDSS* 1:108–17.

Taylor, J., *Les Actes des Deux Apôtres*, vol. 5: *Commentaire Historique (EBib* 30; Paris J. Gabalda, 1994).

Thrall, M., "A Second Thanksgiving Period in II Corinthians" *JSNT* 16 (1982) 101–24.

–, *The Second Epistle to the Corinthians* (2 vols., ICC; Edinburgh: T&T Clark, 1994).

Tiller, P., "The 'Eternal Planting' in the Dead Sea Scrolls" *DSD* 4 (1997) 312–335.

Trobisch, D., *Paul's Letter Collection Tracing the Origins* (Minneapolis: Fortress Press, 1994).

Ulrich, E. and VanderKam, J., eds., *The Community of the Renewed Covenant: The Notre Dame Symposium on the Dead Sea Scrolls* (Notre Dame: Notre Dame, 1994).

VanderKam, J., *The Book of Jubilees: A Critical Text* (Corpus Scriptorum Christianorum Orientalium; Scriptores Aethiopici, t. 87; Louvain Peeters, 1989).

–, *The Book of Jubilees* (Corpus Scriptorum Christianorum Orientalium, Scriptores Aethiopici, t. 88; Louvain Peeters, 1989).

–, *Calendars in the Dead Sea Scrolls Measuring Time* (Literature of the Dead Sea Scrolls series; London: and New York, NY Routledge, 1998).

–, "Covenant" *EDSS* 1:151–55.

–, "Covenant and Biblical Interpretation in Jubilees 6" in *The Dead Sea Scrolls Fifty Years After Their Discovery*, L. Schiffman, et al., eds., 92–104.

–, "Jubilees, Book of" *EDSS* 1:434–438.

–, "Those Who Look for Smooth Things, Pharisees, and Oral Law" in Shalom Paul, et al., eds., *Emanuel: Studies in Hebrew Bible, Septuagint, and Dead Sea Scrolls in Honor of Emanuel Tov*; 465–477.

Vanhoye, A., *L'Apotre Paul: Personalité, Style et Conception du Ministère* (BETL 73; Leuven: University Press, 1986).

Vaux, Roland de., *Archaeology and the Dead Sea Scrolls* (London: Oxford University Press, 1973).

Vermes, G., "The So-Called King Jonathan Fragment (4Q448)" *JJS* 44 (1993) 294–300.

–, *The Complete Dead Scrolls in English* (New York: Penguin Press, 1997).

–, *An Introduction to the Complete Dead Sea Scrolls* (Philadelphia: Fortress, 1999).

Vermes, G. and Goodman, M., *The Essenes According to the Classical Sources* (Oxford Centre textbooks 1; Sheffield: JSOT, 1989).

Versnel, H., *Triumphus: An Enquiry into the Origin, Development, and Meaning of the Roman Triumph* (Leiden: Brill, 1970).

Von Staden, H., "Hairesis and Heresy: The Case of the *haireseis iatrikai*" in *Jewish and Christian Self-Definition*, vol. 3: *Self-Definition in the Greco-Roman World*, B. Meyer and E. P. Sanders, eds. (Philadelphia: Fortress Press, 1982) 76–100.

Wacholder, B. Z., *The New Damascus Document: the Midrash on the Eschatological Torah of the Dead Sea Scrolls: Reconstruction, Translation, and Commentary* (STDJ 56; Leiden and Boston: Brill, 2007).

Wallace, D., *Greek Grammar Beyond the Basics: An Exegetical Syntax of the New Testament* (Grand Rapids: Zondervan, 1996).

Wassen, C., *Women in the Damascus Document* (SBL Academia Biblica; Leiden and Boston: Brill, 2005).

Weinfeld, M., "The Covenant of Grant in the Old Testament and in the Ancient Near East" *JAOS* 90 (1970) 184–203.

–, "Covenant Terminology in the Ancient Near East and Its Influence on the West" *JAOS* 93 (1973) 190–199.

–, *The Organizational Pattern and the Penal Code of the Qumran Sect: A Comparison with Guilds and Religious Associations of the Hellenistic-Roman Period* (NTOA 2; Göttingen: Vandenhoeck & Ruprecht, 1986).

–, *The Promise of the Land: The Inheritance of the Land of Canaan by the Israelites* (Berkeley: University of California, 1993).

Weisenberg, E., "Chronological Data in the Zadokite Fragments" *VT* 5 (1955) 284–308.

Weiss, J., *Earliest Christianity: A History of the Period A.D. 30–150* (Gloucester, MA: Peter Smith, 1970; trans. of *Das Urchristentum*, Göttingen: Vandenhoeck & Ruprecht, 1917).

Welborn, J., "Like Broken Pieces of a Ring: 2 Cor. 1:1–2:13; 7:5–16 and Ancient Theories of Literary Unity" *NTS* 42 (1996) 559–583.

Werline, R. A., *Penitential Prayer in Second Temple Judaism: The Development of a Religious Institution* (Early Judaism and its Literature 13; Atlanta: Scholars Press, 1998).

White, S. A., "A Comparison of the 'A' and 'B' Manuscripts of the Damascus Document" *RQ* 48 (1987) 537–53.

Williams, R. J., *Hebrew Syntax: An Outline* (2nd ed., Toronto: University of Toronto, 1992).

Windisch, H., *Der zweite Korintherbrief* (Kritisch-exegetischer Kommentar über das Neue Testament; 9th ed., Göttingen: Vandenhoeck & Ruprecht, 1924).

Winter, B., *Philo and Paul Among the Sophists: Alexandrian and Corinthian Responses to a Julio-Claudian Movement* (2nd ed., Grand Rapids: Eerdmans, 2002).

Wintermute, O. S., "Jubilees" *OTP* 1:35–142.

Wise, M., "The Teacher of Righteousness and the High Priest of the Intersacerdotium: Two Approaches," *RQ* 56 (14:4) 1990 587–613.

Wise, M., "Dating the Teacher of Righteousness and the Floruit of his Movement" *JBL* 122 (2003) 53–87

Wise, M., Abegg, M., and Cook, E., *The Dead Sea Scrolls: A New Translation* (New York: HarperCollins, 1996).

Wise, M., et al., eds., *Methods of Investigation of the Dead Sea Scrolls and the Khirbet Qumran Site: Present Realities and Future Prospects* (Annals of the New York Academy of Sciences 722; New York: New York Academy of Sciences, 1994).

Witherington, B., *Conflict and Community in Corinth: A Socio–Rhetorical Commentary on 1 and 2 Corinthians* (Grand Rapids: Eerdmans and Carlisle: Paternoster Press).

Wolf, C., *Der zweite Brief des Paulus an die Korinther* (Theologischer Handkommentar zum Neuen Testament, Bd. 8; Berlin Evangelische Verlagsanstalt, 1989).

Yadin, Y., *The Temple Scroll* (2 vols., Jerusalem: Israel Exploration Society, 1983).

Yamauchi, E., *Pre–Christian Gnosticism: A Survey of the Proposed Evidences* (Grand Rapids: Eerdmans, 1973).

–, "Pre–Christian Gnosticism in the Nag Hammadi Texts?" *Church History* 48 (1979) 129–141.

Yarbro Collins, A. *Crisis and Catharsis: The Power of the Apocalypse* (Philadelphia: Westminster, 1984).

Young, F. and Ford, D. *Truth and Meaning in 2 Corinthians* (Biblical Foundations in Theology series; London: SPCK, 1987).

Index of Ancient Sources

1. Hebrew Bible and Apocrypha

2. Pseudepigrapha

3. Dead Sea Scrolls

4. New Testament

5. Mishnah

6. Philo of Alexandria

7. Flavius Josephus

8. Rabbinic literature

9. Early Christian Literature

10. Classical and Other Ancient Writings

Index of Modern Authors

Index of Subjects and Key Terms

Wissenschaftliche Untersuchungen zum Neuen Testament

Alphabetical Index of the First and Second Series

Bock, Darrell L.: Blasphemy and Exaltation in Judaism and the Final Examination of Jesus. 1998. *Vol. II/106.*

Bockmuehl, Markus N.A.: Revelation and Mystery in Ancient Judaism and Pauline Christianity. 1990. *Vol. II/36.*

Bøe, Sverre: Gog and Magog. 2001. *Vol. II/135.*

Böhlig, Alexander: Gnosis und Synkretismus. Vol. 1 1989. *Vol. 47* – Vol. 2 1989. *Vol. 48.*

Böhm, Martina: Samarien und die Samaritai bei Lukas. 1999. *Vol. II/111.*

Böttrich, Christfried: Weltweisheit – Menschheitsethik – Urkult. 1992. *Vol. II/50.*

– */ Herzer, Jens* (Ed.): Josephus und das Neue Testament. 2007. *Vol. 209.*

Bolyki, János: Jesu Tischgemeinschaften. 1997. *Vol. II/96.*

Bosman, Philip: Conscience in Philo and Paul. 2003. *Vol. II/166.*

Bovon, François: Studies in Early Christianity. 2003. *Vol. 161.*

Brändl, Martin: Der Agon bei Paulus. 2006. *Vol. II/222.*

Breytenbach, Cilliers: see *Frey, Jörg.*

Brocke, Christoph vom: Thessaloniki – Stadt des Kassander und Gemeinde des Paulus. 2001. *Vol. II/125.*

Brunson, Andrew: Psalm 118 in the Gospel of John. 2003. *Vol. II/158.*

Büchli, Jörg: Der Poimandres – ein paganisiertes Evangelium. 1987. *Vol. II/27.*

Bühner, Jan A.: Der Gesandte und sein Weg im 4. Evangelium. 1977. *Vol. II/2.*

Burchard, Christoph: Untersuchungen zu Joseph und Aseneth. 1965. *Vol. 8.*

– Studien zur Theologie, Sprache und Umwelt des Neuen Testaments. Ed. by D. Sänger. 1998. *Vol. 107.*

Burnett, Richard: Karl Barth's Theological Exegesis. 2001. *Vol. II/145.*

Byron, John: Slavery Metaphors in Early Judaism and Pauline Christianity. 2003. *Vol. II/162.*

Byrskog, Samuel: Story as History – History as Story. 2000. *Vol. 123.*

Cancik, Hubert (Ed.): Markus-Philologie. 1984. *Vol. 33.*

Capes, David B.: Old Testament Yaweh Texts in Paul's Christology. 1992. *Vol. II/47.*

Caragounis, Chrys C.: The Development of Greek and the New Testament. 2004. *Vol. 167.*

– The Son of Man. 1986. *Vol. 38.*

– see *Fridrichsen, Anton.*

Carleton Paget, James: The Epistle of Barnabas. 1994. *Vol. II/64.*

Carson, D.A., O'Brien, Peter T. and *Mark Seifrid* (Ed.): Justification and Variegated Nomism.
Vol. 1: The Complexities of Second Temple Judaism. 2001. *Vol. II/140.*
Vol. 2: The Paradoxes of Paul. 2004. *Vol. II/181.*

Chae, Young Sam: Jesus as the Eschatological Davidic Shepherd. 2006. *Vol. II/216.*

Chester, Andrew: Messiah and Exaltation. 2007. *Vol. 207.*

Chibici-Revneanu, Nicole: Die Herrlichkeit des Verherrlichten. 2007. *Vol. II/231.*

Ciampa, Roy E.: The Presence and Function of Scripture in Galatians 1 and 2. 1998. *Vol. II/102.*

Classen, Carl Joachim: Rhetorical Criticsm of the New Testament. 2000. *Vol. 128.*

Colpe, Carsten: Iranier – Aramäer – Hebräer – Hellenen. 2003. *Vol. 154.*

Crump, David: Jesus the Intercessor. 1992. *Vol. II/49.*

Dahl, Nils Alstrup: Studies in Ephesians. 2000. *Vol. 131.*

Daise, Michael A.: Feasts in John. 2007. *Vol. 229.*

Deines, Roland: Die Gerechtigkeit der Tora im Reich des Messias. 2004. *Vol. 177.*

– Jüdische Steingefäße und pharisäische Frömmigkeit. 1993. *Vol. II/52.*

– Die Pharisäer. 1997. *Vol. 101.*

Deines, Roland and *Karl-Wilhelm Niebuhr* (Ed.): Philo und das Neue Testament. 2004. *Vol. 172.*

Dennis, John A.: Jesus' Death and the Gathering of True Israel. 2006. *Vol. 217.*

Dettwiler, Andreas and *Jean Zumstein* (Ed.): Kreuzestheologie im Neuen Testament. 2002. *Vol. 151.*

Dickson, John P.: Mission-Commitment in Ancient Judaism and in the Pauline Communities. 2003. *Vol. II/159.*

Dietzfelbinger, Christian: Der Abschied des Kommenden. 1997. *Vol. 95.*

Dimitrov, Ivan Z., James D.G. Dunn, Ulrich Luz and *Karl-Wilhelm Niebuhr* (Ed.): Das Alte Testament als christliche Bibel in orthodoxer und westlicher Sicht. 2004. *Vol. 174.*

Dobbeler, Axel von: Glaube als Teilhabe. 1987. *Vol. II/22.*

Dryden, J. de Waal: Theology and Ethics in 1 Peter. 2006. *Vol. II/209.*

Du Toit, David S.: Theios Anthropos. 1997. *Vol. II/91.*

Dübbers, Michael: Christologie und Existenz im Kolosserbrief. 2005. *Vol. II/191.*

Gregg, Brian Han: The Historical Jesus and the Final Judgment Sayings in Q. 2005. *Vol. II/207.*

Gregory, Andrew: The Reception of Luke and Acts in the Period before Irenaeus. 2003. *Vol. II/169.*

Grindheim, Sigurd: The Crux of Election. 2005. *Vol. II/202.*

Gundry, Robert H.: The Old is Better. 2005. *Vol. 178.*

Gundry Volf, Judith M.: Paul and Perseverance. 1990. *Vol. II/37.*

Häußer, Detlef: Christusbekenntnis und Jesusüberlieferung bei Paulus. 2006. *Vol. 210.*

Hafemann, Scott J.: Suffering and the Spirit. 1986. *Vol. II/19.*

– Paul, Moses, and the History of Israel. 1995. *Vol. 81.*

Hahn, Ferdinand: Studien zum Neuen Testament.
  Vol. I: Grundsatzfragen, Jesusforschung, Evangelien. 2006. *Vol. 191.*
  Vol. II: Bekenntnisbildung und Theologie in urchristlicher Zeit. 2006. *Vol. 192.*

Hahn, Johannes (Ed.): Zerstörungen des Jerusalemer Tempels. 2002. *Vol. 147.*

Hamid-Khani, Saeed: Relevation and Concealment of Christ. 2000. *Vol. II/120.*

Hannah, Darrel D.: Michael and Christ. 1999. *Vol. II/109.*

Harrison; James R.: Paul's Language of Grace in Its Graeco-Roman Context. 2003. *Vol. II/172.*

Hartman, Lars: Text-Centered New Testament Studies. Ed. von D. Hellholm. 1997. *Vol. 102.*

Hartog, Paul: Polycarp and the New Testament. 2001. *Vol. II/134.*

Heckel, Theo K.: Der Innere Mensch. 1993. *Vol. II/53.*

– Vom Evangelium des Markus zum viergestaltigen Evangelium. 1999. *Vol. 120.*

Heckel, Ulrich: Kraft in Schwachheit. 1993. *Vol. II/56.*

– Der Segen im Neuen Testament. 2002. *Vol. 150.*

– see *Feldmeier, Reinhard.*

– see *Hengel, Martin.*

Heiligenthal, Roman: Werke als Zeichen. 1983. *Vol. II/9.*

Heliso, Desta: Pistis and the Righteous One. 2007. *Vol. II/235.*

Hellholm, D.: see *Hartman, Lars.*

Hemer, Colin J.: The Book of Acts in the Setting of Hellenistic History. 1989. *Vol. 49.*

Hengel, Martin: Judentum und Hellenismus. 1969, ³1988. *Vol. 10.*

– Die johanneische Frage. 1993. *Vol. 67.*

– Judaica et Hellenistica. Kleine Schriften I. 1996. *Vol. 90.*

– Judaica, Hellenistica et Christiana. Kleine Schriften II. 1999. *Vol. 109.*

– Paulus und Jakobus. Kleine Schriften III. 2002. *Vol. 141.*

– Studien zur Christologie. Kleine Schriften IV. 2006. *Vol. 201.*

– and *Anna Maria Schwemer:* Paulus zwischen Damaskus und Antiochien. 1998. *Vol. 108.*

– Der messianische Anspruch Jesu und die Anfänge der Christologie. 2001. *Vol. 138.*

Hengel, Martin and *Ulrich Heckel* (Ed.): Paulus und das antike Judentum. 1991. *Vol. 58.*

– and *Hermut Löhr* (Ed.): Schriftauslegung im antiken Judentum und im Urchristentum. 1994. *Vol. 73.*

– and *Anna Maria Schwemer* (Ed.): Königsherrschaft Gottes und himmlischer Kult. 1991. *Vol. 55.*

– Die Septuaginta. 1994. *Vol. 72.*

–, *Siegfried Mittmann* and *Anna Maria Schwemer* (Ed.): La Cité de Dieu / Die Stadt Gottes. 2000. *Vol. 129.*

Hentschel, Anni: Diakonia im Neuen Testament. 2007. *Vol. 226.*

Hernández Jr., Juan: Scribal Habits and Theological Influence in the Apocalypse. 2006. *Vol. II/218.*

Herrenbrück, Fritz: Jesus und die Zöllner. 1990. *Vol. II/41.*

Herzer, Jens: Paulus oder Petrus? 1998. *Vol. 103.*

– see *Böttrich, Christfried.*

Hill, Charles E.: From the Lost Teaching of Polycarp. 2005. *Vol. 186.*

Hoegen-Rohls, Christina: Der nachösterliche Johannes. 1996. *Vol. II/84.*

Hoffmann, Matthias Reinhard: The Destroyer and the Lamb. 2005. *Vol. II/203.*

Hofius, Otfried: Katapausis. 1970. *Vol. 11.*

– Der Vorhang vor dem Thron Gottes. 1972. *Vol. 14.*

– Der Christushymnus Philipper 2,6–11. 1976, ²1991. *Vol. 17.*

– Paulusstudien. 1989, ²1994. *Vol. 51.*

– Neutestamentliche Studien. 2000. *Vol. 132.*

– Paulusstudien II. 2002. *Vol. 143.*

– and *Hans-Christian Kammler:* Johannesstudien. 1996. *Vol. 88.*

Holtz, Traugott: Geschichte und Theologie des Urchristentums. 1991. *Vol. 57.*

Hommel, Hildebrecht: Sebasmata.
  Vol. 1 1983. *Vol. 31.*
  Vol. 2 1984. *Vol. 32.*

Horbury, William: Herodian Judaism and New Testament Study. 2006. *Vol. 193.*

Horst, Pieter W. van der: Jews and Christians in Their Graeco-Roman Context. 2006. *Vol. 196.*

Hvalvik, Reidar: The Struggle for Scripture and Covenant. 1996. *Vol. II/82.*

Jauhiainen, Marko: The Use of Zechariah in Revelation. 2005. *Vol. II/199.*

Jensen, Morten H.: Herod Antipas in Galilee. 2006. *Vol. II/215.*

Johns, Loren L.: The Lamb Christology of the Apocalypse of John. 2003. *Vol. II/167.*

Jossa, Giorgio: Jews or Christians? 2006. *Vol. 202.*

Joubert, Stephan: Paul as Benefactor. 2000. *Vol. II/124.*

Jungbauer, Harry: „Ehre Vater und Mutter". 2002. *Vol. II/146.*

Kähler, Christoph: Jesu Gleichnisse als Poesie und Therapie. 1995. *Vol. 78.*

Kamlah, Ehrhard: Die Form der katalogischen Paränese im Neuen Testament. 1964. *Vol. 7.*

Kammler, Hans-Christian: Christologie und Eschatologie. 2000. *Vol. 126.*

– Kreuz und Weisheit. 2003. *Vol. 159.*

– see *Hofius, Otfried.*

Kelhoffer, James A.: The Diet of John the Baptist. 2005. *Vol. 176.*

– Miracle and Mission. 1999. *Vol. II/112.*

Kelley, Nicole: Knowledge and Religious Authority in the Pseudo-Clementines. 2006. *Vol. II/213.*

Kieffer, René and *Jan Bergman (Ed.)*: La Main de Dieu / Die Hand Gottes. 1997. *Vol. 94.*

Kierspel, Lars: The Jews and the World in the Fourth Gospel. 2006. *Vol. 220.*

Kim, Seyoon: The Origin of Paul's Gospel. 1981, ²1984. *Vol. II/4.*

– Paul and the New Perspective. 2002. *Vol. 140.*

– "The 'Son of Man'" as the Son of God. 1983. *Vol. 30.*

Klauck, Hans-Josef: Religion und Gesellschaft im frühen Christentum. 2003. *Vol. 152.*

Klein, Hans: see *Dunn, James D.G.*

Kleinknecht, Karl Th.: Der leidende Gerechtfertigte. 1984, ²1988. *Vol. II/13.*

Klinghardt, Matthias: Gesetz und Volk Gottes. 1988. *Vol. II/32.*

Kloppenborg, John S.: The Tenants in the Vineyard. 2006. *Vol. 195.*

Koch, Michael: Drachenkampf und Sonnenfrau. 2004. *Vol. II/184.*

Koch, Stefan: Rechtliche Regelung von Konflikten im frühen Christentum. 2004. *Vol. II/174.*

Köhler, Wolf-Dietrich: Rezeption des Matthäusevangeliums in der Zeit vor Irenäus. 1987. *Vol. II/24.*

Köhn, Andreas: Der Neutestamentler Ernst Lohmeyer. 2004. *Vol. II/180.*

Konradt, Matthias: Israel, Kirche und die Völker im Matthäusevangelium. 2007. *Vol. 215.*

Kooten, George H. van: Cosmic Christology in Paul and the Pauline School. 2003. *Vol. II/171.*

Korn, Manfred: Die Geschichte Jesu in veränderter Zeit. 1993. *Vol. II/51.*

Koskenniemi, Erkki: Apollonios von Tyana in der neutestamentlichen Exegese. 1994. *Vol. II/61.*

– The Old Testament Miracle-Workers in Early Judaism. 2005. *Vol. II/206.*

Kraus, Thomas J.: Sprache, Stil und historischer Ort des zweiten Petrusbriefes. 2001. *Vol. II/136.*

Kraus, Wolfgang: Das Volk Gottes. 1996. *Vol. 85.*

Kraus, Wolfgang and *Karl-Wilhelm Niebuhr* (Ed.): Frühjudentum und Neues Testament im Horizont Biblischer Theologie. 2003. *Vol. 162.*

– see *Walter, Nikolaus.*

Kreplin, Matthias: Das Selbstverständnis Jesu. 2001. *Vol. II/141.*

Kuhn, Karl G.: Achtzehngebet und Vaterunser und der Reim. 1950. *Vol. 1.*

Kvalbein, Hans: see *Ådna, Jostein.*

Kwon, Yon-Gyong: Eschatology in Galatians. 2004. *Vol. II/183.*

Laansma, Jon: I Will Give You Rest. 1997. *Vol. II/98.*

Labahn, Michael: Offenbarung in Zeichen und Wort. 2000. *Vol. II/117.*

Lambers-Petry, Doris: see *Tomson, Peter J.*

Lange, Armin: see *Ego, Beate.*

Lampe, Peter: Die stadtrömischen Christen in den ersten beiden Jahrhunderten. 1987, ²1989. *Vol. II/18.*

Landmesser, Christof: Wahrheit als Grundbegriff neutestamentlicher Wissenschaft. 1999. *Vol. 113.*

– Jüngerberufung und Zuwendung zu Gott. 2000. *Vol. 133.*

Lau, Andrew: Manifest in Flesh. 1996. *Vol. II/86.*

Lawrence, Louise: An Ethnography of the Gospel of Matthew. 2003. *Vol. II/165.*

Lee, Aquila H.I.: From Messiah to Preexistent Son. 2005. *Vol. II/192.*

Lee, Pilchan: The New Jerusalem in the Book of Relevation. 2000. *Vol. II/129.*

Lichtenberger, Hermann: Das Ich Adams und das Ich der Menschheit. 2004. *Vol. 164.*

– see *Avemarie, Friedrich.*
Lierman, John: The New Testament Moses. 2004. *Vol. II/173.*
– (Ed.): Challenging Perspectives on the Gospel of John. 2006. *Vol. II/219.*
Lieu, Samuel N.C.: Manichaeism in the Later Roman Empire and Medieval China. ²1992. *Vol. 63.*
Lindgård, Fredrik: Paul's Line of Thought in 2 Corinthians 4:16–5:10. 2004. *Vol. II/189.*
Loader, William R.G.: Jesus' Attitude Towards the Law. 1997. *Vol. II/97.*
Löhr, Gebhard: Verherrlichung Gottes durch Philosophie. 1997. *Vol. 97.*
Löhr, Hermut: Studien zum frühchristlichen und frühjüdischen Gebet. 2003. *Vol. 160.*
– see *Hengel, Martin.*
Löhr, Winrich Alfried: Basilides und seine Schule. 1995. *Vol. 83.*
Luomanen, Petri: Entering the Kingdom of Heaven. 1998. *Vol. II/101.*
Luz, Ulrich: see *Dunn, James D.G.*
Mackay, Ian D.: John's Raltionship with Mark. 2004. *Vol. II/182.*
Mackie, Scott D.: Eschatology and Exhortation in the Epistle to the Hebrews. 2006. *Vol. II/223.*
Maier, Gerhard: Mensch und freier Wille. 1971. *Vol. 12.*
– Die Johannesoffenbarung und die Kirche. 1981. *Vol. 25.*
Markschies, Christoph: Valentinus Gnosticus? 1992. *Vol. 65.*
Marshall, Peter: Enmity in Corinth: Social Conventions in Paul's Relations with the Corinthians. 1987. *Vol. II/23.*
Martin, Dale B.: see *Zangenberg, Jürgen.*
Mayer, Annemarie: Sprache der Einheit im Epheserbrief und in der Ökumene. 2002. *Vol. II/150.*
Mayordomo, Moisés: Argumentiert Paulus logisch? 2005. *Vol. 188.*
McDonough, Sean M.: YHWH at Patmos: Rev. 1:4 in its Hellenistic and Early Jewish Setting. 1999. *Vol. II/107.*
McDowell, Markus: Prayers of Jewish Women. 2006. *Vol. II/211.*
McGlynn, Moyna: Divine Judgement and Divine Benevolence in the Book of Wisdom. 2001. *Vol. II/139.*
Meade, David G.: Pseudonymity and Canon. 1986. *Vol. 39.*
Meadors, Edward P.: Jesus the Messianic Herald of Salvation. 1995. *Vol. II/72.*
Meißner, Stefan: Die Heimholung des Ketzers. 1996. *Vol. II/87.*
Mell, Ulrich: Die „anderen" Winzer. 1994. *Vol. 77.*

– see *Sänger, Dieter.*
Mengel, Berthold: Studien zum Philipperbrief. 1982. *Vol. II/8.*
Merkel, Helmut: Die Widersprüche zwischen den Evangelien. 1971. *Vol. 13.*
– see *Ego, Beate.*
Merklein, Helmut: Studien zu Jesus und Paulus. Vol. 1 1987. *Vol. 43.* – Vol. 2 1998. *Vol. 105.*
Metzdorf, Christina: Die Tempelaktion Jesu. 2003. *Vol. II/168.*
Metzler, Karin: Der griechische Begriff des Verzeihens. 1991. *Vol. II/44.*
Metzner, Rainer: Die Rezeption des Matthäusevangeliums im 1. Petrusbrief. 1995. *Vol. II/74.*
– Das Verständnis der Sünde im Johannesevangelium. 2000. *Vol. 122.*
Mihoc, Vasile: see *Dunn, James D.G..*
Mineshige, Kiyoshi: Besitzverzicht und Almosen bei Lukas. 2003. *Vol. II/163.*
Mittmann, Siegfried: see *Hengel, Martin.*
Mittmann-Richert, Ulrike: Magnifikat und Benediktus. 1996. *Vol. II/90.*
Miura, Yuzuru: David in Luke-Acts. 2007. *Vol. II/232.*
Mournet, Terence C.: Oral Tradition and Literary Dependency. 2005. *Vol. II/195.*
Mußner, Franz: Jesus von Nazareth im Umfeld Israels und der Urkirche. Ed. von M. Theobald. 1998. *Vol. 111.*
Mutschler, Bernhard: Das Corpus Johanneum bei Irenäus von Lyon. 2005. *Vol. 189.*
Niebuhr, Karl-Wilhelm: Gesetz und Paränese. 1987. *Vol. II/28.*
– Heidenapostel aus Israel. 1992. *Vol. 62.*
– see *Deines, Roland*
– see *Dimitrov, Ivan Z.*
– see *Kraus, Wolfgang*
Nielsen, Anders E.: "Until it is Fullfilled". 2000. *Vol. II/126.*
Nissen, Andreas: Gott und der Nächste im antiken Judentum. 1974. *Vol. 15.*
Noack, Christian: Gottesbewußtsein. 2000. *Vol. II/116.*
Noormann, Rolf: Irenäus als Paulusinterpret. 1994. *Vol. II/66.*
Novakovic, Lidija: Messiah, the Healer of the Sick. 2003. *Vol. II/170.*
Obermann, Andreas: Die christologische Erfüllung der Schrift im Johannesevangelium. 1996. *Vol. II/83.*
Öhler, Markus: Barnabas. 2003. *Vol. 156.*
– see *Becker, Michael.*
Okure, Teresa: The Johannine Approach to Mission. 1988. *Vol. II/31.*
Onuki, Takashi: Heil und Erlösung. 2004. *Vol. 165.*

Oropeza, B. J.: Paul and Apostasy. 2000. *Vol. II/115.*

Ostmeyer, Karl-Heinrich: Kommunikation mit Gott und Christus. 2006. *Vol. 197.*

– Taufe und Typos. 2000. *Vol. II/118.*

Paulsen, Henning: Studien zur Literatur und Geschichte des frühen Christentums. Ed. von Ute E. Eisen. 1997. *Vol. 99.*

Pao, David W.: Acts and the Isaianic New Exodus. 2000. *Vol. II/130.*

Park, Eung Chun: The Mission Discourse in Matthew's Interpretation. 1995. *Vol. II/81.*

Park, Joseph S.: Conceptions of Afterlife in Jewish Insriptions. 2000. *Vol. II/121.*

Pate, C. Marvin: The Reverse of the Curse. 2000. *Vol. II/114.*

Pearce, Sarah J.K.: The Land of the Body. 2007. *Vol. 208.*

Peres, Imre: Griechische Grabinschriften und neutestamentliche Eschatologie. 2003. *Vol. 157.*

Philip, Finny: The Origins of Pauline Pneumatology. 2005. *Vol. II/194.*

Philonenko, Marc (Ed.): Le Trône de Dieu. 1993. *Vol. 69.*

Pilhofer, Peter: Presbyteron Kreitton. 1990. *Vol. II/39.*

– Philippi. Vol. 1 1995. *Vol. 87.* – Vol. 2 2000. *Vol. 119.*

– Die frühen Christen und ihre Welt. 2002. *Vol. 145.*

– see *Becker, Eve-Marie.*

– see *Ego, Beate.*

Pitre, Brant: Jesus, the Tribulation, and the End of the Exile. 2005. *Vol. II/204.*

Plümacher, Eckhard: Geschichte und Geschichten. 2004. *Vol. 170.*

Pöhlmann, Wolfgang: Der Verlorene Sohn und das Haus. 1993. *Vol. 68.*

Pokorný, Petr and *Josef B. Souček:* Bibelauslegung als Theologie. 1997. *Vol. 100.*

– and *Jan Roskovec* (Ed.): Philosophical Hermeneutics and Biblical Exegesis. 2002. *Vol. 153.*

Popkes, Enno Edzard: Die Theologie der Liebe Gottes in den johanneischen Schriften. 2005. *Vol. II/197.*

Porter, Stanley E.: The Paul of Acts. 1999. *Vol. 115.*

Prieur, Alexander: Die Verkündigung der Gottesherrschaft. 1996. *Vol. II/89.*

Probst, Hermann: Paulus und der Brief. 1991. *Vol. II/45.*

Räisänen, Heikki: Paul and the Law. 1983, [2]1987. *Vol. 29.*

Rehkopf, Friedrich: Die lukanische Sonderquelle. 1959. *Vol. 5.*

Rein, Matthias: Die Heilung des Blindgeborenen (Joh 9). 1995. *Vol. II/73.*

Reinmuth, Eckart: Pseudo-Philo und Lukas. 1994. *Vol. 74.*

Reiser, Marius: Syntax und Stil des Markusevangeliums. 1984. *Vol. II/11.*

Rhodes, James N.: The Epistle of Barnabas and the Deuteronomic Tradition. 2004. *Vol. II/188.*

Richards, E. Randolph: The Secretary in the Letters of Paul. 1991. *Vol. II/42.*

Riesner, Rainer: Jesus als Lehrer. 1981, [3]1988. *Vol. II/7.*

– Die Frühzeit des Apostels Paulus. 1994. *Vol. 71.*

Rissi, Mathias: Die Theologie des Hebräerbriefs. 1987. *Vol. 41.*

Roskovec, Jan: see *Pokorný, Petr.*

Röhser, Günter: Metaphorik und Personifikation der Sünde. 1987. *Vol. II/25.*

Rose, Christian: Die Wolke der Zeugen. 1994. *Vol. II/60.*

Rothschild, Clare K.: Baptist Traditions and Q. 2005. *Vol. 190.*

– Luke Acts and the Rhetoric of History. 2004. *Vol. II/175.*

Rüegger, Hans-Ulrich: Verstehen, was Markus erzählt. 2002. *Vol. II/155.*

Rüger, Hans Peter: Die Weisheitsschrift aus der Kairoer Geniza. 1991. *Vol. 53.*

Sänger, Dieter: Antikes Judentum und die Mysterien. 1980. *Vol. II/5.*

– Die Verkündigung des Gekreuzigten und Israel. 1994. *Vol. 75.*

– see *Burchard, Christoph*

– and *Ulrich Mell* (Hrsg.): Paulus und Johannes. 2006. *Vol. 198.*

Salier, Willis Hedley: The Rhetorical Impact of the Semeia in the Gospel of John. 2004. *Vol. II/186.*

Salzmann, Jorg Christian: Lehren und Ermahnen. 1994. *Vol. II/59.*

Sandnes, Karl Olav: Paul – One of the Prophets? 1991. *Vol. II/43.*

Sato, Migaku: Q und Prophetie. 1988. *Vol. II/29.*

Schäfer, Ruth: Paulus bis zum Apostelkonzil. 2004. *Vol. II/179.*

Schaper, Joachim: Eschatology in the Greek Psalter. 1995. *Vol. II/76.*

Schimanowski, Gottfried: Die himmlische Liturgie in der Apokalypse des Johannes. 2002. *Vol. II/154.*

– Weisheit und Messias. 1985. *Vol. II/17.*

Schlichting, Günter: Ein jüdisches Leben Jesu. 1982. *Vol. 24.*

Schließer, Benjamin: Abraham's Faith in Romans 4. 2007. *Vol. II/224.*

Schnabel, Eckhard J.: Law and Wisdom from Ben Sira to Paul. 1985. *Vol. II/16.*

Schnelle, Udo: see *Frey, Jörg.*

Schröter, Jens: Von Jesus zum Neuen Testament. 2007. *Vol. 204.*

– see *Frey, Jörg.*

Schutter, William L.: Hermeneutic and Composition in I Peter. 1989. *Vol. II/30.*

Schwartz, Daniel R.: Studies in the Jewish Background of Christianity. 1992. *Vol. 60.*

Schwemer, Anna Maria: see *Hengel, Martin*

Scott, Ian W.: Implicit Epistemology in the Letters of Paul. 2005. *Vol. II/205.*

Scott, James M.: Adoption as Sons of God. 1992. *Vol. II/48.*

– Paul and the Nations. 1995. *Vol. 84.*

Shum, Shiu-Lun: Paul's Use of Isaiah in Romans. 2002. *Vol. II/156.*

Siegert, Folker: Drei hellenistisch-jüdische Predigten. Teil I 1980. *Vol. 20* – Teil II 1992. *Vol. 61.*

– Nag-Hammadi-Register. 1982. *Vol. 26.*

– Argumentation bei Paulus. 1985. *Vol. 34.*

– Philon von Alexandrien. 1988. *Vol. 46.*

Simon, Marcel: Le christianisme antique et son contexte religieux I/II. 1981. *Vol. 23.*

Snodgrass, Klyne: The Parable of the Wicked Tenants. 1983. *Vol. 27.*

Smit, Peter-Ben: Food and Fellowship in the Kingdom. 2007. *Vol. II/234.*

Söding, Thomas: Das Wort vom Kreuz. 1997. *Vol. 93.*

– see *Thüsing, Wilhelm.*

Sommer, Urs: Die Passionsgeschichte des Markusevangeliums. 1993. *Vol. II/58.*

Sorensen, Eric: Possession and Exorcism in the New Testament and Early Christianity. 2002. *Vol. II/157.*

Souček, Josef B.: see *Pokorný, Petr.*

Spangenberg, Volker: Herrlichkeit des Neuen Bundes. 1993. *Vol. II/55.*

Spanje, T.E. van: Inconsistency in Paul? 1999. *Vol. II/110.*

Speyer, Wolfgang: Frühes Christentum im antiken Strahlungsfeld. Vol. I: 1989. *Vol. 50.*

– Vol. II: 1999. *Vol. 116.*

– Vol. III: 2007. *Vol. 213.*

Stadelmann, Helge: Ben Sira als Schriftgelehrter. 1980. *Vol. II/6.*

Stenschke, Christoph W.: Luke's Portrait of Gentiles Prior to Their Coming to Faith. *Vol. II/108.*

Sterck-Degueldre, Jean-Pierre: Eine Frau namens Lydia. 2004. *Vol. II/176.*

Stettler, Christian: Der Kolosserhymnus. 2000. *Vol. II/131.*

Stettler, Hanna: Die Christologie der Pastoralbriefe. 1998. *Vol. II/105.*

Stökl Ben Ezra, Daniel: The Impact of Yom Kippur on Early Christianity. 2003. *Vol. 163.*

Strobel, August: Die Stunde der Wahrheit. 1980. *Vol. 21.*

Stroumsa, Guy G.: Barbarian Philosophy. 1999. *Vol. 112.*

Stuckenbruck, Loren T.: Angel Veneration and Christology. 1995. *Vol. II/70.*

– , *Stephen C. Barton* and *Benjamin G. Wold* (Ed.): Memory in the Bible and Antiquity. 2007. *Vol. 212.*

Stuhlmacher, Peter (Ed.): Das Evangelium und die Evangelien. 1983. *Vol. 28.*

– Biblische Theologie und Evangelium. 2002. *Vol. 146.*

Sung, Chong-Hyon: Vergebung der Sünden. 1993. *Vol. II/57.*

Tajra, Harry W.: The Trial of St. Paul. 1989. *Vol. II/35.*

– The Martyrdom of St.Paul. 1994. *Vol. II/67.*

Theißen, Gerd: Studien zur Soziologie des Urchristentums. 1979, ³1989. *Vol. 19.*

Theobald, Michael: Studien zum Römerbrief. 2001. *Vol. 136.*

Theobald, Michael: see *Mußner, Franz.*

Thornton, Claus-Jürgen: Der Zeuge des Zeugen. 1991. *Vol. 56.*

Thüsing, Wilhelm: Studien zur neutestamentlichen Theologie. Ed. von Thomas Söding. 1995. *Vol. 82.*

Thurén, Lauri: Derhethorizing Paul. 2000. *Vol. 124.*

Thyen, Hartwig: Studien zum Corpus Iohanneum. 2007. *Vol. 214.*

Tibbs, Clint: Religious Experience of the Pneuma. 2007. *Vol. II/230.*

Tolmie, D. Francois: Persuading the Galatians. 2005. *Vol. II/190.*

Tomson, Peter J. and *Doris Lambers-Petry* (Ed.): The Image of the Judaeo-Christians in Ancient Jewish and Christian Literature. 2003. *Vol. 158.*

Trebilco, Paul: The Early Christians in Ephesus from Paul to Ignatius. 2004. *Vol. 166.*

Treloar, Geoffrey R.: Lightfoot the Historian. 1998. *Vol. II/103.*

Tsuji, Manabu: Glaube zwischen Vollkommenheit und Verweltlichung. 1997. *Vol. II/93.*

Twelftree, Graham H.: Jesus the Exorcist. 1993. *Vol. II/54.*

Ulrichs, Karl Friedrich: Christusglaube. 2007. *Vol. II/227.*

Urban, Christina: Das Menschenbild nach dem Johannesevangelium. 2001. *Vol. II/137.*

Visotzky, Burton L.: Fathers of the World. 1995. *Vol. 80.*

Vollenweider, Samuel: Horizonte neutestamentlicher Christologie. 2002. *Vol. 144.*

Vos, Johan S.: Die Kunst der Argumentation bei Paulus. 2002. *Vol. 149.*

Wagener, Ulrike: Die Ordnung des „Hauses Gottes". 1994. *Vol. II/65.*

Wahlen, Clinton: Jesus and the Impurity of Spirits in the Synoptic Gospels. 2004. *Vol. II/185.*

Walker, Donald D.: Paul's Offer of Leniency (2 Cor 10:1). 2002. *Vol. II/152.*

Walter, Nikolaus: Praeparatio Evangelica. Ed. von Wolfgang Kraus und Florian Wilk. 1997. *Vol. 98.*

Wander, Bernd: Gottesfürchtige und Sympathi-santen. 1998. *Vol. 104.*

Waters, Guy: The End of Deuteronomy in the Epistles of Paul. 2006. *Vol. 221.*

Watt, Jan G. van der: see *Frey, Jörg*

Watts, Rikki: Isaiah's New Exodus and Mark. 1997. *Vol. II/88.*

Wedderburn, A.J.M.: Baptism and Resurrection. 1987. *Vol. 44.*

Wegner, Uwe: Der Hauptmann von Kafarnaum. 1985. *Vol. II/14.*

Weissenrieder, Annette: Images of Illness in the Gospel of Luke. 2003. Vol. II/164.

–, *Friederike Wendt* and *Petra von Gemünden* (Ed.): Picturing the New Testament. 2005. *Vol. II/193.*

Welck, Christian: Erzählte ‚Zeichen'. 1994. *Vol. II/69.*

Wendt, Friederike (Ed.): see *Weissenrieder, Annette.*

Wiarda, Timothy: Peter in the Gospels. 2000. *Vol. II/127.*

Wifstrand, Albert: Epochs and Styles. 2005. *Vol. 179.*

Wilk, Florian: see *Walter, Nikolaus.*

Williams, Catrin H.: I am He. 2000. *Vol. II/113.*

Wilson, Todd A.: The Curse of the Law and the Crisis in Galatia. 2007. *Vol. II/225.*

Wilson, Walter T.: Love without Pretense. 1991. *Vol. II/46.*

Wischmeyer, Oda: Von Ben Sira zu Paulus. 2004. *Vol. 173.*

Wisdom, Jeffrey: Blessing for the Nations and the Curse of the Law. 2001. *Vol. II/133.*

Wold, Benjamin G.: Women, Men, and Angels. 2005. *Vol. II/2001.*

– see *Stuckenbruck, Loren T.*

Wright, Archie T.: The Origin of Evil Spirits. 2005. *Vol. II/198.*

Wucherpfennig, Ansgar: Heracleon Philologus. 2002. *Vol. 142.*

Yeung, Maureen: Faith in Jesus and Paul. 2002. *Vol. II/147.*

Zangenberg, Jürgen, Harold W. Attridge and *Dale B. Martin* (Ed.): Religion, Ethnicity and Identity in Ancient Galilee. 2007. *Vol. 210.*

Zimmermann, Alfred E.: Die urchristlichen Leh-rer. 1984, ²1988. *Vol. II/12.*

Zimmermann, Johannes: Messianische Texte aus Qumran. 1998. *Vol. II/104.*

Zimmermann, Ruben: Christologie der Bilder im Johannesevangelium. 2004. *Vol. 171.*

– Geschlechtermetaphorik und Gottesverhält-nis. 2001. *Vol. II/122.*

– see *Frey, Jörg*

Zumstein, Jean: see *Dettwiler, Andreas*

Zwiep, Arie W.: Judas and the Choice of Matthias. 2004. *Vol. II/187.*

For a complete catalogue please write to the publisher
Mohr Siebeck • P.O. Box 2030 • D–72010 Tübingen/Germany
Up-to-date information on the internet at www.mohr.de